D1526745

Bodies of War

Bodies of War

World War I and the Politics of Commemoration in America, 1919–1933

Lisa M. Budreau

NEW YORK UNIVERSITY PRESS

New York and London

NEW YORK UNIVERSITY PRESS
New York and London
www.nyupress.org

© 2010 by New York University

Library of Congress Cataloging-in-Publication Data

Budreau, Lisa M. (Lisa Mary), 1957–
Bodies of war : World War I and the politics of commemoration in
America, 1919–1933 / Lisa M. Budreau.
p. cm.
Includes bibliographical references and index.
ISBN-13: 978-0-8147-9990-1 (cl : alk. paper)
ISBN-10: 0-8147-9990-6 (cl : alk. paper)
1. World War, 1914–1918—Monuments—United States. 2. War
memorials—Political aspects—United States—History—20th century.
3. War memorials—Social aspects—United States—History—20th
century. 4. World War, 1914–1918—Social aspects—United States.
5. United States—Social conditions—1918–1932. 6. Political culture—
United States—History—20th century. 7. United States—Politics and
government—1918–1933. I. Title.
D670.B83   2009
940.4'60973—dc22   2009029205

Manufactured in the United States of America

10 9 8 7 6 5 4 3 2 1

In Memory of
Mary Blanche Richardson
and
Florence Budrow Emerson

Contents

For oh, when the war will be over
We'll go and we'll look for our dead;
We'll go when the bee's on the clover,
And the plume of the poppy is red:
We'll go when the year's at its gayest,
When meadows are laughing with flow'rs;
And there where the crosses are greyest,
We'll seek for the cross that is ours.

For they cry to us: *Friends, we are lonely,*
A-weary the night and the day;
But come in the blossom-time only,
Come when our graves will be gay:
When daffodils all are a-blowing,
And larks are a-thrilling the skies,
Oh, come with the hearts of you glowing,
And the joy of the Spring in your eyes.

But never, oh, never come sighing,
For ours was the Splendid Release;
And oh, but 'twas joy in the dying
To know we were winning you Peace!
So come when the valleys are sheening,
And fledged with the promise of grain;
And here where our graves will be greening,
Just smile and be happy again.

And so, when the war will be over,
We'll seek for the Wonderful One;
And maiden will look for her lover,
And mother will look for her son;
And there will be end to our grieving,
And gladness will gleam over loss,
As—glory beyond all believing!
We point . . . to a name on a cross.

—Robert W. Service, *Rhymes of a Red-Cross Man* (1916)

Preface

Years ago, I embarked on an adventure that has since culminated in this book. Like a true pilgrim, I had no idea what my journey would entail, nor did I realize what a life-changing experience it would be.

In September 2001, I crossed the Channel from France to England after participating in a First World War battlefield tour that I researched and coordinated for the Smithsonian Institution. In those frantic, fearful days just after 9/11, more than twenty Americans still managed to join us in Paris where the French warmly welcomed our group as we made our way across the former Western Front. We visited many of the U.S. cemeteries, monuments, and battlefield sites mentioned in this book and performed the same rituals as our predecessors, swearing enduring remembrance to the dead.

I initially conceived of the tour idea in the mid-1990s while visiting the British battlefields with the renowned military historian Martin Middlebrook. When asked where the American battlefields were, my knowledgeable guide gestured with vague indifference, "they're somewhere *over there*."[1] I could not have imagined then that his reply would serve as my calling, one that found fulfillment on the pockmarked fields of France and Belgium.

Armed with my maps, a compass, a tattered copy of the *American Armies and Battlefields in Europe* guide (1938), Phil Cousineau's *The Art of Pilgrimage* (1998), and a warm pair of gloves, I set off. I am still not certain whether it was an expatriate's national pride or plain curiosity that sustained me as I traipsed across the plains of Picardy and maneuvered along the narrow, winding roads of countless quaint villages along the Hindenburg Line. As I made my way over to the farthest reaches of eastern France, vestiges of the American military presence appeared more numerous with each visit. I was struck by the sheer splendor of each national monument and the manicured perfection of those spacious cemeteries. Yet among all that magnificence and sacrifice, there was seldom anyone there but myself and the dead. Bemused, I wondered if Americans had simply forgotten the war, or perhaps they had just moved on to others?

Unbeknownst to me, those early expeditions would later serve as the foundation for my doctoral dissertation and the point where the distant past became my future. Similar to other pilgrims before me, I began by treading ground. I followed no itinerary, was guided only by a vague sense of direction, and had very little funding to get me there. But, once I started on my path, the road opened before me.

As a child, I was fascinated by old cemeteries, but I had never lost anyone close to me, so I knew nothing about the heartbreaking despair of the grieving. I came from a military family, but I was not aware of any relatives who had served in the First World War, nor had I ever met a Gold Star Mother. Then, I read Jay Winter's classic study *Sites of Memory, Sites of Mourning* and was puzzled by the absence of any mention of American involvement in that war. Apparently, the whole world had forgotten about the U.S. presence overseas from 1917 to 1918. I wrote to Winter, inspired by his suggestion that "the history of the pilgrimage movement is a subject worthy of a book in itself."[2] Winter's response was the catalyst that sent me on my way.

Now, ten years later, I sense that my pilgrimage is complete. I return where I began—older, wiser, and forever changed by the experience. The journey led me across Europe and the United States searching for the missing fragments of this unusual story. But, as I approached the book's final chapter, I found the key insight within myself when both my mother and grandmother died within months of one another. While grieving the tragic loss of those whom I had loved so dearly, I knew viscerally what had previously eluded me—I was no longer a mere observer of grief. Like the people you will meet in the following pages, my innocence was gone. In its place was a new awareness of our human connection and the certainty that each life matters. Although these men and women lived more than ninety years ago, their existence, their legacy, and their death should not be forgotten; they are part of our nation's story and serve to remind us that "no man is an island, . . . any man's death diminishes me because I am involved in mankind."[3]

Acknowledgments

With humility, I recognize the enormous debt I owe to all those who contributed to the completion of *Bodies of War*. I begin by thanking Jay Winter for being so receptive to my original research plans and for his guidance, which ultimately led me to Oxford University. It was due to Winter's intercession that I had the pleasure of working with my first dissertation adviser, Adrian Gregory. I benefited enormously from Adrian's tutelage, which familiarized me with the extensive historiography on European war memory. Moreover, his readings of my earliest chapters provided much-needed support during that crucial phase.

After Adrian's sabbatical from Oxford in 2002, Gareth Davies stepped into that key adviser role, generously offering immeasurable hours of patient guidance, keen perceptive analysis of American politics during the 1920s, and an unwavering belief in my abilities and endurance.

I would also like to thank my friend and mentor, Kurt Piehler, for sharing his vast expertise regarding American war memory, despite his own heavy workload. Kurt always found time to generously share his research and to comment on countless revisions of the manuscript. His input was an integral component that provided greater depth, color, and clarity overall.

Within American military and social history circles, many gracious readers must be thanked for patiently reading, editing, and discussing various sections of this book during its progression. Others freely shared their research and archival materials and generally supported my work in a myriad of ways. In the United States, they include Michael Birdwell, Edward Bliss, Edward "Mac" Coffman, Holly Fenelon, Robert H. Ferrell, John T. Greenwood, Millard Greer, Paul J. Jacobsmeyer, Jennifer Keene, Michael Neiberg, Stephen W. Warner, Allen Weinstein, and Jeremy Young. Overseas, Stephen Badsey, Malcolm Brown, Frederic Castier, Stephen P. Dean, Mark Meigs, Michael O'Brien, Ron Robin, and Gary Sheffield, must all be graciously thanked.

In England, professors Ian Beckett and Jay Sexton with their rigorous analysis challenged me to aim for standards of scholarship I had previously hesitated to demand of myself. I am grateful to them for that gift and for their discerning, insightful comments that have greatly improved this book.

While at Oxford my research benefited from several generous financial gifts including St. Antony's College Arnold Fund (2001), Stahl Fund (2003), and Oxford University's Scatcherd European Scholarship (2002–2003), which enabled me to do the necessary field work in France, where I had the privilege of working with the distinguished French war historian Annette Becker. With her assistance, I managed to navigate the archival holdings at the Bibliothèque de documentation internationale contemporaine, in Nanterre (Paris); the Archives de la Guerre, Vincennes; and the foreign-policy papers at the Ministère des Affaires Étrangères, Quai d'Orsay, Paris. In Calais, the town's Médiathèque staff were extremely attentive to countless requests to review their vast collection of regional newspapers from the postwar era.

In June 2003, the extraordinary Centre de recherche de l'Historial de la Grande Guerre (Museum of the Great War) in Peronne granted me a generous financial fellowship that sustained further field work. I am exceedingly grateful to Annette Becker and Jay Winter for making that esteemed award possible.

This study necessitated research at an array of international archives, but I am particularly grateful to the helpful staff in the documents room at the Imperial War Museum, London, and at the Commonwealth War Graves Commission in Maidenhead, Berkshire. At the American cemetery in Waregem, Belgium, I owe particular thanks to my good friend ABMC assistant superintendent and historian Christopher Sims. Chris commented on various portions of the manuscript and provided a wealth of obscure photographs and other archival materials from his own collection, as well as insights and observations gleaned from many years of faithful service to that organization.

In the United States, I would also like to thank Monte Monroe, archivist of the Southwest Collection at Texas Technical University, Lubbock, Texas (Julia Duggan Hart Collection); Christine Lutz at the Seeley G. Mudd Library, Princeton University (David A. Reed Papers); all the staff at the U.S. Army Military History Institute, U.S. Army War College, Carlisle Barracks, Pennsylvania; and Doran Cart and Jonathan Casey at the Liberty Museum in Kansas City, Missouri (Gold Star Mothers Collection), where the museum also welcomed me as a guest speaker in 2002.

I was fortunate to have received exceptionally valuable feedback from audiences at various venues in the United States and overseas, where I presented papers, including the graduate colloquium at Vanderbilt University, Nashville, Tennessee (2002); the Atlantic World Seminar in Modern History at the Rothermere American Institute, Oxford University (2002); the Society of Military Historians annual conference, Knoxville, Tennessee (2003); and the 92nd Street Y, New York City (November 2005). My research was also given public exposure by Alison Davis Wood, producer of *Gold Star Mothers: Pilgrimage of Remembrance,* a PBS documentary (WILL-TV, Urbana, Illinois, in 2004). Additionally, I would like to thank the editorial staff of the *Journal of Military History* for their efforts to refine my article for publication as it appeared in the spring 2008 volume.

A postdoctoral fellowship at the Joint POW/MIA Accounting Command (JPAC), at Hickam AFB, Hawaii, from September 2005 to November 2006, provided me with the means to earn a living while I wrote. It was administered by the Oak Ridge Institute for Science and Education, in agreement with the U.S. Department of Energy. Those busy months afforded an excellent opportunity to witness the military's identification and recovery process firsthand. I must thank my friends and colleagues there for making that experience so memorable.

More recently, I have had the pleasure of working in the Office of Medical History at the U.S. Army Surgeon General's Office in Falls Church, Virginia. I would like to extend heartfelt appreciation to my employer William T. Gray, of Gray & Associates Consulting. His genuine interest and encouragement, along with that of my colleagues, Christina N. Reinhard, Ellen A. Milhiser, and Lieutenant Colonel Cheryl Y. Capers, were key factors in the book's ultimate completion. My gratitude also goes to Army Nurse Corps Lieutenant Colonel Richard M. Prior for bringing his considerable military experience and balanced perspective to the discussion.

No writer could sustain the long hours of isolation without the support of loving friends and family. My warmest thanks to Serenity Amber, Chris Bayot, Valerie Cribbs, Glory Fox Dierker, Phil Dryburgh, Sharon Fairhurst, Wayne L. Garrett, Frank and Annette Gesoff, Daniel D. Killerlane, Mary Lindquist, Steve Thompson, Jon Woolven, and finally, my dear friend and confidant Quannah Santiago. Thank you, "Q," for sharing your awesome political knowledge, perceptive critical analysis, and a patient ear that got me through all those rough patches.

I also owe a special word of thanks to Mitchell Yockelson for drawing my attention to the bountiful Gold Star Mothers material at the National

Archives. Mitch's perpetual encouragement, generous spirit, and superb wit helped to make this book a reality.

Lastly, I want to thank my dear family, specifically Wayne and Mary Jo Warner for their prayers and warm hospitality, Charles H. Halpert, and the Budrows—Frances, Richard and Joan, Craig and Cori, Jennifer and Rich—for their patient support and boundless love.

Abbreviations

ABMC	American Battle Monuments Commission
AEF	American Expeditionary Forces
CFA	Commission of Fine Arts
CWGC	Commonwealth War Graves Commission (post–World War I)
GAR	Grand Army of the Republic
GHQ	general headquarters
GSM	Gold Star Mothers
GRS	Graves Registration Service
IWGC	Imperial War Graves Commission
JWB	Jewish Welfare Board
LOC	Library of Congress
NA	National Archives and Records Administration
NAACP	National Association for the Advancement of Colored People
NOK	next of kin
NYT	*New York Times*
QMC	Quartermaster Corps
QMG	quartermaster general
RG	record group
SC	Signal Corps
SOS	Services of Supply
UDC	United Daughters of the Confederacy
WRC	Women's Relief Corps

American Battle Monuments and Military Cemeteries of the First World War in Europe

© L. Budreau, 2008

Legend

- ✖ Monuments
- ⬛ Cemeteries
- ✪ National capitals
- —·— International boundaries

GERMANY

NETHERLANDS

BELGIUM

BRUSSELS ✪

Waereghem
✖ YPRES
✖ AUDENARDE
FLANDERS FIELD

LUXEMBURG ✪
LUX.

North Sea

English Channel

ENGLAND

LONDON ✪
⬛ BROOKWOOD

Boulogne

Le Havre

St. Nazaire

BREST ✖

FRANCE

Amiens
BELLICOURT ✖
SOMME ⬛ Bony
St. Quentin
CANTIGNY ✖

Fère-en-Tardenois
Belleau
AISNE-MARNE
SURESNES ⬛
PARIS ✪
Seine

SOMMEPY ✖
Reims
Romagne ⬛ MEUSE-ARGONNE
OISE-AISNE ⬛
Château-Thierry
CHÂTEAU-THIERRY ✖
Argonne Forest
Metz
MONTFAUCON ✖
ST. MIHIEL ✖
Thiaucourt
MONTSEC ✖
St-Mihiel
Nancy

Meuse
Marne
Chaumont

Loire

TOURS ✖
to GIBRALTAR ✖✖

SWITZERLAND
BERN ✪

0   100   200 Kilometers
0   50   100   150 Miles

xviii

Introduction

The years immediately following the armistice in the United States have generally been characterized by massive labor unrest, cultural and class tension, ethnic turmoil, isolationist tendencies, nativism, and racial prejudice—forces that dominated public concern and threatened the core of national unity.[1] Permeating this ubiquitous discontent was the lingering malaise produced by an ambiguous war, exacerbated by America's failure to ratify the Treaty of Versailles or join the League of Nations.

Efforts to unite this fractured society were reinforced by President Woodrow Wilson's appeal to democratic ideals as a primary justification for bringing the country into war. However, attempts to portray a unified nation with a common purpose did not end with the armistice, or with Wilson's efforts to take his cause to the people during a cross-country tour. Instead, they fueled the politics of remembrance in the aftermath of the First World War, which resulted in a story that remains essentially untold, of exploitation and experimentation in the name of honor to America's war dead.

This book explains why the United States commemorated the war as it did and emphasizes the degree to which that course was so remarkable. It re-creates the specific, grounded, textured, and complex political and cultural environment in which the corresponding policies were made, thereby illuminating the character of American politics and culture in the aftermath of the First World War in new ways.

The first mass war of the twentieth century brought abrupt change to the United States as its citizens adjusted to expansive new technologies, a massive surge in their industrial development (and the vast immigration this sparked), the rapid growth of their cities, and a political democracy that became increasingly more centralized and bureaucratized. These broad, wrenching powers of modernization forced Americans to revise former concepts of collective identity and reconsider their obligation to the nation. A modern American ideology emerged, one intent on cohesiveness, in which racial, religious, and ethnic differences were over-looked in favor of national unity. In the process, collective identities were exchanged for the benefits of citizenship.

As the social and political culture of the United States altered, so too did public aspirations concerning former commemorative patterns and symbols. Americans were searching for a fresh vocabulary for mediating grief, one that reflected current points of view, rather than the conventional practices of old-world Europe. Former symbols of mourning were cast aside in favor of expressions that more closely represented a progressive, forward-looking society with its needs based in the present. Their quest led to a modern, secular variety of mourning that attempted to transform grief into glory.

Historically, America's commemorative path had evolved from the nation's responses to previous wars, which had established precedents that influenced practice by 1918. Its distinctive character was also motivated by other aspects of the country's culture: its institutions, its ethno-cultural mix, the legacy of slavery, the evolving role of women in public life, the rise of Jim Crow, and the increasing power of organized interests within an inimitable democratic mass culture. These forces were often in conflict, making it extremely difficult for policymakers to meet the expectations of all groups.

The Great War demanded a revision of former practice since the past could not be relied on to guide future policy. By involving itself in the international conflict at such a crucial juncture, injecting men and resources that ultimately provided a decisive Allied victory, the nation forever altered its global status.

Comforting, well-established traditions that had evolved over several decades, such as the unrestrained erection of monuments and the unquestioned return of the war dead, were abruptly threatened by radical revision. Graves scattered across Europe and the United States, and remains that lay unidentified or simply no longer existed, complicated efforts to collectively mourn the dead just as distant battlefields and government restrictions prevented cooperative efforts to mark the war in a personal and meaningful way.

Nevertheless, the United States joined the international community in the creation of rituals of remembrance after the war with the dedication of a tomb for the Unknown Soldier, the construction of local and regional memorials, the designation of a national day of remembrance, the establishment of cemeteries on former battlefields, and eventually organized pilgrimages. Yet ambivalence and delay marked America's postwar commemorative effort, in which a diverse population, unprepared for war and then late into the conflict, sought to commemorate the experience that led to its new world role. The introduction of these modern practices during the immediate postwar years of instability, debate, and uncertainty made their acceptance all the more difficult.

Attempts to commemorate at home reflected the ambivalence felt within the nation toward this war that seemed to have gained nothing, as efforts to maintain a sense of wartime harmony and social unity dissolved in the postwar determination to reinterpret the past. In this climate diverse partisan factions sought to create war memories that would lend meaning and restore purpose to this tragic ignoble event. Dialogue ensued between the various participants who attempted to negotiate their version of war memory, such as the state, civil society, social groups, and individuals. Women and veterans became especially vocal, particularly as their associations grew in strength and numbers; however, efforts by the state to appease this democratic society merely fostered further conflict.

Heated disagreements raged between isolationists and internationalists, confusion reigned over the ideal path to world peace, and to the majority of Americans, menacing fears over insidious alien forces such as Bolshevism proved to be more pressing concerns than national commemoration. These circumstances contributed to mass indifference toward the memorialization of a war that served such questionable aims, particularly toward plans that involved overseas constructions.

The emergence of the country's new power, wealth, and prestige brought changes to the political realm, affecting foreign policies that marginalized the rights of citizens as guardians of their nation's war memory. But a compromise was deemed necessary since the nation could no longer remain isolated from world affairs; U.S. wealth, global expansion, and military power now demanded a more ambitious diplomatic presence abroad to protect American interests and investments.

Internationally, governments struggled on behalf of their citizens to interpret meaning from the vast death tolls, while simultaneously developing practical measures for coping with remains of the deceased. The decisions reached by nation-states regarding the sensitive issue of the war dead seldom gained the support of their citizenry since negotiations over the rights and ownership of the deceased had never previously taken place. Yet on a personal level the sacrifice of life needed to be fully justified and then mourned and remembered in an honorable way.

Much was at stake in the ensuing debates that raged between governments and their people over the war and its remembrance, primarily the glory of warriors, the grief of the bereaved, the image of the nation, and the needs of the state. These factors influenced the construction of the myth of the war experience by those most concerned with the image and unity of the nation. This sociocultural process was designed to "draw the sting from death in war and emphasize the meaningfulness of the fighting and sacrifice." The myth relied on the cult of the fallen soldier "with the aim of mak[ing] an inherently unpalatable past acceptable, important not just for the purpose of consolation but above all for the justification of the nation in whose name the war had been fought."[2] This myth was not unique to the United States since all thriving nation-states require warriors prepared to sacrifice their lives for a cause greater than individual life. However, in a democratic society, this process became a negotiable one whereby special interest groups affected by the war expected a tangible return for their sacrifice.

Invoking the memory of the war dead promoted solidarity while instilling a willingness to die for an abstract cause; thus, the deceased were imbued with a unique purpose beyond that which their sacrifice had served. But as a valuable and meaningful commodity, the dead required new levels of protection, care, and preservation. In the aftermath of war, a sanctioned memory evolved on heritage landscapes composed of national cemeteries and commemorative battlefield sites.

With few domestic guidelines in place, policymakers looked to the imperial designs and rituals of the former European powers for a precedent. When these processes combined with American commemorative apparatus dating from the mid-nineteenth century, the result was nothing short of a spectacular compromise.

Continuity (or pedigree) is at the very heart of what civilization is. It is the means by which a culture maintains its identity. In the absence of centuries and even millennia by which the life of a culture is usually measured, a young nation thrust into the role of world leader must construct its own identity. In the era of discontinuity ushered in by the First World War, when forces of the old and new worlds ruptured, Americans became alienated from their past. This tendency continues as national innocence is increasingly replaced with "a materialistic creed that celebrates transience, and an electronic faith that worships the present to the exclusion of all other dimensions of time."[3]

This book follows the American response in three chronological stages: "Repatriation," which explains the process of democratic choice regarding the disposition of remains; "Remembrance," the construction of commemorative symbols abroad by a select group of politically motivated individuals; and "Return," which explores the lavish state-sanctioned battlefield pilgrimages in which the full impact of American and European cultural approaches unfolded.

The investigation benefits from this three-pronged methodology that identifies distinct stages within the U.S. commemorative process, whereby each phase impelled the next. Part 1, "Repatriation," explores the roots of historical memory based in previous American wars that still held tremendous influence over the nation in 1917. With Secretary of War Newton Baker's promise of 1918, public expectations were raised that the government would provide a home burial to all who died in its foreign service. In the absence of a firm prewar policy, this promise resulted in a massive operation that cost the government millions of dollars and firmly established a national paradigm that has endured. Despite this extraordinary undertaking and the disruption caused when families were offered an opportunity to decide the burial place of their deceased, the unprecedented exercise remains an obscure event in America's past.

Evidence indicates that repatriation of the dead from overseas battlefields was the catalyst that drove American First World War commemoration. Yet the democratic burial options offered to families, initially proposed to assuage their grief, also contributed to a massive diffusion of memory. Since most of America's war dead lay buried in scattered graves throughout the United States, interest in overseas commemoration was undeniably diluted.

In part 2, "Remembrance," the investigation turns to the establishment of the American Battle Monuments Commission (ABMC) in 1923 and the mounting tension that occurred within an increasingly diverse society, as a result of the group's policies. ABMC efforts to wield political power into grand schemes of commemoration beyond American borders contributed instead to a state of cultural amnesia. I address the causes that led to this unfortunate outcome by first considering how American commemorative practices were shaped by events preceding the First World War.

As the story unfolds, it becomes apparent that national commemorative traditions evolved along a historical path rooted in the western frontier, the Mexican-American War, the Civil War, and the Spanish-American War. Each conflict contributed to the establishment of exceptional practices that eventually influenced post–World War remembrance. Yet America in the 1840s was a very different place from the America of the

1920s. The nation's political democracy became more centralized and bureaucratized through this period as authority moved from local to state and then to federal government. The American Battle Monuments Commission, the military, and civil society all had their own interests and dogmas, and this is a feature of the rise of the modern state. Tracing the story of remembrance between the 1840s and the 1930s, with particular reference to the period after the war, offers an opportunity to probe all these broad, wrenching forces of modernization.

Unlike other governments, U.S. policymakers were accountable to a public that held unique assumptions regarding commemorative practices intended to honor its war dead. By the close of the Civil War in 1865, Americans expected national cemeteries for those who chose not to bring their dead home; they also anticipated an unrestrained right to erect monuments on former battlefields. Moreover, the public had traditionally held their government and military leaders responsible for the care of their deceased to the extent that they presumed the use of modern funeral procedures and advanced search and identification methods. These diverse expectations made the task of commemorating the first modern, international war of the twentieth century an intrinsically complicated one.

Adding to the confusion was widespread disillusionment over American participation in a war that seemed to lack any obvious gains. President Woodrow Wilson's references to democratic objectives as a justification for war had only added to the ambivalence many Americans felt toward another foreign military conflict. Congressional rejection of the League of Nations also reinforced the public's resolve to avoid future entanglements; consequently, many turned their backs on the past, reverting instead to isolationism or detached self-interest. Much of this disenchantment was reflected in an ideology based on what was good for the individual, not the community. This tension between the individual and the collective appears to have increased when exposed to uncertainties regarding the appropriate remembrance of such a questionable and costly pursuit.

Political officials, the military, and even the public were caught unprepared for the new role America would play in postwar international affairs. ABMC members were equally confused as to how a world power should most effectively memorialize its military role, which had contributed to a decisive Allied victory. In the absence of a suitable policy, the government improvised by constructing a modern solution with ties to historical convention. Since individual states and local communities had attempted to pursue their own commemorative plans, national remembrance readily merged with broader foreign objectives. National cemeteries became instruments of public diplomacy, as did monuments, designed to win sympathy and induce a sense of awe and obligation abroad. This political action soon proved divisive at home and abroad as ABMC commissioners promoted grandiose schemes of commemoration beyond American borders.

The ABMC's part-imitative, part-innovative initiatives represented a radical departure from convention. Their project cost the nation millions of dollars but was thought to reflect more accurately the burgeoning prestige and influence held by the United States. It included impressive national cemeteries resembling landscaped gardens that beckoned tourists while advocating a "forgetting" of painful sacrifices for those seeking resolution of their grief. And whereas the federal government had traditionally consented to a fairly unrestrained approach to public commemoration by Americans, in the wake of this war, the state deviated from convention. Grand edifices were erected to the nation's glory on distant battlefields instead of in the United States, where they might have served to remind the nation of its participation and the war's cost. The extent to which this decision altered collective war memory is considered in detail.

Part 2 concludes with an investigation into the responses of those people most affected by the war and by America's policies. In Britain and its dominions, government restrictions prohibited the repatriation of the war dead. Instead, the state chose on behalf of its people to construct national cemeteries near the former battlefield. In doing so, the government faced dissension and angry protest at this imposition of state authority, yet it ultimately preserved a comparatively more dignified and enduring symbol of remembrance. By contrast, the war dead of France and the United States were subjected to a macabre process that involved the mass consolidation of remains into national "Fields of Honor." U.S. practices caused further chaos in France by triggering dissent among a grieving population that demanded the state acknowledge their sacrifices in a similar manner.

One of the most striking contrasts between the American experience and that which occurred in other nations is the degree to which the U.S. military and political elites were expected to respond to mass opinion expressed through newspapers and organized groups. In this regard, the investigation considers civil society's role as agent of memory, specifically, that of the American Legion and the Gold Star Mothers. These collectives offer a rich, multidimensional model of ethnic, cultural, economic, and religious diversity prevalent in America during the interwar years while providing scope for exploration into racial, gender, and political issues within the context of national mourning.

Perhaps in response to the limitations imposed on group participation in overseas commemoration, civic affiliations within the United States of women, war veterans, and African Americans proliferated in the immediate postwar era. These groups claimed a stake in the nation's victory and expected something in return for the sacrifices they had made. As civil societies, they were practicing their democratic right to unite as enfranchised units that wielded greater authority in a nation increasingly dominated by group politics. Together, they forged a common voice that exalted their unique contribution to war's official memory.

By the late 1920s, Britain and the United States had nearly completed a massive phase of commemorative construction, primarily in Belgium and France. This triggered the third integral part of remembrance: the battlefield pilgrim, the focus of part 3, "Return." For Americans, an ocean and thousands of miles separated them from the cemeteries and monuments erected on behalf of their nation and its heroes. As a consequence, only the more affluent could afford the long voyage to Europe. Yet ABMC commissioners were certain that generations of Americans would make the pilgrimage across the sea. The fact that this mass exodus never materialized disturbed those people most determined to ensure a lasting memory of the war: veterans and families of the deceased.

In 1927 thousands of veterans from the powerful American Legion and its auxiliaries paraded through Paris to mark the tenth anniversary of the war. Away from the United States, the group's zealous marching bands, lavish colorful costumes, and uproarious performances appeared to European observers as a mockery of war's memory. These events, dedicated to the celebration of victory rather than war's painful losses, bore a marked resemblance to the behavior of Civil War veterans during their annual encampments at Gettysburg.

Although the Legionnaires' pilgrimage appears to have warranted a place in several contemporary historical accounts, the Gold Star Mothers pilgrimages have remained in relative obscurity. These women, named for the gold star they were urged to display on armbands and service flags in their homes, were accorded greater recognition for having lost loved ones in the war. Many people believed these mothers and widows deserved an opportunity to see the graves of their sons and husbands overseas. So between 1930 and 1933, with much of the nation experiencing severe economic hardship, these pilgrims enjoyed a luxurious voyage to Europe as guests of the U.S. government. However, African American women invited to participate in the pilgrimage did so on the same segregated basis as their sons and husbands who had fought and died.

The Gold Star Mothers pilgrimages emerged from a decade-long struggle marked by effective political lobbying by white, Anglo-Saxon, Protestant women's organizations that had largely supported President Wilson's early war effort. As auxiliary units of the American Legion, they benefited not only from experience gained in earlier women's reform movements but also from their elevated position within society as "sacrificial mother." This status was reinforced by an ideology that perceived blood ties as the fundamental basis for reckoning kinship, which excluded adoptive mothers and widows. That kinship also excluded black mothers, who had hoped to employ motherhood as a means of building a coalition with their white counterparts.

Whereas white women used gender to their advantage, exploiting stereotypes in a way that gave them greater power, African Americans had no power. Yet black outrage at the treatment of African Americans during and after the war, and then in response to the segregated pilgrimages, hints at a kind of cultural assertiveness that was also evident in the contemporary phenomenon of the Harlem Renaissance. In that sense, the reaction of blacks to the pilgrimage discrimination prefigured the civil rights movement that burgeoned after the Second World War.

Gender and ethno-racial fissures ran throughout American life, not just between black and white but also between Christian and Jew. Despite this disparity, the pilgrimages, like the newly constructed monuments overseas and the segregated veterans' groups, were presented to the world as symbols of American solidarity and classic democratic egalitarianism.

Organized pilgrimages represent a point of intersection between individual loss and national community. Ideally, they can serve to unite groups and their nation in remembrance, while offering an opportunity for participants to come to terms with grief, thus consigning the dead to memory. The Gold Star pilgrimages were crafted by Congress, the military, and some of the more politically savvy "pilgrims" into a mission with political and diplomatic aims that misconstrued their original intent. As such, their value as an instrument of closure for grieving mothers and widows is questionable.

I have pieced together what I believe to be an accurate account of this epic journey. References from private collections, mothers' diaries, and letters animate the vivid memories of numerous participants. In tandem, logistical and administrative documents from public archives highlight the elaborate detail and expense the government incurred to ensure smooth, efficient sailing. Occasionally, the sparks flew from pages of confidential documents revealing the hidden uneasiness ignited when motherhood and the military establishment collided.

Why did these women choose to leave their loved ones buried overseas? Why were they so emotionally restrained when they knelt at their loved ones' gravesides? Had they felt their sacrifice to have been worthwhile? After sifting through all the rich material left behind, the answers soon became clear.

Despite their ability to influence domestic policy, veterans and other postwar organizations were unable to alter the nation's commemorative strategy overseas. Instead, civil society was essentially prevented from participating in the overseas remembrance process to the extent that they were discouraged from attending the dedication ceremonies held in the 1930s. While those most affected by the conflict struggled against rapidly fading memories, others grew increasingly indifferent.

Today, most Americans are likely unaware of the repatriation work of the army's Graves Registration Service, the Gold Star Mothers pilgrimages of 1930–1933, and perhaps even the presence of First World War overseas monuments and cemeteries. Yet the military's mission to search for, recover, identify, and return American soldiers killed in war continues, funded handsomely by U.S. taxpayers. This effort emerges as one of the key historical legacies stemming from America's approach to commemorating the first major war of the twentieth century.

Offered here is a rich and fascinating story featuring a remarkable range of characters who animate an enormous body of historical data drawn from numerous international sources. The result is a faithful depiction of the complex political cultural environment in which the policies of American commemoration were shaped and the quirky irony that results when governments respond to the current wishes of its citizens.

It is my hope that this book will highlight the lasting significance of the war's aftermath on the nation, the dangers facing a society that ceases to remember its past, and the process by which a democracy remembers war.

PART I

Repatriation

1

The Journey's End

On a warm morning in late May 1933, Mrs. Estella Kendall of Shenandoah, Iowa, walked anxiously through the Meuse-Argonne American Cemetery in northern France. Many summers had passed since that day in 1918 when she first learned of her son's death: as a member of the 168th Infantry, 42nd Division, First Sergeant Harry N. Kendall had been attempting to move his men to a safer position during the opening hours of the Champagne sector battle; before they could find shelter, a shell exploded, killing him instantly.[1] Now, on row 12, grave 16, mother and son were reunited as she knelt before his white marble headstone.

Mrs. Kendall's choice to leave her son buried overseas had not been an easy one. Like thousands of families across the United States, she struggled with this thorny decision offered by the War Department in 1919. The choice had been unexpected because the government had assured her that once the war was over, the remains of all American soldiers who died abroad would be returned to their homes.[2] The pledge was followed by consoling letters, including one from the regimental chaplain, offering solace during her dark hour. The chaplain encouraged Estella Kendall not to think of Harry as dead but rather as having given his life for his country and the "Great Cause." "His body only lies buried," he claimed with certainty. "I believe that he is with God." The chaplain described the dignified wooden cross that marked Harry's temporary grave and the honor that had been bestowed on him during the initial battlefield burial service. "Such courage and disdain of death's toll when in line of duty can point to but one thing, that such dauntless spirit is immortal. When it was needed your son gave his body for his country. His spirit is safe in the everlasting arms."[3]

The chaplain's well-intentioned expressions echoed those written to thousands of other families during the eighteen months America participated in the Great War, as it became known. The rhetorical phrases celebrated the glory of victory and sacrifice for democratic ideals and aimed

Estella Kendall of Shenandoah, Iowa, at her son's
grave during her pilgrim-
age to the Meuse-Argonne
cemetery at Romagne-
sous-Montfaucon, France,
in May 1933. First Sergeant
Harry N. Kendall, 168th Infantry, 42nd Division, was
killed in 1918. (Courtesy of
Liberty Museum, Kansas
City, Missouri)

to solace the grief of the bereaved. In the process, each of the deceased
became a cult figure, an embodiment of national identity, thus deserving
of preservation and honor by its citizens.

So it must have been surprising to Mrs. Kendall when, in the war's aftermath, the government asked her to decide whether Harry's final resting
place should be in her hometown or at Arlington National Cemetery or
on the former battlefield in France.[4] Despite the options presented and
the chaplain's previous attempts to assuage her grief, in April 1919, Estella
Kendall requested that the body of her son be sent home to Iowa, rather
than remain in an overseas American cemetery.[5] Here, she believed she
could care for his grave as only a mother could.

Then, in June 1921, nearly three years after Harry's death, Estella Kendall mysteriously reversed her decision and wired the army's Quartermaster Corps' Graves Registration Service that he was to rest instead within

one of the new national military cemeteries constructed thousands of miles from American shores. Two full years passed before the summer of 1923, when she received word that her son had finally been laid to rest in a permanent grave at the Meuse-Argonne American Cemetery, Romagne-sous-Montfaucon, France.[6]

Perhaps it was the interminable wait for the return of her son's body that convinced Estella Kendall to leave him buried overseas, or it may have been the perpetual care and reverence promised by the American government. Either way, nearly twenty-five thousand other families made a similar additional sacrifice that seemed to guarantee everlasting remembrance. Like Mrs. Kendall's, their choice was not made without further pain and indecision. The weight this sacred burden represented to many families is apparent from the steady stream of cable dispatches from Washington, DC, to France, when, by 1921, thousands of families had changed their minds regarding the final disposition of their deceased. Ultimately, more than thirty thousand American dead of this war were buried in U.S. cemeteries overseas, including those without a known identity.[7]

For Americans, the anxious uncertainty that accompanied the government's immediate postwar indecision over the disposition of its war dead was a heartbreaking period for all concerned. Once resolved, the agonizing wait for the body's return could take years. For others, the decision to leave their deceased overseas came at an equally high price. There would be no funeral service, no headstone in a local cemetery, nothing left to venerate, and no closure so necessary in the grieving process. For those whose sons or husbands were officially termed "missing" or "unknown," the relentless passage of time seldom offered any solace or resolution. Although the government was in the process of returning the identifiable deceased, countless bodies remained unidentifiable, and scores of others were never found. Their loved ones would receive no benefit from the government's offer of a personal headstone as a site of memory. In honor of approximately forty-five hundred of these American "unknowns," political and military leaders in the United States followed the example of England and France and buried one unidentified soldier in 1921.[8]

While the democratic options presented to families may have appeared to be the best policy at the time, the outcome did little to promote national solidarity as intended. On the contrary, impassioned debate raged across America as to whether it was best to leave the deceased in foreign soil or to bring the bodies home for burial. Repatriation of the dead eventually proved enormously costly and divisive, and it placed an extraordinary burden on the bereaved, leaving doubts that often lingered years after the daunting choice was made.

It may have been partially due to this uncertainty that mothers and widows of loved ones buried overseas argued so persuasively during the postwar years for a government-sponsored pilgrimage to the gravesites. Gold Star mothers and widows, so named for the emblem they were urged to display on armbands and service flags in their homes, believed their sacrifice warranted a further debt of gratitude that could best be rewarded with a visit to the graves of their sons (or daughters) and husbands.[9]

The incomparable tale of the Gold Star Mothers and Widows pilgrimage was the result of years of effective lobbying by white, Anglo-Saxon women's organizations, testing their budding political power in a new arena while attempting to capitalize on a unique era when mothers held the moral high ground. Their extraordinary achievement resulted in a series of unprecedented pilgrimages between 1930 and 1933, when mothers and widows traveled in luxury to cemeteries in Europe as guests of the U.S. government. Originally, the offer was intended to give women— regardless of race, color, or economic status—an opportunity to find resolution with death at the faraway graveside of their loved one. Whether the pilgrimages, as crafted by Congress, the military, and some of the more politically savvy "pilgrims," met that objective is for the reader to decide.

But when Estella Kendall and thousands like her made their painful decision, there was no assurance of a future pilgrimage. Instead, an ocean and thousands of miles separated them from the cemeteries and monuments being erected overseas throughout the late 1920s on behalf of their nation and its heroes. As a consequence, only the more affluent could afford the long voyage to Europe. So why, then, did these families choose to leave their loved ones buried in foreign lands, and did they feel that the additional sacrifice had been worthwhile?

Fifteen years after Harry Kendall's death, his mother sailed to France as one of more than six thousand women who accepted the government's offer.[10] Her recorded memories vividly describe the striking hat she wore most days, the luxurious accommodations aboard ship, and the cathedrals she visited, with occasional embellishments of French history gleaned from the day's sightseeing. The former battlefields, although no longer scenes of death and devastation, still held enormous fascination for the pilgrims, as they did for many tourists. Mrs. Kendall mentions seeing the Bayonet Trench, "where 250 soldiers were buried where they fell" (in fact, there were less than one hundred),[11] a British tank captured by the Germans, and plenty of barbed-wire entanglements, trenches, and shell holes. But what of her visit to the cemetery, the key purpose of her pilgrimage?

Estella Kendall's presence at her son's final resting place coincided with Memorial Day weekend, when "the cemetery was beautiful with its decorations of United States and French flags and poppies." Yet, following her visit to Harry's grave, Estella's diary simply reads, "Went to the Meuse-Argonne cemetery where we placed large wreaths on our sons' graves." Nothing more. As she knelt by his headstone and looked out over the perfectly manicured gardenlike setting of this, the largest of the American World War I cemeteries, Estella must have wondered why it took more than a decade for the War Department's invitation to arrive. Why indeed? Like the on-screen mother in the popular 1933 Hollywood film *Pilgrimage,* Estella Kendall had been invited to France to revisit her son's death after spending more than ten years "remembering to forget."[12]

Whereas the history of the First World War has been told repeatedly in various forms, the saga of the dead and the efforts of the living to honor their heroes has remained dormant far too long. What follows is the staggering, often-macabre tale that brought Estella Kendall and thousands of women like her on a journey steeped in the pathos and human drama of a democratic nation struggling to find meaning in war. As the political dynamics of this venture unfold, we sense that although times may change, much remains remarkably the same.

2

Origins

After more than ninety years, the First World War still evokes gruesome images of No Man's Land, where bodies lie dead or slowly dying amid the chaos of battle as machine-gun bullets crackle and whiz across the parapets of mud-filled trenches. We think of the Western Front, a hellish place where intrepid soldiers trek across churned-up battlefields pitted with craters to assault the enemy through a barrage of rapid gunfire. Shell fire illuminates the night skies, exposing the ever-present barbed wire, and noxious chlorine or phosgene gas wafts across the battlefields, bringing the slow death of asphyxiation to countless men destined to suffer in places with familiar names such as the Somme, Ypres, Verdun, Belleau Wood, and the Meuse-Argonne.

This ghastly global conflict, responsible for the death of over nine million people, took place primarily in Europe from August 4, 1914, to November 11, 1918, and resulted chiefly from the breakdown of powerful political alliances. The Entente Powers comprised France, Russia (until 1917), Great Britain, and later Italy (from 1915). These nations were joined by the United States on April 6, 1917 (as an "associate" power, according to President Woodrow Wilson, rather than as an ally), in the defeat of the Central Powers of the Austro-Hungarian, German, and Ottoman empires.

The Great War undoubtedly had a devastating impact on the history of the twentieth century in that millions of individuals suffered fatal or often disabling wounds and injuries. Moreover, each belligerent nation bore immeasurable and long-term social, financial, and psychological costs and scars; pervasive disillusionment among people of all combatant nations endured for generations.

The Treaty of Versailles in 1919 severely punished Germany as the alleged instigator of the war and required its people to pay enormous war reparations while awarding vast territory to the victors. Despite the passage of time since the armistice, historians have continued to argue persuasively over countless aspects of the war, including its causes, the

Lieutenant Finnel, chaplain of the 124th Machine Gun Battalion, identifying the dead of the 33rd Division. Bois de Chaume, southeast of Sivry-sur-Meuse, France, October 14, 1918. (SC Photo 111, No. 27088, RG 92, NA)

effectiveness of commanders and operations, and even the outcome. Nevertheless, one indisputable consequence was the depth and intensity of grief that engulfed the bereaved, who struggled to find meaning from their painful and often questionable loss.

In the United States, war losses were substantially less than those suffered by other nations. For example, by 1919, there were approximately 722,785 British war dead, compared with U.S. figures well under 100,000, and many of the American dead were actually flu victims. In May 1919, the Graves Registration Service (GRS) stated with unreserved precision that 34,063 had been killed in action, 14,215 had died of wounds, 23,210 had died of disease, and another 4,588 had died of "other causes." With a further 4,102 noted as "missing in action," total overseas losses for the American Expeditionary Forces (AEF) were documented at that time at 80,178.[1] This relatively low number cannot compare to other nations' figures for the First World War, or to the over 600,000 dead of the Civil War,

General John J. Pershing, commander of the American Expeditionary Forces, and Secretary of War Newton D. Baker begin their inspection tour at Bordeaux, France, February, 1918. (SC Photo 111, No. 7819, RG 92, NA)

when the United States had a population a third of its 1918 size.[2] Yet, after the cessation of hostilities in the First World War, the War Department found itself with no defined policy for the disposition of its war dead.

Because of the scarcity of shipping space aboard transports crossing the Atlantic, General John J. Pershing, the AEF commander, and Major General Henry G. Sharpe, the U.S. Army's quartermaster general, agreed that it was "impracticable" to use valuable shipping space for coffins and burial equipment. Thus, it was decided that Americans who died in Europe would be interred there, and no attempt would be made to bring them back until after the close of hostilities.[3] This directive was the extent of the War Department's prewar planning concerning the disposition of American remains.

Then, in early September 1918, just as General Pershing was amassing nearly half a million inexperienced American doughboys near the Saint-

Mihiel salient on the Western Front in France, Secretary of War Newton D. Baker publicly pledged to the nation that the government would ensure a home burial to all who died in its foreign service.[4] This promise, made in lieu of a clear policy concerning the deceased, was announced in the newspapers that autumn. It would place the government in an awkward position once peace was declared.

President Wilson had appointed Baker, a lawyer by profession and former mayor of Cleveland, in March 1916, because he was considered an acceptable candidate for politicians on both sides of the war question. An avowed pacifist, Baker suffered merciless criticism for his conduct of the war during its early months, and this may have influenced his decision to make this public pledge.[5] However, the passing of two unprecedented years of modern technological warfare occurring thousands of miles from American shores, the extent of casualties, and shifting trends in public opinion undoubtedly combined to make the disposition of bodies an issue worthy of reconsideration.[6]

Despite the straightforward simplicity of Baker's promise, it triggered a massive and highly controversial repatriation of war dead from the battlefields in Europe to the United States between 1919 and 1922. Neither the United States nor any other nation up until that time had ever attempted such a colossal task, one that eventually cost the government thirty million dollars and set an enduring national precedent for generations.[7]

3

A Daunting Pledge

Although the guns were silenced in November, the months following the signing of the armistice in 1918 brought an increased awareness of the extent of death and destruction caused by the war. Nowhere was this devastation more apparent than across the Western Front, in Belgium and northern France. While politicians debated reparations and the future League of Nations, armies buried their dead and counted the cost of victory or defeat. The painful process of reconstruction had begun.

Allied efforts to sanitize the former fields of carnage began with the consolidation of cemeteries once peace was declared. The American Graves Registration Service, created in 1917, was largely responsible for this work, but during hostilities, sanitary squads and Pioneer Infantry units following the advancing armies were usually assigned the task of burying the dead.[1] By war's end, the GRS had assumed responsibility for the formidable work of identifying, exhuming, and registering burials left in more than twenty-three hundred cemeteries across Europe where American dead were temporarily buried. Even more astounding is that of the total seventy thousand burials in France, approximately fifteen thousand were in isolated graves.[2] Yet, despite the burial process gradually taking place overseas, Americans at home were growing increasingly intolerant since 1919 brought no evidence of any effort being made to return their loved ones.

Impatient pleas began arriving at the War Department within days of the cease-fire, with friends and families clamoring for the return of the war dead. Most letters were not as cordial as the one from a Mississippi woman who wrote to the quartermaster general's office regarding infantryman Clifford Greenwood, who died of pneumonia just days after reaching Liverpool, England, in October 1918:

Dear Sir,

   Am writing you of a serious proposition. A dear boy Mr. Clifford Greenwood of Co. D, 150th Inf. who passed away Oct. 22, 1918 of pneumonia in Liverpool England overseas only lived a few days after reaching overseas. Now, I am going to ask a favor of you to please send him home. He was struck conscious to the very last and his dear mother was in his words until he died and his last word was send me home to Mama, and he very often said when he died, he wanted to be buried on his own soil. He was also a good boy of good standing, and was going over to do his bit and died before succeeding. And now is your time to do your bit—is [*sic*] to send him home as his request. . . Am yours as ever, Miss Lola Seyton.[3]

As a family friend, Miss Seyton's attempt to bargain with the War Department does not seem to have carried much weight, since it was followed by a more fervent plea from Greenwood's mother in January 1919: "Now, what I want to know—will the dead be sent home after a while and can I have my sons [*sic*] body shipped to me at Ellisville, Miss?" She concluded by saying, "I can rest satisfied if I know he would be sent back and sent [to] me." By August, Mrs. Greenwood's tone was one of increased intolerance: "I want to know when the U.S. government will begin sending our dead home. We Mothers of America are getting very impatient and anxious. . . . I am so anxious for mine to come, so please let me hear from you at once." Greenwood's burial file contains seven similar inquiries sent to military officials between November 1918 and July 1920, but only one response. In August 1919, the quartermaster general's office replied to Mrs. Greenwood that the War Department could not return the bodies at that time; however, it reiterated the promise that "when permitted, the bodies will be returned to the U.S. and shipped to their families for interment at public expense."[4]

   Others wrote with similar pleas and just as frequently with requests for information concerning their deceased, which they presumed the War Department, or the military leadership, could readily provide. Writing from New York City in December 1918, Mrs. Ethel Goldman asked her son's former commander for further details concerning his death, since previous letters to the War Department had remained unanswered. Her anxious letter questioned whether or not her son had died in a hospital and pleaded for further details concerning his burial, especially the place of his interment. Still others wanted photographs of their loved one's grave as early as March 1919, when the burial process remained in the earliest stages of consolidation.[5]

It was reasonable for Americans to assume that the government would return the bodies of their loved ones because the enduring imagery of the Civil War dead had continued to serve as a touchstone for subsequent generations. That national apocalypse had led to a dramatic shift in the American pattern of commemorating war, when, in its aftermath, the federal government built an elaborate network of cemeteries for those who fought for the Union. President Abraham Lincoln delivered one of his most famous addresses at the Gettysburg Cemetery in 1863, evoking the soldier dead as an enduring symbol of the ultimate goals of the war. Efforts were made to maintain individual soldier identity after death, and remains were concentrated and placed in government-maintained graves. A national bureau was organized to maintain records for missing soldiers in an attempt to keep families informed; this system, although primitive, thus aided in the eventual preservation and return of bodies for home burial for those who could afford it. In defeat, white Southerners, through private Ladies Memorial Associations, also sought to locate and inter the Confederate war dead in permanent cemeteries.

Changing attitudes toward death and burial practice continued to influence cemeterial location, design, and care of the dead in nineteenth-century society. Similarly, contemporary developments in scientific technology created new means of preserving death through innovative embalming methods and photographic imagery. These were timely and welcome advances to a culture that placed high value on modernization and progress.

Public expectation concerning the level of accountability that the government should assume over the health, welfare, and death of its troops escalated after the Civil War, strengthened largely by the proliferation of national cemeteries. By September 1917, when the federal government once again assumed its role as caretaker for the dead, patterns of war remembrance were principally established within the nation's collective memory.

Five months after the United States entered the First World War, Major General Henry G. Sharpe, the quartermaster general, wrote to Secretary Baker regarding the number and frequency of inquiries from relatives of soldiers killed overseas: "It is recommended that a definite policy be adopted," the memo began, that bodies "be disinterred and shipped to their homes" after the war, "*if practicable.*" Then, as if to justify this proposal,

General Sharpe reminded Secretary Baker that "this course was pursued after the War with Spain [when] the remains of all United States soldiers . . . that could be recovered, who died in Cuba, Porto Rico and the Philippines, were brought to the United States and interred in National Cemeteries or sent to their homes."[6] Far from fading, post–Civil War practices resurfaced after the Spanish-American War, accompanied by newly improvised policies made to fit this major conflict fought outside national borders.

The federal government responded by taking a more active role in sponsoring national memorials, promoting the observances of holidays, and administering for the care of the dead once more. With the country's increasing involvement in the affairs of other nations, remembrance practices and the construction of commemorative symbols soon became a powerful tool for building crucial national unity.

Just as American participation in the First World War had divided the United States, the Spanish-American War two decades earlier had been equally controversial, with its motives and outcomes similarly ambiguous. And, although prior expansion across the American frontier was considered crucial to national interests, wars beyond U.S. borders were thought contrary to the longstanding ethos of self-determination for all people. Americans had traditionally resisted becoming involved in the affairs of other nations, so it was essential for the government to justify military interference as something other than an imperialist action by a bellicose force.

To gain public support, war's purposefulness was emphasized rather than its tragedy, as death in battle became a noble deed for a worthy cause. At the same time, the notion of heroic death was readily invoked to assuage the grief of the living while furthering the interests of the nation. Within this process, war death assumed a mythical, cultlike status in which each soldier was worthy of tribute. To meet this debt of honor, soldiers' remains had to be preserved, even when identity could not be guaranteed. In time, it seemed that the greater the need for solidarity, the more resources the government willingly invested in locating and recovering the dead.

The War Department's promise of 1918 was deeply rooted in the commemorative practices of previous American conflicts, particularly those involving the retrieval of war dead from far-flung battlefields. This precedent began with the Mexican-American War in the mid-nineteenth century, when the federal government subsidized the earliest American cemetery in Mexico City for those who died in that engagement, then evolved to ensure an honorable burial for the Civil War dead. Yet the attempted return of all American war dead from foreign shores in the wake of the bloody insurrection that followed the Spanish-American War represented an undeniably more challenging experiment than anything previously attempted. That such an act of remembrance should have been carried out never seems to have been publicly debated in 1900, although it undoubtedly remained a politically viable proposition. Similarly, the details of this costly, perilous, and problematic operation were not widely questioned or explained to the military or the general public.

As no attempt was made to relate the complexities and enormity of this task to the American people, expectations were perpetuated on to the first great war of the twentieth century. Had the details of these recovery missions been made known, it might have prevented the political snafus and much of the anxiety and indecision that occurred just twenty years later.

The people appointed by the U.S. government to perform this gruesome work assumed their role with fierce and stalwart determination in the midst of enormous obstacles. Like Charon, the mythological ferryman of Hades whom the Greeks once believed responsible for rowing the deceased across the river Styx, these men were paid handsomely for the souls they transported.[7] Given the profound impact of their daring efforts on future policymakers and the public, it is worth pausing to give their exploits apt consideration, as I do in the next chapter.

4

Charon's Price

On February 15, 1898, a massive explosion shattered the American battleship *Maine* in Havana Harbor, killing 260 men. Although the exact cause was unknown, the sinking was widely attributed to deliberate sabotage by Spain. By April 1898, Republican president William McKinley had asked Congress for a declaration of war. Although short, the Spanish-American War resulted in territorial gain, the occupation of the Philippines, and a bloody insurrection by the Filipinos that lasted more than three years and cost thousands of lives.[1] In its aftermath, the war was portrayed as a necessary conflict that had strengthened the nation, but many Americans remained doubtful of what had actually been accomplished.

The preliminary success of American forces abroad had done little to soothe the national conscience once the fruits of victory were tainted by local reprisals and after the public realized that more than four thousand service members had died. During the initial war against Spain that lasted sixteen weeks, Secretary of War Russell A. Alger reported 345 combat-related deaths among the U.S. forces, and another 2,565 men had died of disease.[2] In the face of ambiguous war aims, public focus shifted toward an increased concern over the care and treatment of the dead.

Confronted with the public's anger against the War Department, which included allegations that food and medical provision for troops was mishandled, President McKinley launched a military investigation that placed the Quartermaster Corps under close scrutiny. With midterm elections looming and the press hammering the White House for action by autumn, McKinley attempted to use the investigation to contain the public's revulsion against further military intervention.[3] By 1899, the federal government could not afford to ignore popular demands, particularly in view of the imminent need for additional volunteers to assist with the planned annexation of the Philippines.

The investigators' conclusions "blamed most of the war's administrative mistakes and supply shortages on the country's failure to maintain a well-equipped force in peacetime," and they insisted that "intelligent planning and proper management could have prevented these and other misfortunes."[4] Their findings illustrate the potential political power to be gained by evoking the memory of the dead, in this case, as justification for the war-preparedness movement.

In the midst of the public outcry over the military scandal, the American transport *Crook,* the first funeral ship to sail into Brooklyn, returned to New York Harbor in March 1899, bearing the remains of nearly seven hundred bodies of men who had died in the recent conflict.[5] A burial corps composed of civilian morticians and their assistants had just completed the first disinterment of soldiers' remains in Cuba and Puerto Rico for shipment home.

The press ensured a hero's welcome awaited the crew and their cargo, one befitting the dead from America's costly attempt to annex territory beyond the shores of its own continent. The *New York Times* greeted the *Crook's* arrival with headlines proclaiming that for "those who died in another land . . . it was fitting that with the advent of peace won by their sacrifice, their bodies should be gathered with tender care and restored to home and kindred."[6] This bringing home of the dead to the land of their birth or adoption was to be regarded "as an innovation in the world's history of warfare."[7]

The public's reaction to the ship's arrival seems to have been more subdued since there was no music and no display of flags or emotion from the dockside. Instead, men and women dressed in black reportedly stayed "only long enough to learn conclusively that the missing ones they sought had been found."[8] Afterward, rail transportation was arranged for the remains of 350 men whose bodies lay in flagged-draped caskets bound for Arlington Cemetery in Virginia. Included among the dead were 110 whose bodies were unidentified. Rather than dwelling on individual identity or lack of it, the press reflected on the "promiscuous comradeship of the dead," claiming that here black men mingled with white, as did the regular and volunteer troops. That black soldiers had been segregated into separate regiments and fought apart from their white counterparts was not mentioned, nor was it apparent that their bodies were destined for burial in segregated lots at Arlington, a practice that continued throughout the First World War.

Civilian employees, the military, prominent passengers, and hired undertakers all rubbed shoulders aboard the returning funeral ship. In the postbellum era, those in the funeral trade had managed to establish an "aura of professionalism around the treatment of the dead" that helped legitimize their industry as a "respectable and authoritative enterprise."[9] Then, in 1882, in one of the earliest trade journals of the century, *The Casket,* the National Funeral Director's Association announced its status as a professional society for the care of the dead.[10] From the pages of its appealing and effective advertising grew a constituency that became politically potent after 1918.

Basing the journal's title on a burial receptacle was more than a clever marketing gimmick; it was immensely appropriate, since the century's industrial technology had created new developments in the casket's design and construction. But it was the lucrative practice of embalming that legitimized the industry as respectable and its members as "well-trained experts" who had the necessary knowledge and skill to alleviate anxieties over the care of the dead.[11]

Generally, undertakers enjoyed enormous popularity among civilians waiting on the home front. Not only did they promise that, for a fee, they would expeditiously return the bodies, but their trade secret—embalming—contributed to their popular mystique and created the illusion of life in the body, making it easier for the living to accept death.

It had been impossible to preserve the remains of soldier dead in the Spanish-American War with embalming methods as they were then known. Experiments to do so were a failure, and in the warm weather decomposition was rapid. Further embalming attempts were soon stopped because of the risks involved to the health of the Philippine inhabitants. An early cablegram sent to Washington explained that of the twelve embalmed bodies already sent to the United States, it was doubtful whether all reached the port in worthy condition. Even as the public was applauding the honor being shown to the *Crook*'s precious cargo unloaded that day in New York Harbor, Major General E. S. Otis, a former Civil War officer and American commander in the Philippines, ordered that there would be no further shipments for at least six months.[12]

Preserving the corpse reflected more than the advancement of scientific methods; it was an attempt to demonstrate honor to those who had sacrificed their lives as well as to ease the grief of the living. In addition to ensuring hefty profits for undertakers, embalming also promised a way of maintaining not just a name but an identity. This desire to name individually all those citizens who died in service to the nation had begun decades earlier in the United States, whereas no similar collective attempt was made by other nations until the First World War. For Americans, distant wars coincided with rapid changes in cultural attitudes toward death just as science was discovering a means of meeting that demand.

By 1900, embalming was still the exception rather than the rule in civil society and was generally done in the home. Increasingly, it became more common to take the body after death to be dressed and embalmed at the funeral parlor, where the public would then come and gaze on it. In turn, the appearance of the deceased became an important factor during the period since, as one industry publication pointed out, "There is no doubt that people view the dead out of curiosity."[13] This cultural ritual would cause families and the War Department great difficulty by the end of the First World War.

Even professionals are bound to err, and those in the burgeoning funeral industry were frequently blamed in reported cases of misidentification. Others were guided by a new policy for the identification of remains that was eventually written into U.S. Army regulations. Several corpsmen, under the direction of David H. Rhodes, superintendent of the U.S. Burial and Disinterment Corps, were contracted by the government to work jointly with the army on the search and reburial mission. Their system called for a corked bottle to be placed alongside the buried body of the deceased with a card containing his name, regiment, and date of death. Rhodes's efforts were crucial in recognizing the importance of accurately marking and registering graves within a minimum time after the original burial. Eventually, the bottle idea evolved into the standard identification tag issued to all soldiers by the First World War.

Just weeks before the national presidential election in 1900, the army's quartermaster general gave Rhodes new instructions to venture abroad once again in pursuit of soldiers' remains. A party of fifteen assistants accompanied him in October, when he sailed from San Francisco bound for Hawaii, Guam, and the Philippine Islands on a remarkable voyage of several months. Their perilous journey took them nearly eight thousand miles by land and water to the various points necessary to disinter the remains of 1,422 bodies and escort them back to the United States. In Rhodes's report to the quartermaster, he meticulously described the extremely hazardous, often laborious and frustrating ordeal he and his men endured to accomplish their macabre mission.[14] Those details are particularly noteworthy because they bear a striking resemblance to similar operations that took place after later wars.

Rhodes's remarks begin with the corps' arrival in Hawaii, where he and his men were met by superstitious islanders repulsed by the idea of handling the dead, thus preventing him from hiring additional local workers who were so crucial to his mission. Undeterred, the resourceful superintendent paid a visit to the Japanese consulate, where he successfully obtained the services of laborers, but when the men reported for work the next morning, within three hours they struck for higher wages. They demanded $5 a day instead of the $1.25 agreed on, and when Rhodes refused to comply with their request, they refused to work. As a last resort, volunteers were sought from the American soldiers onboard the ship that had brought them to Hawaii. Within a few days thirty-seven bodies had been exhumed and placed on the transport.

In Guam, bull carts were used to haul caskets and other tools over miles of rough terrain to disinter another seven American bodies, before the corps departed for Manila just days later. There, Rhodes's team received a frustrating reception from military bureaucrats stationed on the island who refused to cooperate with their attempts to ascertain the burial places of several sailors and marines who they believed were buried nearby. After locating the cemetery, Rhodes discovered twice as many American graves as he expected, with the names on his list carelessly recorded, making his task all the more complicated. Cases of mistaken identity, incorrect spellings, transposition of rank and burial dates, and graves where multiple bodies lay mysteriously buried were common. Rhodes also quickly discovered that many among the local U.S. hospital staff were indifferent toward his mission rather than supportive. He was repulsed by the disdain and uncooperative manner of others who he believed should have felt as strongly as he did about this sacred work.[15]

Throughout the islands, repugnance regarding such treatment of the dead made the availability of local labor a constant challenge as Rhodes led his men across this disease-ridden region. Nevertheless, the team continued to navigate its way through unchartered, treacherous reefs and, when necessary, waded through the water carrying caskets and other materials ashore. With monsoons unavoidable and nothing in the way of a pier, the safety of the dead, as well as of the living, was risked as bodies and caskets were transferred onboard. Once on land, they used pack mules and ponies to reach American graves, as they trekked miles across remote territory infested with armed Philippine insurgents. The extreme inconvenience, discomfort, cost, and ever-present danger that Rhodes and his men were willing to endure for the dead is nothing short of staggering. Surprisingly, there are no reports of losses among his corpsmen.

Yet, despite all their brave attempts, Rhodes was forced to concede that the burial team had been unable to reach every American grave. In some instances, the dead were left for reasons other than accessibility, such as the decision to leave two exhumed corpses in the ground once it was discovered that they were deserters. Officers present at the disinterment requested that the dead men be left in this state of disgrace, and Rhodes apparently complied.

Although physical and logistical trials proved surmountable, interaction with military officials continued to be the greatest challenge for Rhodes. As a civilian without benefit of rank, his authority was tested at every turn. He did not hesitate, however, to document the complacency of army officers whose pugnacious attitude toward the fate of the dead and the mission of the burial corps was, he reported, "a disgrace to all concerned." An outspoken, resourceful, and apparently brave man, Rhodes remarked frequently on the "gross carelessness" and "rank stupidity" of the individuals he met, comments eventually edited out of the quartermaster general's final report.[16]

Rhodes's difficulties intensified when General Otis, the American commander of the Philippines, stretched protocol by establishing an Army Morgue and Office of Identification at Manila, with Chaplain Charles C. Pierce as the officer in charge of the service. When the historian Edward Steere chronicled the Graves Registration Service in 1951, he noted the animosity between Pierce and Rhodes. Steere wrote that the enraged Rhodes alleged that Pierce's final operation report was "indecent in its claims. . . . Simply bosh."[17] Their rivalry might have threatened the success of burial operations had these efforts not been officially discontinued in 1901. Later War Department policy forbade any similar civilian-military division of authority within an active theater of command.

Ill will and resentment notwithstanding, the Pierce-Rhodes mission did manage to assert a positive influence on the course of burial policy in the twentieth century. Two basic tenets, primarily credited to Chaplain Pierce, were eventually enacted by the War Department. The first recommendation called for an identity disk of aluminum as a required item of the field kit for all servicemen, to be worn constantly around the neck. Additionally, it was suggested that one central office should be responsible for the collection and preservation of all mortuary records, acting as a central agency for burial information.

The military's adoption of these proposals illustrates its recognition of the importance of individual identity to citizen soldiers and its attempt to develop efficient, modern methods. The army seems to have accepted another principle, albeit an unwritten one—that war preparation and planning was no longer a matter of choice but a national necessity.

It is difficult to establish whether D. H. Rhodes's captivating report, brimming with more than fifty pages of gripping observations, useful recommendations, and travel lore, was ever widely circulated within the army. Given his criticisms of military personnel, his accusations regarding pilfered supplies, and references to the steady flow of cash necessary to accomplish the government's mission, it is doubtful. In his typical forthright manner, Rhodes also felt that censorship by the authorities was another factor worthy of change. Details of the hardships and dangers involved in the recovery and return of the dead had repeatedly been kept from public awareness. As Rhodes explained, "Relatives, friends, and others . . . can hardly realize what a tremendous task it is to reach many of the graves of our soldiers and return their remains safely to their homes."[18] Had Americans and the military hierarchy been aware of these details, such insights might have informed future policy.

In spite of Rhodes's patriotic fervor for country and mission, this determined government employee concluded his report with cautioning words that seemed to question whether the end truly justified the costly means required for such an ambitious endeavor. Aside from all the inevitable difficulties with terrain, materials, monsoons, and disease, Rhodes believed this policy of recovery, however sacred the intention, became "an extremely hazardous operation for the safety of the dead, as well as the living."[19] Despite the accuracy of his statement, public acknowledgment of these dangers by the authorities might have jeopardized the entire repatriation process.

Throughout the intervening years of the Spanish-American War, the Philippine insurrection, and the outbreak of the First World War, the War Department continued to maintain garrisons outside the United States. But, despite the ongoing repatriation of these American dead from overseas, army regulations concerning policy and procedure were not updated. Civil War veterans attending their fiftieth reunion at Gettysburg in July 1913 would have recognized many of the same military policies that they had known during their service. For example, it was not until August 1917, four months after the U.S. declaration of war against Germany, that regulations were adjusted to require the identification tag as a necessary part of the field kit.

Although the more experienced David Rhodes outlived his rival by many years, it was Chaplain Pierce who was chosen for the job of Charon,

America's twentieth-century ferryman of the dead. With the emergence of hostilities in Europe, a Graves Registration Service of the Quartermaster Corps was authorized, and retired Chaplain Charles C. Pierce was recalled to active duty. He was appointed the rank of major and assigned commander of the fledgling GRS, to be based in Tours, France. His team was inadequately staffed, however, with only two officers, sixteen noncommissioned officers, and various support personnel.[20] Nevertheless, Major Pierce trained this initial GRS unit in Philadelphia for service overseas and did so on the basis of his previous war experience in Manila.

With the expedient decision to recall Pierce out of retirement to head the new service, burial practices of another era were perpetuated into a new kind of warfare. Technical procedures such as embalming had largely been left to civilians in the past, and methods of evacuating remains from active battlefronts to the rear had never been attempted in a theater such as existed on the Western Front. Adding to these challenges was the lack of a clear and well-defined policy for administering to the needs of American dead at the onset of the war. Moreover, Pershing's participation as commanding officer in earlier wars does not seem to have equipped him with the knowledge or experience with which to inform and guide burial methods for his own army.

With America's entry into the First World War, John J. Pershing, known as "Black Jack" for his leadership role with the black soldiers of the 10th Cavalry during the Spanish-American War, assumed command of the American Expeditionary Forces. In this new role, he and Pierce entered the century of American expansion as veterans of a nineteenth-century conflict, with experiences and perceptions shaped accordingly. They bridged the generations from Cuba and the Philippines to the trenches of France as others had done in previous wars.[21] And with this continuum came the exportation of established methods, attitudes, and assumptions that informed future military policy while shaping American remembrance practice.

The repatriation efforts of 1898 were initiated just as far-reaching reforms were getting under way within the military establishment. This revolution resulted in a total transformation of the institution during the two decades between the end of the Spanish-American War and the First World War. Much of the impetus for change came from young, Staff College–trained officers who gave serious thought toward the professionalization and administration of a modern military organization. By 1918, many of these young military reformers found themselves with key authority in high-ranking positions within the AEF.

Lieutenant Colonel Charles C. Pierce, Quartermaster Corps, Chief of Graves Registration Service, Office of the Quartermaster General, at his headquarters in Tours, France, October 2, 1918. (SC Photo 111, No. 25877, RG 92, NA)

The highly specialized funeral industry challenged the ambitious and possibly premature efforts of military officials to cope with death in an efficient and professional manner. American undertakers were a formidable contender with years of experience, marketing panache, generous fiscal resources, and widespread public approval. Military officials resisted reliance on these civilians, who did not hesitate to remind them of their inexperience and ineptitude in matters beyond warmongering.

The U.S. Army, for its part, remained skeptical toward the motives of these death specialists, whose efforts to locate isolated burial places appear to have gone largely unappreciated. Consequently, men such as D. H. Rhodes failed to gain recognition for their heroic adventures because such missions were not thought worthy of manly heroism, nor were they publicized. Like grave digging, this task was assigned to civilians and to people perceived as inferiors. So, while the military dwelt on the statistical precision of its identification rates, others performed the contemptible recovery work. In the process, the public continued to believe that their loved ones had died a beautiful death and that their sacrifice reflected dignity, heroic virtue, and patriotism.

Regardless of the efficiency or rationality of a nation's collective memories, they are, like those of an individual, created by layers of events deposited one on top of another that often obscure the original experience.[22] In turn, these memories are regularly subjected to selective recall as one event is highlighted in favor of another or eclipsed by subsequent occurrences. In this way, a culture maintains its identity by passing on the sum of its values and experiences from one generation to the next.[23] This foray into the years preceding the First World War illuminates the far-reaching yet unmistakable components that were crucial to the construction of American remembrance, namely, a moral obligation to the dead and the recognition of commemoration as an instrument of authority and solidarity.

For Americans struggling with their personal loss and the ambiguity of war after 1918, repatriation was no longer an innovation but an established and resolute pact with the government. This practice symbolized the nation's gratitude and offered those in mourning a measure of consolation, however costly and inconvenient the process. For a young country still forming its collective identity, the custom had weathered the test of several wars and was entrenched in the minds of Americans as a unique and honorable birthright. In the aftermath of the century's first global war, democratic choice was added to the formula that has since become an unquestioned component of the American commemorative process.

5

A Problem of Policy

No nation was ready for the devastation of the First World War, but in the aftermath of slaughter, each remained accountable for its dead. The United States was equally unprepared for a war of such magnitude and distance, despite the brevity of America's overseas encounter and the benefits which might have been gained from prior military experience. Nevertheless, for over a year after the armistice, the War Department possessed no firm, well-defined policy for the disposition of thousands of buried soldiers' remains in countless locations across Europe.

Just as the majority of civilians were generally unaware of the demands that efficient burial practice and repatriation required, so it seems were those in command of the U.S. Army. That is surprising given the many innovations carried out since the Civil War and the progressive efforts made throughout the early twentieth century to professionalize the military establishment.

The apparent lack of preparedness was evident even in 1916 during America's Punitive Expedition into Mexico. From March 1916 to February 1917, John J. Pershing led an expedition numbering over fifteen thousand men across the border four hundred miles into Mexican territory in pursuit of the bandit Pancho Villa. When recalling his Mexican experiences in relation to the war in Europe, Pershing states, "It is almost inconceivable that there could have been such an apparent lack of foresight in administration circles regarding the probable necessity for an increase of our military forces and so little appreciation of the time and effort which would be required to prepare them for effective service." Pershing acknowledges that Congress had appropriated more than three hundred million dollars in August 1916 for military expansion and improved administrative organization, but he insists that "scarcely a move was made to carry it out prior to our actual entrance into the war."[1]

Pershing's primary regret relates to the loss of the strategic value of an additional five hundred thousand American combat troops ready to assist the Allies by the spring of 1917, due to the "erroneous theory that neutrality forbade any move toward preparation."[2] Equally regrettable was the missed opportunity to prepare firm policies and procedures for the eventual handling of American war dead once the American Expeditionary Forces arrived overseas.

Two months after Pershing left his duty in Mexico in early 1917, the War Department began expressing concerns to army personnel at Fort Sam Houston, Texas: "What provisions, if any, have been made for preparation of remains of soldiers dying in Mexico and shipment home of same?" and "How long before bodies already buried in Mexico can be removed and shipped home?" These questions illustrate the pervasive ambiguity surrounding army policy on this issue. The authorities were not making the proper provision to handle such cases, and the suggestion followed that perhaps licensed professional embalmers should be employed. Fearing public reprisals similar to those that followed the Spanish-American War, one Quartermaster Corps official wrote, "I am afraid it will subject our Corps to criticism if remains of soldiers temporarily interred in Mexico are not brought home at the earliest opportunity."[3]

When, in September 1917, the bodies of seven American soldiers buried in Mexico still had not been recovered, proposals were invited from private undertakers in El Paso for the disinterment and return of the soldiers' remains. But these hired professionals attempted to charge the War Department more than was budgeted, thus creating further delays. In a foretaste of events to come, the War Department was inundated with emotional letters from impatient and distressed next of kin, imploring officials to send a search party immediately. Sadly, by the time a burial team finally reached Mexico in 1925, it found only empty graves. Local residents who were interviewed claimed that at least one of the bodies had been removed from its temporary burial place shortly after the withdrawal of American troops and then had been hanged to a tree and burned.[4]

This grievous experience may explain why, with America's entry into the First World War in April 1917, the U.S. Army's quartermaster general, hoping perhaps to avoid any future scandal, recommended that Secretary of War Newton Baker appoint a civilian burial corps rather than a military unit. The government's official history is vague on this point, but within a month the chief of staff was formulating plans for a militarized burial team instead.[5]

Some members of Congress felt that civilian burial organizations were a more promising choice. In mid-July 1917, J. Hampton Moore, a House

Republican from Pennsylvania, introduced a bill to the Committee on Military Affairs recommending that the secretary of war accept what appears to have been a generous offer made by the American Purple Cross Association.[6] This group, likened to the American Red Cross (which came to the aid of the U.S. Army Medical Department that year), volunteered to recover, embalm, and care for the bodies of those who died in battle. The association even offered to raise, equip, train, and maintain—at its own expense—units of embalmers with automobiles to ensure that the bodies of soldier dead could be preserved for their eventual return home for burial in "recognizable condition."

The proposal would have placed responsibility for the dead largely on a noncombatant organization, which is reasonable given the links between the GRS and civilians in former conflicts. Despite the association's generous offer, it is difficult to imagine how these men might have coped with the realities of modern warfare while riding in their hearses across the trenches of the Western Front. Regardless, the committee voted instead to make the GRS solely responsible for this task. Moore's bill never made it beyond a brief debate within the committee's chamber, and little was heard of the Purple Cross Association again until after the war. By 1920, the promise of preserving soldiers' bodies with their identity intact became a matter of considerably greater importance.

However, in July 1917, when this bill was introduced, the United States had been at war for barely four months and had, as yet, no knowledge of the devastating impact that twentieth-century weapons would have on the dead. Americans were also understandably confident that, as in past wars, their dead would be returned home for burial. They were still relatively unprepared for the heartache of missing men, massive unidentified dead, and the eventual complications wrought by a policy that advocated leaving bodies buried on or near distant battlefields during hostilities.

Moreover, Americans assumed that after the war the French government would assure the transport and return of their soldiers buried over there, but the situation changed dramatically in late February 1919, when the Ministry of the Interior passed a decree forbidding all exhumations and transport of bodies for three years.[7] The French were anxious to consolidate isolated graves (due to the difficulties they otherwise represented to the resumption of French agriculture), but lack of transportation and hygiene dangers were cited as justification for delaying any further removals.[8]

The French government's position may have affected America's ability to produce a clear plan, but equally, it provided the War Department with much-needed time to formulate a strategy. The implications of this unexpected legislation were significant since work had already begun by late 1918 to exhume and assemble remains from thousands of isolated graves and temporary cemeteries into organized, concentrated burial grounds. "Isolated" graves—those outside a cemetery, in some obscure French burial ground or in a detached field—required greater care, as they could easily be overlooked. Restrictions against the removal of these bodies for three years risked serious logistical problems of space, misidentification, administrative chaos, and fierce public outcry from Americans anxious for the return of their deceased.

Discussions between the French Office of Military Burials and the recently promoted Lieutenant Colonel Pierce occurred frequently in early 1919 and included at least one conference where both the American and French services agreed that the return of American soldiers' bodies to the United States was not contemplated "for a long time yet."[9] This outcome is surprising given that at an earlier Anglo-French conference, the French government claimed that it was "impossible under existing French law to prohibit exhumation and removal" of bodies.[10] According to the British Imperial War Graves Commission (IWGC) chief, Major General Fabian Ware, and unbeknownst to the American public, it was the U.S. War Department that requested the French government to insist on no bodies being moved at that time.[11] Thus, although the French were publicly blamed for banning the immediate repatriation of the dead, both governments may have been partially responsible.

News of the French decree seems to have shocked General Pershing when he read of it in a Paris newspaper rather than through official channels. In a confidential cablegram notifying Washington of the recent ruling, the commander expressed his fear over the increased difficulties such action would have for the preservation of identifications.[12] Pershing must have recalled that just weeks before, his staff officer in charge of Services and Supply (SOS), Major General John G. Harbord, had, in a rather routine manner, ordered that authorization be obtained from the French to return bodies of American soldiers or sailors buried in France. Harbord suggested that the French government be asked to designate an officer to assist with "the *minor details*" of the operation.[13]

It was later disclosed that General Harbord had entirely underestimated the importance of this undertaking and was not pleased that General Pershing had seen fit to assign him to this post.[14] Harbord appointed another officer, Colonel Joe S. Herron, to oversee the work, and Herron

The American Graves Registration Service was largely responsible for the formidable work of identifying, exhuming, and registering burials left in more than twenty-four hundred sites across Europe where American dead were temporarily buried. This is an example of a trench burial. Undated. (*History of the American Graves Registration Service*, Volume 1, 22.A)

in turn "failed to appreciate the responsibilities of his duty."[15] Later, Herron prematurely reported that the cemetery work was complete and on a "maintenance only" basis when, in fact, it was far from being finished. When transportation and labor were taken away from the task, some families of the dead were quick to criticize the GRS and the burial conditions they observed while visiting the graves in France. Consequently, no work was accomplished during the summer of 1919 until trucks were again available.

While winter weather halted the military's progress for the next several months, French officials wrestled with the precise terms of their new legislation in a published Ministry of War pamphlet. "If the situation is clear about the British, Italians and Belgians," it stated, "it is still uncertain on the political point of view for the Americans."[16] Although officials recognized that the U.S. government was "bound by obligations," lawmakers had their own internal matters to consider. According to the pamphlet,

French officials felt public opinion would be "painfully affected" to see the Allies receive their war dead before French families. With an eye toward successful postwar Franco-American relations, the burden of such an unprecedented decision must have been enormous. In an effort to reach a compromise, officials offered land as "Fields of Honor" for the American dead and agreed to assist with maintenance and care of these cemeteries. They explained that although the American government may have preferred an exception be made, the French wanted "no gruesome horrors of millions of bodies of dead on their trains."[17]

France was not the only nation affected by American intentions. In Brussels, the "insistent demands" of the U.S. government for the removal of soldiers' remains buried there were said to be causing "considerable embarrassment to the Belgian government."[18] An equally difficult strain was placed on policymakers in London. "The American decision and announcement makes our responsibility much more difficult than it would have been," wrote an official at the IWGC. "I do not know what, if any, negotiations took place between Washington and Paris before the decision was taken, . . . but we have already received letters referring to it from relatives who desire a similar concession and I do not know what answer to give."[19]

The British government did not permit the repatriation of their soldiers' remains. Instead, plans were made for the construction of military cemeteries on the battlefields even before the war's end.[20] The nonrepatriation decision originated with the IWGC's chief, Major General Fabian Ware, who arrived in France in September 1914 to command a mobile Red Cross unit with casualties at the front.[21] Ware was struck by the absence of any official organization responsible for the marking and recording of British graves and, accordingly, assumed that task in 1915, when units were reorganized as a Graves Registration Commission. Ware, "conscious of the greater democratic mood of Britain at war," prohibited private, and thereby selective, exhumations from the battlefield in March 1915 and then forbade personalized monuments in May 1916.[22] By this time, two hundred cemetery sites had already been chosen, and plans for more were in progress. Ware was cognizant of the effect American repatriation would have on the British mood and was prepared for the backlash. In September 1919, he wrote, "if any such removals are allowed the general demand will be very large and while it may be possible for the Americans to take back their 50,000 dead to America (appalling as the thought of such a procedure is), it will be utterly impracticable for us to bring back the greater 500,000."[23] As a result of Ware's action, scattered bodies were to be gathered together, reinterred, and individually marked for the first time in British military history.

After inspecting American graves at a British cemetery, Assistant Chief of the GRS Colonel W. P. Coleman expressed impatience and apparent discomfort that Britain had progressed more rapidly in these efforts. Colonel Coleman wrote, "The I.W.G.C. is eager to know what is the adopted policy regarding our dead. They would like to have our dead left in British cemeteries. However we must agree to their adopted plans."[24] Acting on Coleman's suggestion, Colonel Leon Kromer of the Paris GRS office recommended that a policy be adopted as soon as possible so that the GRS might have "something more definite . . . to go on."[25] As the months passed, Britain was kept waiting, not just by the U.S. War Department but by the same French restrictions that prevented all countries from moving their dead.[26]

Lieutenant Colonel Pierce met regularly with French officials throughout early 1919 to discuss the ban on removal of the deceased. In April, he relayed their response to Pershing: "Should an exception be made in the case of American dead it would at once involve each of the other nations in clamorous agitation for like action to satisfy its own people." Pierce pointed out that France would become a "veritable charnel house" if the United States proceeded with its plan for removals. On behalf of the French, he pleaded that such "ghastliness" be avoided.[27] Having witnessed the horrendous exhumation work of a previous war, Pierce would surely have preferred to avoid a repetition of similar events on a much greater scale.

In March 1919, the War Department, with increasing ambivalence regarding its ability to fulfill its pledge, sent a letter accompanied by a ballot card to families of the deceased (referred to as "next of kin" or NOK), in an attempt to ascertain their wishes regarding the permanent disposition of bodies overseas. As a preemptive measure, the government's ballot warned that it was not "deemed practicable to grant requests for relatives, friends, or undertakers to go to France to superintend the preparation and shipment of, or to accompany bodies back to the United States."[28] No date was given regarding the transfer of bodies, nor did the government attempt to sway public opinion or explain the difficulties involved with recovery and return of the deceased. The letter did, however, clarify who could rightly determine disposition of remains, and this honor rested first with the father if the deceased was an unmarried man. If the father was dead, the mother would decide on her son's final resting place. In the case of a married man, the wife had the right to decide, followed by his parents if she had remarried, then any children of the marriage.

The War Department sent 74,770 ballot cards, and 63,708 answers were received by January 1920.[29] Confusion was inevitable after these cards were mailed back from NOK to several different offices in Washington, DC, and overseas, rather than to one central location. In exasperation, Pierce tried to reconcile these various requests (often from the same family) with conflicts of "all sorts and changes back and forth, sometimes as many as five alterations."[30] Family differences complicated the process further, particularly when those involved were disgruntled wives and mothers who could not agree. In thousands of cases, letters were returned to the quartermaster's office months after initially being sent because of an improper address or people having moved or having died.

In these instances, groups of veterans such as those from the New York Department of the American Legion often stepped in to offer their assistance in locating NOK, using their own questionnaires to other legion posts and former army buddies all over the country.[31] George Mosse speaks of this new solidarity among veterans as that which occurs with loss. Through their efforts, the memory of war is refashioned into a sacred experience with the cult of the fallen at the center of what he terms the "myth of the war experience."[32] This democratic myth was reinforced when the whole community welded a common identity capable of giving meaning to the familiar symbols of the war myth: monuments, a sense of patriotic mission, camaraderie, and the war cemetery. Yet that solidarity faltered when exposed to a democratic process based on individual demands, as the ballots demonstrated.

Wanting to obtain the most up-to-the-minute wishes of the families, Pierce and his team sent a follow-up "shipping inquiry" to NOK asking for their final decision regarding the disposition of their deceased. In some cases, families had already written that they did not want the body returned. Sometimes, as many as two years had passed since the NOK sent their instructions. Consequently, letters such as that received from an impatient New York father were not unusual: "We have received already two of these forms and have filled them out and sent back. We have told you that we don't want the body of Walter Kowalewski to be sent here. We wish his body to remain in London where he is buried now. And we wish not to be molested with any more telegrams or any other forms as to the shipment of the above."[33]

In other instances, letters were sent to families in anticipation of their loved one's being located or identified, thereby prematurely creating hopes that their deceased would be returned. Sadly, this was not always the case. One father of a New York private who died in October 1918, after being assured that his son's body would be recovered, wrote, "If [this] letter means that the body of our dear one will not be returned to us, it is surprising. After the many requests I have made [to] the War Department, they have replied assuring the return of the body when conditions will permit. The enclosed letter is a shock to the family."[34]

Evidently, the public's response was overwhelming, as an anxious communication from Washington attested in the spring of 1919: "This office is in receipt of many communications containing inquiries relative to the death and burial of our soldiers overseas, and it is requested that the office be furnished with such information as will enable it to make a definite reply." Eighteen pointed questions were listed reflecting the public's concerns, such as "Are the bodies of the soldiers who die now embalmed?" "What kind of casket has been used for burial?" "Will it be possible to allow relatives to have caskets, containing bodies returned to this country, opened for inspection?" "Can a tentative date for starting removal of bodies to this country be given?" "Will it be advisable to approve requests to have the bodies returned to other countries than the U.S.?" An expeditious reply was requested so that a War Department response could be made at once.[35] The extent of public inquiry into this complex and controversial dilemma had prompted another flustered attempt to reach a timely compromise.

Neither the church nor the state nor anyone in military or political circles could agree on the best course of action. Just after the armistice, Major General John F. O'Ryan, senior commander of the 27th Division, questioned all his company commanders "unofficially" as to "what the sentiment [was] in relation to the removal of bodies of our men who fell in battle." The general explained that he was having difficulty answering the many letters from families asking for the most desirable or practical response from the soldier's standpoint. Years of military service had rendered O'Ryan incapable of providing a comfortable or informed response; however, his recent battlefield experience forced him to acknowledge privately that in many cases, there was "very little to ship back in the way of remains as many bodies were blown into fragments."[36] A prompt and emphatic reply from the 107th Infantry Regiment headquarters stated that "all of the Company Commanders are of the opinion that if it is practicable such bodies as are requested by relatives should be returned without delay."[37]

Conversely, a senior chaplain from general headquarters claimed to be speaking for the majority of GHQ chaplains "almost unanimously" when he asserted that the bodies should rest in France.[38] Those in the military's higher echelon tended to agree. Most reflected the views of General Harbord, the SOS commander, who wrote to the chief of staff in 1919, "It would be better to concentrate the bodies of American dead in central cemeteries in France than to undertake to remove them to the United States." He further warned that the War Department be advised of the many reasons for leaving bodies in France and suggested that a "propaganda [campaign] be started in an endeavor to create a sentiment against this removal." Harbord reported that "bodies could not possibly be shipped home for some time," but this, he stated, "would allow the grief of relatives and friends [to become] less acute." Whereas, if the bodies were sent immediately, "the result would be funerals all over the United States."[39] Consequently, the French government's ban against the movement of remains had thus allowed for everyone to consider their stance and, more significant, for factions to consolidate.

In the midst of this maelstrom, a congressional committee arrived in France in April 1919 to help decide the question of disposition. According to General Harbord, the committee concurred that it would be better to leave the American dead in France, and members promised to publicly promote this stance once they returned to the United States.[40] As an inducement to families considering an overseas burial, plans were announced for the beautiful cemeteries soon to be built there. Within two months, the U.S. Senate appropriated five hundred thousand dollars for the establishment of a national cemetery in France, but still the French resisted political pressure.[41]

France, for its part, had just cause to delay American repatriation efforts. War had devastated the rich northern regions of the country, where the best coal and iron fields were located and where most of the factories and big iron and steel works operated. Twenty-five percent of the total taxes paid in France had been raised in this territory before it was ravaged by war. But more significant for the American question was the lack of transportation. Over fourteen hundred miles of main railways had been demolished, along with nearly one-half of the total one thousand miles of canals. What is more, extensive destruction to France's thirty-two thousand miles of roads made travel even more difficult for nearly 2,728,000 refugees attempting to return to their war-torn homes. Perhaps the most demoralizing statistic of all was that by 1920, the beleaguered nation was indebted between three and four billion dollars to the United States.[42]

Nevertheless, the official GRS history claims that although French arguments appeared to be based on reasons of public policy—alleged interference with reconstruction, sanitary dangers, insufficient modes of transport—these explanations were, the author asserted, "a reaction against a policy not understood or sympathized with, a natural tendency to say 'No' to a country to whom they had been continually saying 'Yes' for two years or more." The GRS historian claimed that this state of things was normal since "familiarity breeds close acquaintance with each other's faults."[43]

From this perspective, many in military and government circles continued to place relentless pressure on the French to lift restrictions on the exhumation work. This course of action was believed to be the only just one, since whereas French families could visit their dead, distance deprived the majority of Americans of that consolation.[44] No thought seems to have been given to others across the British Empire—in South Africa, Canada, and India—grieving their losses in faraway IWGC cemeteries on the Western Front. For instance, North America is thirty-five hundred miles from Western Europe; Australia and New Zealand are twelve thousand miles. According to Australian historian Bart Ziino, "distance from the battlefield actually defined grief as a shared experience" for those grieving the sixty thousand Australians who died in the Great War, of which only thirty-eight thousand were ever identified.[45]

At home, the American people continued to debate the hotly contested repatriation issue from an "Atlantic-wide sense of security," without the distress of a powerful border enemy and as the principal beneficiary of the war.[46] France, on the other hand, lived in daily fear of repeated, vengeful German aggression. With that fear in mind, ministerial officials may have felt that the presence of British and American cemeteries might serve as collateral if French soil was ever invaded again.

By November 1919, forty thousand next of kin had responded to the War Department's ballot (an estimated half of the total number of American dead), with an overwhelming majority asking that their loved ones be returned home as soon as arrangements could be made.[47] In anticipation of this action, Congress allocated five million dollars, authorizing the secretary of war to make all necessary arrangements, and still the French desisted.[48] Ever reluctant to arouse public resentment, Secretary Baker urged Secretary of State Robert Lansing to reach an agreement with the

French as soon as possible. He explained that it could be a "very embar-rassing situation to inform next of kin that France refuses to permit such action."[49] On December 10, 1919, France relented marginally by modifying its three-year ban. The revised decree permitted exhumations within the interior zone only—that is, outside the former battle zone.[50]

Despite repeated official reports and eyewitness testimony that it was "almost impossible" to bring these bodies to the United States due to the "insurmountable difficulties" that moving them presented, the govern-ment proceeded to satisfy the wishes of its people. As one congressman reminded his audience, "We promised the parents that we would bring the bodies of their loved ones home. We certainly cannot fail in this sol-emn duty."[51] Joining him but stopping just short of relating all the sordid details of battle death and burial, Secretary Baker implored Americans to consider the well-kept cemeteries in France as a "wiser and better course to leave those bodies."[52]

National cemeteries overseas offered the ideal opportunity for the state to preserve the myth of the fallen soldier while maintaining mili-tary esprit de corps. Here, on the adorned landscape of camaraderie and memory, the United States could leave its footprint of national might and influence abroad. Conversely, the reality of human sacrifice, with its vivid horrors and gruesome imagery, was clearly visible to the military and postwar travelers to France, who witnessed the exhumation of mangled, decomposing bodies for transport. But this practical, more ghastly side of war and death was minimized in favor of abstract ideologies that glorified sacrifice for the nation.

The rhetorical language of sacrifice undoubtedly solaced the grief of many families who received repeated assurances that their loved ones had died a noble death, one necessary for the nation's survival. Efforts to prevent the erosion of this illusion were crucial, as exemplified by under-takers offering preservation of the bodies, military leaders clamoring for undisturbed comradeship, and authorities everywhere warning against opening returned coffins. Nevertheless, most Americans were less con-cerned about preserving the nation's presence overseas than about con-firming the identification of their deceased.

By May 1920, the War Department received a deluge of requests, pri-marily from undertakers and health officials, for policy guidance regard-ing the opening of coffins by family members eager to view the remains of their returned loved ones. This unforeseen crisis represented yet an-other breach in the evolving repatriation policy, a situation that became so

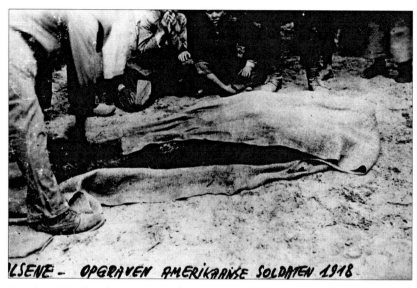

American labor battalions opening the graves of soldiers for reinterring in concentrated cemeteries, with local Belgian children looking on. Olsene, Belgium. (Courtesy of Christopher Sims, Waregem, Belgium)

serious that Secretary Baker requested an emergency session between the quartermaster general and the surgeon general's office. He asked them to determine what measures could be taken to prevent the opening of these caskets. It was thought that the Public Health Service might use its authority to prevent such action by affirming the dangers that open coffins allegedly posed to the health of the living. Much was at stake for the government if the public came face to face with the harsh reality of the coffins' contents. Whereas Americans at home had hoped to verify their loved ones' identity with a final glimpse of a recognizable image, more than likely, what they risked seeing was the shocking remnants of earth and skeletal fragments that hardly resembled the human form they expected.

Men of the GRS, a number of congressional leaders, and many in War Department circles knew of the burial conditions in France and were aware that bodies had been buried in ordinary wooden caskets (or blankets) without being embalmed, in some cases for more than two years, and were in various stages of decomposition. As one medical corps officer commented, "[They are] almost invariably a mass of decomposing material, and are at

best a gruesome spectacle."[53] Families underestimated the horrifying realities of modern warfare, believing death in battle to be a beautiful and heroic event; their expectations reflected this ignorance.

Ultimately, the American public's stronger inclination to have their
loved ones near them even in death determined the national response,
despite hopes that time might diminish public pressure for repatriation.
Even in countries without historical traditions similar to those of the
United States, mourners were no less anxious to have their dead home—
preferably in a recognizable condition.

6

Make Way for Democracy!

Americans were appalled that the French would disapprove of the immediate and complete removal of bodies from all regions. Newspaper editorials and congressional debates reflected the indignant spirit of impatience, such as that of Representative Clement C. Dickinson of Missouri, who addressed the House: "The French Government will not refuse to do what this Government asks and urges to be done; to refuse would be an unfriendly or hostile act."[1] Under renewed pressure, the War Department continued to appeal to the French government to modify its restrictive policy throughout most of 1919.

While awaiting further policy guidance, the GRS continued its work of locating, consolidating, and reburying the dead. Earlier procedures that assigned burial responsibility to regimental units and forbade the shipment of embalming supplies or coffins now had grim consequences. The task of preserving identity and grave locations within the battle zone had been particularly difficult since the war dead were frequently given only a simple, hastily marked burial that did not withstand enemy fire. This experience was true of all armies.[2] Equally troublesome to the GRS were those graves that had been dug to accommodate multiple bodies in the same trench without individual identity markings. Normally, the dead were buried in blankets wearing an identification tag and lain beneath a cross bearing their name, but circumstance and necessity often complicated an all-too-hasty burial process.

After the war, the army's surgeon general wrote that burial of the dead was a "painful duty" that became a serious sanitary problem during battle, one closely connected to questions of morale. Acknowledging that although prompt burial of the dead was essential, he explained that combat line troops could not be spared from the front for this purpose during the fighting. After battle, these soldiers were so "mentally and physically exhausted" that seeing "evidence of the recent engagement" had a depressing effect on them.[3] The intolerable conditions of warfare during the summer of 1918 were intensified by the horrific sights such as those in Fere-en-Tardenois, where troops advanced in the midst of dead bodies of men and animals strewn over the terrain. Many had lain on the ground for ten days or longer during the intense fighting, and the "stench from these bodies was intolerable."

> Dead horses lay at short intervals along the way, many having died from exhaustion. The weather was hot and the bodies of both men and animals had become black, swollen, disorganized masses of organic matter, alive with maggots. Flies bred in millions and soon became an intolerable nuisance as well as a more or less serious menace to health. Other insanitary conditions existed, and there was much reason to apprehend an outbreak of intestinal diseases.[4]

The effect on the esprit of troops must have been a challenge to military commanders, particularly to the corps surgeon, who requested that five hundred men be assigned directly to his corps for the sole purpose of burying the dead. He suggested that these men work with the GRS so that proper identification and care of the personal effects of the deceased might be assured. This appeal was disapproved at general headquarters, but when the surgeon resubmitted another request that Pioneer Infantry be allotted for this purpose, the recommendation was approved and thereafter became the norm. These men apparently performed their work so well that similar conditions never occurred again, but in giving of their service to this arduous work, often performed so close to the front, the living lost their own lives on several occasions.

Within the U.S. Army, as in other armies, the lines of advance were so close together, with fighting taking place in the same spot for days at a time, that it was not unusual for graves to be opened repeatedly by shell fire and for burial parties to be hit in the process of their duty. Orders strictly prohibited burials in remote, inaccessible places or sites of unsuitable drainage, but the circumstances of battle were frequently such that any available location might be used for temporary burials. Following the cessation of war, a complete rechecking of all graves in France was made so that isolated burials could be assembled into large cemeteries "where maintenance would be simpler and the location not forgotten."[5]

The postwar concentration of dead was itself a process prone to confusion and chaos as bodies were often exhumed several times and relocated miles from their original burial place, before finally being laid to rest in a national cemetery. Many were moved yet again to another cemetery in the United States, at the request of NOK, who seldom had any idea what the concentration of the dead entailed. Others, such as Etha May Jackson, of West Philadelphia, knew all too well. Mrs. Jackson, the mother of three sons who had all volunteered for service overseas, asked the War Department where her son's name would appear at the new cemetery in France. "I am a mother of unknown," she wrote. "My son, Sgt. Winfield A. Jackson, was buried three times and then lost."[6] Sergeant Jackson had first been a victim of enemy fire, then of a bureaucracy that, though well intentioned, was not equipped to deal with the ever-changing demands forced on it.

Burial parties of various nations experienced the same macabre disinterment scenes as they endured January's severe frosts, which eventually brought work to a standstill. By February, muddy thaws made the work "by necessity slow," recorded Field Marshal Douglas Haig, commander in chief of the British Armies. "Shell craters full of water, mud and tangled belts of barbed wire render it difficult to find graves which are known to exist and the ground has to be carefully searched to discover others which have not been registered."[7] Commenting on the immense effort involved in the widespread concentration of large cemeteries, one War Graves Commission official noted,

> It involves the great labour of opening perhaps a hundred and fifty thousand graves and removing the bodies for a distance varying from a few yards to three miles or more. It is a task repugnant to both the personnel employed on it and to the relatives who imagine it; but, except in the chalky soil of the country immediately north of the Somme, a few months after burial are sufficient to reduce the body to a skeleton.[8]

British policy called for the establishment of a cemetery wherever forty or more bodies were interred, thus necessitating the creation of more than fifteen hundred cemeteries, involving what the American GRS considered "a proportionately high cost of maintenance and care."[9] The British commission relied primarily on volunteers for this work, a force that continually declined, owing to demobilization.

For General Pershing's army, more than six thousand African American soldiers were detailed to the GRS to perform the gruesome reburial work. One Graves Registration unit and one hundred labor troops were assigned a section of ground, over which there had been combat activities.

Bodies retrieved from outlying areas for reburial at the Meuse-Argonne
cemetery, April 18, 1919. (SC Photo 111, No. 160211, RG 92, NA)

Twenty men would form a skirmish line at intervals of fifty meters, and in
this fashion these troops would cover an average of sixty-four square kilometers a day. The majority of bodies had to be disinterred and reburied, as
few were originally laid more than two feet underground. Three sites were
initially selected as the principal points of concentration in France, one at
Beaumont, one at Pont-a-Mousson, and the third at Romagne, near the
Meuse River and the Argonne Forest.

Labor battalions considered this the "worst job of all Services of Supply assignments."[10] Troops appointed to this task were expected to live in
primitive housing without modern conveniences, often enduring unpleas-
ant weather while they performed their grisly duty. Despite the desolate
conditions and the nature of their reburial work, black laborers found and
reburied at least twenty-three thousand bodies there. As historian Mark
Meigs notes, "Soldiers could view the task of picking up the dead of their
own unit with a sense of duty and humanity," but for the whole army, the
task encompassed much more than the digging of some trenches and laying in the bodies.[11] The digging and burying went on for years.

The GRS official history makes only passing reference to the burial work of African American soldiers, referring to them more often only as cemetery workers or "men of the G.R.S."[12] Where references do occur, specific comments made in the GRS history about the black laborers are suggestive of the general mood of this dreary mission and the times in which these men found themselves: "The handling of the bodies was entirely new work to the colored men, but, after witnessing the manner in which the white personnel performed the various operations, they proved to be efficient in the disagreeable task."[13]

However, the draft version of the service's history contains a revealing passage written by a *New York Evening Post* journalist who visited the Argonne cemetery at Romagne in May 1919. He presents a poignant account of the grave-digging process, describing the work of "sturdy negro troops" living in tents and "droning out those weird tunes that are known in the South as 'the blues.'"[14] His observations were crossed out of the GRS final report.

Graves Registration Servicemen removing bodies from graves for reburial in a larger concentrated American cemetery. A detail of men from Company A, 322nd Labor Battalion, is assisting in the work in a battlefield near Grandpre, France, February 20, 1919. (SC Photo 111, No. 153214, RG 92, NA)

It remains one of the inexorable ironies of the war and its aftermath that African American soldiers were members of a Jim Crow army, denied the right to fight in combat with their white compatriots and used primarily as work gangs. Many laborers were stevedores; some worked in construction jobs; others quarried stone, built railroads, or tended stables; and quite a few found themselves as mess men. Those with previous experience were frequently pulled to serve as cooks and waiters on the private trains of General Harbord and General Pershing himself.[15]

Equality for the black soldier eluded him while he was alive, yet his efforts ensured a democratic process for the dead. The injustice of this contradiction did not go unnoticed by the black community, as the following newspaper excerpt indicates:

> The national administration at Washington has taken pains to see that reports of the alleged atrocities of the Germans generally, and effectively, circulated throughout the length and breadth of this country. But we challenge a denial of the state that no member of the present national administration has even much as publicly commented upon the fiendish atrocities common in the Southland upon members of our race.
>
> What atrocious act of the Germans, thus far reported, can pass, for brutal atrocity, the awful burning alive of that poor . . . ignorant Colored man last week, in this, "the land of the free and home of the brave?"[16]

Despite such media reports, or perhaps because of them, Secretary Baker felt it necessary to thwart any notion of a potential shift in the nation's future views toward racial equality. "I want to impress upon you men, that if you feel that things have not been as you would like them . . . you must try to forget them and go back to civil life with the determination to do your part to make the country what it should be."[17]

Given the era in which the graves registration history was written, it is perhaps understandable that the role of African American soldiers received little or no mention. However, Emmett Scott's failure in his *Official History of the American Negro* to reveal their role in caring for the dead is more surprising. Scott, a conservative African American, was an assistant to Secretary Baker and an adviser on black affairs. He was thought a traitor by many returning black veterans who felt he concealed the truth about their wartime service.

These men felt similarly justified in their disgust of Robert Moton, Booker T. Washington's moderate successor, whom President Wilson had sent to

African American soldiers from the 301st Stevedore Regiment attached to the 23rd Engineers enjoy a respite from their labor in a sing-along near Legney, France, on May 13, 1918. (SC Photo 111, No. 14598, RG 92, NA)

France after the armistice to "quiet unrest and to forestall trouble" when the black soldiers returned to the United States. Despite the black troops' splendid record, Moton told them to exercise self-control and suggested they settle down quietly "as farmers" once they got back to the States.[18]

What could have been spun into a public-relations coup for the black community seems to have gone unrecognized. An article hidden within the back pages of the *New York Times* in April 1919 revealed that "10,000 Negro Troops" were assembling bodies at Romagne cemetery.[19] No further mention of the subject followed. When the *Cleveland Advocate* ran a similar story, entitled "Colored Yanks Bury Dead as They Sing Old Song," the black readership responded. A reporter claimed that "these black men who thus sang songs of their Zion in a strange land must indeed have understood the meaning and full significance of the fact that Death is swallowed up in victory."[20] Singing, a traditional form of collective expression, offered solace in the face of such morbid, backbreaking work. Perhaps it also served as an anodyne, freeing the mind while adding honor to the task at hand.

Instead of seizing this opportunity to publish praises to the glorious and sacred labor of black soldiers, Scott attributed the singing to "that gaiety which characterizes a cheerful race."[21] Similarly, the *New York Times* commented, "Officers in charge say that the negro troops take the work good-naturedly, but under no circumstances will work there after nightfall."[22] Although popular American opinion placed such great importance on the disposition of its dead, burial being a sanctified duty, no one but the black man was asked to do the job.

When that *New York Times* article appeared in 1919, racial violence in the United States was on the upsurge, as discharged soldiers, still in uniform, were beaten out of towns throughout the South. After several years in which the number of lynchings had declined, the curve started upward in 1917, and again in 1918, and by 1919, eighty-three people were killed by mobs (seventy-seven were black).[23] Understandably, the summer of 1919 has been called the Red Summer because of the quantity of blood spilled in race riots throughout the country. At least thirty-eight clashes (classified as race riots) occurred that year, and as in previous years, some of the most vengeful mob activity took place in northern cities (including St. Louis, Chicago, New York, and Newark).

During the war, President Wilson had been asked to speak out against lynching and violence, but he replied that he had no authority in such matters and suggested that they be left to state control.[24] Despite his appeals to democratic principles as justification for American participation in the war, Wilson declined to support racial democracy at home. In the summer of 1917, over five thousand members of New York's black community showed their solidarity against a recent outbreak of riots in East St. Louis by marching in silent parade. A black delegation attempted to see Wilson, but the president refused, claiming pressing urgent business. In response to Wilson's snub, an open letter to the president appeared in several newspapers, asking, "The Negro, Mr. President, in this emergency, will stand by you and the nation. Will you and the nation stand by the Negro?" There was no reply.[25]

Although the underlying causes of the riots were profoundly economic, social, and psychological, historians Arthur Barbeau and Florette Henri contend that it was the return of black veterans that triggered them. In their words, much of this violence was attributed to a "surge of racial pride" and "a new attitude among black people, born of the military experiences of the recent war."[26] Memories of wartime injustices undoubtedly lived long after the hostilities ended, often serving as a reminder that democracy eluded the black man overseas and at home.

Some of the more than six thousand African American soldiers who were detailed to the GRS to perform the gruesome reburial work, December 1, 1918. (SC Photo 111, No. 36192, RG 92, NA)

In February 1922, men exhuming American dead from the French cemetery at Bar-sur-Aube uncovered the remains of William Buckner, a black private from Company B, 313th Labor Battalion. When his body was disinterred, it was found with a black cap over the head, a rope around the neck, and legs bound in straps. Buckner, originally from Kentucky, was court-martialed on September 6, 1918, for "willful misconduct and was ordered to be shot by a firing squad of American troops which was done."[27] Mercifully, Buckner's mother, Mary, was never informed of the true circumstances surrounding her son's death, nor did she ever receive any government compensation or insurance benefits.

Disturbing testimony such as this from returning black veterans served to stir racial pride, as well as memories, among black veterans in the United States, as did the deeply resonating sentiments expressed through the pen of W. E. B. Du Bois, the brilliant African American writer, editor, and civil rights activist. Du Bois had backed Wilson in the 1912 election, a choice that later proved a bitter disappointment. Throughout 1918, he once again supported the government by urging blacks to "Close Ranks" and put aside their grievances in their country's time of need.[28] But in the spring of 1919, he welcomed returning black soldiers with the defiant proclamation, "Make Way for Democracy! We saved it in France, and by the Great Jehovah, we will save it in the United States of America, or know the reason why." Du Bois declared the Great War to be "the jealous and avaricious struggle for the largest share in exploiting darker races" and claimed that it was not an aberration or insanity but "the real soul of white culture."[29] His sharp attack stunned many white readers but offered an alternative, albeit a distinctly audacious perspective, on the First World War for countless African Americans. Regardless of their limited role in combat and their demeaning burial work, the experience of the Great War had become the race war for an emerging self-reliant but much-less-innocent new Negro.

The treatment accorded to the African American soldier remains, as historian Kurt Piehler suggests, "one of the most glaring contradictions in efforts to portray the First World War as a struggle for democratic principles."[30] In those difficult, racially tense postwar years, families in mourning were not spared the same indignities that had been imposed on their loved ones who risked and often sacrificed their lives for the freedoms reserved for others. In June 1921, two African American families attending a funeral service at Arlington Cemetery were asked during the ceremony to move to the "colored section" when it was discovered that both of their deceased were about to be mistakenly buried in the white section. An officer observing the regrettable incident claimed that this request had been "necessary in plain view of all mourners and particularly the relatives of the colored men mentioned."[31] Despite injustices such as these, the government's attention remained focused on the dead overseas and the potential embarrassment they posed, while problems with the living at home continued to fester.

As in previous wars, the federal government could not afford to ignore the demands of Americans it had relied on for enlistments. Like their white counterparts, African American citizen soldiers and their families, in effect, negotiated terms with the government that exchanged their service to the nation for the assurance that their personal sacrifice would be reverently remembered. But what of the surviving veterans and those African Americans who lived on after mourning the loss of their husbands and sons?

Many soldiers who survived the Civil War and those who had witnessed it were still alive when the nation marched off to Europe in 1917. Within the shadow of these memories, the Civil War continued to serve as a touchstone for American remembrance, particularly among black citizens. Although people of all races reverted to the Civil War commemorative model that was established when Abraham Lincoln dedicated Gettysburg Cemetery in 1863, the site held added significance for African Americans, who perceived Gettysburg as the birthplace of their emancipation. There, the president had defined the nature of American democracy and announced a "new birth of freedom" for all Americans. But in the months preceding that famed public dedication, black laborers had been forced to exhume the remains of the war dead from their scattered burials in crude, shallow graves for reburial. The lowest bidder, awarded a contract for the most economical exhumation work, supervised those whose hands had performed the macabre work since the earliest days of the war. This discriminatory and repressive treatment appears in direct opposition to the democratic spirit depicted on the landscape of America's first national cemetery, but it was still the policy enforced during the construction of the nation's First World War cemeteries.

The remains of those who had died of disease were left undisturbed in Civil War cemeteries, while the graves of black soldiers (like the enemy's dead) were less fortunate. They were segregated into plots away from those of their fellow comrades in battle. This separation of bodies even in death demonstrates the continuing extent of disunity that existed within the nation. Although efforts were made to construct cemeteries that depicted noble death for a justifiable cause, sectional and racial unity was still, in reality, a myth. War had not changed that.

Years later, black soldiers serving in the Philippines during the Spanish-American War had hoped that their military service might help them win political rights; instead, they found that the color line had followed them despite their meritorious achievements. In battle, their status was generally typified in the epithet "nigger," which they shared with the enemy, the Filipinos.[32] Upon their return to the United States, they discovered that white men remained resistant to accepting black men as military heroes, thereby marginalizing African American memory in this war, as had been done in the Civil War.

President Wilson, like his predecessor, William McKinley, avoided the equal-rights question in order to further national reconciliation in 1918. Similarly, in both the Spanish-American War and the First World War, many Americans tolerated disenfranchisement and lynchings of African Americans in their own country while supporting wars intended to defend democracy and end suffering abroad.[33]

The racial violence and political anxiety over the civil rights issue suggests yet another aspect of the inherent tension between the individual and the community within a democratic state. Allowing this situation to go unchecked threatened the nation's potential military manpower as well as the stability and solidarity of the union. This would not, however, be the last time racial disharmony disturbed the collective memory of the First World War in the United States.

7

Troubled Waters

Immigrant soldiers played a key role in the American military force that went to war in 1917, especially since no legal provision forbade the voluntary enlistment of registered aliens from enemy nations. Tens of thousands of the citizens and subjects of other countries joined up, an appreciable fraction of them natives of Germany and Austria.[1] Foreign-born troops, eager to express their loyalty and make their ethnicity acceptable to the United States, readily offered their service to the nation, but their willingness to sacrifice was not without auxiliary aspirations. Many nationalities utilized the popular patriotic rhetoric and imagery employed by both reigning nativists and the government propaganda machine to "achieve their own international goals and express ethnic pride," as Nancy Gentile Ford has written. Even before the nation entered war in April 1917, "German and Irish immigrants attempted to pressure the government to keep America out of the conflict and actively promoted a course of strict neutrality." Their intentions were matched by other immigrants who staunchly advocated a prowar position. Eventual U.S. entry into war, for example, "provided American Czech, Slovak, Polish, and Jewish immigrants an opportunity to fight for the independence of their homeland from the bondage of the German, Austro-Hungarian, and Turkish Empires," Ford explains.[2]

In this war of global participation, America's multiethnic fighting force contributed enormously to its military strength, but it also complicated an already complex repatriation process of the war dead. Many next of kin to the deceased lived in foreign countries and, accordingly, requested that loved ones be buried in their native homeland. Their desires did not go unnoticed by the deceased's adopted country. On January 1, 1920, in an attempt to honor the contributions of all Americans, the War Department decided to deliver, upon request of the families, the bodies of American servicemen buried overseas to their homes, wherever they may be.[3] Replies were received from some of the most remote parts of Europe in response to letters sent out from the Paris GRS headquarters. They usually conveyed the same desire as that expressed by thousands of Americans living in the United States, that is, to have the body returned "home." Doing so required an elaborate series of formal negotiations with a substantial assortment of foreign governments, a process that continued well into August 1920. The Italian government proved the most complex of all negotiating countries since there were more Italians than any other nationality who desired foreign burial, followed by those originating from Ireland.[4] Interestingly, the same indecision that afflicted families in the United States over the disposition question often found its way into the hearts of foreigners trying to choose between personal desires and conflicting national loyalties.

When Private Pietro dePalma of the 311th Infantry Regiment was killed in the Argonne Forest just weeks before the armistice, his mother, an illiterate woman living in Italy who spoke no English, was adamant that her son should rest in America's national cemetery at Arlington, Virginia. DePalma's brother, on the other hand, wanted the body brought home to New Jersey.[5] When the coffin arrived in Brooklyn, the family was still undecided. Finally, in February 1922, Mrs. dePalma acquiesced to her eldest son's wishes and relinquished her right, as assigned by the War Department, to decide Pietro's final resting place. It seems family pressures and obligations trumped national ones.

The extent of the government's efforts to accommodate NOK requests is surely without precedent, particularly in Italy, where many of the bodies had to be transported long distances into the mountains after they reached the last railroad point to which they could be carried. Some were then sent further on, as far as ninety kilometers. One body was even delivered to a small island about fifty miles from Naples aboard an Italian naval vessel.[6] The GRS history claimed that 454 bodies were ultimately shipped to foreign countries for burial by 1922.[7]

Not all requests were so readily honored, however. In July 1918, Wasil Kovaswick, a private with the 32nd Division, died while serving in France. His only surviving relative, a sister in Russia, wrote to the GRS requesting that her brother's body be brought there for burial. The Paris GRS never responded to her wishes but notified the newly formed branch office in Washington, DC, that "correspondence is not undertaken with relatives residing in Russia, and consequently, this case will be considered as one for concentration [burial in France]."[8] Regardless of the next of kin's request, government policy stated that no bodies were to be left in

Germany, Luxembourg, and Russia.[9] These nations were not considered "friendly" to the United States and, as such, were not fitting resting places for American heroes.

During the war, Woodrow Wilson had agreed to the U.S. Army's intervention in Russia, at Archangel and Siberia, for several reasons, primarily to placate the Allies and to help the Czecho-Slovaks consolidate their forces against the Bolsheviks. U.S. soldiers began arriving there in the summer of 1918 and remained, basically abandoned, until the spring of 1919 without achieving their mission, which was never made quite clear to them by the War Department. The British, Italians, Japanese, and French also had forces in Russia.

News of the government's intention to exhume the dead outside of France appeared in American newspapers in the autumn of 1919, but behind the scenes, work on recoveries beyond the war zone had already begun. In June of that year, Second Lieutenant V. M. Conway was ordered to proceed to northern Russia to command a detachment of ten GRS men sent to exhume American dead from the 111 graves registered there. After his military discharge, Lieutenant Conway documented the experience he endured while carrying out the dismal Russian assignment, as others on similar missions had felt compelled to do. A brief summary of that sworn testimony follows.

Before leaving France, three of the team were lost to illness and not replaced. The remaining group arrived in Archangel on a British transport, but no coffins were available and none were delivered until an American vessel, the SS *Lake Daraga,* arrived more than one month later. While awaiting coffins, Conway and his men exhumed bodies from surrounding regions and consolidated them in Archangel. Their work was performed under extremely adverse conditions including cold, rainy weather, barges that continually sank under the weight, and no materials to seal the coffins once the containers finally arrived. Conway had no support from the American government since those authorities had evacuated the country shortly after his arrival. British and Russian military authorities were reportedly "opposed to the project" and gave him no additional labor or cooperation in his task. Conway was forced to hire local civilian labor, Bolshevik prisoners, who often proved "unreliable and unmotivated."[10]

When British authorities inexplicably ordered the commander of the *Lake Daraga* to leave by the next morning, Conway claimed he and his men worked through the night to load bodies onto the steamer. During the crossing, coffin lids caved in and broke open, "the ooze resulting from

the mud and rain at time of disinterment, together with the decomposition of the remains," causing Conway enormous concern, especially for
the health of his men. Upon arrival in France, coffins were not unloaded
but taken directly back to the United States for burial. In Conway's testimony, he summarized the hellish circumstances surrounding the burials
in Russia:

> Wrong crosses over graves. Very few identification tags on crosses or
> bodies; Americans buried with French and Russians; cemetery located in
> a swamp. It was impossible to locate these bodies, they were not buried in
> the spot marked by their caskets. I am not absolutely certain of the cor-
> rect identification of any of the bodies which were buried without tags.[11]

The Archangel episode is reminiscent of circumstances previously
documented in reports by D. H. Rhodes during his attempts to retrieve
the dead after the Spanish-American War. The details are significant for
several reasons. Despite the importance placed on the disposition of
American dead, a low-ranking second lieutenant was asked to perform
this mission with so few men and without any governmental support or
materials. The gruesome ordeal they endured in the process of providing
the dead with an honorable resting place is sadly ironic. Like Rhodes and
his corpsmen decades before, the hardships these men were willing to endure to locate remains is astonishing. These events were never publicly
exposed. Instead, the media invented a polished, rhetorical version of the
episode in a further attempt to perpetuate the cult of the fallen soldier.[12]

The *New York Times* applauded the ship's arrival from Russia, calling it
"right and proper" that bodies of the American soldiers killed in the Archangel campaign were brought home for burial. "That desolate land has no
associations for them or for us to make it a suitable resting place for such
as they, nor would their graves there have had the care or the honor deserved."[13] Only England, France, and Belgium were considered appropriate resting places for national heroes. Russia was seen as unfit, yet Russian
hands were there to do the dirty work during the grisly process of exhumation. Like the grave-digging Bowery thugs who buried the remains of
returning Spanish-American War heroes who died of disease in New York
hospitals and the black laborers who dug the burial trenches in Europe,
the resented task was similarly assigned to the despised Bolsheviks.

The *Times* did not mention that Conway was, by circumstance, forced
to leave eighty-five American dead behind in Russia.[14] The military, for its

part, was more concerned with the recent arrival of 105 coffins at the port of Hoboken, New Jersey, when it was learned that a key had been provided with each casket. In a last-minute attempt to avoid public scandal, an official from the GRS's Cemeterial Branch suggested that each key be thrown away. "It may be impossible to prevent the opening of the casket by the relatives in the home of the deceased," he wrote, "but this should not be facilitated by furnishing them with a key." In closing, he added, "This need not apply to embalmed bodies."[15] Ninety-eight of the deceased were shipped to relatives, and five were buried in national cemeteries; none of the Americans who died in Russia were buried in the permanent American cemeteries in France.

Most nations cooperated fully with American plans, but relations between the United States and Great Britain over this issue were somewhat more delicate. It was the policy of the U.S. War Department to return all bodies from Great Britain and Ireland to America, unless a specific request to the contrary was made by the NOK. Since the British were not allowing their own citizens to reclaim their loved ones, the IWGC was understandably cautious about parading American bodies bound for home before the British people. Instead, it offered a permanent cemetery at Brookwood, England, for the more than two thousand American bodies left in Great Britain; or families could elect to leave the deceased where they were originally buried.[16] Widespread disinterment and repatriation of Americans who died while in the service of the British Crown was not permitted; rather, the government agreed to take up each request from NOK on a case-by-case basis.[17] Those families that chose to have the bodies of Americans (temporarily buried in France, Belgium, and other points) shipped to Britain for burial caused considerably greater objections from the British War Graves Commission. Following formal embassy discussions, it was agreed that the caskets would be shipped in plain wooden shipping cases without being draped with an American flag, and soldiers accompanying the bodies would do so in civilian clothes.

The complex multinational strategy involving the exhumation of American dead from ten different nations, some with multiple cemeteries in each, began within weeks of the French modification that permitted exhumations outside the former battle zone.[18] Internationally, efforts to negotiate these complex but effectual compromises appeared to be progressing seamlessly, but within the United States, fissures were rapidly widening. Maintaining open communication between the War Department and family members proved particularly difficult.

In an attempt to honor the contributions of all Americans, the War Department decided to deliver, upon request of the families, the bodies of American servicemen buried overseas to their homes, wherever that residence was. (SC Photo 111, No. 28137, RG 92, NA)

Lack of coordination between the U.S. Army's GRS and the Navy and Marines contributed significantly to the misinformation that families frequently received, events that were readily exploited by the press. In England and Scotland, the Navy disinterred its own dead entirely independent of the Army, but in France, the GRS exhumed deceased members of the Navy and Marine Corps, at a cost to the other service branches. But communication broke down in Washington when the Marine Corps began handling its own dead without waiting for the GRS. Similarly, the Navy began concentrating its dead at Brest, France, believing it more cost effective to evacuate one cemetery at a time and then to ship all sailors home together. As a result, the GRS sent inquiries to relatives in the United States asking their decision regarding disposition of remains when, in fact, the Marine and Navy bodies were already with their families and interred at home.[19]

Newspapers became a veritable battleground for bitter debate when announcements of the government's decision to begin bringing the dead home first appeared. Controversy intensified as the dead became pawns in a game of power that excluded few players. The loudest voices were those of politicians competing for a distinct voice above the crowd. By January 1920, fourteen congressional bills had been introduced in favor of repatriation. Perhaps the most creative solution came from New York's Representative Fiorello LaGuardia, who introduced legislation that would have provided transportation to France for the nearest of kin of all soldiers buried overseas. That, he thought, would be preferable to the plan of attempting to return all bodies to America.[20] LaGuardia, a former war veteran, would have to wait several years before seeing his suggestion implemented with the passage of the Gold Star pilgrimage legislation in 1929.

The newly formed Gold Star Mothers groups expressed no collective response to the repatriation issue. Perhaps these women believed (as did many in the American Legion) that this was an individual decision. Organizationally, they may have also felt that it was not in their best interest to speak against the government's plans. While some mothers were privately writing the War Department for their sons' return, the more vocal expressed "more than reluctance—something like horror—when discussing the proposed removal."[21] One mother, who had been to France to observe the care given American graves, begged others to join her in "organized and combined movement against repatriation."[22] Yet letters from other mothers insisted that their sons had specifically requested a home burial. The anxiety this unprecedented decision caused families unfolded daily on the pages of national newspapers.

The press also exhibited a noticeably strong antirepatriation bias as policymakers in Washington exerted pressure to steer public sentiment accordingly. One powerful vehicle for this campaign was the American Field of Honor Association, counting among its members John Pershing, former president William Howard Taft, Samuel Gompers, Cornelius Vanderbilt, senior AEF chaplain Bishop Charles H. Brent, and others who supported overseas cemeteries.[23] The organization mounted a widespread and fierce campaign to convince the American public that "as the men had fought and died in France they should lie in France."[24] Association members advanced a number of convincing arguments against repatriation, including the obvious problems of disinterring bodies that had been buried for several years, the expenditure of millions "drawn from the public treasury," "the risk of returning the wrong body to mothers," and the value of "preserving the comradeship of the war."[25]

At the onset of the debates in 1919, the newly formed American Legion, the largest affiliation of First World War veterans, passed a resolution stating that the bodies of the dead should not be returned from France except in cases where specifically requested.[26] The Legion's founder, Colonel Theodore Roosevelt, Jr., vigorously backed the arguments of the Field of Honor Association. Undoubtedly, he felt obliged to support the firm stance taken by his father who, upon hearing that his son Quentin had died after being shot down in aerial combat in July 1918, had insisted that the body remain in France. "We feel that where the tree falls there let it lie," wrote the elder Roosevelt.[27]

Abiding by the organization's official position, legionnaires throughout the country joined in lengthy editorial debate against the removal of their dead comrades in France.[28] But, once the bodies began arriving back in the United States, the Legion became the self-appointed keeper of the fallen. Veterans participated in the reception of remains from overseas, arranged services throughout the country, and ensured that the graves of these men and those from former wars were not forgotten.[29]

General Pershing was perhaps the staunchest advocate of overseas cemeteries. In his zeal, he offered to establish these grounds even before the government had endorsed the idea.[30] Senior AEF chaplain Bishop Charles H. Brent, a supporter who shared Pershing's vision, explained that the "American central field of honor" would be a place where "commemoration of the dead will be observed." Apparently visualizing one central cemetery, Brent spoke of the project as "a work of love carried through by a sense of reverence for that sacred dust which, though mingled with the soil of France, is forever American."[31]

Brent's evocation is that of a national shrine of worship, an attempt to find the sacred in the secular, and it is a key element in the perpetuation of the myth of the war experience.[32] "Pershing was not particularly religious," writes biographer Donald Smythe, but he "wanted each cemetery to have a chapel in order to provide it with a religious atmosphere, changing it from a mere burial ground to a sacred site."[33] However pious, this sanctity required a further sacrifice that many Americans felt was too much to ask, that of surrendering loved ones forever to foreign soil.

Alternative views were represented by the Bring Home the Soldier Dead League, which promised a "Tomb in America for every US Hero." The group's democratic vision was based on what was good for the individual. It insisted that people preferred to mourn and remember their loved ones privately in local burial grounds, where graves could be tended personally. The league's membership was predominantly people from the wealthy classes "who also happened to be parents, widows and relatives of American Hero Dead."[34]

The league's manifesto was based primarily on the government's former pledge to return the dead, and it reminded the public of that promise repeatedly. Its method was to appeal directly to the nation, particularly through petitions emphasizing the "principles of American Motherhood: peaceful death at home, free from the turmoil of War, with solace of a grave within easy reach" and "no tragic memories."[35] The league highlighted popular claims that, unlike the British, Americans were too far away to visit the graves of loved ones. It alleged that the presence of American bodies overseas would involve the United States in future wars abroad, and it suspected that unscrupulous French morticians and coffin makers wanted the bodies to remain overseas.[36] Conversely, the Field of Honor Association (which claimed a significant military membership) defended the French and "suspected a plot by American morticians."[37]

The ubiquitous disdain held by the military toward civilian undertakers is consistent with that of other nations. In England, Fabian Ware wrote scathingly of members of the American funeral industry, claiming they were "capable of anything." Ware insisted that they caused considerable trouble for the military authorities and were "given practically a free hand to bring back the American dead."[38] In France, undertakers were equally despised by the military. There, where exhumations of war dead remained illegal until September 1920, private French gravediggers engaged in illegal financial arrangements with wealthy clients in exchange for the return of their sons' bodies. Jay Winter claims, "This form of private enterprise infuriated the army, which had to deal with bribery and churned-up cemeteries, as well as the anger of poor parents, irate at the crassness and privilege of wealth."[39]

Whether the funeral industry deserved the derision heaped on it by so many people is difficult to say. More readily apparent is that undertakers seem to have been the targets of wrangling between various factions caught up in the tension and discord inherent in democratic free choice. In both France and the United States, where families were given the opportunity to have their loved ones returned, undertakers stood ready to serve the individual in exchange for financial gain. Myths transformed the painful reality of war into an abstraction; undertakers threatened the solidarity of the collective by bringing the harsh realities of capitalism into direct confrontation with the intangible principles of nationalism and citizenship.

America's nationalist ideology was constructed with two essential components: unity and the obligation of citizens to national service. This language of American militarized nationalism was articulated and promulgated by influential voices in the culture, along with the press and war veterans, to unite the nation around an "unusually strong sense of patriotism."[40] Although patriotic pride was based on principles of equality and democracy, it was implicitly a raced nationalism in which African American contributions were marginalized while ethnic nationalities were rewarded.

8

Bringing Them Home

The year 1920 brought increased impatience and renewed attempts by Congress to flex its political muscle. In February, Charles Pierce was called to testify before a House expenditures subcommittee, where, as chief of the GRS, he struggled to justify delays abroad in response to questions from his harsh interrogators. Indiana Republican Oscar E. Bland posited, "I am of the impression that . . . practically all the high officers in the A.E.F., not only were of the opinion that it was not advisable to bring these bodies home, but that no provisions at that time [were] made to do it. Am I right in that?" Pierce attempted to remain circumspective, but Bland repeated the accusations more forcefully the second time: "The whole bunch, Connor, Pershing, . . . did not consider that we would undertake the job of bringing these bodies home and were not in sympathy with it![?]" Pierce replied, "I would rather not answer that question in that way."[1]

Over fifty professional embalmers, supervisors, and assistants had been sent to France in December 1919, Pierce explained, so that they might be used as replacements for the forces maintaining cemeteries. "Why the necessity for these men in Paris—in France—expert embalmers?" Bland asked, as if to doubt the service chief's explanation. "You were not embalming anyone," the congressman asserted.

The GRS repeatedly expressed concern within the organization that a public demand would be made for the embalming of all the AEF dead. Aside from the practical conditions of combat, doing so would have incurred additional costs for supplies and involved a sizeable increase of trained staff.[2] In Pierce's early plea for overall control of the cemetery work, he insisted that his current staff include a large percentage of embalmers and undertakers who could perform these tasks quite well.[3] Although the public was repeatedly told that embalming was practiced, it seems it seldom was. The issue became increasingly relevant once families began pressing for permission to open coffins as bodies began arriving home.

"Commercialized patriotism" was how Pierce referred to the funeral industry's rhetoric when he wrote to the AEF's chief quartermaster. In an attempt to obtain policies and procedures regarding the disposition of the dead, Pierce feared the government would dispatch undertakers to France to "take over." Memories of antagonism between himself and Rhodes must have been on his mind when he wrote in 1918, "It is presumed that this Service [GRS] may be able to give to the project of removal more intelligent and practicable supervision than any imported corps of inexperienced civilians could possibly do." He concluded with a warning of the political agitation that would soon be occurring in the States, "in view of the vast financial profits involved."[4]

The need to maintain control seems to have been Pierce's priority, although one can understand the War Department's reluctance to incur the steep costs of contracting work to eager morticians. Perhaps this animosity was an inherent disinclination bound to occur between two antithetical professions, made all the more acrimonious by the potentially lucrative position of funeral directors likely to profit from inevitable military losses.

Nevertheless, Bland's patience reached its limit once Pierce admitted that his team of experts had yet to do anything with the dead, claiming it had been impossible to get the materials with which to do the work. "Do you really know whether or not there was any real French objection to the removal of the bodies from the interior of France?" he asked Pierce pointedly. In his defense, the colonel simply replied that it was an "utter surprise" to him when the French claimed recently that they had no objection to the removals.

Pierce reluctantly told the committee of the many delays his service encountered: the lack of caskets and coffins, restrictions on railway use in France, problems obtaining local labor, the lack of serviceable trucks for transporting coffins, and the objections many servicemen felt toward having their dead moved to central cemeteries so far from where they had fallen. He went on to explain that there were so many dead that the one cemetery planned for Suresnes (Paris) was now clearly insufficient for American needs and that more land would be needed. Pierce presented his idea of establishing several primary cemeteries in each of the regions where Americans fought, to include Château-Thierry, Belleau Wood, and the Argonne, but admitted that there were problems endemic with a large cemetery so close to the German border. Romagne was in the Verdun sector and "in a dangerous land, so far as battle traditions are concerned."

Shown here are the wooden crosses of the early 1920s, after most of the concentration of graves was complete. They were replaced with the more familiar marble cross headstones of the present. Location unknown. (SC Photo 111, No. 86150, RG 92, NA)

"It was in the path of contending armies in the future," he continued, and a permanent cemetery there was "liable to be torn up, first by one army pressing on and then by another."[5]

Pierce's prophetic testimony illustrates not only the tremendous number of practical obstacles facing the military officials responsible for carrying out this immense reburial effort but also the vast range of unknown factors, political and military, that could play out in the future. Apparently, there were already doubts afloat that the recent war would not be the one to end all wars. He concluded his testimony by admitting that in fact, as Representative Bland posited, there was "no plan developed yet, or settled upon, by the War Department as to what is to become of those dead over there."[6]

By March 1920, it was estimated that at least 70 percent of the dead would have to be returned from abroad at the request of their families. Secretary Baker's plea to the Senate to "leave the care of the dead in the hands of the War Department" was followed by a request for an appropriation of thirty million dollars for the project. This estimation was based on a figure of five hundred dollars for each body returned, but if the body remained overseas, the cost was halved.[7]

Within a week of Baker's report, the first of three Franco-American conferences on the repatriation of remains was convened. Pierce and Assistant Secretary Ralph Hayes negotiated with the French (1) to transport to the United States only those bodies whose return was demanded by the next of kin (this excluded the unknown), (2) to move only "homeward bound dead," leaving the rest in temporary cemeteries to be reburied later, and (3) to begin work in September 1920.[8] Transportation problems were resolved when the United States agreed to pay rental charges to the French for the use of their railway system. A similar decree two weeks later made the transfer of French dead to their homes also possible and fully legitimate.

Transportation of the bodies across France was a logistical dilemma requiring a generous allowance of trucks, canal boats, and railway cars. Coffins had to be procured and more labor was required to complete the task on a time scale that would keep the American public content. Administratively, requests from the next of kin had to be matched with bodies buried in hundreds of sites, and even as the logistics were being worked out, changes were continuous.[9] Before the number of repatriated dead reached a peak in mid-1921, newspapers were reporting that more than thirteen thousand families had changed their minds and decided to leave the remains overseas.[10] The GRS official history documented the opposite phenomenon, citing the first six months of 1922, when it received 633 requests to change from permanent burial in France to home shipments to the United States.[11] Either way, a steady stream of cable dispatches from Washington to France frequently requested changes even as a body was being exhumed or had been placed aboard ship for the homeward voyage, thus adding to the confusion. In exasperation, the secretary of war informed the public that after August 15, 1921, it would definitely not authorize any further changes to previous instructions.

Despite the GRS's best attempts to deny allegations against its efficiency, those allegations mounted as press surveillance reports struggled to meet the insatiable demands of an increasingly suspicious public. Letters arrived at the War Department daily, expressing fears similar to those of Mr. and Mrs. Isaac Smith of Newton, Massachusetts, who wrote, "everybody that we talked to said we would never get the right body from France."[12] From Brooklyn, New York, another mother claimed, "I heard so many conflicting stories about over seas that I thought America was the best place for his body so as myself and my family could take care of his grave and no doubt there are lots of other parents to next a kin [*sic*] felt the same way."[13]

Preparing coffins for their return to the United States. Here the cases are being re-moved from the makeshift morgue to be loaded onto transport ships. (*History of the American Graves Registration Service*, Volume 2, 81-A)

Similar views were indeed expressed across the country. In July 1919, the parents of August Sudbeck, of the 363rd Infantry Regiment, received news in Nebraska that their son had been killed the previous October and bur-ied in a field behind a Belgian farmhouse. The deceased's father wrote to ask for further details of his son's death but claimed he did not want the remains returned because "it is very doubtful, whether you get the right person." Years later, a relative of Sudbeck wrote that many of the caskets sent back to America had rocks in them, so the family decided to leave their loved one in Belgium.[14]

Efforts to appease the American people occupied an inordinate amount of time for the GRS. Correspondence reveals distinct expressions of apprehension and anxiety as the fledgling service struggled to adapt to changing expectations under the watchful eye of the media that fur-ther complicated its plight. Popular author Owen Wister visited France and reported on "the mistake" of disturbing graves of American soldiers, which he described as "poor fragments of humanity" being taken up and "dragged from the soil of their sacrifice."[15] Writing in defense of overseas cemeteries, Wister claimed it was "extremely improbable that the families

Aboard the transport as the coffin is lowered into the ship's hatch. (*History of the American Graves Registration Service*, Volume 2, 82-B)

receiving bodies of soldiers actually got the remains of their own sons."[16] In a relentless attack, Wister revealed that upon arrival, "unclaimed bodies of soldier dead were piled at the Hoboken pier" and that "many went to Potter's Field.[17] The army admitted difficulty in its efforts to provide sufficient notice to relatives informing them of a body's arrival, but this was attributed to frequently changing addresses.

The government requested that people refrain from intrusion but did not enforce that restriction.[18] The *New York Times* regularly reported the efforts of private citizens who chose to take matters into their own hands. In May 1921, for example, a seventy-year-old father sailed to France, where he spent months attempting to locate his son's grave, claiming he could not be content until the body rested in the family plot in Mississippi.[19] Although this article praised the work and assistance of the GRS, other accounts were extremely critical.

By April 1921, more than 14,800 bodies had been returned to the United States, but these success figures were overlooked in the profusion of criticism heaped on the GRS.[20] Characteristically, newspapers were quick to highlight evidence of negligence, such as that which occurred during the summer of 1921 when a New Jersey father returned home and unexpectedly found his son's coffin sitting on his front porch. "Four soldiers just backed the truck to the curb and carried the coffin to the porch," neighbors reported.[21]

The national president of the Bring Home League, A. B. Pouch, reminded the government that although the new cemeteries overseas were being nicely cared for, "if the parents are physically or financially unable to visit these cemeteries the work cannot be appreciated."[22] League petitions called for increased motor transportation, faster delivery of caskets, more work crews, and progress reports to the public. President Pouch and League Chairman J. D. Foster spoke of the "aggravating conditions, customs and regulations of the French Government and people" and urged Secretary Baker to deal more aggressively with them.[23] On several occasions, the newly promoted Colonel Pierce was recruited to attend public meetings, at the Bring Home League's expense, to "help console those who are not fully informed."[24]

While Pierce's public endorsement of the Bring Home League seems inappropriate, J. D. Foster's rogue tactics reek of self-interest and profiteering. Not only was Foster the chairman of the Bring Home the Soldier League, but he was also the owner of Foster & Son, sellers of disinfectants and fumigators. It is unclear whether the son mentioned in the company title is the same soldier son buried in Belleau Wood, France, a site Mr. and Mrs. Foster planned to visit in April 1920.[25] Prior to sailing, Foster arranged to have Pierce provide letters of introduction to "those in charge of the Service" in France, Italy, and England. Ingratiating his favor, Pierce's letters referred to Foster as "an exceptionally good friend to us in many ways" who should receive "anything you can do to facilitate the work he has in hand."[26] In exchange, Pierce received Foster's assurance that he would petition some of his friends in Congress to actively support pending legislation in favor of Pierce's keeping his appointed colonel's rank upon retirement.[27]

The American democratic process, as instituted by the government, genuinely attempted to respond to the wishes of the people, despite the delays and costliness of the venture and the considerable hardship it imposed on other nations. Unfortunately, the outcome inadvertently opened the way to greed, corruption, and an expediency that spawned public suspicion and irreverence to the dead. These traits were not restricted to the funeral industry, despite the military's longstanding accusations of its avaricious practices. Postwar army investigation files reveal the sworn testimony of several Quartermaster Corps officers who claimed that the GRS was "the most lucrative field for graft in the Army." One army captain told investigators, "Graft is obtained by someone in Washington obtaining names of the persons asking expeditious return of bodies to the U.S." He explained that in return for this service, some people would pay as much as twenty-five hundred dollars to get bodies back from overseas. The officer revealed that he would then "divide the proceeds with Col Pierce."[28] Although it may not be possible to determine the extent of such foul play, this testimony suggests that the postwar repatriation process engendered a profound and recurrent tension between the individual and the greater community. Contrary to political intentions, freedom of choice did not create unity within the United States; rather, it deepened the divisiveness already present.

The gruesome character of burial work combined with the pressure and conditions under which it was performed took their toll on the morale of the GRS and also affected its efficiency. One GRS officer commented that he felt that the GRS was "more or less despised because of the nature of [its] work."[29] Pierce does not appear to have expressed such views publicly; instead, he seems to have resigned himself to the situation at hand. Could opposition to the return of American dead have caused his reticence, or was it the chaos caused by democratic choice that he silently resented? In previous wars, Pierce supervised the repatriation of American war dead when no alternative existed, whereas the establishment of cemeteries abroad represented an exceptional ideology to this officer from the "old school." Regardless of his personal perspective, Pierce died of pneumonia in Tours, France, in May 1921, without living to see the last of America's dead returned home. In his will, he requested that his body be returned to the United States for burial in Arlington National Cemetery, "without the assistance of an undertaking establishment."[30]

Although figures vary slightly, the GRS stated that it shipped 45,588 dead to the United States and 764 to European places of birth.[31] Ultimately, the price of uniting American dead with their families was $30 million, or $658 per body, far in excess of the 1920 estimate of $160 per body, or $8 million.[32] Despite the enormous financial cost, attempts to construct an image of national cohesion abroad faltered as most Americans chose to mourn privately and at government expense. For those who died with their individuality intact, democracy offered a choice, as next of kin (by proxy) determined their final resting place. This could often be a lengthy process, as it was for Estella Kendall, who waited five years after Harry's death to learn that her son had reached his final resting place in 1923. Ten more years would pass before she would kneel at his grave.

Those whose identity died with them forfeited their right to choose. The unknown (except for the body destined for the Tomb at Arlington National Cemetery) were all buried overseas without benefit of identity or choice. Their individuality was exchanged for a far loftier perception of national identity that would rest forever on foreign soil. In the words of one mother returning from her son's grave in France, "To remove the known dead would be unjust discrimination against the many unknown dead, who made the supreme sacrifice and cannot be honored by name. If the unknown dead alone were left," she implored, "they would be forgotten."[33] Despite these prophetic words, the government devoted the next decade to ensuring their eternal remembrance.

PART II

Remembrance

9

Republican Motherhood Thrives

On a rainy November in 1917 three Americans serving with the U.S. 1st Division were brutally murdered in their dugouts during a German raid within a supposedly quiet sector east of Verdun. That night, Private Thomas Enright, Private Merle Hay, and Corporal James Gresham became the first U.S. Army combat fatalities in the war, but they are now all but forgotten at home and most certainly in France.[1] At that time, the event was honored by both nations in a small French cemetery near Bathelémont, close to where the men died. The French military arranged a dignified burial for the soldiers with an honor guard ceremony presided over by French general Paul Bordeaux. Looking back on that day, Pershing recalled "the common sacrifices our two peoples were to make in the same great cause."[2] General Bordeaux thanked the three who gave their lives and vowed that the local citizens would erect a monument over their graves.[3] His promise was kept in 1918.

Within days of the soldiers' funeral, letters began arriving at the War Department from the men's families asking when their sons' bodies would be returned. In Pittsburgh, Private Enright's relatives were particularly anxious to retrieve his body and managed to persuade their congressman, Guy Campbell, a former Spanish-American War veteran, to write Secretary Baker on behalf of the town. Campbell was asked to endorse a resolution drawn up by county commissioners for the return of Enright's body to Pittsburgh so that his people could honor his memory. The congressman penned his request accordingly: "While I appreciate that as the casualties increase, it will be impossible to forward the remains of stricken soldiers . . . it would be a fitting and just tribute to the first of the fallen to return their bodies to their friends, for burial at home."[4]

Before these first American casualties occurred, Quartermaster General Henry G. Sharpe had written to the secretary of war, recommending that a definite burial policy be adopted and made known to the public; nevertheless, it seems the government was caught unprepared. General

Funeral of Thomas Enright, Merle D. Hay and James B. Gresham, the first three American soldiers from the 16th Infantry Regiment, 1st Division, to be killed in action near Bathelémont-lès-Bauzemont, Moselle region, France, November 1917. (SC Photo 111, No. 67133, RG 92, NA)

Sharpe was forced to explain to Pittsburgh officials that it would be "impracticable to comply" with their request.[5]

Some people in the town were pleased with the War Department's response, chiefly parents of other soldiers, who wasted no time voicing their disapproval of the preferential treatment being considered. One woman, identifying herself simply as "a very patriotic Pittsburgh Mother," thought it unjust that "Young Mr. Enright" should receive "special priviledge [sic] when he only did his duty as was expected of him."[6] This mother, whose own son was also serving in France, claimed that she would not think for a minute of asking the government to bring him home. In a rather disdainful tone, she recalled the attention afforded "young Enright's people" and relayed to Secretary Baker in detail the town's commemorative plans. Apparently, arrangements were already in progress for a grand military funeral, and petitions had been drawn up to have a local street named in Enright's honor. While implying that others would not receive the same treatment, this patriotic mother reminded the secretary that if he agreed to return the body, his office would be besieged with more requests, and families "would be justified in making them."[7]

Years of post–Civil War ceremonies, speeches, parades, and grave decorations influenced collective efforts to mark the loss of loved ones in battle. By the early twentieth century, a soldier's death had shifted from being an occasion of mournful private seclusion to one of communal respect within a triumphal context. Pittsburgh's anonymous mother recalled such an occasion when the body of the first local boy was killed at the Mexican border during the Punitive Expedition of 1916–1917. "When . . . young DeLowry was brought home," she explained, "St. Mary's church . . . made a gala day out of the funeral." On that occasion, local dignitaries attended a parade for the benefit of cameras that were filming the event, and then later the movie was viewed by audiences in the town's theater. With Enright in mind, she concluded, "the family certainly found he was more valuable dead than alive, as he was a regular scamp when living."[8] This festive spirit of remembrance lived on from traditions practiced during lively Civil War reunions and continued for years after the First World War.

Pittsburgh's plans were eventually abandoned since the bodies of Gresham, Enright, and Hay were not returned home until 1921. During the interim, they had been laid to rest with their comrades amid ritual gunfire and evocative oration from an appreciative nation. Yet, on the home front, Americans were determined to bestow on them a different glory.

The beleaguered debate that soon embroiled the entire nation at war's end had begun with women's voices offering the most vocal commentary. These were not the docile tones of protective maternal pampering, however, as Pittsburgh's patriotic mother demonstrates. A new Republican Mother had emerged with this war, one anxious to participate in and support the nationalist dialogue in dramatically profound ways.

Public support is crucial to a successful national war, as victory depends less on professional armies than on the "extent to which an integrated social unit composed of democratic committees [can] sustain a collective will."[9] As the nation began its military mobilization during the early months of 1917, many women were quick to voice publicly their support for the war and to suggest ways that its lost servicemen might be remembered. Their authority was instinctively based on their traditional status as mourner, nurturer, and sacrificial mother—an active role they had assumed immediately after the Civil War.

Women's groups such as the United Daughters of the Confederacy (UDC) and, later, the Women's Relief Corps (WRC), an auxiliary to the

Grand Army of the Republic (GAR), believed it their moral and religious duty to serve as purveyors of community memorial work and custodians of the dead. In doing so, they aided the mobilization effort with their patriotic discourse and innovative remembrance practices by producing what has since been termed a "romanticized militarism." These women affiliated themselves closely with veterans' organizations, and regardless of their differing objectives and divergent pasts, the state still "benefited from nationalist impulses and abetted them at certain points."[10]

Memorial Day, or Decoration Day (as it was originally known), is one popular example that still lives on. This holiday, dedicated to remembering the Civil War dead, had been a much earlier tradition in the South in which women's groups decorated the graves of Confederate soldiers and held memorial services there each spring.[11] On May 5, 1868, General John A. Logan, commander of the newly established Union veterans' association, the Grand Army of the Republic, officially designated May 30 for strewing flowers and decorating the graves of comrades.[12] Impressive ceremonies were held throughout the nation, featuring prayers, hymns, and patriotic anthems while the names of the community's war dead were read aloud. Orators, usually former generals or clergy members, "described how the sacrifice of the dead had paved the way for a united nation and brought the blessings of liberty."[13]

Years later, an American Legion publication explained to its First World War readers, "The Civil War was fought on the South's own soil." And "like the mothers of Belgium, the mothers of the South were actual witnesses to the bloody spectacle of war."[14] The implication here is that those who have personally experienced war are best qualified to determine how it will be remembered. Within this retelling of history, women's customary role as guardians of memory is intrinsically linked with the active participation of the veterans. Although women were responsible for initiating remembrance rituals such as Memorial Day, it was not until their efforts were recognized by the larger, politically prominent male organization that the initiative became a widely accepted national holiday. Jointly, veterans and women's auxiliaries determined to remember the dead were sufficient to shape the rituals of national commemoration beyond the Civil War years into the late twentieth century.

Clara Barton (who later became president of the American Red Cross) serves as another example of the powerful influence of women on national war memory. Interestingly, popular history continues to define Barton's role within the more feminine realm of nursing and not for her service to more than twenty-two thousand soldiers whose memory would have been permanently lost without her contribution.[15]

In 1865, Barton initiated an Office of Correspondence with the Friends of the Missing Men of the U.S. Army, where she maintained lists of missing soldiers and their last known whereabouts. She then transmitted the information to correspondents, who were nearly all women and who in most cases had waited years for news of their sons or husbands.[16] Public reaction to the search project was overwhelming. Letters eventually totaled some 63,182 inquiries about missing men and burial locations. Barton's diary records her shocked reaction to "the intense anxiety and excitement amounting in many instances nearly to insanity which characterized those letters." She regarded their "poignant grief" as the "most pressing necessity at the moment."[17]

The extent of the public response to Barton's project strengthens the premise that loss of a loved one in battle is magnified by the uncertainty of burial place and the inability to connect a name with a grave or body. The War Department nevertheless refused to support Barton's efforts and even declined to reimburse her costs until Congress intervened on her behalf. Barton approached the War Department again in 1866 with a plan to concentrate, register, and identify the Union dead at Andersonville prison. Once more, her efforts were thwarted when Quartermaster General Montgomery C. Meigs assigned the task to Major James Moore instead. Clara Barton was begrudgingly granted permission to accompany Moore on this military assignment, where he allegedly treated her "with studied disrespect." Barton refers to a "hosts of errors" during this mission that she believed to be the result of "indecent and criminal haste" on Moore's part.[18] The officer never mentioned Barton's presence in his official reports, nor is she credited in the army's Graves Registration Service history.

Bearing the torch of welfare reforms into the twentieth century, the Women's Relief Corps (WRC) worked to keep Memorial Day a reverent day of sorrow and loss. As an auxiliary of the GAR, the women enjoyed political power and success unmatched by other fraternal organizations until the formation of the equally successful American Legion in the aftermath of the First World War. When the WRC received official status in 1883, membership rules required women to be relatives of those who had served in the Union army or to be married to a GAR member. The WRC was primarily a service organization dedicated to helping the veterans by serving refreshments, sewing flags for the post halls, and raising charity funds that the GAR distributed. They became increasingly involved with improving the lives of veterans' widows and orphans through social-welfare reforms. The two associations complemented one another and together dedicated themselves to the perpetuity of the Union army.[19]

Years later, women volunteered again in both sections of the nation during the Spanish-American War to serve the needs of the military. Whereas some women provided nursing care under the army's authority, others such as Clara Barton tended the sick and wounded under the auspices of the Red Cross.[20] A determined Barton used aggressive tactics by going directly to the offices of the secretary of state and the president to personally request permission to lead a Red Cross mission to Havana.[21]

Clara Barton was welcomed with celebrity status upon her arrival home in November 1898.[22] She had successfully assumed leadership in a distinctive form of social-welfare work centered within the dangerous, masculine arena of confrontation and death. Building on her Civil War experience, Barton was again able to provide a key service to the military, one they were unable (or neglected) to perform satisfactorily for themselves. In doing so, she defied popular perceptions of women's wartime activities, which were narrowly defined within a supporting role. Her success may be further attributed to her dedication to socially acceptable women's work that rested safely within the realm of a compassionate nurturer, healer, consoler, and mourner. Barton was educated and of middle-class background, and as a single woman she avoided potential allegations that she neglected her own family's needs. Perhaps most remarkable is Barton's prevailing presence within national memory, despite the army's former attempts to marginalize her contribution largely on the basis of her status as a civilian and a woman.

Traditionally, women were excluded from the public stage largely because of their perceived abstract feminine qualities that ideally "transcended class, party, and indeed politics."[23] Nevertheless, with time and experience, Barton was able to maneuver through this complex masculine system with sagacity and aplomb. Speaking before the New England Woman's Suffrage Association, she reminded women that they need not ask men to confer rights, since men did not possess the privilege of bestowing rights. "He [man] depended upon woman for his being, his very existence, nurture and rearing. . . . Who furnished the warriors; who but the mothers? Who reared the sons and taught them that liberty and their country were worth their blood? Who gave them up and wept their fall, nursed them in suffering, and mourned them, dead?"[24] As spokeswoman for the values of republican motherhood, her noncompetitive views threatened neither prevailing myths of womanhood nor existing masculine ideologies. Thus, she was able to claim her rights on the basis of citizenship, birth, and her humanitarian contributions.

By contrast, suffragists openly challenged the superiority of male service and were quick to point out that women's military assistance, like men's, was also worthy of political rights. They were generally critical of the conduct of the war in an attempt to show that their women's energies were needed in all aspects of political life. The women who were the most successful appear to have been those who could convincingly demonstrate that achieving their special-interest goals would also benefit the country. Women soon recognized that they would have to work within the political context to win the rights they desired.

In the South, there seems to have been an earlier and more persistent determination among Confederate veterans to forget the war, since it was not until 1889 that the United Confederate Veterans emerged.[25] But their unification may have had less to do with trends than with the work of Confederate women's groups such as the United Daughters of the Confederacy, who assumed postwar responsibility for the rehabilitation of southern war memory.[26]

Women claimed for themselves the responsibility of documenting a public history in which the ideals of republican motherhood extended beyond the home. Through their organizations, they crafted a eulogy to the past that portrayed a genteel "moonlight-and-magnolia" South where contented slaves thrived on patriarchal plantations under benevolent masters. This historical imagery, popularly known as the "Lost Cause," depicted a triumphal version of the war that sought to wholly vindicate the Confederacy.[27]

Recent scholarship has shown that it was elite white women throughout the South who "donned the mantle of 'guardians of the past' to a degree without precedence in the region's history."[28] They were, as David Blight acknowledges, "activists eager to fight to control America's memory of slavery, the Civil War, and Reconstruction."[29]

Men conceded, rather than objected, to the women's newly assumed responsibility, despite gendered interpretations that placed an increasing significance on women's historical roles. As one recent study notes, "For many white women, their gendered identities could not be separated from their ties to the past—not just their personal, familial past, but also the collective 'history' of the South." Thus, white women used history to "fashion new selves without sundering links to the old," primarily by insisting that women of culture were integral to human progress.[30] Greater emphasis was then placed on the contributions of women pioneers, colonial women, and women who participated in the American Revolutionary War—all were instruments of a useable past.

The women's activities directly affected public life in southern communities as historic homes previously destined for destruction were preserved, museums were opened, oral histories were selectively recorded, and town squares were left permanently adorned with stone memorials dedicated to the deeds of Confederate heroes. Southern women effectively molded an authoritative historical memory by conducting letter-writing campaigns (including to the press), lobbying Congress, delivering speeches, fundraising, and even ensuring pro-southern textbooks in schools. Through the transformation and dissemination of history, southern white women had legitimized their role while establishing a firm voice of authority over what became a powerful and enduring collective memory.

With the passing of the post–Civil War years, the terms of reconciliation eventually eased divisions between the scarred nation, but they did so by fostering a deliberate forgetting of slavery. While African Americans struggled to keep emancipation centered within their collective memory, others in the reunited nation felt the subject was best kept out of national discourse. Maintaining selective control over the construction of monuments was one method of keeping the issue of slavery out of public memory.

Monuments were crucial to the longevity of memory since, as permanent public images, they had the power to legitimize collective remembrance. In the South, memorial sites assumed an added dimension by serving as places where African Americans and whites struggled over history and collective memory.[31] In the midst of this tension, motherhood, as a universal experience, had the capacity to be a racial equalizer and a potent catalyst for change, or so many black women thought.

The contest for ownership of black memory reached new proportions by the early twentieth century, when the UDC pressed Congress for permission to erect a Mammy Monument in the nation's capital.[32] The monument was intended to honor the "faithful colored mammies of the South" as a warm, maternal figure that represented the supposed contentment and loyalty of African Americans within the paternalistic slave system.[33] To white women, Black Mammy represented the harmonious relationship that existed between the races in the plantation South.[34]

But African American women believed that the Black Mammy depicted an inferior woman without a life and family of her own beyond that of servant to the master's family. They saw this as an opportunity to defend their womanhood and their homes, arguing that "the race could rise no higher than its women."[35] With no competing image, such a monument would stand as a perpetual vision of African Americans as slaves.

Joan Marie Johnson asserts that black women "had a particular stake in defining images of themselves that drew attention to their motherhood and love for their own children." They believed that this common factor could serve "as a basis for the possibility of cooperation with white women in the future." But African Americans would have to struggle to compete with white southerners, who held the wealth and power to ensure that only their monuments were raised.[36] The emotive power of motherhood imagery is revealed here within the national discourse of war memory, particularly in its ability to speak to both races, albeit in distinctly divergent terms.

Reaction to this purportedly nonthreatening monument was swift and vociferous from the National Association of Colored Women's Club (NACWC), founded in 1896. Incensed members perceived the Mammy figure solely as a testament to white slaveholders, and ultimately, their nationwide letter-writing campaign ensured that the bill was rejected by the Senate.

In the evolution of African American civil rights, it is significant that black women succeeded in their protest against the powerful UDC, but as Kirk Savage explains, it also suggests that "public monuments do not arise as if by natural law to celebrate the deserving; they are built by people with sufficient power to marshal (or impose) public consent for their erection."[37]

Black men also contributed significantly to the Civil War, yet few, if any, monuments were constructed to their memory. Of the 188,571 black soldiers and sailors who served in the Civil War, 20 percent perished (a rate 3 percent higher than that of white troops), primarily from disease.[38] In an effort to stake a claim on black memory, monuments were periodically proposed, but to assist with their remembrance would have threatened the collective forgetting necessary to nationwide reconciliation.[39]

Not surprisingly, black war stories were conspicuously absent from the popular literature of the 1880s that connected war memory with nationalism and citizenship.[40] Wartime experiences and memories of white veterans, by contrast, shaped a distinct genre of American literature, involving travelers' accounts of excursions into the South that included war-torn battlefields. "By the 1870s, the South had emerged as a major tourist attraction for the growing middle class of Northerners who could afford to travel."[41] Often, these travels were transformed into guidebooks that included tourist itineraries of Civil War battlefields embellished with enticing tales of farmers' plows disturbing the bones of buried Union soldiers.

With the decision not to recognize the memory of slavery, four years of the worst bloodshed in American history remained inexplicable, while its intrinsic cause lay ignored for the sake of national harmony. Ultimately, "many Americans increasingly realized that remembering the war . . . became, with time, easier than struggling over the enduring ideas for which those battles had been fought."[42] Naturally, this perception had an enduring impact on the memorialization of that bloody conflict.

The effects of women's grassroots partisan activism also extend beyond the construction of southern Civil War memory. A tradition of republican motherhood strengthened during this period, as did a political savvy born from an awareness of women's power to create desired reforms. Future generations of southern white women (like their counterparts in northern communities) built on this valuable political experience and their elevated status as mothers to gain support for even greater acts of national remembrance in the 1920s.

10

A Star of Recognition

Within days of the St. Mihiel Salient deaths in eastern France, a women's movement to abolish traditional black mourning dress was launched on the editorial pages of the American press. It began when Mrs. Louise D. Bowen, the chairman of Chicago's Women's Committee of the State Council of Defense proposed a gold star as a substitute for black mourning dress in memory of the American soldier dead.[1] Bowen's appeal was launched in a *New York Times* editorial, in which she claimed that the "glory of the death should be emphasized rather than its sadness." Bowen added that the psychological effect of "multitudes in mourning" was not good for the country and that the majority of soldiers were also against such demonstrations of grief. "It is not too early to consider this subject now," she concluded.[2]

The notion that wearing mourning garb was somehow mentally and physically injurious to the bereaved triggered a quick succession of editorials that wholeheartedly supported the patriotic chorus. The "lugubrious uniform once felt to be compulsory" was observed to have been in decline in recent years, due to change in taste and sentiment.[3] Instead, it was believed that the adoption of the gold star emblem would "show a higher appreciation of what death in the country's good cause really [was]—an honor even more than a misfortune, and one reflecting something of honor on those whom the bereavement directly and personally affects." Thus, sadness for the tragic, premature end of a life and the natural grieving process for that death were exchanged in favor of recognition for the living. "There is no better death than this and none so good," the editorial espoused, "and manifestation of its glory rather than of a private grief becomes the patriotic citizen."[4]

Pressure to change longstanding traditions emanated from the male domain as well as from women's groups. Speaking before an audience in Washington, DC, James W. Sullivan, assistant to the labor leader Samuel Gompers, described his experiences overseas and exclaimed, "All France is in mourning." Sullivan's concern went beyond the depressing sight of mourning garments to more practical questions of cost. He reasoned that if the French had declined to wear mourning attire, "the poor would have saved tens of millions of dollars." Sullivan went on to suggest that mourners wear a black band on the sleeve rather than a gold star. "If we are in for a two or three years' war, it is worth considering," he added.[5]

In May 1918, President Wilson wrote to Dr. Anna Howard Shaw, head of the Women's Committee of the United States Council of National Defense, suggesting that the group publicize its advice on mourning to other women. He urged the committee to promote service badges "upon which the white stars might upon the occurrence of a death be changed into stars of gold."[6] Wilson confided to Shaw that it would be unwise for him to "make any public utterance in this delicate matter," since it might appear that he was suggesting high death tolls.[7] He therefore urged the committee to publish his ideas through its own voice, which it did. On May 26, the *New York Times* published an endorsement letter from the president that stated, "American women should wear a black band on the left arm with a gilt star . . . for each member of the family who has given up his life for the nation."[8] His suggestion was derived from countless letters received from women across the nation who wrote to the White House seeking a meaningful alternative to painful mourning. "We should not *dare to mourn*, lest those seeing our insignia and knowing of that supreme sacrifice, might think we felt it a precious life thrown away," wrote Caroline S. Read, the widow of a prominent New York banker.[9]

The precise evolution of the service flag in connection with the black mourning armband and star is unclear, but by early 1918, a service flag (or window banner) was considered de rigueur in homes across the United States. "In every home in this wide land is now a service flag, or explanations for the embarrassing lack of one," one woman stated.[10] The choice of an easily recognizable gold star, rather than white for purity and sacrifice or purple (the traditional color of mourning), reflects a need to see the loss in terms of preciousness and as a valuable contribution.

Mourning symbolism also assumed gender affiliations, as men increasingly chose to wear the armband without a star, while the service flag with star was the preferred choice for women in their homes. Presumably, as guardians of the home and hearth, women's pride was better reflected there than on their sleeves while engaging in the external, masculine sphere. Service flags required no costly financial outlay since they could be handmade or purchased in local shops, an added benefit. On each flag a blue star was displayed for every family member in the service. If that family member died, a gold star was superimposed over the blue star.

When Wilson wrote to Shaw in that spring of 1918, he undoubtedly recognized an opportunity to gain a public endorsement from women for the war effort. Mothers readily willing to sacrifice sons for the nation lent extraordinary support and unity to the cause. In his letters, Wilson expressed a belief that the British were treating mourning more wisely than the French, which no doubt strengthened his approval for the gold star emblem.[11] Turning to the British example provided added credibility for ideas already being discussed at home.

Wilson's comment about British and French mourning practices is an intriguing one that beckons closer scrutiny of cultural trends in both societies. In a study of family mourning in Britain during the First World War, Pat Jalland suggests that family attitudes and responses to death were profoundly affected by an accelerated prewar trend away from religious adherence.[12] Due to the decline in Christian belief and practice, spiritualism became a popular movement, funeral rituals were reformed, and simpler mourning fashions were encouraged. In Britain, it was argued within social circles that "national morale and patriotism would suffer if thousands of widows all wore full mourning-dress, especially after the mass deaths from 1916."[13] According to Jalland, people rejected the depressing effect of black dress. As one observer noted, "funereal gloom increased the fear of death by making it black, mysterious and awesome."[14] Enthusiasm for cremations grew as nineteenth-century funeral and age-old mourning customs were largely condemned.

America's powerful funeral industry would probably have resisted a popular movement toward cremation, but one striking similarity does span the cultural Anglo-American divide. "Death," Jalland writes, "was effectively removed from the domain of the family and became instead a communal sacrifice for the nation—death could no longer be readily mourned by individual families."[15] The unique and tragic circumstances produced by a war that left masses of unidentified and missing dead (who had died prematurely for questionable aims) meant traditional mourning rituals were inadequate, irrelevant, and generally impossible.[16]

Interestingly, France's predominant Catholic culture remained true to traditional mourning rituals and expressions despite casualty figures that surpassed those of Britain and the United States. By contrast, Protestant Anglo-Americans facing a decline in religious faith and practice embraced a transformational process that minimized public expressions of grief during the First World War. Similar trends in French society were not noticeable for several decades. Philippe Ariès, in his 1977 landmark study of changing French attitudes toward death, appears to support this claim with recollections of "women in mourning . . . invisible under their crepe and voluminous black veils." Ariès adds that his mother wore full mourning dress for her son, killed in the Second World War, long after his brother's death in 1945.[17] The avoidance of physical expressions of grief among Americans experiencing loss was not, therefore, unique, since it paralleled British experience, but the gold star remained a strictly American badge of recognition.[18]

Sigmund Freud wrote that mourning and its more maligned form of melancholia share distinguishable features, but the primary distinction is mourning's ability to heal, which occurs when "the ego becomes free and uninhibited again."[19] Jay Winter suggests that it is problematic to consider remembrance in Freudian terms, since mourning does not always lead to healing. He suggests that for some people, the burden of bereavement is bearable; for others, it is crushing. For the nonmelancholic mourner, the ability to disengage from the departed or to "forget" paradoxically leads to healthy recovery. Winter believes that ritual is a means of forgetting, as much as of commemoration, and that war memorials are there to help in the necessary act of forgetting.[20] The validity of this theory was soon tested when thousands of American mothers began journeying to their sons' graves more than a decade after their loss.

Much of this theoretical conjecture fails to address the implications for society when the natural processes of mourning and forgetting are replaced with stars of recognition, particularly in the absence of a body or grave or, indeed, in the outright societal disapproval of the conventional displays of grief. In the United States, a reliance on traditional rituals familiar since the Civil War was substituted with modern pressure to conform to public demonstrations of patriotic support. American women had traditionally taken up guardianship over the dead, but with the nation's entry into the First World War, they assumed an increasingly active role in the modification of practice, as death became an occasion for a gold star reward. This emblem of exclusivity brought not only recognition of a sacred sacrifice but also a means of unity among the grieving. Ideally, the gold star represented a bond that surpassed ethnic or racial orientation. Such a gesture was significant and politically useful in wartime for an exceedingly diverse society, unlike that which existed in Europe.

In Britain, the government ban against the return of the dead brought voices of outrage, forcing issues of equality and democracy to surface. Distinctions between socialism and citizens' rights were blurred along with rigid class boundaries as modernity clashed with tradition. However, the British state remained stronger than the individual, even after death.

In France, as in Britain, there was no precedence for government repatriation of the war dead, but the state acquiesced to public demands nevertheless. This giving way to modernity did not produce a similar shift in public mourning practices, which remained steeped in religious and cultural traditions of the past. Territorial aggression by Germany gave further clarity of purpose to the people of this embattled nation. In France, a homogeneous society mourned collectively with no need to forge solidarity with glittering gold stars. These differences were apparent even before the armistice, but they became more pronounced in the immediate postwar years.

Clearly, memory did cause divisions among society, but it could also unite groups as well.[21] Those most directly affected by the war, veterans and mothers (and widows), kept patriotism and past memories alive by forming organized collectives with others with whom they shared a common bond. Since loss was experienced within a larger community, people who had joined together helped one another validate interpretations and construct memory. Personal or collective, cultural, and public, memories are selected and interpreted to serve present needs, and often negotiation within a wide context is necessary to locate a meaningful interpretation.[22]

Together, veterans' groups and women's organizations attempted to transform personal grief and doubt over the war's achievements into full allegiance to the state. In return, they received political recognition, financial and social benefits, and perhaps most significant, national assurances that the sacrifice of life had not been in vain.

11

A Reluctant Giant

On November 11, 1921, the United States followed the example set by France and Great Britain when it laid the body of an unidentified soldier to rest at Arlington National Cemetery and designated it the "Unknown Soldier."[1] The body had been chosen amidst elaborate ceremony in France that October, and with its arrival in America, thousands filed past the casket to pay homage to the soldier as he lay in the Capitol rotunda. Assurances of anonymity mattered more than rank, race, or social status, since the remains symbolized the ideal of national community. This democratic practice of "part invented and part copied" symbolism recognized the loss of life and the replacement of individual identity with a national identity.[2]

Despite the solemn pageantry and hero worship that marked First World War memorialization, such symbols failed to mask the postwar tension, divisiveness, and political rancor of a disillusioned society. Once the repatriation debate was settled, tension began anew over where the Unknown Soldier should be buried, how many unidentified bodies might be returned, the suitability of Arlington because of its isolated location, and the best day for burial.[3]

Months before the ceremony, Charles Pierce sent a heartfelt entreaty to the War Department not to rush the body of an unknown soldier back for burial at Arlington. "The great danger in this movement lies in the haste with which it may be consummated," wrote Pierce to the army's quartermaster general. "In my judgment this [Memorial Day] is too early," since "it is utterly impossible for any person to make certification that an individual body is impossible of identification."[4] Pierce concluded with a startling appeal to have all the unknown bodies returned to Arlington. In doing so, they might receive "fitting honor" and could remain "in custody" until their final identity was determined.[5]

Secretary Baker's disapproval of this idea had an enduring impact on the nation's memory of the First World War. Had all the dead been

The chosen unidentified American soldier being returned from France to the United States to rest in the Tomb of the Unknown at Arlington National Cemetery, 1921. (SC Photo 111, No. 104183, RG 92, NA)

returned, the presence of their graves in the United States might have served as a resounding reminder of America's sacrifice and key participation. Instead, Baker decided to "mark the advance line of freedom," thus using the dead as a stake in "the farthest advance yet of the American ideal."[6] The war dead as impersonal entities again remained useful as political tools for the sake of the nation.

Events surrounding the burial of the Unknown Soldier highlight patterns and practices that continued to characterize American remembrance throughout the interwar period. Rhetoric that emphasized America's homogeneity as the model representation of a true democracy claimed to transcend individualism, diversity, and sectionalism.[7] Yet the commemorative forms chosen usually "defined the ideal American as a white, most likely Protestant, Christian," as demonstrated by the rituals and symbolism surrounding the Unknown Soldier's burial.[8] Even the marble tomb placed over the Unknown Soldier caused tension when people were undecided as to whether it should symbolize war or peace. Five years passed before Congress authorized a white marble compromise that supported three allegorical figures of Peace, Valor, and a dominant central Victory, all depicted on a simple sarcophagus. America, an ambivalent nation struggling with the memory of war, repeatedly focused its remembrance on victory and not on death. This policy served as the underpinning on which the nation's commemorative symbols stood for decades—both literally and figuratively.

Burial of the Unknown Soldier at Arlington represented the primary official means by which the United States collectively memorialized the war. There were local parades and wreath-laying ceremonies at the base of new monuments throughout the country; however, there were no plans for the construction of any national monuments in Washington, DC, to accompany those that honored previous wars. Instead, policy planners turned to foreign fields for the construction of commemorative symbols. As political architecture abroad, monuments were linked to evolving foreign-policy objectives considered appropriate reflections of America's growing status and military might.[9] This process appears inconsistent with the long-held concept of isolationism, which is believed to have existed throughout America during this period. The contradiction deserves further analysis.

The Arlington ceremony followed one year after the Senate voted against President Wilson's League of Nations. The country had crushingly rejected his prospective Democratic successor, James M. Cox, hoping instead for a return to normalcy with its new president, Warren G. Harding. Wilson had wanted the 1920 election to be a "solemn referendum" on the issue of the League, but before the campaign even began, "it was a foregone conclusion that Harding would win."[10] On January 12, 1919, when the Peace Conference opened in Paris, Wilson's fight for the passage of the League began. Faced with criticism at home by a Republican majority in both houses of Congress, the president strove to convince the Allied leaders to accept a "peace without victory." According to William Leuchtenburg, Wilson's hated opponents, Theodore Roosevelt and Senator Henry Cabot Lodge, believed in a more aggressive "balance of power politics and were contemptuous of Wilson's idealism." Both men would stop at nothing to undermine the president's standing abroad, with Roosevelt going so far as to issue a statement that the president had no credibility at home.[11]

Although Senator Lodge declared in March 1919 that the constitution of the League of Nations "should not be accepted by the United States," a majority of Americans are believed to have favored entrance into the League by that summer.[12] Despite these statistics and Wilson's failing health, the president embarked on a strenuous nationwide tour in September to seek support directly from the people. Audiences were moved to tears as they listened to Wilson's reference to the graves in France. He promised that similar deaths on foreign fields could be avoided with American entrance and acceptance of the League. Since the repatriation issue remained far from settled by the autumn of 1919, war death would have been a sensitive and painful topic for many Americans. On the other hand, the news of French legislation forbidding the removal of bodies from overseas, announced in mid-1919, may have caused some Wilson supporters to reconsider their position.

Time was not on the president's side, nor were the returning doughboys who swelled isolationist numbers with antiforeign, anti-French sentiment that increased their determination never to fight over there again. Ships returning the war-weary troops brought "tales of being fleeced by French storekeepers," and others voiced their disillusionment over anticipated French gratitude that was not forthcoming.[13]

When dispatches from newsmen at the Peace Conference reported on Europe's rapacious appetite for colonies, enlarged boundaries, or reparations, the anti-League reaction mounted. Others were simply indifferent to foreign affairs amid a general feeling of malaise with League business and a desire to get back to domestic affairs.

Isolationists argued that the League would "cripple or destroy the Monroe Doctrine," thus challenging the exclusive American control of the Western Hemisphere that had been welded to the older policy of isolationism. The isolationists were confronted by internationalists, who saw the League as a means of preventing future war by assuming responsibility for ensuring "territorial integrity and existing political independence of all members of the League."[14] Although public opinion favoring the League may have been strongest in 1919, most people did not understand the consequences implied by collective security. With concerns and confusion over foreign affairs such as the Bolshevist threat from Russia and the petty wars and turmoil following the formal end of fighting, it is not surprising that many Americans preferred to rest in the feeling of "smugness, superiority and safety" of their own borders.[15] American opinion remained in this polarized state over foreign-policy objectives until, unable to reach a settlement with the president, the Senate voted against the League on March 19, 1920, for the last time.

Europeans were united in their surprise and disappointment when the U.S. Senate failed to consent to the Treaty of Versailles. Historian Robert Ferrell tells us that the "heart of the world was broken" as the international community struggled to understand Wilson's failure at home.[16] The war debt issue only exacerbated misunderstandings as Europeans attempted to justify their expectations that these payments should be "forgiven." Eventually, after much ill feeling and mutual recrimination, an arrangement was worked out that greatly reduced payment.

The extent of American loans in the postwar global economy demonstrates the rapid and extensive shift of power. By 1919, the U.S. government had altered its status of five years prior, from a debtor nation to a firmly established position as a creditor nation. Private individuals had loaned almost three million dollars, and the government had extended over ten million dollars to foreign governments.[17] By March 1921, when Warren G. Harding assumed the presidency, the nation's military apparatus had similarly altered to meet the increasing challenges of its new status. Harding inherited a formidable establishment, with a modern army that was more than twice the size of any force the United States had ever before fielded in peacetime and a navy that was at least arguably the most powerful in the world.[18]

Despite sentiments to the contrary, the nation could no longer remain isolated from world affairs. Leuchtenburg refers to America's ambivalence toward its rising position in international affairs as that of a "Reluctant Giant."[19] By involving itself in the world war at such a crucial juncture, injecting men and resources that ultimately provided a decisive Allied victory, the nation forever altered its global status. This wealth, expansion, and military growth also required a more ambitious diplomatic presence abroad to protect American interests and investments. The United States quickly developed a professional foreign service, embassies, and an unmistakable foreign policy that reflected a strong, positive national image. Commemorative architecture was also clearly linked to these new and evolving policy objectives. According to Ron Robin, the process of "implanting artifacts of American power in far-flung corners of the globe" represented a compromise between the "simultaneous demands for a return to isolationism on the one hand, and expansionist government aid for capturing foreign markets on the other."[20] After all, it was much easier to accept a few embassies, overseas monuments, cemeteries, and an emerging diplomatic corps than the foreign entanglements that could result from pursuing commitments to collective security agreements.

The resolution to repatriate American remains after the war was standard military practice by 1919. The political decision to deviate from that policy at a time when the nation was already mired in acrimonious debate between isolationism and internationalism served to trigger further divisiveness. Robin has identified the government's cemeteries and grand monuments overseas as a clear departure from the isolationist sentiment that dominated much of foreign policy prior to the late nineteenth century. He suggests that the divergence from this norm indicates a "deliberate turn of events" rather than a spontaneous reaction to the disposition of war dead after cessation of hostilities.[21]

Robin's assertions raise two critical factors that deserve further consideration. The first—that the establishment of cemeteries, monuments, and other instruments of the American foreign presence was a departure from a dominating isolationist sentiment—must be questioned. To what extent can the precise nature and degree of isolationism in America during the aftermath of the First World War be measured? The renowned Wilson scholar John Milton Cooper persuasively challenges the prevalent view that isolationism dominated American thinking throughout the 1920s. Cooper claims that "only a small minority of people held to isolationist views and rejected overseas commitments out of hand." He asserts that "there was no 'retreat into isolation' during the League fight, and almost no one expressed disillusionment with the war or its outcome. Those things came later."[22] Admittedly, there was a strong isolationist element (Cooper argues that it was a small sect) of politicians and intellectuals who played an "interesting and often constructive role in American foreign policy"; this group promoted disarmament and noninterventionist policies that coexisted and sometimes clashed with policies favoring "discretionary involvement in international power politics."[23]

Whether Cooper has underestimated the power and extent of the isolationist movement in the country at that time cannot fully be addressed within the scope of this study. However, consideration must be given to the possibility that rather than mass isolationism, what may have existed was a collective desire to temporarily *disengage* from Europe and the recent war. Whether the dominant voice throughout the nation was isolationism or disengagement, evidence shows that few Americans believed it should obscure an obligation to commemorate the services of their forces on the former battlefield.

To address the second aspect of Robin's argument one might ask whether commemorative practices such as the establishment of overseas cemeteries and the construction of monuments need imply a broader commitment to internationalism. When Americans commemorated the end of the Civil War, they turned to the former battlefield as a fitting location for their memorials. The most profuse testimony to decades of communal remembrance is the landscape at Gettysburg.[24] Represented there is a sprawling, eclectic merger of the sacred and secular on the former field of battle, which happened to be on American soil.

Similarly, attempts at collective memorialization began to flourish across the Western Front even before the armistice. American military units were quick to improvise hastily built monuments of field stones and concrete in the middle of nowhere and often on private property. They were an inconvenience to farmers, who were forced to plow around them, and without maintenance, most of them deteriorated.[25] In time, complaints were heard within government circles that these unsightly images projected an uneven, conflicting impression that required intervention and regulation. Efforts to avoid a repetition of the haphazard Gettysburg landscape were thus motivated by an awareness that a nation of rising power and prominence required revised guidelines.

Several key observations are apparent from the government's metamorphic approach to international affairs: the rapidity of the nation's transformation, an increase in federal authority beyond American borders (once primarily in the hands of private commercial investors), and a measure of uncertainty concerning the precise nature of overseas objectives. With few domestic regulations in place, policymakers looked to the imperial practices of former European powers for a precedent when determining a national commemorative response.[26]

To that end, the government turned to its new commemorative instrument, the American Battle Monuments Commission, to initiate and oversee the construction of a grand scheme of national monuments on the former battlefield. Regardless of public sentiment favoring international intervention or complete withdrawal from European affairs, America's overseas commemorative strategy ultimately reflected the aspirations of its politically prominent members.

This ambivalent coterie of appointed commissioners (nearly all civilians) were similarly guided through most phases of their American overseas commemorative strategy by their influential European counterparts. When these processes combined with traditional American practices dating from the mid-nineteenth century, the result was nothing short of a dazzling compromise. Nevertheless, this powerful new nation, created by its own mighty military machine, was determined to appear as though it acted independently on behalf of a peaceful consensus.

12

A Commission Is Born

Suggestions as to how the nation might best remember its heroes were not publicly solicited after the war, but that did not prevent Colonel Webb C. Hayes, son of former president Rutherford B. Hayes and the chairman of the Cuba-China Battlefield Commission, from sharing his ideas with the U.S. Army's Quartermaster General in December 1918.[1] Hayes presented a detailed proposal for commemorating the "Great War of Democracy versus autocracy," with recommendations that closely resembled efforts to memorialize the former Spanish-American conflict and the "American China Relief Expedition of 1900."[2] Revised plans deriving from that former era called for a series of battle monuments marking major engagements, which would be visible from a driveway along the entire line of American trenches, and then a memorial observation tower with accompanying large bronze tablets dedicated to those killed in action.

The strategy that Hayes proposed in 1918, which was eventually rejected in favor of a military planning board, assumed that the state would not repatriate remains as it had done after the Spanish-American War.[3] Hayes was convinced that the First World War would follow patterns of the past: "in all our domestic battles or wars . . . , the American dead have been buried in national cemeteries near the battlefields where they fell and few indeed have been buried at their homes."[4] Although resolution of the repatriation debate proved Hayes wrong by 1922, his strategy based on traditional practice still posed a formidable threat to the War Department's own plans.

No one had a greater stake in ensuring that the efforts and sacrifices of the AEF were remembered than its commander in chief, General John J. Pershing. Before leaving Europe, Pershing advised his chief of staff that the army should "thoroughly mark the battlefields in a semi-permanent way" so that if in the future "it should be our desire to erect monuments or to mark them more permanently, we could do so."[5]

After several weeks and much discussion, military officials decided that temporary markers were impractical because of the unsettled conditions where fighting had occurred. Personnel in the army's Historical Section nevertheless attempted to record troop movements and positions, conscious of the need to document its role in the recent global conflict. Evidence on the ground was rapidly disappearing when General Fox Conner suggested that it might be better to select a prominent battlefield site where a marker might be erected at a later date.[6] Ultimately, General George Van Horn Moseley, assistant chief of staff, made the final decision and ordered personnel to "fix the most important points by measuring the coordinates with accuracy."[7]

Pershing, who once fought stridently for the autonomy of the U.S. Army while serving as its commander, now fought to ensure that its valiant efforts were honored and remembered. His "scholarly" general, John McAuley Palmer, diligently studied and compiled historical battlefield details, photographed the sites of primary engagements, and then outlined a comprehensive strategy for remembrance based primarily on this research.[8]

By 1920, the need for central supervision of overseas memorials was evidenced by the large number of markers that overrepresented some divisions while other units went unrecognized. Moreover, the army's battlefield researchers claimed that the historical accuracy of these markers was highly questionable. To address this need Assistant Secretary Ralph Hayes recommended the appointment of a War Memorials Council in May 1920. Secretary of War Baker authorized the council accordingly, which consisted of twenty-one individuals who met for the first time on June 9, 1920.[9] But just as the army's commemorative approach was beginning to take shape in early December 1921, word came of a competing plan that threatened to gain congressional approval.

Frank B. Willis, former Republican governor of Ohio, introduced the Memorial Highway bill to the Senate, outlining a proposal that would largely transform France and Belgium into a memorial park.[10] Days later, the same bill was brought before the House by Representative James W. Husted (R-New York).[11] The Husted Bill, as it became known, was the same previously rejected plan that Webb C. Hayes had originally proposed in December 1918.[12] Undaunted, a persistent Hayes had successfully persuaded members of a New York City preservation society, and the Ohio State Archaeological and Historical Society (represented by Husted and Willis), to resurrect the plan. Both men agreed that theirs was "a more appropriate memorial" than the army's version.[13]

The Husted Bill called for the revitalization of preexisting roads in Belgium and France, linking them together to trace the path of the victorious armies. It also proposed a series of mounted historical tablets depicting the area's recent battle action and the relevant positions of American and Allied divisions engaged there. Memorial markers, rather than elaborately constructed monuments, were planned for areas of special distinction. The highway would incorporate each of the American cemeteries along its path and pay tribute to the sites where temporary cemeteries had been. Groups in the United States could also participate with prior approval from a governing body. To fill this organizational void the bill called for a Memorial Highway Commission with authority to coordinate and regulate all aspects of the project. "Associate commissioners" would be appointed by all state governors and the District of Columbia. Jointly, they would raise state funding for the project to ensure that the federal government incurred no expense other than an initial ten-thousand-dollar appropriation. Lastly, the bill called for cooperation with the French and Belgian authorities on matters of construction, and it invited those nations to mount their own historical tablets along the highway's route.

Hayes's plan reflects much of America's former prewar innocence. By current standards and perhaps even to some of Hayes's contemporaries, this attempt to forge another Gettysburg-like memorial park in Europe appears naive, idealistic, and internationally intrusive. The scheme had its commemorative roots in the past, and as such, it looked to precedence for guidance following a war that had no parallels. It also reveals optimism that modernity could be stifled in favor of a more comfortable status quo. Hayes's bill granted authority to the states, with few expectations of the federal government. Moreover, it was functional. Hayes outlined a clear strategy for honoring the war dead and their sacrifice, while offering an opportunity for international cooperation. Despite aims to precisely document the battle action and grant credit to the respective fighting units, the War Department's Battle Monuments Board vigorously opposed the highway bill. Both strategies presumed that the proper place for memorialization was on the former battlefield, though other similarities were few.

In the midst of fears that America's contribution to the war effort was being overlooked by its allies, proponents of the military believed that the War Department should retain control of war memory, in addition to national cemeteries.[14] In response, Pershing's board asked for an array of bronze maps and tablets in addition to twelve special monuments at a cost of $540,000.[15] If sufficient funds remained after the historical memorials were complete, three separate monuments were also proposed for areas considered most important to American operations. Military board members believed their maps and monuments should be the only markers on the battlefield, fearing that private and state efforts would distort historical authenticity. No precise plans to honor the war dead were included in the board's strategy; rather, it placed priority on historical integrity and on Pershing's desire to ensure that all units were accorded equal recognition.

President Harding did not question the board's perspective when he agreed to the military's proposal in its original form in February 1922. Similarly, Stephen G. Porter, a Republican representative from Pennsylvania and chairman of the Committee on Foreign Affairs, also proved an ardent supporter. In March, Porter introduced the legislation to the House of Representatives, but two days later, he returned with a revised bill that included the participation of the Veterans of Foreign Wars (VFW), founded in Pittsburgh in September 1914. The military considered this change "undesirable" since the original legislation had suggested that membership be restricted to active-duty officers only.[16]

Hearings for the nation's First World War commemorative strategy were held before the Committee on Foreign Affairs in March 1922, and had it not been for the intercession of its chairman, Husted's highway bill would surely have defeated the War Department's proposal. Instead, Porter did not allow a vote to be taken on the government's plan, simply because "the sentiment of the Committee was not favorable toward it."[17] Due to some confusion over the committee's agenda, no member of the military's Battle Monuments Board was present at the hearing.

Afterwards, Pershing and his colleagues were shocked that Congress had responded with such hostility to their proposal, but Porter attributed this reaction to the bill's origins within the War Department. He was convinced that the committee would have disapproved of the bill if the question had been brought to a vote. This proved to be merely the first hurdle in what became an exceedingly difficult struggle for supporters of the military's plan. Pershing believed that their bill "was badly needed" and had been "an exceedingly fair one," but evidence proves it was poorly timed.

Ships were returning daily from overseas, bearing the last of America's repatriated war dead, and newspapers were filled with scathing details of the Veterans' Bureau scandals that were revealed in 1923. But corruption was not the only cause for public vehemence. Anger also stemmed from what veterans perceived as the government's inability to recognize its social and financial obligation to them. Whereas veterans of earlier wars could look to their war bonuses to give them a new start, the post–First World War administration was determined to avoid the colossal expenditures of the past.[18] Congress remained divided over the appropriate reward for veterans' services, and veterans, in turn, remained bitter toward the government. In 1922, when the War Department's commemorative bill was introduced, the campaign for adjusted compensation had intensified as high unemployment fueled the veterans' discontent. Consequently, the men bore a heavy grudge against all levels of government.[19] The matter was not resolved until 1924, when Congress passed a veterans' benefit measure over President Calvin Coolidge's veto.[20] Thus, circumstances might have favored military control of overseas remembrance had the Battle Monuments Board introduced its bill immediately after the war; but as the years passed, antipathy toward the War Department increased.

In order to receive a second hearing, Congressman Porter advised the board to secure the backing of veterans' associations, "which, by reason of their character," would be interested in marking the American battlefields.[21] Steps were taken to secure the support of the American Legion, Veterans of Foreign Wars, and the National Guard Associations, despite the military's firm stand against their inclusion.

After a bitterly contested, four-hour debate, the Committee on Foreign Affairs approved the War Department's plan with changes that included the veteran community. On March 4, 1923, President Harding signed the bill into law, and the American Battlefields Monuments Commission (ABMC) was created. However, this success brought military planners little cause for celebration. Although Congress had ratified the memorial legislation as proposed by the War Department, there was one critical deviation: originally, the commission's membership specified a strong military majority, whereas in the version passed, this choice was left to the president's discretion.[22] Consequently, Pershing and his officers anticipated civilian interference as a potential threat to military control.

Dismayed, John Palmer, Pershing's appointee, urged the chief of staff to consider the enormous importance of the commission and those chosen to serve on it. Speaking on behalf of the military's war board, he claimed it was of the greatest importance that the secretary of war assume chairmanship, and he provided the president with a list of suggested "prominent men." But when the first meeting of the ABMC was convened in September 1923, those present included John J. Pershing, as chairman; David A. Reed, Republican senator from Pennsylvania, as acting chairman; a Republican Gold Star Mother; and three civilians who represented each of the national veterans associations.[23] The state of Pennsylvania was overwhelmingly represented on the commission, as was the Republican Party.

President Harding's appointment of civic representatives is understandable, whether prompted by choice or pressure, but regardless of the outcome, Palmer need not have feared that the glory days of the AEF would be overlooked. As time passed, the path to overseas remembrance taken by the ABMC far exceeded the modest plans first anticipated by the War Department.

This heated contest over the nation's ideal commemorative strategy offers a revealing glimpse into the political dynamics of Congress, the Executive, and the military as they played out in the immediate postwar era. The episode also illustrates the escalating power of American interest-group pressure. Although distrust of the military establishment undoubtedly played a key role in the selection of ABMC members, Congress may have been hesitant to relinquish its control over the formation of the nation's war memory. As it was and continues to be repeatedly demonstrated, those who can successfully seize and maintain authority over the instruments of remembrance hold enormous power.

13

Sacred Space and Strife

Within weeks of the ABMC's founding, the secretary of war relinquished chairmanship over the new commission and named General Pershing in his place. The intention may have been at least partially calculated to foster public support by separating the agency from the War Department's direct control. Regardless, Pershing and his secretary, Major Xenophon H. (X. H.) Price, were the only military members of the new governing body.[1] Once it became clear that Pershing's other duties (he was still the chief of staff, for example) would prevent him from attending regular meetings, Senator Reed assumed an increasingly prominent role as "acting chairman," leaving Major Price as the lone military representative.

The decision to appoint Senator David Aiken Reed, a lawyer by profession, to such a key role undoubtedly proved a crucial factor in determining America's commemorative legacy overseas. No individual exerted more influence than Reed over the shape and intention of the nation's memorialization efforts; consequently, the senator's personality, biases, and political leanings, as well as his extravagant, grandiose architectural schemes, are still apparent across the battlefields today.

David Reed was born into a wealthy Pittsburgh family, educated at "expensive private schools," graduated Princeton in 1900, and entered his father's law firm in 1903. His practice dealt chiefly with corporations and public utilities, interests that *Time* magazine claimed were closely associated with his friend and mentor, Andrew W. Mellon. Reed was commissioned a major in the First World War and won several medals in the Argonne campaign. Following his overseas service, he returned to his law office in Pennsylvania until he was appointed senator in 1922.[2]

The *Time* article described Reed as a "thin, lean, wiry man of medium stature" who possessed a "supercilious" manner and walked very rapidly in expensive cut suits, swinging his arms with an "air of great preoccupation." His unsmiling eyes, set in a long and deeply lined face, gave him the appearance of a man well beyond his years. With his thin brown hair slicked back across his head, he spoke with a "vibrant intensity" on the Senate floor while leaning forward, every muscle taut.[3] Politically, Reed was known as a "vigorous Republican partisan" who voted for tax reductions, farm relief, and increased prohibition penalties. More significant, in 1923, he voted against the Soldier Bonus bill, which would have authorized adjusted pay benefits and insurance for veterans. For that reason, war veterans were reportedly suspicious of Reed, making him the government's "man of the hour" but certainly no friend to the "common man."[4] Reportedly, the senator maintained his aristocratic airs and made no effort to appeal to average Americans.

Senator Reed later claimed that President Harding "really exercised very little choice in making the [ABMC] selections, because . . . [they] were practically forced upon him by the decision of these various organizations that everybody wanted recognized."[5] Warren G. Harding, the first American president to take office after the First World War, is remembered mainly for the scandals that clouded his administration, which lasted barely two and a half years. By midterm, Harding's popularity had greatly diminished due to the collapse of the war boom, wage cuts, unemployment, distress among farmers, and urban resentment of prohibition.[6] Thus, the president might have viewed the ABMC appointments as an opportunity to appease special interests.

Reed's comment hints at raised public expectations that greater civic participation on the commission would lead to an enhanced public voice in the outcome. If so, these hopes were soon dispelled. The passage of the ABMC legislation unarguably moved control of the nation's war remembrance out of the hands of the War Department into the laps of public representatives; however, it is unclear whether this action reflected narrow political calculation by the Harding administration or was a genuine attempt to give the public a stronger voice in commemorative policy.

The months between the ABMC's creation in March and Harding's death in August 1923 (just before the first ABMC meeting in September) were tumultuous ones in Washington. Corruption, political disgrace, and subsequent investigations (particularly those concerning the Veterans Bureau) plagued the administration, and "for a time it was not clear that the President's death . . . would be sufficient to save his party from the feared political consequences."[7] Senator Reed's participation in the Veterans' Bureau investigations were said to have "helped expose graft" that ultimately sent the director, Charles Forbes, to the penitentiary.[8] Perhaps that made Reed's appointment somewhat more acceptable to disgruntled veterans.

Although a Gold Star Mother was appointed to the ABMC, the choice of a Republican female supporter as a member of this commemorative board, against the wishes of the military establishment, seems to have been geared toward similar political advantage. No ethnic or racial minorities were invited to serve, nor were there any naval personnel appointed. When a Navy Department official did appear before the ABMC to inquire about plans for deceased sailors, he was given polite but vague assurances and then promptly dismissed.[9] Regardless, ABMC membership did not necessarily guarantee one a voice in the decision-making process, as members soon discovered.

Evidently, a successful bid for representation on the commission was dependent on the cohesiveness and finally the power of the organized interest requesting it. Political appeasement was then exchanged for support from the collective, and in turn, these groups responded with their own demands for services. Such an exclusive arrangement invites one to question the efficacy of the ABMC during this period, particularly as members had neither clear guidelines nor a precedent to follow. No matter a commissioner's group affiliation, the subsequent decade placed all ABMC members squarely in the firing line of discontented veterans, state officials, and private citizens who resented iron-fisted restrictions against their right to memorialize. Ultimately, the ABMC did not reflect the wishes of those Americans who expressed a desire to remember the fallen, nor was it inclusive of all those who had served.[10]

Once appointed, members wasted no time preparing plans for America's memorialization abroad. Despite the lack of initial funding, the commission hastened to consolidate control over all planned memorial construction in Europe.[11] The foreign ambassadors of Belgium, Britain, and France were notified of the appointments and directed to refer all requests from Americans for memorials to the ABMC for approval.[12] By December, authority was complete, when even the secretary of state agreed to transfer to the commission all matters pertaining to war memorials and monuments in Europe.[13] The commission also voted to defer a decision on monument proposals that had been previously received from private individuals, states, and associations, which inevitably resulted in further delays and a slackening of public interest.

On June 14, 1924, the entire commission sailed out of New York Harbor bound for Europe, where they planned to inspect conditions at American cemeteries and formulate plans for a national strategy. Their entourage included spouses, children, valets, and maids who accompanied several

The leadership of the ABMC pictured in Brussels, Belgium during their investigative tour in Europe. *Left to right:* Secretary Price, General Pershing, and Senator David Reed. (SC Photo 111, No. 86161, RG 92, NA)

members, many of whom remained in Europe until mid-August. The group spent more than a month visiting sites, meeting with members of foreign graves commissions, and viewing military cemeteries in England, Italy, Belgium, and France.[14]

By 1924, much of the grave consolidation work in Europe was complete, and eight final cemetery locations had been designated for the 31,508 American bodies that would eventually be buried there.[15] As General Pershing accompanied the commissioners on their overseas tour, he undoubtedly shared with them his memories of the work that he and his GRS chief, Colonel Pierce, had previously undertaken to formulate plans for the cemeteries. It might prove helpful to pause for similar reflection of those years before the arrival of the ABMC, when Pierce and members of the Commission of Fine Arts prepared tentative plans for the American cemeteries.

In the fall of 1923, Pershing had made a six-month tour of the burial sites, then given his approval to a further revised strategy. The final scheme established French cemeteries at St. Mihiel and Meuse-Argonne, which were associated with the victories of the AEF, whereas the five other cemeteries (located in Bony, Belleau Wood, Fere-en-Tardenois, Suresnes, and Waregem, Belgium) were affiliated with areas where American divisions fought in joint operations under British and French command.[16] For those Americans who had died in Great Britain, a portion of England's Brookwood military cemetery was chosen as their final resting place.[17]

Despite a prevailing sentiment abhorrent to the process, plans for consolidation of the dead proceeded. Such disturbance of buried human remains has historically been considered disrespectful to the deceased, since the space they inhabit is thought to be consecrated ground. This veneration is ancient, but according to Philippe Ariès, the hesitation to move cemeteries may also have origins in the epidemics of the sixteenth century. Doctors of that period were convinced that a connection existed between cemeteries and disease, but they were unsure of the real causes, although they were not altogether uncertain that the link might be the work of the devil. Thus, "the plague, the devil, and the cemetery form a kind of unholy trinity of influence," writes Ariès, noting that burial grounds fell increasingly within the realm of the Church. The ground is still sacred, and as such, "man cannot defile it with profane hands." Hence, the practice of moving cemeteries came to be seen as "unworthy" of Christians. The dead are sacred, and like altars and temples, "they should not be moved."[18]

This reverence of the ground where remains were initially placed caused immense frustration for the Graves Registration Service, since it resulted in numerous isolated graves that fell into disrepair when families stubbornly refused to allow the body of their loved one to be removed. Even threats that the government would not take responsibility for the "not to be disturbed" graves could not persuade families to move their loved ones to national cemeteries. One Connecticut father requested repeatedly that the Cemeterial Division "refrain from urging [his wife] to permit her son's remains to be moved anywhere." He pointed out that she had "never wavered in her desire to leave her son's body where it [was]." Consequently, the military's repeated urgings only tended to "open up sorrow that time is healing."[19]

During the postwar repatriation period, NOK were not officially given the option of leaving bodies in their original grave, although this was a recurrent request. One repeated justification for this ruling was that the French urgently needed their land back for cultivation.[20] Provisions under a French Law of December 29, 1915, had vested the Allies with burial rights in perpetuity, but when the French Ministry introduced this bill, the extent of this costly gesture would not be realized for several more years.

The French government gave the Americans two cemeteries, one at Ro-magne-sous-Montfaucon and the other in Paris (Suresnes), but U.S. funds were still required for expansion, improvements, and additional cemeter-ies.[21] Initially, Congress authorized one million dollars "to permit the ac-quisition of exclusive rights of burial . . . when title to such land could not be secured." By June 30, 1922, the United States had spent $111,000 on land for burial places in France, England, and Belgium.[22]

To ensure tax-free status, the American government reimbursed the French ministry after it purchased the required land from tenants and landowners. In turn, the property was transferred to the U.S. government for its "free and perpetual use."[23] Transactions similar to these had been conducted with private landowners since the conception of national cem-eteries after the Civil War. (In 1926, the same system was enacted toward the purchase of land for American monuments.)[24]

France's land-use legislation was met with reluctance among some French citizens who held a traditional view that an ossuary was the proper receptacle for a soldier's remains.[25] That method offered a less expensive alternative to the provision of separate graves. Perhaps even greater re-luctance toward the bill resulted from the compulsory expropriation of private land by the government if the owner was unwilling to sell. The Belgian government also granted land for cemeteries to the Allies in Sep-tember 1917, triggering disputes such as that surrounding wealthy land-owner Mademoiselle Melvina Delespaul in her rural Flemish village of Waregem.

In October 1921, Waregem's mayor was instructed by the War Graves Commission in Bruges to inform Delespaul that a certain parcel of her land was judged the ideal location for the interment of American soldiers. Despite numerous letters of resistance and a complaint filed by Delespaul that the proximity of the cemetery to one of her farms would risk con-tamination of its water supply, the wheels of bureaucracy were already in motion. The final documents were signed on January 10, 1922, when the land was reclaimed by the Belgian government for use by the Allies.[26]

This episode depicts the weakened voice of the individual when faced with the will of the state, particularly when that state is a dominant global power determined to mark its political presence. Reason suggests that Delespaul's wealth meant that the usual financial incentives offered by the U.S. government would not have been sufficient inducement for her to readily relinquish her property. For some people, paying their debt to the fallen was more than mere metaphor.

ABMC members visiting the American cemetery at Waregem, Belgium. (SC Photo 111, No. 86153, RG 92, NA)

Imposition of state dominion over the rights of the people reflected similar struggles occurring among international governments as the terms of preserving sacred space for the dead were vigorously tested and negotiated. Questions of cost and long-term maintenance for cemeteries, such as those that arose between Britain and the United States, had never previously been raised.[27] In August 1920, a British treasury official wrote to the IWGC chief, Fabian Ware, asking for policy guidance regarding land and maintenance for American graves in Britain. Sensing some discrepancy, the official pointed out that since the British government was maintaining its own graves in Allied countries, it was difficult to see why it should now offer the upkeep of Allied graves in the United Kingdom. The official admitted that France did offer to care for British graves, but he reminded Ware that this offer was turned down. "[W]e decided to do it ourselves and thereby relieved them of enormous expense." He added, "If it be argued that they will have to spend much more on purchasing sites than we shall[;] I think the reply really is that the sentiment of the case is all on our side, since we fought in defence of their soil in the first place."[28]

In Ware's response, he recalled that the War Office had adopted the same procedure with the Americans that France had offered Britain by

A battlefield cemetery entirely underwater with eighty-three bodies to be disinterred. Fleville, Argonne, France, February 20, 1919. (SC Photo 111, No. 153213, RG 92, NA)

proposing to maintain their graves. "To . . . my surprise and discomfiture the Americans immediately closed with this offer, probably at the moment regarding merely the dollar aspect of the question."[29] Ware's response is perhaps understandable considering that the United States had fewer graves to maintain.

Across the spacious fields of uniformly lined American crosses, intermittent Star of David headboards marked the dead of the Jewish faith. During the war, orders were issued that triangular headboards, instead of crosses, should be placed over known Jewish graves, but many people claimed it was nearly impossible to enforce those regulations.[30] "[G]reat difficulty is experienced in determining whether a dead soldier is Roman Catholic, Protestant, or a Jew," explained a chaplain in 1918.[31] But the mistakes did not go unnoticed by other soldiers. "Yesterday, I visited the cemetery where our dead comrades were laid to rest, and there were our Jewish boys, the sons of Moses and Jacob with a cross at the head of their graves," wrote an AEF private to his rabbi.[32]

Although the army agreed to use the Magen David double triangle—or Star of David, as it is better known—the War Department was not so easily persuaded when Jewish organizations protested against their chaplains wearing the cross insignia. Yet, when the Operations Division drafted an order that all chaplains, Christian or otherwise, should wear the shepherd's crook in place of the cross, Newton Baker had the order immediately suppressed. The cross was still to remain the symbol of religious faith in the army, but Baker allowed chaplains of Jewish faith to wear the triangle where the Christian chaplains continued to wear the cross.[33]

The total number of American Jews in service to the AEF may have amounted to as many as two hundred thousand, with approximately fifty thousand serving overseas.[34] The Jewish Welfare Board (JWB) served them all, regardless of race, creed, or color, believing it to be its "patriotic duty to help the army while carrying on its distinctive religious and social activities for the troops."[35] On August 1918, the Overseas Headquarters of the JWB were opened at No. 41 Boulevard Haussmann, in Paris, where the organization worked in close liaison with the Young Men's Christian Association (YMCA). Eventually, forty-four new centers were opened throughout France, where volunteers distributed cigarettes, candy, and literature consisting of Bibles, prayer books, and newspapers, along with other forms of entertainment and refreshment.

According to Rabbi Lee Levinger, who served in France during the war, there were only twelve Jewish chaplains in the entire AEF.[36] One necessary part of their work and that of the JWB was to care for the graves of Jewish soldiers, but that effort was complicated by the lack of identification tags bearing the additional letter for religion ("H" for Hebrew). The alphabetical indicators were issued on the tags after most soldiers went overseas; consequently, it could often take months, Levinger explained, to verify the lists of Jewish dead. So it was not surprising that in May 1919, when the Red Cross began sending grave photographs home to families, many of the dead had not been identified as Jewish and still bore the symbolic cross. The image proved shocking to recipients of both faiths.

Once again, the political power possessed by some elements of American civil society had been sufficient to compel the government to yield to their demands. Yet no topic managed to stir more controversy than the use of religious symbolism on headstone designs. Although the United States espoused religious and ethnic tolerance, the nation maintained a predisposition toward Protestant Christianity in its commemorative ceremonies and symbols, a stance that was repeatedly challenged. The political wrangling over this issue continued long after the war, causing a series of frustrating delays that prevented the placement of permanent grave markers over the soldier dead for more than a decade.

Charles Pierce was evidently aware of these sensitive issues when he drew up the original recommendations for American cemeteries immediately after the war. In July 1919, Pierce had written to the Quartermaster General's Office explaining that he did not recommend that another cross be substituted for the temporary wooden markers then in use. His justification was that

> Hebrews object to the use of a cross, and their desire having been made mandatory by official action, it is necessary for us to employ a different marker for Jewish graves. This introduces the element of diversity in grave marking and prevents the desirable harmony which should characterize national cemeteries. Whatever substitution is made should conform as nearly as possible to the designs used in national cemeteries in the United States and when such markers are officialized they should be standardized and all references to a man's peculiar religion should be prohibited. When the crosses are eliminated, such reference, by words or symbols, will become unnecessary.[37]

Months later, on June 9, 1920, Pierce proposed a headstone model to a subcommittee of the War Memorials Council that included representatives of the National Catholic War Council, the American Legion, the American Institute of Architects, General John A. LeJeune, commandant of the U.S. Marine Corps, Mr. Charles Moore of the national Commission of Fine Arts (CFA), and AEF chaplain Bishop Charles H. Brent. He explained that the standardized flat marker, as designed by the CFA for use in Europe, had been officially approved by the quartermaster general and was to be made of the best American white marble. It featured a rosette engraved at the top of the headstone but otherwise resembled the traditional markers used at national cemeteries in the United States. Secretary Baker liked the new model and expressed his desire that it should be used overseas and in the European Section at Arlington Cemetery.[38]

By the close of 1920, the council had unanimously adopted the new model with the slight modification that "the rosette specs on the military headstone be utilized for religious designation—a cross or Star of David."[39] The secretary of the council, the quartermaster general, and the secretary of war all agreed that "there should be no variation in the governmental headstones recently approved for graves of all world-war dead."[40] The plans as agreed by the council also allowed for relatives to place an inscription on the reverse side of the stone at their own expense, provided it did not exceed sixty letters. Pierce also requested and received approval for the placement of commemorative markers at the sites of abandoned American cemeteries in France, but after his death in 1921, the plan seems to have lost momentum. All efforts to mark these burial grounds, which many people deemed sacred, were later cast aside.

What was once thought settled was overturned in one motion during the third ABMC meeting, on November 8, 1923, when without Pershing's presence, Senator Reed announced that "it was the sense of the commission that the form of the headstone used in the cemeteries abroad should be that of a cross."[41] Thus, members formally agreed even before embarking on their first overseas tour, to erect cruciform headstones in the cemeteries abroad. Senator Reed and Congressman John Philip Hill were commended by the commission, which was evidently in such unanimous agreement "that the matter required no further congressional action."[42] On this, the Gold Star Mothers associations and the American Legion were reportedly in favor, but their concurrence did not extend to the use of Italian Carrara marble or the French white stone when it came up for consideration. Both the Gold Star Fathers Association and Mrs. F. Bentley, the GSM representative, preferred American granite and specifically requested that the letting of contracts be postponed until the matter could be further discussed. Instead, Chairman Reed ended the discussion with the curt announcement that "as far as the Commission was concerned, the matter was closed."[43]

Although ABMC commissioners reached an agreement on the question of headstone design, a degree of their dissatisfaction returned once they arrived overseas in 1924. ABMC visitors witnessed the uniform rows of white wooden crosses, each bearing the name of a deceased American soldier or nurse, in black stenciled letters. Yet members grumbled because gaps were noticeable among the otherwise consistently spaced headstones where bodies had been removed for return to the United States. The equal spacing was said to give a "very effective" appearance that added greatly to the cemetery's layout, but the intermittent gaps were clearly "disturbing."[44] In general, members agreed that the overall condition of the American cemeteries was satisfactory but much more remained to be done.

They claimed that American standards were too plain and that every cemetery gave them the impression that the work had been done "with a minimum expenditure of funds." This was felt to be in direct contrast to the effect gained from a British cemetery, "where everything is of the best."[45] Members were determined to correct this inadequacy with united resolve. As a result, the flat rosette headstone was not the only modification to the hard-won resolutions that Pershing thought had been previously secured.

While the ABMC members were meeting with Britain's Major General Fabian Ware during their 1924 visit, the IWGC chief explained to them that his organization was primarily concerned with cemeteries and "only incidently [*sic*] with battlefield memorials." They listened as Ware clarified his view that "the British cemeteries, inasmuch as the soldiers are still buried where they fell, are their real monuments on the battlefields."[46] But even as he spoke, the Menin Gate at Ypres, Belgium, Britain's memorial to the missing soldiers of the Empire, was under construction. ABMC members observed the IWGC's majestic tribute that eventually bore the names of 54,896 Commonwealth soldiers, many of whom had marched down this road to the front line, never to return. Thousands of people would eventually attend the unveiling ceremony in July 1927, a full year before Pershing announced that the designs and sites for America's monuments had been approved and "all that remained was to erect the memorials."[47]

Britain's Menin Gate must have had a powerful effect on the American commissioners, who decided that they too needed "some sort of memorial" to honor their missing. But their approach was considerably different from that of their allies. Instead, the ABMC voted to inscribe the names of American missing inside cemetery chapel walls in a manner that met their definition of "Christian symbolism" without any "excessive austerity." After greater consideration, members formulated the criteria that would guide the many commemorative decisions they would make on behalf of the nation and its war memory:

> After discussing at great length the question of the interiors of the chapels, it was unanimously decided that . . . , as the United States is a Christian nation, the interiors of these chapels should be Christian in character. It was also decided, by unanimous vote, that the interiors of these chapels should be made as beautiful as they can be made and that additional funds would be allotted for this purpose if necessary. Symbolical panels, mosaics stained glass, etc., were suggested as some of the means of accomplishing this purpose.[48]

Several more years passed before the commission finally completed its chapels, however; not everyone welcomed the cross into the memorial's design.

Cyrus Adler, founder of the JWB, wrote to the Commission of Fine Arts in 1928 to argue that the cross was more than mere aesthetic; it was in itself a symbol. Charles Platt, the New York architect who designed the memorial's interior, claimed that his instructions were that though the chapels "should not be sectarian, they were Christian." He added, "if the Jews are strong enough to prevent us from using any insignia of the Christian religion, I suppose I shall have to comply with their desire."[49] But Platt's reluctant concession was unnecessary because the ABMC ultimately determined that the cross would be retained in the chapel's design.

The desire to compromise with the demands of the JWB appears to have been strongest during the war, when victory was most dependent on solidarity between those of all creeds, hence the War Department's compromise on the chaplains' cross insignia and the Star of David headstone. But during the postwar years, efforts toward conformity took precedence over the specialized interests of those organizations that no longer offered a politically worthy exchange. Anti-Semitism was on the rise in the United States by 1924, as evidenced by the passage of several immigration laws that strongly affected the Jewish population. Legislative schemes were called for that would preserve "a distinct American type," and in response, temporary legislation was enacted in 1921 that imposed numerical restrictions on European immigration.[50]

As the economic slump subsided by late 1922, a new age of prosperity seemed imminent and with it the need for increased labor. To resolve the issue, Senator David Reed intervened by leading a revised bill that would retain the quota system but permit the entry of additional immigrants in periods of labor shortage. The result was the Johnson-Reed Act, passed by Congress in 1924, which carried the policy of immigration restriction to new lengths and stung the Jews, Italians, Slavs, and Greeks especially hard.[51]

That same year, ABMC Secretary Price wrote to Chairman Pershing to update him on the commission's recent business. When relaying the news of the group's decision to use the cross headstone, Price confided to Pershing that members could not control Senator Reed's personal actions.[52] Since Reed was so impressed with the beauty of the cross, Price implied that the others were powerless to object. Such a telling statement brings into question the repeated assurances that members were so often in unanimous agreement on issues that might have benefited from some internal debate.

The use of religious symbolism in a secular setting may have appeared to give the ABMC a higher sacred authority; it might also have served as a precautionary measure to guard against any suggestion that the cemeteries were an attempt to glorify war.[53] By contrast, the centuries-old Church of England, that nation's officially established Christian church, does not seem to have shown any interest in mobilizing the IWGC toward a similarly religious national statement. Instead, Britain's chosen headstone resembled the U.S. Civil War flat version in that it occupied less space and allowed for more graves in each cemetery.[54] The badge of the deceased's regiment or his nationality was inscribed within a rosette at the top of the marker with rank, name, unit, and date of death at the bottom. A cross or other religious symbol also appeared at the bottom of the headstone. In this way, Britain concentrated more than a million graves into cemeteries across France and Belgium, whereas American cemetery plans called for more space between graves to compensate for the thousands who were repatriated.

For the U.S. war dead, all remnants of individuality were similarly erased in favor of a simple uniform epitaph that consisted of name, rank, unit, state of origin, date of death, and any honors or distinction.[55] Paradoxically, officers and enlisted men were buried in separate plots at Arlington Cemetery, as were black soldiers, and the flat headstone, rather than the cross, was deemed more appropriate in the United States.

Before this mandate was publicly announced, families often assumed privileges to which they were no longer entitled. Many, like one New York mother, were informed that the specially designed headstone she had ordered for delivery to her son's grave in France was not authorized. "If private headstones of all sizes and designs were permitted, it would destroy the symmetry of the cemeteries," a government official wrote.[56] Whether this mother found comfort in the government's intentions to make the permanent American cemeteries "the most beautiful in the world" is not apparent.

Traditionally, women had assumed the role of mourner and believed it their moral, patriotic duty to tend and mark the graves of soldiers and loved ones; the inability to do so after this war was frequently cited by many mothers as justification for not leaving their son's body overseas. Although women continued to remember the dead in Memorial Day activities across America, distance now prevented thousands of them from tending the grave of their own. For mothers such as Emily Ann Mossop of Sewickley, Pennsylvania, the choice had not been theirs. Her son, a twenty-one-year-old sergeant, was killed while serving as a member of the British Expeditionary Force in December 1917 and was buried in a British cemetery outside Calais, France.[57] The War Department did not recognize the deaths of those Americans who chose service with other nations' military forces, however, so it did not repatriate their bodies. Thus, the Mossops were left to mourn, like many others, without benefit of a grave during the town's forty-first annual Memorial Day ceremony.

At that ceremony, veterans of several generations presided over rituals that were repeated in countless American towns, with hymns being sung, prayers being said, and patriotic speakers imploring their tearful audiences to remember their dead. After leaving the cemetery, the ladies auxiliary prepared supper for the veterans at the school hall, rendering the same nurturing service they had provided since the Civil War.[58]

But in this new age of international war a unique response was needed, and in the absence of these women's organizations, the American Overseas Memorial Day Association was formed in 1920. Myron T. Herrick, the American ambassador to France, presided over the commemorative agency, and Francis Drake, the commander of the American Legion, chaired this group whose sole aim was to render homage to those who rested far from home shores. With the formal dedication of the national cemeteries approaching in February 1923, and no federal appropriation available for floral decorations, Drake turned to General Pershing for help. He wrote to the former AEF commander and asked him to help raise the three hundred thousand dollars necessary and to honor them with his presence in France at the ceremonies. But Pershing replied that he was "up to his ears in work" and that when he did go to France, he hoped it would be "for a real vacation."[59]

To assist with the grieving process, civic groups often attempted to work out their own strategy for dealing with remembrance. Frequently, tense negotiations among a multiplicity of organizations were required, sometimes alongside the state, sometimes against it. For Americans desirous of commemorating abroad, distance proved a frustrating complication, as were their attempts to adhere to conventional practice when the rules seemed to change without public consent.

While some aspects of national remembrance proceeded down uncharted paths, the federal government remained consistent after the First

World War by once again assuming control of the nation's military cemeteries. Accordingly, practice followed precedents established decades earlier in Mexico City—that is, government representatives negotiated with local landowners for grounds; bodies were reinterred by concentrated groupings, each individually marked with a standard-issue headstone (and named when an identity was known); high walls encircled the grounds; and a caretaker's cottage usually stood nearby. All were constructed of durable materials requiring the barest of maintenance. Throughout the process, delays and cost concerns persisted. What had occurred without forethought after the Mexican-American War with a ten-thousand-dollar purchase had eventually determined an enduring national policy. By 1930, when the First World War cemeteries finally reached a maintenance-only basis, the U.S. government had spent $2,446,973.47, including the purchase of land.[60]

In contrast to the military cemeteries, which remained within the domain of the federal government, the work of monument construction had traditionally been assumed by local communities, private individuals, and state governments. But that too was about to change. As instruments of power, monuments can preserve memory and promote harmony, or they can disrupt that cohesion and foster disunity or, worse, a forgetting.

14

We the People

By the latter half of 1920, net alien arrivals into the United States averaged fifty-two thousand a month, and "by February 1921, the jam at Ellis Island had become so great that immigration authorities were hastily diverting New York–bound ships to Boston."[1] This massive influx of immigrants collided with a wave of unemployment and general economic depression that followed on the heels of tremendous wartime prosperity. Recently demobilized veterans competed with this flood of immigrants for fewer jobs in a declining employment market, adding to a virulent hatred of the new arrivals. In such an environment disillusionment found expression in a "general revulsion against all foreigners."[2] Prewar hopes of assimilating the immigrants into their new culture were believed to have failed as Americans turned their disenchantment onto the foreigners in their midst. The Ku Klux Klan, an organization that dated its founding from 1915, was rejuvenated, as was an accompanying resurgent racism and bigotry. Semi-scientific racism, inspired by Madison Grant's *The Passing of the Great Race*, championed an antiequalitarian outlook by using eugenics and scraps of historical data to "prove" the inferiority of dark-skinned races and some people of white European stock. This harsh racial doctrine spread beyond intellectual circles and combined with a crude Anglo-Saxon nativism, characterized by prevailing hatred that included Jews and Catholics.[3]

Forgetting the contributions of the Irish to the war effort, when more than two-thirds of the military's volunteers hailed from the immigrant population, George Creel, himself an Irishman, denounced them as "so much slag in the melting pot."[4] Creel had been a newspaper man before becoming head of Wilson's Committee on Public Information, where he was responsible for molding public opinion in favor of the war. This master salesman believed the war was "the world's greatest adventure in advertising" and, accordingly, set about to "weld the people of the United States into one white-hot mass instinct with fraternity, devotion, courage, and deathless determination."[5] Unfortunately, in carrying out this mission, historian Elizabeth Stevenson believes Creel's campaign also "manipulated the genuine love of country that was in plentiful supply." By war's end, she claims, "patriotism, real or false, seemed to leave a bad taste in the mouth."[6]

Unable to thrust this hyped-up feeling onto a common enemy, many Americans transferred their tightly held hatred and fear to domestic issues and individuals. Like a prize fighter poised for a match then deprived of a contender, the war's abrupt end left Americans spoiling for a showdown. Prior to the cease-fire, factories operated at full strength and prosperity abounded, while another two million men prepared to join Pershing's army when it struck further into German territory. The unexpected surrender stopped these plans almost overnight, and the war "became a myth almost as soon as it was over, both to those who had stayed home and to those who had gone abroad."[7] Generally, Americans backed the war while it was being fought, but it grew to be highly unpopular afterward.[8] Thirty-one months after Wilson's voyage to the Peace Conference, a separate American peace was concluded by Congress in a joint resolution of the House and Senate on July 2, 1921. Meanwhile, a tremendous surge of nationalistic feeling swept over the country.

"The war experience had been stripped of glory and idealism and revealed as stark death, bestiality, and filth," wrote Jules Abels in his biography of the man they called "Silent Cal," Calvin Coolidge. What had initially been seen as a "quixotic adventure to save democracy" soon became a sacrifice and a costly chore to "pull Britain's and France's chestnuts out of the fire."[9] Americans believed that they had saved Europe from "starvation and ruin," a conviction encouraged and shared by the nation's new leadership.

The Republican Coolidge had arrived in Washington as Harding's vice president in 1921, and upon Harding's death in August 1923, Coolidge was sworn in as president, an office he held until 1929. It was, by many accounts, a period of "ebullient optimism and robust living," an era of hyperactivity that has often been called the Jazz Age or the Roaring Twenties.[10] The times are remembered today by classic scenes such as the hot, July courtroom in Dayton, Tennessee, where that state's antievolution law was tested in the famous John Scopes trial of 1925. One year later, Gertrude Ederle swam the English Channel, and by 1927, Babe Ruth had hit his sixtieth home run. Improvisation was the key note for African American musicians such as war veterans Noble Sissle and James Reese Europe, big-band kings who helped create a curiously popular new jazz sound. Speakeasies proliferated even though prohibition had become the law of the land. Women were embracing an increasingly liberated lifestyle with their newly acquired freedoms that offered far greater opportunity for self-expression. Cigarette-smoking "flappers," sporting bobbed hair and a shorter hemline, were sharing interpretations of Freud's latest theories while Will Rogers delivered his snappy witticisms to the nation. "Washington mustn't forget who rules when it comes to a showdown," he once quipped.[11]

As the country's needs altered after the war, efforts to create a distinctly "American" image took precedence over the demands of minority groups, whose political power was weakened by shifting national priorities. Those new priorities were generally centered on big business, under the extremely powerful industrialist, banker, and financier Andrew Mellon, the U.S. secretary of the treasury. Coolidge inherited Mellon, who had also served in the same post under President Harding. He had been recommended by his lifelong friend and fellow Pennsylvanian Senator Philander Knox. Up until that time, Mellon was an unknown figure outside Pennsylvania, despite his being one of "the fattest of the fat cats in support of the Republican Party."[12]

Andrew Mellon, a Scotsman like Coolidge, remained treasury secretary and the leading cabinet member for eleven years. But, of the three presidents in whose administrations he served, none gave Mellon fuller support than Coolidge, who announced in 1924 that he would "back the Mellon program to the hilt." Mellon was considered the Rock of Gibraltar in the Coolidge administration and an important reason for the general confidence in the president.[13]

Coolidge and his secretary shared more than just their Scottish ancestry. Both were rather shy, quiet men with a dry demeanor and a dark, irritable, and secretive side that often strained personal relationships.[14] More significantly, they possessed a firm belief that business alone produced wealth and national well-being. In Coolidge's 1924 inaugural speech, he espoused his faith in Mellon's philosophy that surtaxes on the income of the rich should be cut so that wealth could be invested in business.[15] But their idea of business was one left alone to correct its own way, leaving the government free to advance from problems of reform to those of economy and construction. Moreover, both were against organized labor and believed that just because abuses existed, it was not necessarily the federal government's responsibility to attempt change. Reform had become associated with revolutionary thought and was tantamount to Bolshevism.

Within this political climate, fear and suspicion spread that foreigners were inferior and were largely Communists contaminated with radicalism. Consequently, Americans of differing classes, ethnicity, race, and religion were pitted against one another in vicious battles; however, both the Democrats and the Republicans avoided choosing sides in this melee lest they alienate a constituency whose loss might ensure their own defeat. Instead, politicians intervened with legislation against a collective, anonymous foe: future immigrants.[16]

Although former president Woodrow Wilson had vetoed a bill to establish quotas on immigration, by 1921, the Quota Act was welcomed under the Harding administration. But the more stringent Johnson-Reed Act of 1924 curtailed European immigration still further. The legislation bearing the name of Pennsylvania's Senator Reed sought to create domestic conformity; this same ideology was extended overseas in an attempt to project an image of national solidarity, void of diversity and discord. Even as the legislation he championed was being enacted, the senator used his power within the ABMC to further influence the spread of American nativism abroad. Despite the heightened xenophobia at home, the preservation of a united national identity was considered crucial to the power and authority of the government abroad.

In January 1920, the U.S. Census found 106.5 million people living in the United States. Of this number, almost 45 percent of the white population had either come to the United States themselves or were the children of immigrants.[17] Census figures also identified 9.9 percent of Americans as black, 0.23 percent as Native American, and 0.17 percent as Asian. Others were of mixed races, with those of Hispanic origin making up 12.5 percent. The demographics show that although the foreign presence in the United States was strong at the beginning of the decade, more than 83 percent of the white population and almost all nonwhite residents had been born and raised in the United States.[18]

Pennsylvania would have been bulging with recent arrivals in the early decade, since many immigrants tended either to stay in the city of debarkation or to cluster where their countrymen already resided. Slavic and Serbian enclaves gravitated toward Pittsburgh, home to Senator Reed and Secretary Mellon, while Italians generally preferred south Philadelphia.[19] That did not deter Reed from provoking the immigrant voters that made up such a large percentage of his state. He was often heard denigrating various groups, such as when he described Italians as "an inferior race."[20] Other times, his criticisms fell indiscriminately, as when he referred to his Pennsylvania constituents as "dunderheads."[21] Few were safe from the senator's acerbic tongue, including his fellow veterans, whom Reed once accused of being "loafers."[22]

Andrew Mellon, like his protégé Reed, was equally hostile and unforgiving toward the less fortunate in American society. Mellon dominated Pennsylvania, yet in his native Pittsburgh, "workers lived 'amid ugliness and dirt, in congested quarters, next door to vice and crime,'" and Catholics, Jews, blacks, and Slavs played no serious part in the city's industry or commerce.[23] Journalists of the period noted that the city's elite were largely "anti-democratic" and, indeed, "possessed no sense of responsibility" for the poor. Instead, Mellon and his class had "used the labor of the poor as just another raw material, to be bought as cheaply as possible." No doubt the elder gentleman remained unmoved by these reports, since he was said to have been indifferent toward, and indeed contemptible of, public opinion. In his biography of the cunning financier, David Cannadine adds that Mellon was devoid of warmth or empathy, and incapable of feeling or expressing emotion.[24]

The close similarity between Reed's personal biases and political agendas and those of his mentor, Andrew Mellon, did not go unnoticed by his contemporaries or by more recent observers. His political legacy as "Mellon's puppet" and as someone "who did what Mellon told [him] to do" lives on.[25] The resemblance was no coincidence. Mellon's biographer states that he effectively anointed the son of James Reed in 1922, with the idea that he would "carry the secretary's standard in the Senate" after the death of his friend, Senator Knox.[26] With Mellon's support, David Reed was elected, "on the clear understanding that he would take on the task of supporting and defending the secretary and his policies on the Senate floor."[27] Reed was a loyal Mellon man, and he remained so for the decade. In turn, Mellon considered Reed part of his extended family, and under his watchful eye the senator's career swiftly prospered, ensuring a successful and mutually beneficial relationship that continued until the early 1930s.

The junior senator's appointment to the new Battle Monuments Commission in the spring of 1923 came only months after he was elected to a full six-year term. Reed's nomination to acting chairman of the ABMC followed immediately, due chiefly to the presence of Captain Robert G. Woodside, another Pittsburgh resident on the committee, who ensured

many a vote for the senator's copious motions.[28] Although General Pershing was officially the organization's chairman, he rarely attended meetings.
These absences meant that more than two years' previous study and preparation by the general and his military advisers was jeopardized, along
with hopes of close cooperation between the War Department and the
commission. Under Pershing's close supervision, the Battle Monuments
Board (appointed by Secretary Baker in 1921) had already outlined an
overseas commemorative project, prepared financial estimates, conducted
historical research, and devised a formal strategy that was in the final
phase of planning by 1923.[29]

Whichever commemorative scheme Congress chose, one issue dominated American servicemen's concerns, regardless of their race or ethnic
origins; that was the preservation of those monuments of remembrance
erected on the battlefield before they returned from abroad. Although the
quality and composition of these structures varied from concrete boulders with bronzed plates mounted on them to obelisks bearing the division's insignia, each was constructed with care and reverence. At the time,
preservation of the memory and deeds mattered more than the prospect
of future deterioration, the eventual rusting of the war relics incorporated
into the designs, or the minor details of property ownership. Some units
inscribed dates onto their monuments, and others even recorded the time
of its informal dedication.[30]

ABMC commissioners visited several of the more than fifty-five unit
markers while overseas in the summer of 1924. One monument was
erected to the 5th Corps, and the others were primarily those of four divisions (the 1st, 2nd, 5th, and 27th). Nearly all were said to be in poor condition, obscured by weeds, and as members noted, not always resting on
historically accurate ground.[31]

Of equal concern were the more permanent monuments, those erected
during the authoritarian void that preceded the ABMC's appointment.
Pennsylvania, Missouri, and Tennessee had acted quickly to erect memorials to their troops, just as various regiments and larger military units
had done, once they were back in the United States. Commissioners noted
that although the 3rd Division monument in Château-Thierry was "one of
the most attractive monuments erected by Americans in Europe," the four
monuments erected by Tennessee were small and too close to roads and,
thus, were "not particularly impressive."[32]

Pershing's former military board had considered these problems in
1921 when they interviewed returning veterans who had witnessed the

Wartime battlefield monument erected by the men of the 1st Division. (SC Photo 111, No. 160027, RG 92, NA)

27th Division
monument, near Bony,
France. (SC Photo
111, No. 86043, RG 92,
NA)

monuments' construction. Most reports were similar to that of Colonel Frank Parker, a 1st Division infantry officer who replied that no arrangements were made for the land use; however, the local French mayor was consulted, and he had agreed to appoint a resident to act as the monument's guardian. The individual was offered fifty francs per year for his service and was made an honorary member of the division.[33]

But Pershing expressed little or no opinion on this matter once the commissioners returned to the United States with their final report. Members acknowledged that although the temporary markers had retained their historical interest and a "sentimental appeal" that other monuments lacked, their future could not be guaranteed. They were causing interference to French landowners, and no arrangements had been made for their upkeep or for the use of the ground. Therefore, the ABMC decided that it would accept responsibility for only a few of these shrines, since the acts they commemorated would, they rationalized, be remembered "on larger and finer monuments."[34] This last point was significant since the commissioners had expressed repeated concern that the unsightly appearance of these structures would reflect poorly on America's image.

"I have consulted members of the . . . division," wrote the president of the First Division Society, and "all are extremely opposed to obliterating any of our monuments or to moving the sites now occupied by them."[35] His response arrived in early 1926, after the ABMC's Secretary Price wrote to ask each of the various military groups to remove its monuments from the former battlefield. Most, like Major General Charles P. Summerall of the 1st Division, had declined to do so. With characteristic determination, Reed asked Price to write again to the 1st Division to suggest a "personal conference" with General Summerall to decide this question. "General Pershing has heartily approved this suggestion," Price added, hoping to persuade the 1st Division's representative with a higher authority. In defiance, Summerall's rebuttal was polite but taunting: "no funds are available to defray expenses incident thereto and I am compelled to regret my

The 3rd Division monument in Château-Thierry. The monument was damaged during a bombardment in 1940 and now stands in a new location within the town. (SC Photo 111, No. 86044, RG 92, NA)

inability to appear." Within weeks of Summerall's response, the ABMC voted that all memorials erected in France by the 1st Division should be removed from the list of permanent memorials previously approved.[36]

The veterans' determined resistance toward parting with tradition was reflected in their repeated efforts to preserve their war markers. Pleas from regimental veterans' groups in the United States to the ABMC were numerous, as were vociferous articles that appeared in the press by the late 1920s and into the following decade.[37] The men looked in vain to their government for the maintenance of the monuments, which one source called "the step-children or rather 'nobody's children,' of the war."[38] Most soldier-built monuments, though simple in design, were nevertheless considered "striking and solitary records of historic events, commemorating the capture of strategic points."[39] As a former officer of the 5th Division remarked, "One might indicate a riverbank that our soldiers reached under heavy shell-fire; another, a wooded height that they recaptured from the enemy, and yet another, a little town that they restored to its French inhabitants. It is with the aid of such simple markers that, in the words of Lincoln, 'We can never forget what they did here.'"[40]

This Civil War reference illustrates the desire among veterans to establish a link with tradition that would validate their own war experience. However, Charles Moore, in his capacity as chairman of the Commission of Fine Arts (CFA), advised Americans that the generation that fought the Civil War was passing away. "With them the dead past had buried its dead," he insisted.[41] Instead, monuments to the First World War dead should look to the future rather than to the past. Moore attempted to steer his countrymen through the maze of domestic memorial construction in 1922 with an established set of guidelines, aptly published in the *American Legion Weekly*. The CFA chairman had been instrumental in the design of national cemetery construction in France directly after the war and now turned his aggressive nationalist ideology homeward.

Many towns chose to connect their remembrances of First World War dead with those of the Civil War by adding names to monuments already occupying a central location. This practice offered a sense of continuity and tradition for a society uncertain of what the war had accomplished. But Moore discouraged placing memorials that commemorated the two wars in close proximity with one another. He mocked the grotesque figures of Civil War soldiers, claiming that future generations would do the same to countless depictions of identical doughboy statues. "If the Civil

War monument is bad, as most of them are, the new memorial should be placed beyond the pernicious influence of the old one," Moore advised.[42]

Time has shown Moore's counsel to be quite wide of the mark, however. The mass-produced *Spirit of the American Doughboy* statue, designed by Ernest Moore Viquesney (1876–1946), a second-generation French immigrant, was perhaps the most popular and enduring memorial of the decade.[43] Normally, the figure was erected outside museums, on courthouse lawns, and in cemeteries, town squares, and parks; but Viquesney, an aggressive self-promoter, also created several smaller versions of his famous work, including lamps made from a twelve-inch-high statuette of the doughboy holding up a light bulb. Regardless of Moore's comments, Viquesney's works seems to have met with widespread approval throughout American communities, despite its purported lack of originality.

The chairman's guidance contained two elements he believed crucial to a war memorial's distinction; the first was location. "Like the dome of the United States Capitol," a memorial must be located at a prominent intersection so that it forms an object of interest and can occupy a prominent "point of vantage."[44] To illustrate his point, Moore referred to the Kansas City memorial site where residents began their community-based fundraising drive in 1919, perhaps the earliest of such postwar efforts. The local memorial association raised over $2.5 million in less than two weeks by public subscription in the city and across the nation.[45] Their tremendous success reflects the public's enthusiasm immediately after the war, and an earnest desire to preserve the memory of American participation. In 1921, while nationalistic fervor was still running high, Marshal Foch and General Pershing presided over an elaborate dedication ceremony attended by two hundred thousand people (although the structure was not completed until 1926).

"Kansas City has found and utilized such a commanding location, but most of the larger cities are still groping for a suitable site," noted Moore, in a reference to the prevailing monument-building rivalry occurring among large American cities.[46] Much of this competition occurred in urban areas dominated by political bosses such as Democrat Tom Pendergast, whose political machine ruled Kansas City throughout the 1920s.

Presumably, the classical Beaux-Arts Kansas City War Memorial would have received equally high marks for meeting Moore's second vital requirement: originality. Architects merged utility with artistic classical sculpture to erect a "crowning light 360 feet above the surrounding country" atop a shaft of masonry that rose triumphantly from the terrace.[47]

Less prominent was the distinction noted in the site's title, the Kansas City Liberty Memorial, named, amid much debate, not in celebration of war but of the peace won by the war.[48]

The soldier-built monuments in France offered true originality in design and construction, and their location supported the memories of those who had done the fighting, but they were considered remnants unworthy of preservation or attention from the ABMC. The same year that the organization ruled against the preservation of most wartime relics, it issued severe restrictions on all future monument proposals. Only those structures that would be useful to the French inhabitants, such as fountains, public buildings, bridges, gateways, and other utilitarian projects, considered "public improvements," were welcome; all overseas monuments of strictly commemorative nature would not be approved.[49]

Pershing supported the authoritarian measure and attempted to persuade the public that too many memorials would "exceed the bounds of good taste."[50] He reminded audiences that the nation had only entered the fighting during the latter part of the war and had fewer troops and lighter losses than France, England, or Italy. He implored Americans to express their gratitude and love for the soldiers by erecting memorials in the United States.

Pershing's guidance on this matter, although undoubtedly welcomed by some Americans, had arrived rather late. Nearly ten years had passed since the nation's entry into the war, and cities across the nation were already well advanced in their commemorative planning, if not in the actual construction. Back in 1921, Washington, DC, citizens began their campaign to raise nearly two hundred thousand dollars by popular subscription to build a white marble Doric temple to honor the city's twenty-six thousand residents who had served in the war. The crusade was led by the local Noyes family, already known for their lobbying efforts to gain an amendment to give District citizens representation in Congress. Frank B. Noyes, president of the local *Evening Star* and the nation's Associated Press, led the fundraising committee that included Baltimore's Mrs. John Philip Hill, wife of the ABMC commissioner.[51]

The memorial was intended as a venue for military concerts, as the setting promised to lend itself perfectly to performances. Speakers at the memorial's eventual dedication on Armistice Day 1931 noticed that extraneous noises were minimal and the location offered plenty of grassy space for audiences who enjoyed unlimited nearby parking. The acoustics were tested when none other than the aging John Philip Sousa, dressed in a navy officer's uniform, led the U.S. Marine Band in a rousing *Stars and Stripes Forever* that was broadcast by radio across the nation. Mrs. George Seibold, the national president of the American Gold Star Mothers, placed a wreath below the carved names of 499 local men and women who lost their lives in the war.

To reach the committee's financial goal, the District's civic organizations had sponsored local events for months, and seventy thousand schoolchildren were pressed into donating five cents each. Even President Coolidge's cabinet members and all his government workers were instructed to contribute to the cause. But, despite their tenacity and ultimate success, an American Legion committeeman criticized residents for not having acted sooner to build their memorial. "Washington lags behind every state in the union in expressing its appreciation of the services of its sons and daughters who 'went to war,'" he told audiences.[52]

The veteran's disgruntled remarks may have had less to do with the District's monument than with other more pressing concerns affecting ex-servicemen and the debt they felt was owed them by the nation. Unbridled forgetfulness of their wartime service posed a genuine and solemn menace to America's veterans throughout the 1920s and into the following decade, one that surfaced in a variety of ways. In their ongoing battle to preserve their overseas monuments, the men insisted it was "unfair to burden [them] with maintenance costs," particularly when, as they saw it, a greater price had already been paid. But their perception of the country's lack of respect for their wartime service, and its forgetfulness of those who had made the ultimate sacrifice, went beyond their quest for financial remuneration. The threat seemed particularly acute after the veterans had returned from personal pilgrimages to the former battlefield.

"[W]e were entirely disgusted to see the initials of someone carved into the monument erected to the memory of our comrades," wrote one 27th Division veteran to the *New York Herald Tribune*. "Large pieces of this monument have already tumbled to the ground. On one side of the monument some degenerate has carved a picture of a man's privates (penus and testicals [*sic*]). I was utterly disgusted and would have torn this piece out of the monument myself had it not been for the restraining powers of my companion."[53]

Similar complaints and potentially misplaced blame were often directed toward the French, whom some American servicemen believed were ungrateful for their wartime involvement. Protests against the raucous noise from a café across the street from the Meuse-Argonne cemetery at

Romagne-sous-Montfaucon prompted another returning member of the VFW to appeal to the secretary of state for action. "We regret very much that the French Government has admitted this commercializing upon our departed Comrades by granting a license for [this] café." That drinking and dancing should be permitted so near to the sacred spot where "14,000 brave 'Buddies' lay buried" was completely unacceptable to the VFW members, who wanted the café's license revoked. The local French mayor was sympathetic but explained that the café had been there for years and had only a small dance area with a single "victrola and mechanical piano."[54]

Although capable of flexing some political muscle, the VFW never managed to match the size and strength of the largest veterans' group to emerge from the First World War, the American Legion, founded in 1919. As David Kennedy notes, "the very name 'Legion' perpetuated the romantic idiom in which the official culture had taught the doughboys to think of themselves."[55] Even the organization's moniker was a reminder of what its members represented, and it reflected their insistence that the war should not be forgotten. To risk the loss of memory would have threatened the very core of the Legion's raison d'être, the myth of the fallen soldier and the glories of America's victories.

The Legion's instruments for maintaining what would become a national "civil religion" were similar to those of the past and included much flag waving and many parades and marching bands that served to instill patriotism while establishing the idea of a national identity in the minds of Americans.[56] Public remembrance ceremonies were another significant commemorative tool, particularly when presided over by celebrated orators who recalled the war's memory and praised the men for their valor and bravery. Armistice Day observances provided the ideal occasion for these events, and the promotion of this day as a national holiday was one of the veterans' earliest initiatives.

Since the Civil War, Memorial Day had traditionally been a day when the dead of all conflicts were honored, whereas Armistice Day was designated as a national day to commemorate America's participation in the First World War. Ceremonies in the United States were similar to those observed in France and Great Britain, with processions, wreath-laying ceremonies, and a moment of silence in homage to the war dead. On the third Armistice Day after the war, the burial of America's Unknown Soldier reinforced the rituals promulgated by the Legion, which were designed to unify a nation still ambivalent about its involvement in the former conflict. Although Americans were united in their desire to pay tribute to those who fought and died, they could not agree on the precise nature and intent of Armistice Day rituals.

The American Legion endeavored to ensure remembrance of the dead through hymns and prayers, but their ceremonies also emphasized the cost of war and the need to work for a more harmonious world order. Ceremonies and political speeches throughout the country often emphasized the peaceful nature of the day, echoing the theme of national unity. Despite the strong message of peace, Legion parades also included a military component, with participation from the various branches of the armed forces and rifle or artillery salutes to the dead.

Other parade organizers preferred to completely rid Armistice Day of its militaristic character, emphasizing instead the tragedy of war and the preservation of peace. A series of disarmament treaties and pacifist promises such as those of the Kellogg-Briand pact of 1928 created a sense of optimism that there might never be another war.[57] Members of national peace movements believed war could be stopped only through disarmament and pacifism, while the Legion insisted that military preparedness provided the best assurance against future wars. This lack of consensus revealed the ambivalence still prevalent regarding America's intervention in the war, with political polarities playing out most vividly in commemorative ceremonies.[58]

Such an occasion rose in 1927 when displeased veterans in Plainfield, New Jersey, boycotted dedication ceremonies of the town's memorial because the inscription read, "Nation shall not lift sword against nation, neither shall they learn war any more."[59] Similar storms and upheaval were repeated in ceremonies across the country during the latter part of the decade as communities struggled to reach a compromise.

In 1927, Owen Wister (author and outspoken advocate of overseas cemeteries) led a vigorous campaign at Harvard University for the construction of a war memorial to commemorate the dead of his alma mater.[60] Unaware of the controversy that awaited them, the university board acquired a memorial before any plans had been drawn up for housing it. At their request, the distinguished sculptor Malvina Hoffman created a pietà, depicting a dying crusader being cradled by his mother. Wister, characteristically provocative, was opposed to religious memorials and led a strident protest against construction of a chapel to house the sculpture. Student involvement broadened the controversy by asking just who should be commemorated. Lacking any criteria for the memorial's construction, university officials remained unresponsive to student challenges regarding their authority to insist on an Allied Memorial when four former students had been killed while serving in the German Army. By January 1928, sufficient funds had been pledged for the erection of a war memorial church. Harvard president A. L. Lowell finally settled the dispute by insisting that the memorial would honor the Allied dead but a plaque containing the names of the German soldiers would be placed nearby within the memorial building.

Monuments and the accompanying rituals designed to pay homage to the dead often served instead as a political platform for the voices of the living. Throughout the 1920s, the nation witnessed a surge of memorial and monument building that seems to have eclipsed efforts solely dedicated to the construction of war remembrances; the year 1927 was particularly popular for such projects. For instance, in that year sculptors began work on the peaks at Mount Rushmore, the Wright Brothers Memorial project was launched in North Carolina, the Peace Bridge between Canada and the United States was opened, and the Jefferson Davis Memorial Highway in Texas was dedicated. Cities also undertook massive building projects such as the ambitious Veterans Memorial Auditorium in Providence, Rhode Island, that took shape in 1927; and Washington, DC's neoclassical designs for Andrew Mellon's vast Federal Triangle scheme were also begun. Despite intentions, construction was often shrouded in controversy and acrimonious debate over design, functionality, and appropriateness.

Feminine allegorical forms regularly appeared on monuments to men, but there seems to have been insufficient momentum to dedicate any monuments to the memory of American women who gave their lives for the Allied cause.[61] African Americans fared slightly better. The World War I Black Soldiers' Memorial in Chicago was erected in 1927 to commemorate Illinois's 8th Regiment, which was reorganized in France as the 370th U.S. Infantry of the 93rd Division. The unit was one of only two black combat divisions during the First World War. Critics complained, however, that it was "not truly representative of a fighting unit, but more like a classic statue representing a passive group."[62] In response, an African American doughboy was placed atop the monument in 1936.

Chicago's memorial to black soldiers was situated on the city's South Side in the Black Metropolis district, where African American migrants had continued to congregate after the war. Like Chicago, New York's combat unit, the all-black 369th Infantry Regiment, was organized from the heart of the city's black ghetto, Harlem—"supreme among all the new black communities."[63] Harlem became the center of black cultural and intellectual life and the birthplace of the Black Renaissance that characterized the 1920s. In this climate, solidarity against the white community spread as demands for political, economic, and social freedom increased among the *New Negro,* as black leader Alain Locke dubbed them.[64]

Although the military newspaper *Stars and Stripes* proclaimed the American Legion a "true democracy," a notion perpetuated by the organization, members were unprepared to take a democratic stand for black veterans.[65] Despite the proud, heroic service of African American soldiers during the war and feats of heroism such as those of Sergeant Henry Johnson of the 369th "Hellfighters" (winner of the Distinguished Service Cross), black ex-servicemen were not generally accorded the same benefits as their white counterparts.[66] Many of them turned to the National Association for the Advancement of Colored People (NAACP) with their grievances.[67] Letters resembling the one written by a black sergeant to W. E. B. Du Bois in 1918 about the terrible conditions he and his men endured at Camp Alexander, Virginia, were common. As members of stevedore and labor units, they "loaded the ships with food and ammunition . . . for those that have been sent over." "Last winter men died in this camp like sheep," he wrote, after having been "forced to sleep in tents on the bare ground with a little straw for bedding and only a thin blanket." He claimed that they all believed President Wilson's democracy to be "a farce."[68]

After the war, many black servicemen were refused treatment in veterans' hospitals, barred from joining Legion posts, and often refused a charter to start their own organizations. The Legion's position was directly at odds with its self-proclaimed status as a heterogeneous organization that united veterans from different religions, classes, ethnic groups, and races.[69] Local black veterans' groups could have affiliated themselves with the VFW or the Disabled American Veterans organizations, but as one Louisiana veteran explained, only "under the American Legion banner" would they learn "just what the Government is doing for us in the way of benefits for ourselves, our wives, mothers and children."[70]

Despite frequent appeals, officials remained adamant that charters could only be granted by the state and that if membership was refused, the Legion's national headquarters had no authority to act. By 1934, Walter White, the NAACP secretary, achieved limited success through his group's intervention, but the NAACP was powerless to act against the Legion's discriminatory policy favoring states' rights. Black ex-ser-vicemen, in defense of their war memory and torn between patriotism, civic pride, and their struggle for racial equality, found their collec-tive voice too faint to be heard among the nation's more audible, white Legionnaires.[71]

In 1927, the Legion combined Pershing's recommendation with its own predominant stance against federal domination of state power by dedi-cating the Indiana World War memorial in Indianapolis as the site of its national headquarters. The delegation argued that the location should be near to the center of the country and not in Washington, DC, where "the legion would be overshadowed by federal institutions."[72] Ten million dol-lars was allocated for the construction of a memorial building and plaza to house the Legion while simultaneously honoring the dead. Despite protests from veterans that the money could be better spent on benefits, "the initiative of economic and political leaders could not be repressed."[73] Historian John Bodnar writes that the dedication, led by General Persh-ing, was "probably the greatest patriotic ceremony in twentieth-century Indianapolis."[74] More important was the portrayal of a united city steeped in emotional patriotism and loyalty to the nation.

This harmonious façade masked deeper concerns and a pervasive am-bivalence that was occurring nationally about the war, its ultimate gains, and the most appropriate way to honor the dead. While organizations such as the American Legion and the ABMC attempted to disguise the increasingly fractious nature of American society, continuity with the past was also being severed by preoccupation with the present. Moore's em-phasis on location was an aesthetic one that overlooked the void created when the link between memory of an event and its physical remains is destroyed. Thus, the veterans' compelling desire to place their memorials on the ground where they had fought remained a vexing issue for years. As French sociologist Maurice Halbwachs posited, memory is more apt to endure if it can be attached to a fixed point in the terrain.[75] In sharp contrast, the ABMC's ruling attempted to transfer the soldiers' sense of battlefield ownership to a communal memorial in the United States or toward the eventual support of monuments in France that would not be completed for more than a decade after the fighting. This interference was bound to detract from the loyalty and enthusiasm that the new monu-ments were designed to imbue. Thus, it is not surprising that veterans often turned their hostility toward those they deemed responsible for de-stroying valuable memory traces, as the Pennsylvania American Legion did in 1927 when it recommended the expulsion of Senator David A. Reed from the organization.[76]

Given the lingering disillusionment over America's involvement in the war, the span of time since the armistice, and the earlier return of most American war dead to the United States, public indifference toward the government's overseas plans is not surprising. But without the support of those directly affected by the war—that is, families of the deceased and veterans (including ethnic and racial minorities)—the success of overseas memorialization would be seriously threatened.

ABMC members, for their part, sought to balance the diverse and frequently conflicting demands of the military, the preferences of the CFA, the shifting international climate, and the desires of veterans and families. Too often, commissioners responded by tightening their authoritarian grip, attempting a compromise solution whenever possible; however, their efforts failed to respond sensitively to the diverse needs of their constituents. If they had done so, they might have risked the consensual support of the majority. Even so, can a collective war memory based on exclusivity really be effective, particularly one intended to represent a democracy?

15

Americans Make Waves

By 1925, the ABMC had radically altered Pershing's original scheme for memorialization because the project handed to them was, they insisted, unsuitable. "There are too many monuments," members complained after returning from their overseas inspection of the Allied cemeteries.[1] Moreover, they felt that the monuments called for in the existing plan were "of such a small size that they would not be seen," nor would they be accessible or easy to maintain. Instead, the commission chose to construct three colossal monuments for each of the primary sectors of American operations. They were situated in commanding locations high upon French hillsides as a testimony to the world of the "widespread use of American troops who were in constant demand by the allies, lest their efforts be forgotten."[2] These three edifices became the nucleus of the U.S. memorial project overseas.

The largest and most imposing of all monuments was to be erected at Montfaucon in the Meuse-Argonne region, scene of what was perceived as "the greatest battle in American history."[3] The proposed site was a dominating height on the former German defensive position. It overlooked the jump-off point for the Meuse-Argonne offensive that began in September 1918. Slightly less money was allocated for the St. Mihiel monument at Montsec and for a third structure at Château-Thierry, which would commemorate the American operations in the Marne region. Three historical markers of "modest design" were specified at other locations, but plans altered over the ensuing years, reflecting the shifting winds of political change and resources. Ultimately, eight minor monuments completed the hierarchical project. The entire appropriation totaled $3 million, or "less than $1.50 per soldier who served abroad," prompting members to agree that a more "suitable, complete and economical project [could not] be made."[4]

The secretary of the navy also approved plans for commemorating U.S. naval operations, including a large memorial monument at Southampton, England, and another at Brest, France. It was agreed that an inscription would also be added to the Montfaucon monument acknowledging the American naval guns that assisted in that attack. Additionally, a Naval Arch was later to be erected at Gibraltar.

Once ABMC members had decided on a revised plan, they set about hiring the most prominent architects in the country, in consultation with the Commission of Fine Arts (CFA), the nation's advisory body. It was the CFA's duty to counsel Americans on the design and structure of public images, so it was presumed that its approval might also benefit overseas plans. The CFA recommended Paul P. Cret of Philadelphia as chief architect of the project, and in him the ABMC vested full authority to interpret its ideas.[5]

Cret had emigrated from France to the United States in 1903 to teach the École des Beaux-Arts style of design at the University of Pennsylvania. Although a foreigner, Cret appealed to commissioners because he had been in the country most of his life and had served in the recent war for two years. Thus, he was thought to be "a good man to keep in mind."[6]

Paul Cret seemed the ideal complement to the goals and standards of the ABMC. He had been singled out for his national reputation as a civic architect, but he also had an "impressive record" in architectural competitions. Cret had designed the Pan American Union (now the OAS) building in Washington, DC, but more impressive to the commissioners was his previous work for the Pennsylvania Battle Monuments Commission, where his designs were enthusiastically employed on memorials honoring troops from that state.[7]

In November 1924, this ambitious state body led by General William G. Price, Jr., submitted plans to the ABMC for three memorials to be erected in France and one in Belgium. Pennsylvania had been one of the earliest states to organize a postwar commemorative agency, a move prompted by General Price's return from France, whereupon he was given command of the 28th National Guard Division.[8] Pennsylvania's commission, established in 1921, had nearly completed its overseas plans while the federally funded ABMC was still being formalized.

The state's elaborate and costly commemorative project called for an ornamental stone bridge at Fismes dedicated to the 28th Division, a stone fountain at Nantillois to the 80th Division, and a monument at Audenarde, Belgium, to the 28th Division. The fourth element in its impressive three-hundred-thousand-dollar plan called for an altar and colonnade in the public square at Varennes, in honor of all the troops from the state who served in the war.

Pennsylvania's commission was anxious to have immediate approval of all its planned construction and justified its urgency by claiming "state legislative reasons." The commission requested an impromptu Saturday meeting with the ABMC, but Secretary Price was unable to contact all members on such short notice (including the ABMC chairman, John Pershing). Price later explained in a letter to Pershing that the state's designs were "so good that the members present, feeling that the absent members would approve of their action, decided to . . . act upon them."[9] General Price's Pennsylvania Monuments Commission was duly congratulated, and once approval was granted by the CFA, the governments of France and Belgium were notified that these memorials had been officially sanctioned.

The state commission had plans for yet a fifth memorial dedicated to the 79th Division, to be situated within a few miles northeast of Varennes, on the arresting hilltop at Montfaucon. Although eager to obtain approval, the Pennsylvania men were willing to wait for the ABMC to finalize its designs for the popular site to ensure that the two monuments would harmonize. While they waited, other groups were busy making their own plans.

The 79th Division comprised the 313th, 314th, 315th, and 316th Infantry Regiments, men drawn from northeastern Pennsylvania, Maryland, and the District of Columbia. Members of the 315th regiment had also applied for the right to construct a memorial hall in the village of Nantillois. The 316th planned to erect two monuments, one near Verdun and another in Montfaucon, where they had already received the mayor's permission. The regiment had begun planning early in 1920 and had managed to raise sufficient funds. However, after giving the matter further consideration, the ABMC decided that the services of the 316th regiment "were not of a more distinguished character than those of the other regiments of the division," nor were they "of more distinguished character than the average American regiment that served."[10] So, on the basis of the ABMC's previously agreed policy to refuse any request to honor units smaller than a division, it denied approval to all infantry regiments of the 79th Division. The decision soon became a source of increased rancor among American veterans determined to claim their right to memorialize their fellow soldiers.

In May 1925, Paul Cret returned to Europe as the ABMC's paid consultant to survey the proposed memorial sites and to supervise the commission's designs. Construction of the monuments was scheduled to begin by the summer of 1926, once Cret's preliminary findings were completed. However, in the ABMC members' architectural brief to Cret, they did not address their intention that the monuments should correspond with each site's historical operational significance. Instead, members chose to emphasize tourist appeal, accessibility to the region, and a commanding view as chief priorities. Although the sites chosen met these requirements, the terrain was "too varied to facilitate architectural comparability," which resulted in designs that did not accurately reflect the hierarchy of battles anticipated by the ABMC.[11] Consequently, sites of lesser military significance were often chosen for the grandest monuments with the most impressive views.

All the architects chosen by Cret were classicists known for their civic architectural works throughout the United States, a preference Cret later vigorously defended in the midst of international debates concerning modernism and classicism that engaged the profession during the 1920s and 1930s. Classicism, Cret insisted, represented a "symbolic affirmation of America's traditional democratic ethos," and through it he and his client found an "artistic idiom for representing a sense of continuity with the past."[12] According to Cret, America's classical civic architecture abroad would "bridge the end of *Beaux-Arts* historicism and the rise of modernism."[13] Thus, the structures closely paralleled the nation's struggle to build continuity between the past and the complex contemporary world it had inherited. Cret and his team of skilled architects helped shape an illusion, with chapels reminiscent of medieval castles and classic Athenian-temple-like features that "assured continuity of western political and cultural traditions across the rupture of the Great War."[14]

The commission relied on these men of prominence and repute who were certain to follow their clients' every desire rather than risk fresh, innovative designs through a competitive process. ABMC commissioners briefly considered sponsoring architectural competitions for the overseas memorials but eventually decided against it, despite the increased public interest doing so might have generated.[15] Plagued once more by indecision, this inexperienced cohort looked abroad for guidance rather than chance the inevitable negotiations that public consultation would have invited. The commemorative designs of the old world represented enduring authority, elegance, and dominion and, as such, were thought worthy of imitation by the nation's elite.

In retrospect, such a deference to "Old World" Europe seems misplaced given America's postwar transformation into a global superpower, with the

accompanying entitlement that its wealth had assured. But this did not necessarily guarantee friends abroad. By the mid- to late 1920s, ties between the
United States and France were tenuous at best. The issue of the war-debt repayment continued as a primary cause of friction, despite the intervention
of the Dawes Plan of 1924. This brilliant piece of improvisation, named for
Charles Dawes, Harding's director of the Bureau of the Budget, orchestrated
enormous loans from American banks to Germany. This enabled Germany
to make its reparations payments to the British and French, who, in turn,
used these funds to repay their war debt to the United States.[16]

A period of relative stability and prosperity resulted across Europe, but
it did not sufficiently clear the tension inherent in the American commemorative process. Instead, the ABMC's frequent demands aggravated
relations with its host nation and threatened meaningful joint commemoration. In its single-minded determination to maintain control of overseas
remembrance, the ABMC imposed strict mandates, often with insensitiv-
ity toward Americans and with flagrant disregard for French sovereignty.
French officials repeatedly attempted to accommodate the commission's
requests, but that nation's citizens no longer seemed so warmly inclined
toward their former ally.

Money and power were often at the root of these Franco-American
misunderstandings, as evidenced in the ABMC's ability to persuade the
French government to waive customs taxes on Italian marble being imported for the American cemeteries. That request resulted in a sizeable
loss of revenue to the country still in the midst of economic recovery. The
commission's decision to forbid the erection of U.S. monuments abroad
caused similar problems when angry French stonecutters petitioned their
government over the significant loss of wages they would suffer.[17]

Complicating matters still further were the messy tangles in which the
French invariably found themselves when American groups vied with one
another over land rights. If the veterans of the 26th Division are to be believed, the French were admittedly "antagonistic to American monuments
erected promiscuously," but there were numerous agencies that "had the
right to pass on locations and designs" and were willing to work with the
Americans to plan appropriate sites. As part of the 26th Division's memorial effort, the unit's men planned to use their funds to rebuild the thir-
teenth-century village church in Belleau since, during the war, the original
structure had been partly destroyed by gunfire from the 26th Division's
own artillery. The veterans also hoped to construct "something else—a
shaft or a monument on some hill-top"—nearby.[18]

They eventually landed themselves in difficulties when their unit unwittingly negotiated a better deal with French landowners than the ABMC, over property on a hilltop in Château-Thierry. The veterans' competitive bid effectively drove up the cost of land per acre, causing a furious Secretary Price to write the unit's chairman that the ABMC had been trying to purchase that land for over six months. "Our work in obtaining these options has been very difficult, due to the . . . present hostile attitude of the French towards Americans and the fact that all Americans are considered to have plenty of money and consequently should pay much more for what they get than other people."[19] He complained that everything had been going smoothly until the representatives from the 26th Division appeared on the scene.

Things were anything but steady between the ABMC and the veterans as the squabbling continued over disputed claims to wartime engagements that were rapidly disappearing into history. In 1925, Douglas MacArthur, who later saw fame in the next war, added his voice to the disgruntled crowd. The former chief of staff for the 42nd Division was angry because he had seen a letter from one of the ABMC members suggesting that plans for the monument to his old division were to be eliminated. Justification was based on the composition of this National Guard unit, which, it was asserted, "did not operate as a unit but served brigaded with French Divisions." Moreover, the commission believed that one monument in the region was sufficient.[20]

MacArthur questioned the commission's reasoning. "As I understand it, the purpose of the law was to commemorate the services of American units," he insisted. "I should suppose that the monument would be placed where the troops were engaged and not according to some checker board scheme which fits the fancy of an architect or the convenience of a landscape gardener." He insisted that it was the ground that was "holy and hallowed" because of the events that occurred there and that these factors, and not aesthetics, should determine a monument's location.[21]

MacArthur's distressed words point to the confusion that can arise when the purpose and priorities of a commemorative structure are never made clear and agreed on. Commissioned architects were working to one set of guidelines while veterans were holding stubbornly to another unwritten code, one based on their connection to the ground and to those who fought and died there. At the same time, the ABMC was attempting to maintain a larger perspective while balancing the multitudinous demands of the living. The result was frequently chaos and delay.

These setbacks did not escape the cost-conscious gaze of General Herbert Lord, director of the Bureau of the Budget, when the ABMC presented estimates for its 1927 appropriation. Secretary Price was informed that General Lord was "frankly skeptical" about the work of the commission, since "after 27 months of existence," it still had not started any construction work and was "without even so much as a single completed design for a monument."[22] Lord's office compared the ABMC to the Arlington Memorial Bridge commission, which had started excavations within twenty-four hours after receiving its money. In defense, Price's assistant explained that they had not received their first funding allocation until April 1924, that their project covered a much wider area, and that it was all taking place more than three thousand miles from Washington.[23] Price might have justifiably added that they had spent much of their time settling disputes, both foreign and domestic.

Conflicting proprietary rights over Montfaucon had been percolating between various associations for years, as each demanded the right to erect a monument on the once-vital hilltop in the Meuse-Argonne. Prior to the ABMC's appointment, the War Department had attempted to ignore an increasingly heated debate created in Congress when several units, including Pennsylvania's 79th Division and Ohio's 37th Division, each tried to convince the other that it was they who had captured the glorified summit. Senator David Reed, no stranger to controversy, entered the fray when he introduced a resolution to the Senate authorizing the erection of a monument by his state's 79th Division.[24] Ironically, the site of America's proudest victory in the Meuse-Argonne had become the cause of much discontent among those struggling to secure a lasting legacy there.

ABMC officials chose to place the matter in abeyance, where it rested until March 1926, when an equally difficult crisis was raised before a House Committee on Foreign Affairs. The proceedings were chaired by Stephen G. Porter (of Pennsylvania), who had worked tirelessly to get Pershing's military-monuments strategy through Congress in 1923. On the basis of this involvement, he had been a favored nominee to the ABMC panel, but the appointment was instead filled by Senator Reed.

Hamilton Fish, Jr., of New York, a former officer in the 93rd Division, introduced a bill before the committee to memorialize the services of three "colored" regiments in that African American AEF unit (specifically the 369th, 371st, and 372nd Infantry Regiments). Both the 92nd and 93rd Divisions were distinct in that they were the only black fighting troops in the U.S. Army to be attached permanently with the French Army. They did not, however, serve as a full-strength military contingent overseas. Although the ABMC had decreed that no monuments would be approved for units smaller than a division, Fish hoped that the black unit might qualify as an exception.

The 93rd Division that Fish intended to honor was termed "provisional" because it consisted solely of four infantry regiments, three of which were composed almost entirely of National Guard units, and the fourth, of black draftees.[25] Fish strongly believed that the excellent combat record and heavy casualty figures (40 percent killed or wounded) of the three National Guard regiments should not have been overlooked.

Congressional members called Senator Reed to give testimony concerning the ABMC's ruling that the 93rd Division did not deserve a monument. Reed argued vigorously that though he had "great sympathy for their feeling," he did not see any reason "why we should treat those people better than we treat whites."[26] He reasoned that the unit could not be considered a proper division because its artillery never made it to France and its regiments were parceled out to the French. Therefore, ABMC members agreed that the "colored" soldiers would have to be content to receive mention on one of the commission's combined regional historical monuments. House Representative Fish was quick to point out that approval had been granted for a monument to two white American divisions that had served with the British in Flanders and on the Hindenburg Line. "You have gone out of your way for these troops attached to the English and the Belgians but have ignored these three regiments attached to the French."[27]

Zealous efforts to establish factual accounts meant that casualty figures became fixed indicators on the barometer of martial efficacy. In the process, remembrance of the dead was often overlooked. The bitter debate intensified when Fish reminded the congressmen that the 27th Division had fewer casualties, yet they were granted a monument because they were attached to the British. Addressing Reed directly, Fish noted that the "particular group of people" under discussion were "very sensitive." "If I were on the commission . . . I would be very careful that there should be no reasonable ground for them to think they were discriminated against."[28]

The committee debated for three days. Members listened as Reed, for the first time, was held accountable for abandoning the previously approved War Monument Board's legislated plans, in favor of a more costly, ambitious project. Reed entertained the committee with amusing details of his attempts to locate the military's designated markers and the forlorn relics left by veterans. He compared those efforts with the revised plans to create "something that could be seen." Reed emphasized the ABMC's policy to place future monuments "near a road that everybody goes on" and the equally crucial intention "to make it so beautiful or important in itself that people will go out of their way to find it."[29]

Before Senator Reed could leave the hearing he was asked to justify another apparent inconsistency, the ubiquitous Pennsylvania monuments. Candidly and without apology, Reed replied that the commission had nothing to do with the building of that state's monuments, "except to approve the design." Unchallenged, Reed ended his testimony by boldly reaffirming the ABMC's plans and achievements.[30]

Attempts to check the ever-growing power of the federal government against the perceived authority conferred on the states by the Constitution were prevalent throughout the mid- to late 1920s. To restrict Pennsylvania's right to liberally commemorate its soldiers as they chose may have been interpreted as an encroachment by the federally appointed ABMC. The state undoubtedly held the upper hand, with Pennsylvania's representatives composing a majority on the ABMC board. Pittsburgh's David Reed was not only its acting chairman, but by 1925, he was also chairman of the Expenditures Committee under the aegis of his fellow Pennsylvanian the secretary of the treasury. Pershing had persistently expressed his objections to the state's dominating presence on the former battlefields, but he was no match for the politicians of the period. In 1926, despite the general's well-known disapproval of Pennsylvania's request for a memorial fountain in Nantillois, Senator Reed took advantage of Pershing's unexpected absence from an ABMC meeting to sanction the state's 79th Division application. Afterward, Paul Cret and Secretary Price promptly wrote to the Pennsylvania commissioners asking them to reconsider their plans and to relay Pershing's opinion that the state had already "erected too many memorials in France."[31]

Once again, the people invested with the authority to consent or deny commemorative structures ultimately select which memories will be preserved. In this case, the African American regiments had to wait several decades to receive the distinction that Congressman Fish believed they had earned.[32] Rather than rule against the ABMC, congressional leaders at the hearing agreed with the commission that it would be sufficient to mention the deeds of the black servicemen on an intended memorial at Nancy. There, they would inscribe the words "Ninety-third Division" and in parentheses add the name of the regiment, along with the other 120 regiments that saw service at that front.[33]

But these plans were not to be. Just as the path of commemorative intention in the United States was neither smooth nor straightforward, efforts to construct memorials overseas were equally disruptive. Months after the 1926 congressional hearing took place, the ABMC requested permission from the mayor of Nancy to construct a fountain of classic design in the town center. Commissioners had proposed the monument the year before because they believed that "all American divisions should be commemorated in some way."[34] The Nancy monument would record the "sector occupation" of troops who had contact with the enemy but had not seen service in battle.

In response, an angry exposé appeared in two local French newspapers sharply criticizing the American "monument of arrogance." It began,

> So, the Gentlemen of America, who were our Allies and who cultivate . . . the loathsome thirst for gold, have decided in their superb arrogance to impose upon several cities of France, among them Nantes and Nancy, colossal monuments in order to commemorate for the benefit of the generations of French people whom they intend to oppress, the glory of their armies during 1917–1918.

The Frenchman stated emphatically that his own nation's veterans, "wounded and otherwise, who have no monument to themselves, do not want this thing at any price."[35]

ABMC officials visited Nancy the following month in an attempt to convince the city's authorities that the monument was intended to honor the American soldier dead and to recognize Franco-American cooperation. In vain they argued that it was completely "unconnected with the debt situation."[36] But the timing was inopportune. Nanciennes, like the rest of France, were faced with debt repayments for sixty-two years and believed the idea of spending sixty thousand francs on a monument of dubious value was intolerable. "I would like to see this monument . . . [in] ten or twenty years from now, when the unhappy French people will be crushed beneath the burden of taxes in order to pay millions of dollars each year—which, in all justice they do not owe!"[37] The commission eventually agreed with officials in Nancy that this hostility was widespread and that the debt settlement had "profoundly disillusioned the mass of the French people as to the meaning of American friendship."[38] Ultimately,

ABMC plans for a monument to the American forces in Nancy never came to fruition, and with its demise went the memory of Hamilton Fish's 93rd Division African Americans.

In 1927, the state of Pennsylvania was just completing its vast memorial park in the small village of Varennes when the ABMC finally informed the French Ministry of Foreign Affairs of its plans to erect three major monuments to America's "most important" battlefield victories. Without any previous experience or precedence to guide them, ABMC members faced repeated delays as they improvised on a range of policies covering memorial design, placement, and authority, as well as in dealings with their host nation.

Through the years, a series of ongoing, terse negotiations with the French had ensued over the location and purchase of land for numerous American monuments, resulting in frequent concessions by both nations. Pershing's favored monument at Montfaucon had proven to be the general's most difficult battle once more, not least of all because the French had their eye on the same site and for similar purposes. In rather imperious fashion, the ABMC decided that it would refrain from building there "unless proper assurances were received from the French government that they did not intend to erect a memorial on Montfaucon later on."[39] To ensure ownership of the site and the success of its designs, the commission purchased the property several months later and then destroyed a new house that had just been built there, so as not to obstruct the intended view.[40]

Decisions concerning the memorial's size, location, and design were frequently altered over time, reflecting an array of shifting priorities and ambiguous intentions. However, Pershing remained consistent in his efforts to ensure that no other monument compete with the two-hundred-foot Doric column, surmounted by symbolic Liberty, that marked his army's triumphal campaign.[41] The honor of transforming this complex dream into reality was bestowed on John Russell Pope (1874–1937), perhaps the most distinguished American architect of the time.

Pope was master of the classical Beaux-Arts style so favored by Cret and the CFA. He was also engaged by Andrew Mellon during the late 1920s to design the West Building of the National Gallery of Art, as part of the secretary's pet government building project, the Federal Triangle, in Washington, DC. But in France, Cret had given Pope a relatively free hand in the monument's design by inadvertently passing on to him the same ambiguous directives he had received. Cret instructed Pope, "For the major monuments there is absolutely no program. . . . The principal thing is to have it suitable for the site. . . . Do something beautiful."[42]

One element of the memorial that did not alter over time was its inscription. On the terrace was to be inscribed a dedication to the 1st Army and each of the twenty-seven divisions that fought there. But with the granting of lands for this and other monuments, the French foreign minister had another message in mind. The United States was asked to consider including the words "To the French and American Armies" on the Montfaucon memorial.[43] Reasoning that the British government planned to inscribe its Thiepval monument "To the Allied Armies," it was thought that the Americans would be equally willing to share the glory and the credit. But when the request was passed on to General Pershing, it was accompanied by a confidential note from the embassy advising him that the best course of action was to "let the matter slumber."[44] Years later, the French government was more insistent when it authorized land for the American monument at Bellicourt on the Hindenburg Line. Officials added the condition that it must mention the British and French units that took part in the same action. To date, the monument bears no such inscription.[45]

While Cret and his team of architects carried on their work, civic groups within the United States were busy plotting creative methods to circumvent the ABMC's restrictions in Europe. Veterans of the 315th had surreptitiously erected their memorial structure in the village of Nantillois and then given it to the local people to be used as a community hall. The building was discovered by an ABMC official, who noticed the prominent inscription on the exterior: "Erected in memory of the glorious dead of the 315th infantry, USA." To resolve the difficult, sensitive situation a compromise was reached when new wording was added that emphasized a collective victory over death; it read, "In memory of the high *achievements* of the American troops who *fought* in this region."[46]

Members of the former 316th regiment were also reluctant to concede to the ABMC when they failed to obtain permission to erect their monument in Sivry-sur-Meuse, near Verdun. Instead, they made a large donation to the village hospice. That being a French rather than American institution, its volunteers felt justified constructing the monument without making any formal arrangements with the commission. Following the unveiling ceremony, which was attended by both French and American dignitaries, General Pershing issued a formal protest to the French government for the removal of the monument.[47]

Gold Star Mothers were outraged and claimed that Pershing had "desecrated" their monument to the dead, just as the people of Sivry-sur-Meuse were equally "incensed at the action of the commission."[48] Mrs. Frederic Bentley, the ABMC's Gold Star Mother, might have prevented the misunderstanding, but she died the previous September, and her position was not immediately replaced. However, as the only woman on the commission, she does not appear to have been a particularly active or vocal member.

The extent to which commissioners responded to public demands seems at times rather arbitrary, but as the episodes presented here show, the ABMC reacted more readily to those groups with the loudest, most powerful voices. Evidence for this assertion repeatedly emerges from the minutes of countless meetings, such as the commission's refusal to grant a monument to the Adjutant of the Siberian Veterans at Vladivostok and to the Americans who had served in Russia. Their request was denied when the ABMC claimed it had no legal authority to erect monuments there.[49] On the motion of Senator Reed, the state of Oklahoma was advised to put its statue to Native American Indian service members "some place" in the United States, rather than overseas.[50] Similarly, in 1926, it was decided that the inscription on the American memorial in Rome should not include mention of the Italians who served in the U.S. Army during the war, "on account of the precedent which would be established."[51] And when Emmett Scott wrote to the ABMC objecting to its prejudicial decision not to build a monument to the 93rd Division, David Reed responded that it was Congressman Fish who had drawn the color line, not he.[52]

Without the support of the powerful American Legion, which had chosen not to take a position on the erection or removal of its overseas monuments, minor veterans' groups did not hold much sway over the ABMC abroad. Similarly, families of the unknown and missing dead, various racial and ethnic minorities, and women were all unable to successfully manipulate the ABMC's policies in favor of their memory. The ongoing tension between the individual, the interest groups, the state and federal governments, and the ABMC is apparent here, as each grappled with the intrinsically complicated challenge of satisfying a multitude of diverse and conflicting demands. These features are indicative of a distinctively democratic mass culture during the rise of the modern state.

By the close of 1930, plans for the overseas dedication ceremonies were still being discussed. However, ABMC members had already decided that invitations would be sent only to European dignitaries and a select group of families. Commissioners' concerns that no extra effort should be undertaken to ensure that all the deceased's relatives were invited proved unwarranted by 1931, when Pershing revealed that several of the memorials (including the column at Montfaucon) would not be completed in time for the planned 1932 dedication.[53] The chairman recommended that the ceremony be postponed, citing such delays as economic conditions, the international debt question, the upcoming presidential election with its accompanying campaign season, and anxiety over the imminent Disarmament Conference.[54]

Years passed while the veterans' organizations grew increasingly impatient. ABMC commissioners often dismissed inquiries, as they did at one VFW meeting when the audience was reminded that there was a depression going on in the United States and that, in any case, the dedication of monuments concerned primarily the active servicemen.[55]

But in 1932, veterans were occupied with other concerns when thousands of angry men, dubbed the Bonus Army, descended on Washington, DC, and demanded the immediate payment of the soldier's bonus promised for 1945. They had three particular enemies, for each of whom they dug symbolic graves at their encampment: the headstones were labeled Herbert Hoover, Andrew W. Mellon, and Senator David A. Reed.[56] In July, when police ordered squatters to evacuate buildings on Pennsylvania Avenue, it was Douglas MacArthur who led the violent assault on horseback in full uniform and medals, forcing fellow veterans away at bayonet point.[57]

The ABMC was never designed to be a permanent body, and by 1933 the Quartermaster Corps had assumed control of the cemeteries and memorials in Europe once more. That decision was mysteriously reversed in 1934, when an executive order returned control back to the civilian commission, where it remains today.[58] Senator David Reed lost his seat in the midterm election that year, despite his efforts to distance himself politically from his mentor, Andrew Mellon. The former secretary was now a "loathed leader" and, like Herbert Hoover, had lost public confidence.[59]

Reed was not listed as the ABMC's vice chairman in Pershing's celebrated 1934 article "Our National War Memorials in Europe," published in the *National Geographic Magazine*.[60] Likewise, photos of Pennsylvania's grand and omnipresent monuments are absent from the twenty-five illustrations depicting the completed monuments and cemeteries that Pershing had so long anticipated. His obligation to his men fulfilled, the aging general reported in the *American Legion Monthly*, with apparent satisfaction,

Meuse-Argonne American Cemetery, Romagne-sous-Montfaucon, view of memorial chapel. Architects of chapel: York & Sawyer, New York. (SC Photo 111, No. 101600, RG 92, NA)

"we leave to posterity a record in stone and bronze, modest, but I think adequate, to the part we played in the great conflict."[61]

Regrettably, posterity has judged the ABMC's efforts less kindly. When John Russell Pope died in 1937 (the day after Andrew Mellon had), his death prompted a ferocious assault on the architect's reputation and the classicism he represented. Pope's buildings were considered "anachronistic irrelevancies" representing "tired architectural deceit," while his aesthetics were denounced as "elitist, reactionary, and dishonest."[62] As David Cannadine perceptively notes, "it is not coincidence" that this reaction "so clearly echoes many of the political attacks mounted on Mellon [and Reed] during the 1920s and 1930s."[63]

Later generations were no more favorably inclined than their predecessors toward the memorials. By the 1950s, critics referred to the structures as "characterless and lifeless as direct imitation."[64] A decade on, they were described as "old-fashioned" and "just plain bad": "These memorials do not say 'Remember.' They do not even say 'Forget.' They simply give no sign of awareness that anything at all ever happened."[65]

Monuments—regardless of their size, the money invested in their construction, their design, or their location—have a limited shelf life.[66] Changing political circumstances, the effects of weather, the passage of time and generations all contribute to the fading of memory. Within a few years after the last ABMC monument's dedication in 1937, enemy artillery shells from another war destroyed the 3rd Division Monument at Château-Thierry, the 28th Division bridge at Fismes, and the Navy Memorial at Brest and, moderately damaged the St. Mihiel Memorial at Montsec.

Nevertheless, the sacrifice of life needs to be fully justified on a personal level, then mourned and remembered honorably. In the aftermath of the First World War, the United States was not alone in its uncertainty as to how it might best memorialize the war and its sacrifices in a fully satisfying way. However, America's unique past and its distinctive democratic mass culture, driven as it was by demanding organized interests, had combined to forge an idiosyncratic compromise on foreign fields.

PART III

Return

16

A Country for Heroes?

Organizers of the 1927 American Legion excursion billed it "the occasion of a great and solemn pilgrimage" and expected participants to arrive in vast numbers.[1] Special rates were offered to all 713,000 veterans and their auxiliary members, who numbered nearly 300,000. Their coalition caused one excited legionnaire to boast, "we are the biggest thing in the world today."[2] Yet, from the Legion's inception in January 1919, membership figures never represented more than one-quarter of the men in uniform in 1917–18.[3] Concerns that the government would use the Legion as a tool for the military kept many veterans away, and their fears were not completely unfounded.

In his 1944 study of the Legion, Dixon Wecter points out that the organization was created in the spirit of Teddy Roosevelt rather than of Woodrow Wilson and that its keynote, "One hundred per cent Americanism," came straight from the lips of the aggressive, fighting Roosevelt spirit.[4] Pressure from military headquarters for the Legion's formation was aimed at a growing restless and radical mood among soldiers overseas. The world had already witnessed a soldiers' and workers' party revolution in Russia, and fears that such radicalism could spark another in the United States during the transition from war to peace bolstered the government's plans for a controlled nonpartisan veterans' group.

Anti-Bolshevism appears to have been the cement that held the Legionnaires together during those early years, just as public attitudes toward veterans and the war began to alter. Upon soldiers' return home, they were greeted by a glutted job market, inflated currency that rapidly emptied their pockets of the government's stipend, and a society transformed by wartime prosperity. Gradually, the soldier's high-spirited idealism turned to disillusionment, as a prosperous country "had already begun to dismiss his war as something of a bore."[5] One returning veteran claimed with disgust that he could almost hear the nation saying in unison, "So long as the damn thing lasted we had to take an interest in it. Now it's over, and we'd better get to work and pay for it."[6] Some returning soldiers believed, with near religious conviction, that because they had risked their lives to maintain America's liberties, they were the true guardians of Americanism. Their more potent efforts were demonstrated by the Legion's active and extreme determination to rid the United States of the "Red Peril" of Bolshevism.

Immediately after the war, the Legion declared that its sole aim was to "inculcate the duty and obligation of the citizen to state."[7] Red baiting was an extension of that objective, a way to discourage disloyalty and social indiscipline wherever it was found. Legionnaires resorted to vigilante tactics that were often brutal, such as what occurred on May 6, 1919, when an ex-sailor in a patriotic crowd noticed that one man had not stood up during the singing of the "Star Spangled Banner." In response, a veteran shot him three times in the back, to the cheers of onlookers.[8]

African Americans were not immune from suspicion; rather, they were increasingly suspected of Bolshevik inclinations to the extent that the U.S. Army recruited a black officer to conduct surveillance on suspected black subversives.[9] There may have been just cause for these assertions, since white radical groups were actively encouraging blacks to join their ranks, whereas the Legion was less welcoming. Claims that the organization had been founded on American democratic ideals were questioned at meetings, where controversy swirled over the acceptance of black veterans into its ranks. Although black veterans constituted over half the veteran population of the southern states, white delegates there threatened to walk out if forced to recognize black membership. They reasoned that if blacks were admitted, they would have to be allowed to vote in the Legion, even though they could not vote in general elections. It was also feared that the sheer numbers of black members would dominate the southern states' representation. Although blacks protested sporadically during the interwar years, the Legion persisted on a states'-rights policy on the race issue. Elsewhere, black veterans could join either segregated or integrated posts, with northern black veterans usually forming their own posts.[10]

The Legion's membership was said to fall into three general categories: "lots of average Americans looking for a good time," many of whom had never belonged to a fraternal organization before; those with political ambitions, "go-getters and smooth talkers" fascinated by the "vast potential of the soldier vote"; and young professionals and businessmen, "hopeful that Legion contacts would stand them in good stead."[11] After the initial rush to join in 1919, membership began to dwindle in the early 1920s. To remedy the situation, the Legion was forced to modify its mission from one of idealism to power politics and the promise of individual benefits. With its Legislative Committee headquarters set up in Washington, DC, the Legion had introduced 473 bills on Capitol Hill by 1921.[12] Social-welfare legislation, particularly that which was beneficial to children and veterans, highlighted the Legion's efforts, but it was the "Bonus Bill," passed by Congress in 1924 (over President Coolidge's veto), that marked its greatest victory. Known officially as the Adjusted Compensation bill, the legislation called for veterans' bond certificates that would reach maturity in 1945. By the late 1920s, the bill exceeded the Red Scare as the cohesive glue of the Legion.

From then on, escalating membership throughout the decade meant increasing power for the organization when even the local veterans' post became a veritable political machine, with its hand-picked leaders enjoying extraordinary power and prestige. The Legion presented a countenance of striking uniformity, firmly controlled from the top. According to Wecter, "The delegates who transacted its business were always hand-picked; the many thousands of others who came to reunions were more interested in a good time than in matters of policy, discussion, and debate."[13]

Legion events had a reputation that preceded them, to the extent that rowdy state and national conventions eventually soured many soldiers and civilians. Cities clamored for the Legion's trade but were forced, by necessity, to count smashed windows, splintered furniture, streetcars derailed, and broken bottles everywhere. At the Kansas City convention of 1921, a Texas steer was driven into the lobby of the Hotel Baltimore, and in Boston in 1930, automobiles circled the Statler Hotel lobby, armchairs were tossed out of high windows, and 358 revelers were hospitalized (with two fatalities) from alcohol poisoning.[14] Observing the Legionnaires' antics, the public increasingly came to view them as drunkards and buffoons.

Whether other nations were aware of the veterans' behavior is uncertain; however, news of the Legion's political potency certainly extended beyond American borders, as an internal French Cabinet memo indicates: "The American Legion is comprised of 3,000,000 voters [a generous overestimate] capable of influencing public opinion and the American government." The memo noted that this was a "diverse group" who happened to look favorably on French "interests in the financial inter-allied negotiations." Moreover, it was thought that the French government should do all in its power not to endanger the Legion's "positive sympathies."[15] Thus, the French government readily accepted the Legion's proposal to hold its 1927 commemorative convention in Paris, regardless of how *un*conventional it might be.

Pilgrimages represent a point of intersection between individual loss and national community. They can serve to unite groups and nations in remembrance while offering an opportunity for participants to come to terms with grief, thus consigning the dead to memory. Just as modern warfare blurred ethnic, religious, class, and cultural distinctions, pilgrimages offered a similar opportunity for diverse groups to bond through their grief. Within this context of community and social dynamics, memory (both individual and collective) was constructed.

Pilgrimages to the former battlefield sites allowed visitors to exchange memories with those who shared a common identity; their memories in turn contributed to a nationally shaped historical narrative. Despite the grassroots origins of the American Legion pilgrimages (and later the Gold Star pilgrimages), those who made them traveled under the auspices of the state; consequently, their memories were influenced by a foreign-relations component not traditionally experienced by pilgrims traveling alone or in smaller clusters.

Historians of American diplomacy have identified a "national policy of cultural relations . . . that became more firmly established and extensive" in the years preceding the Second World War.[16] Within this context, college students' study-abroad programs, like the pilgrimages, served as an alternative approach to international diplomacy in the late 1920s. They occurred at a time when internationalism consisted primarily of "private individuals and organizations spreading American business practices and mass culture to the rest of the world, notably to Europe." This process was commonly referred to as Americanization.[17]

Both the French and American governments were engaged in separate policies intended to disseminate their language and culture throughout the world; however, France lacked the means to transfer its culture to the United States as successfully as American hegemony traversed French borders. In contrast to the Gold Star and veterans' pilgrimages, students lived independently in France for an extended period and would have returned to the United States with a deeper understanding and, potentially, greater empathy for the citizens of their host nation. Their impressions were enriched from visits to battlefields and war-torn cities, Armistice Day observances, and daily contact with the French people.

By contrast, American participants in the mass pilgrimages to France lacked this transnational perspective and were, for the most part, passive spectators whose cultural experience was more controlled. Travel in large groups limited the participants' opportunity to mingle socially and to challenge national stereotypes. Generally, the minimal interaction pilgrims had with the French due to their often lacking language skills, their highly structured itineraries, and perhaps a self-conscious intimidation would have colored their impressions accordingly.

The primary objective of the U.S. government-affiliated battlefield pilgrimages during the mid- to late 1920s was to honor the war dead, but the experience was marked by a touristy mood that seems incongruous with their true purpose. Ultimately, theirs would prove to be a distinctly different approach to remembrance, one that reflected a nation on a modern and divergent commemorative path.

17

Pilgrim or Tourist?

In the years immediately following the First World War, the ground over which visitors journeyed still reflected unprecedented carnage and devastation previously unknown in warfare. David Lloyd describes one traveler's testimony upon seeing the battlefield for the first time: "We could barely conceive how thoroughly the agents of death leveled the ground . . . leaving nothing emerging more than a foot or two above the surface except for a few former tree trunks bowled over sideways and shattered and splintered until they mimicked ghoulish stalagmites."[1]

Human curiosity was piqued rather than deterred by the grim spectacle as tourists eagerly joined commercial tours to northern France that began as early as 1919. Travel companies and guidebooks directed the inquisitive to shell craters, buildings in ruins, and countless ravaged towns. They enticed them with offers to "view the sites of woods, chateaux, villages and even a cemetery of which no vestiges exist, all blown away by shell fire!"[2]

Many of the more affluent Americans had, by the mid- to late 1920s, already traveled to the former war zone.[3] Some went overseas to view the reconstruction taking place there, while others had ulterior motives. Despite the War Department's restrictions, it was not uncommon to hear of Americans who chose to sail to Europe independent of the government, to locate and retrieve the bodies of their deceased.

Years after the remains of the war dead had been returned to the United States and the number of visitors to the former war zone had greatly diminished, General Pershing publicly expressed his concern over the lack of national interest in the ABMC's commemorative project.[4] The American sector of the battlefield did not comprise the most attractive region of France, and even in the mid-1920s evidence of the war was disappearing rapidly. Consequently, it was feared that the new memorials would fail to attract tourists. With the help of architects, the commissioners therefore decided to place the monuments on well-traveled paths "as nearly as was consistent with the military operations" and "of such outstanding significance that travellers would go out of their way to see them."[5]

The ABMC's concern prompted a resounding invitation to all Americans in the commission's *Guide to the American Battle Fields in Europe*, published just in time for the American Legion pilgrimage in 1927: "No American who travels in Europe should fail to visit them [cemeteries]."[6] Since cemeteries were easily located, the implication here is that tourists would not be inconvenienced in their efforts to pay their respects. Anxiety over the potential neglect of American graves was not completely unwarranted.

Although it seems a rather indecorous aspiration, ABMC members were guileless in their efforts to ensure that visitors had "something" of beauty and magnificence to draw them to the graves of the war dead. If people could be lured to the site, members were optimistic that the memory of war's hard-won victories and sacrifices would be kept fresh rather than lost to time.

Pershing undoubtedly recalled the immediate postwar years when the number of visitors to the cemeteries was noticeably lower than anticipated, particularly in August 1920, when the American Red Cross was forced to discontinue its bus service. The transport had been established in 1919 to carry relatives of American soldiers buried in France from adjacent railway stations to the cemeteries. One year later, the Red Cross commissioner explained that when the service was first initiated, it was believed that a large number of relatives would wish to visit the cemeteries during 1920. However, those visitors taking advantage of this service was from the beginning "far below anticipation."[7]

Practical considerations such as the high cost of overseas transportation in 1919 undoubtedly prevented many Americans from visiting France, still too disrupted for tourism to develop.[8] Fuel shortages, poor roads, and lack of suitable overnight accommodation near the former American battle zones similarly discouraged all but the most determined travelers. In some instances, tourists near the Verdun sector were seen sleeping in the streets before hotels could be built.[9] Those who did venture to the battlefields and cemeteries by independent means would ordinarily have done so with the aid of a driver familiar with the terrain.

Although figures fluctuated dramatically during these years, British trends seem to mirror those of American tourists, according to David Lloyd. He explains that, in 1919, British travelers who could afford it went on guided tours to the "Devastated Regions" and "ate picnics in the trenches with old ammunition boxes as makeshift tables." Those who could not afford such independence traveled with the Church Army, the Salvation Army, and the YMCA. In 1920, one British travel company claimed that "there had never been such a demand for tickets to the Continent at Easter," but by the mid-1920s, interest in the battlefields had already begun to wane.[10]

French preparations for an American invasion of tourists in 1920 never materialized, despite the new tourist offices at major ports, published guidebooks, the French government's entreaties to build hotels, and its efforts to commission souvenirs. According to Harvey Levenstein, "financial instability in America and stories of overcrowded trains, inadequate accommodations, and price-gouging in France" discouraged tourism. "The American invasion of the battlefields turned out to be one of the great nonevents of 1920."[11]

As remnants of the battlefield devastation disappeared, so did tourism. The *Army Quarterly* advised tourists that little of the "handiwork of the combatants" remained, as trenches were falling in and buildings were being rebuilt all across northern France. Although a few places still showed traces of battle, one guidebook noted that a tour of the front ran "the risk of becoming tedious or somewhat meaningless."[12] Despite dramatic prophecies that the Argonne Forest would always bear scars of battle, the vestiges of war began disappearing within months of the armistice.

The decline in the number of visitors supports the claim that tourism is characterized by the search for an authentic or genuine experience. In a study of European tourism, Tobias Döring links the effects of modernization on travel, and the increasing mobility it offered, with a decline in authenticity. Organized mass activity, "along beaten tracks and in regulated modes, precludes the possibility of a singular experience and of true encounters with a place."[13] Thus, the value of large group travel as a genuine experience comes into question, particularly as an opportunity for emotional healing.

Cemeteries offered visitors a potential encounter with the authentic on a personal level, particularly in the presence of a loved one's grave. There, on what may have been the former front line, memories of the deceased could mingle with the imagination. The grounds became a place "set aside for collective memory, where the present [tried] to come to terms with the past."[14]

The government's efforts to make U.S. cemeteries more colorful and spectacular than those of other countries encouraged leisure seekers to visit them as showpieces rather than as places of solemnity and reflection. Accompanying these visitors was behavior thought not entirely in keeping with the somberness of the sites, such as the often-criticized picnics in the cemetery.[15] Although themes of sacrifice and Christianity were emphasized in American cemeteries (as in other nations), their distinct characteristics—namely, high stone walls encompassing dignified chapels and immaculate rows of marble crosses set in landscaped settings—inevitably drew comparisons with other cemeteries. America's cemeteries were "worthy of note owing to their size and their remarkable plan," claimed one tour guide, whereas the French, with their "flimsy wooden crosses," were reportedly far less striking.[16]

The grand cemeteries, despite their role as fields of remembrance and defenders against indifference, seemed destined to overpower the very memories they were designed to preserve. "The whole grim tragedy seems to be forgotten," remarked one observer. Dead soldiers were said to "sink into the artistic oblivion of the green and glory of well-ordered garden craftsmanship."[17]

The remarkable size, symmetry, and beauty of American cemeteries concealed more than the remains of the dead and their memory. Hidden were the conflicts that had beset ABMC members, such as rancor over budget allocations, the ubiquitous use of the cross, and the use of Italian marble against the wishes of many parents who implored officials to engrave Vermont stone instead.[18] The majority of American overseas cemeteries were completed by the late 1920s, but the search for missing bodies and isolated graves continued.

Sir Fabian Ware, Chief of the Imperial War Graves Commission (IWGC), reported that by October 1927, one hundred bodies a week were still being uncovered in France. Even into the next decade, the newspapers would occasionally feature incidents such as that of an aviator whose remains were found sitting in his crashed machine in a French forest.[19] Such stories kept the memory of the war alive just as a new surge of pilgrims prepared to return to France in search of their own authentic experience.

18

Commemoration or Celebration?

Originally, the "Second AEF," as it was termed, was scheduled to set sail on the tenth anniversary of the signing of the armistice, but months after the American Legion confirmed its plans, French officials were informed that the convention had been rescheduled. It seems that 1928 was a presidential election year, and although the Legion's charter touted a nonpartisan agenda, the organization remained politically involved. First World War Missouri veteran Harry Truman later recalled the year that the newly organized American Legion held its convention in St. Joseph, just outside Kansas City. The event exposed the future president to the hurly-burly of politics and introduced him to Tom Pendergast, the "big Boss" of the political machine in Kansas City (which was also home to the Liberty War Memorial erected in 1927). "The legionnaires," Truman said, were "the cream of the country, every one of them, a man's man." He went on to predict that "the next twenty years will see them running the country, and it will be in safe hands."[1]

Taking a pragmatic approach, the Legionnaires agreed that 1927 would be an equally appropriate time to schedule their overseas convention since that was the anniversary of the AEF's creation. Using evocative phrases that no politician could resist, they reassured the French that this event would "wield a tremendous influence for world peace" and strengthen "the bonds of friendship between France and the U.S."[2] However, there were conditions attached.

American officials wanted adequate accommodation in Paris held exclusively for the Legion; they also insisted on a 50 percent reduction in railroad rates, an adequate auditorium, and the waiver of passports and visas. Once these points had been negotiated, the French government expected its costs for hosting the event to be an estimated 1,350,000 francs, but it was nevertheless determined to make this "a great experience to be remembered."[3]

The *American Legion Monthly* began an aggressive campaign to encourage members to start saving for the pilgrimage. Initially, only veterans were eligible to participate, and auxiliary women faced restrictions according to their years of membership.[4] These tight constraints loosened as enrollments proved fewer than anticipated. By mid-1927, the publication's approach altered again as sponsors became increasingly insistent that readers had an *obligation* to participate: "Thousands of American pilgrims—men who but for the chance of war might be themselves sleeping at [overseas cemeteries]—will visit those cemeteries in September as a sacred obligation imposed upon them by their attendance at the Paris convention of the American Legion."[5]

Was it indifference, economics, or other factors that kept enrollment lower than anticipated? The Legion's magazine began publishing entreaties to its readers asking them to consider organizing "a universal campaign against the would-be 'forgetters.'" Fearful that Americans were turning away from war's memory, the article warned, "If the World War were really over and forgotten, what a dismal horrible failure it would have been."[6]

As guardians of war memory, the Legion was understandably anxious to ensure that Americans remembered the efforts and sacrifices of battle and the veterans' place therein. By keeping their self-appointed mission of consecrating the war's memory and sanctifying comradeship, Legionnaires attempted to preserve an idealized version of the Great War on the nation's behalf. Indifference within the organization to this nurturing of collective memory threatened the Legion's very survival and the preservation of the war experience.[7]

Optimism, prosperity, and confidence generally characterized the nation on the tenth anniversary of the First World War. New Era Americans were typically full of exhilaration for the future and enchanted with the comforts, entertainment, and conveniences of the present. Years of postwar prosperity had forged a society obsessed with material wealth and gratification, while the past became a fading memory.

As interest in the war waned, civic groups became more politically adept. Those with the greatest desire to remember the war turned to the one institution that remained consistent in America's short commemorative history, the veterans' association. Strong federal support and an ambitious public-relations campaign boosted the American Legion's power and membership. During the 1920s, when the Legion experienced such enormous power, it essentially chartered the national course of war commemoration within the United States.

The immediate postwar years were vibrant ones for the Legion, when concerns over the Bonus Bill, veterans' benefits, employment rights, and

Vol. 4, No. 31   AUGUST 4, 1922   10c. a Copy

The AMERICAN LEGION Weekly

"It was right around here—"

An "unofficial" voyage to France, Belgium, and England was authorized by the American Legion during the summer of 1922. This issue came out while readers were in Europe. (Holly Fenelon collection) other incentives pushed membership to new levels. Once the fruits of those labors were available to all veterans, however, apathy set in, forcing the organization to craft distinctions between its members and other veterans. Legionnaires were expected to uphold a commitment to the war's memory that allegedly set them apart from their counterparts. The anniversary reunion in France would determine the validity of that claim.

As the date for the pilgrimage drew near, Legionnaires spoke of their "sacred obligation" to honor their comrades at their graveside; however, fears that participants might be put off by the solemnity of the occasion forced organizers to clarify their intentions. "This does not mean that the September pilgrimage will be an affair of sackcloth and ashes— the men who lie in England and Belgium and France would not like that—any more than it will be, as some timorous prophets foresee it, one grand debauch."[8] Organizers hoped that this casual approach would also counteract the pessimistic newspaper reports that had appeared with regularity.

Anticipating events the year before, a 1926 editorial in the *Washington News* suggested the Legion reconsider what it termed a "celebration." "France is still a house of mourning," the author claimed, whereas "America has forgotten the war and become the greatest, richest, happy-go-luckiest country on earth."[9] Skeptics questioned the wisdom of twenty thousand veterans and their wives descending on Paris during that summer of social unrest. In 1927, debt repayment, a devalued franc that continued to plummet, and reports of widespread attacks on Americans figured prominently. Potential participants were equally intimidated by the mass protests of France's popular Socialist Party against the execution of Italian American anarchists F. Nicola Sacco and Bartolomeo Vanzetti, which had occurred on August 23, just weeks before the convention gathered in Paris.[10]

Undaunted, twenty-seven ships including the former troop carrier the SS *Leviathan* sailed off that September for French shores, bearing their cargo of enthusiastic Legionnaires and their families.[11] Government employees received an added bonus when Congress granted them a vacation of up to sixty days' duration to join the pilgrimage.[12] Such incentives prompted the State Department to predict that an estimated thirty thousand people would take part in this "Second AEF," but the reality was something much less than expected.[13] After 3,500 people inexplicably cancelled their reservations just before sailing, the number of pilgrims who disembarked in France peaked at 18,244.[14]

En masse, the new arrivals paraded down the Champs Elysées to mark the opening of the convention, strongly defended by reinforced police protection. More than thirty marching bands entertained the crowds as all of Paris witnessed "a wildly colorful river of Americana." For five hours the boulevards echoed with the sounds of the "Iowa Corn Song," the Pennsylvania Keystone song, Montana's Powder River yell, and the Texas roundelay as the Legion made a "swimming panorama of movement and sound."[15] For those who remained at home, the *American Legion Monthly* described the women's auxiliary clad "in their fetching blue capes with yellow lining" that "enhanced the profusion of the color scheme" in a Paris that had not dressed so lavishly since the Victory Parade of July 1919.[16]

Only two African Americans marched in the parade that day, and they had come on their own because the Legion's travel bureau had refused to accept reservations from black veterans.[17] The official excuse was that steamship companies would not accommodate blacks on the same ship as whites; a similar claim was used three years later by the War Department to justify its policy of segregating mothers and widows during their pilgrimage.

As French spectators watched, a vast onslaught of what appeared to be a typical cross-section of white America descended on their city that autumn. Yet, as powerful as these agents of collective remembrance seemed, they were a minority of citizens trying to keep alive a memory that the rest of their country had nearly forgotten. Although this may have resembled an invasion of extraordinary proportions to Europeans, those attending the convention represented a mere 3 percent of the total Legion membership (excluding the auxiliaries).[18]

What had been an attempt to replicate the successful reunions of the Civil War had not gone exactly as planned. As in those earlier celebrations, colorful fancy costumes were paraded before the crowds and irreverent victory celebrations and songs replaced doleful requiems for the dead. But in contrast to those days in Gettysburg when townspeople eagerly anticipated the veterans' burlesque antics and harmless revelry, Europeans generally clung to the memory of the sacred.[19] America's modern commemorative rituals had collided with a more traditional and culturally varied mind-set. Depicted there on the streets of Paris was a remarkably distinctive and idiosyncratic remembrance path.

The unprecedented event was reported in newspapers across the globe, but in England and France, journalists generally agreed that "America should be shown they were not the only ones who had won the war!"[20] State Department documents claim that "in general the atmosphere of the celebration was very cordial, and . . . was all that could be expected."[21] Similarly, an American Embassy official in Paris reported, "The population has steadily maintained a most sympathetic attitude and I am greatly pleased to be able to record that cases of intoxication and disorderly conduct have been rare and of a harmless nature."[22]

The public's response to the veterans' cavalier spirit varied, as some were said to be shocked and horrified by the "lack of excessive dignity which mark[ed] the usual European convention." As David Kennedy notes, some Frenchmen thought that the Americans were "making fun of Europe's age-old militaries" and that the parade was "America's big laugh at Europe."[23]

Yet the poignant words of a former French officer imply a more tolerant reaction. He asked, "why the devil should you make your trip to France into a pilgrimage? That is the idea of our old civilizations which are always looking backward, thinking about our traditions and our dead." With fervor he added, "For you, the dead are dead and that's all there is to it. They did their bit, they ran their risk, and why should any one be always worrying about them? These people are young," he said without apology. "Let us love those who love us."[24]

The degree of solemnity during the "Second AEF" is difficult to gauge, but there was sufficient concern for General Pershing to remind the Legionnaires that this was a solemn occasion. He asked them to show reverence as they stood on "that sacred soil forever hallowed by the sacrifice."[25] Most contemporary accounts claimed that rather than a pious pilgrimage, what resulted was a drunken, rowdy, carnival atmosphere best characterized by a souvenir ashtray with a picture of a drunken American soldier balancing a champagne glass in one hand and kissing a naked Frenchwoman.[26] Notwithstanding dire predictions, the event seems to have contained an equal measure of uproarious good humor and enthusiasm balanced with purposeful reverence.

Although other nations' monuments were nearing completion in the late 1920s, work on America's commemorative structures had only just begun. In the absence of a memorial site where collective memory might be focused, American cemeteries offered pilgrims the only place of meaningful remembrance. These grounds were unsurpassed for their size, beauty, and uniformity, as visitors repeatedly commented, yet their parklike setting obscured their more sacred purpose. Suresnes Cemetery, located only five miles outside Paris, held just over fifteen hundred graves, but the majority of Legionnaires lost their comrades in the Meuse-Argonne region, so the Romagne-sous-Montfaucon cemetery was their final resting place.[27] However, visiting that cemetery required a train journey of several hours, and accommodation in the area was sparse.

Nevertheless, many Legionnaires did make the journey to their comrades' graves when thirty special trains left Paris crowded with veterans.[28] Without doubt, many of them benefited from guidance found in the ABMC's *Guide to the American Battle Fields in Europe*, published that year. It remains the only officially endorsed history of the American participation in the Great War.

Whether in Philadelphia or Paris, Americans commemorated as they were accustomed to do at home. There, it was considered an honor to bestow the convention's pageant on a city that had competed for that privilege. Granted, state conventions could be rowdy affairs, and the Legion's raucous behavior often worked against its favor, but so did its failure to take a position against the discrimination of black members. Ironically, while the Legion chose to practice segregationist policies that were incongruent with its espoused democratic ideals, women were welcomed as partners.

In alliance with the veterans, women found increased recognition and a platform for their collective voice. As their liaison progressed, the Legion's conservative agenda was broadened to encompass a wider range of public-welfare issues, thus strengthening the position of both groups. The women who composed the American Legion Auxiliary were experiencing the power of enfranchisement and the results of proactive lobbying. These gavel-wielding women were flexing political muscle, and they were getting noticed. When three thousand of them marched down the Champs Elysées, the crowds were said to marvel at the significance and "importance" that American women held in "everyday affairs." Speaking at the Hotel Continental, where conference business sessions were held, National Commander Howard P. Savage told the audience that "the wisest thing the Legion had ever done was to take women into partnership" and referred to them as "the true helpmate of the Legion."[29] In addition to promoting numerous child-welfare resolutions, the auxiliary's agenda closely complemented the work of the Legion, thus carrying on the precedent set by GAR women before them. And although the convention of 1927 brought two clearly contrasting approaches to memorialization into sharp perspective, the presence of the women's auxiliary may have bridged this cultural divide.

Mrs. Levi Hall, a keen and sensitive eyewitness who vividly recorded her visit for auxiliary members back in Minnesota, echoed these sentiments: "We could not help but feel the sincere welcome that came from the hearts of the French people."[30] She described the women's disappointment when they were advised not to wear their colorful orange uniforms, in an attempt to honor the expectations of their hosts. Instead, women respectfully "turned [their] capes wrong side out, showing the black linings, and wore [their] black hats" before joining the parade formation.[31] Collectively, the women seemed to exhibit sensitivity to the cultural variances around them and tried to conform accordingly.

Although politically savvy, these women had not totally relinquished their role as chief mourners and guardians over the dead. Hall was an attentive witness to the human drama swirling around her, and the lingering presence of death and the shocking accompaniment of grief did not go unnoticed. Her animated report of a funeral procession reveals a dark fascination with the somberness of the occasion, highlighted as it was by descriptions of the black-plumed horses that drew the hearse through Paris. For the benefit of those at home, she recorded how the chief mourner wept bitterly into his handkerchief as two other men helped him along. She commented several times that all the women in France "were dressed in very heavy mourning."[32] The observation included titled women in committee chambers such as Mrs. Churchill, Madame Poincaré, and Madame Foch; all attended in mourning dress.

With their newfound power and influence, mourning differences between the old and new world were not the only contrasts auxiliary members witnessed. "Women always seem to be an afterthought in Europe," observed Hall. During a guided battlefield visit, she commented on the "pitiful" sight of so many very old women out in the field doing men's work.[33] Away from the familiarity of the United States, the differences must have been striking.

Women became an increasingly valuable asset after winning their voting rights in 1920, but their role as mothers was equally significant. As an auxiliary force in a predominantly male realm, women were able to exercise authority without appearing to challenge traditional female roles centered on the home, morality, patriotism, and fervent motherhood ideals. "Republican Motherhood," a unique form of patriotism with forceful rhetoric that predates the American Revolution, seems to have reached a pinnacle during the post–First World War period. It revered women who thrust their men bravely into battle, as doing so reflected dedication to the nation and honored their obligations as citizens. More specifically, the "model republican woman was a mother," and her life "was dedicated to the service of civic virtue."[34]

Wearing the recognizable gold star badge, mothers were frequently paid special tribute during tearful convention ceremonies, including the one held in 1927. There, mutual expressions of respect and gratitude were exchanged between American mothers and French women, particularly over the care given to American boys' graves. So perhaps it is not surprising that in 1928, one year after the Paris convention, the American Legion upheld motherhood's moral high ground by voting overwhelmingly to approve the Gold Star Mothers pilgrimage to France.[35]

The pilgrimage response that occurred in the war's aftermath offers a compelling example of humanity's struggle to articulate meaning from the ambiguity of death and suffering. A commemorative language accompanied by somber ritual developed as organizers of traditional pilgrimages strove to articulate this solemn narrative. At least, that was the experience of other nations whose pilgrims defined their battlefield return as a spiritual journey to a sacred place with the intention of having an authentic experience.[36]

By contrast, organizers of the American Legion pilgrimage made a deliberate attempt to minimize grief and the somberness of mourning. Consequently, the "Second AEF" of 1927 is best remembered as a *sensation,* in that it created a revival in battlefield travel among ex-servicemen throughout Europe, Great Britain, Canada, and Australia that lasted throughout the interwar period. Before turning to the journey of the American mothers and widows, I pause briefly here to consider the pilgrimages of other nations; doing so will offer a more expansive perspective from which to appreciate the exceptional nature of the American commemorative experience.

19

Pilgrims' Progress

On May 6, 1930, the SS *America* prepared to steam out of Hoboken, New Jersey, with 231 women onboard, all guests of the U.S. government. The Ziegfeld chorus girls had sent a large wreath in honor of the mothers' departure, and airplanes flew overhead dropping poppies onto the decks below, where each woman stood holding a bouquet of forget-me-nots. The pilgrims wore tiny stars of real gold and waved little U.S. flags as they listened to the War Department's parting message telling them to "Go, not in sorrow but in pride."[1] With band and drum corps playing to hundreds of friends and relatives lining the flag-bedecked pier, the inaugural party embarked on its long-awaited voyage to Europe. This was the first of an eventual twenty vessels dispatched that summer to transport mothers and widows to American cemeteries in France, Belgium, and Great Britain.

Previously, only Gold Star Mothers (GSM) with sufficient means were able to travel to France, and many did so as members of auxiliaries to veterans' organizations such as the American Legion.[2] Collectively, the women received increased public recognition, but perhaps more significantly, they provided one another with companionship, support, and comfort. But, as auxiliary members, the women received no organizational voting rights, nor could they hold office. Gradually, clusters of women began to form larger groups such as the American War Mothers and the Gold Star Association, organized in March 1920. As distinct from the GSM, this latter, more expansive group included next of kin, comrades, and friends of those killed in war.[3] By June 1928, a group of Washington, DC, mothers had created their own organization, known as the American Gold Star Mothers, Inc. They opened membership on a local level but ultimately became the largest and most politically powerful GSM group in the nation.[4]

Although some media attention accompanied the latter Gold Star pilgrimages, publicity focused primarily on the earliest voyage in May 1930, and then the final sailing in September 1933; the intervening period drew scant public notice. Unlike the American Legion pilgrimages three years before, the journey of the mothers and widows triggered no such benevolent imitations from other governments abroad.

In 1919, Australia's grieving war mothers were also honored with a star badge for each son or brother who died, but the government denied their request for a subsidized pilgrimage, despite numerous appeals.[5] Motherhood had attained a prized status among Australians during the war, when public displays of grief were considered a weakness to be resisted. But, as Joy Damousi explains, the "eulogy of the 'sacrificial' mother did not endure in the collective memory."[6] Stoicism did not prevent a markedly dissimilar lack of political recognition for Australian women from that enjoyed by their American counterparts. When their requests for a subsidized pilgrimage went unheeded, women pursued other avenues of meaningful remembrance as an outlet for their grief.[7]

The gates at Woolloomooloo in Sydney, for instance, became a "substitute" commemorative site where women gathered to memorialize their dead. There, where they had previously waved their sons and husbands off to battle, bereaved widows and mothers dressed in mourning clothes, gathered each Anzac Day to lay their wreaths and weep. These "Gates of Remembrance," as they became known, served as a place for collective ritual in the absence of a grave or monument.[8] By contrast, it would be difficult to imagine American women gathering at the docks in Hoboken (the embarkation point for U.S. servicemen) to mourn their dead in this manner. That is not to suggest that American women felt any less grief over their losses, but unlike their counterparts in Australia, they enjoyed a political advantage. Although mothers in both nations desired a pilgrimage, American women were more successful in their appeals. As organized interests in a wealthy democratic society, they possessed the power to influence such decisions—particularly in a nation where motherhood held the moral high ground. Moreover, there was no need for American women to improvise, since the U.S. government honored mothers' sacrifices by returning their dead home.

According to David Lloyd, the First World War served as a passage to nationhood for both Canada and Australia. Each of these young countries suffered approximately the same number of losses and served throughout the entire war in similar battles, and yet in the war's aftermath, the Australians chose a form of commemoration that emphasized the achievements of its servicemen while marginalizing the bereaved.[9] By the 1930s,

Australian women were considered an intrusion at local remembrance ceremonies by veterans who asked them to stay away from Anzac Day public observances.[10] Thus, whereas American widows and mothers were invited to participate in the creation of collective war remembrance, the memory of similar sacrifices made by Australian women went largely unrecognized.

But even in the United States, there were voices of protest from those who would have been equally pleased if the Gold Star pilgrimages had never been sanctioned. Some Americans considered the government's previous offer to repatriate the dead as sufficient acknowledgment of a moral debt. Others felt they, too, deserved some form of compensation. As one embittered mother of a severely disabled soldier wrote, "The gold-star mothers got their insurance and bodies before this pilgrimage," whereas "what compensation have we mothers received for the . . . years we have put in at our own expense and labor to rehabilitate our disabled sons . . . ?"[11]

Families that had declined the government's repatriation offer nevertheless believed that they were still entitled to further remuneration. Neither Arlington Cemetery nor its Tomb of the Unknown nor the government's maintenance of battlefield cemeteries could provide sufficient solace for those women who actively lobbied for the mothers' pilgrimage. As one mother explained, "The body of my only son lies in Romagne Cemetery, France, because I trusted my Government to forever care for and guard the ground in which these heroes were placed." In pleading tones, she added, "not until I saw for myself did I realize the wonderful preparation, care, and protection the United States has provided. . . . I have been anxious ever since that every mother whose son's body lies overseas should have this great boon granted her, so that she may [be] forever satisfied that her decision to allow the tree to lie where it had fallen was the wise one."[12] The women's ultimate success demonstrates the effectiveness of collective action among grieving relatives, war participants, and political sponsors in obtaining what may have been the most extravagant, controversial, gender-based legislation since suffrage.

Battlefield pilgrimages were not unique to the United States, as thousands of people across several continents joined in this centuries-old ritual, but the experience varied widely, becoming increasingly popular with veterans after 1927. In France, the government agreed to return the dead home for burial after the war, but for next of kin who chose to leave their loved ones where they lay, transportation was provided each year between their homes and the burial place. Beginning in September 1920, French families were given only three months to apply for the transfer of their soldiers' remains from the cemeteries at the front to their own communities.[13] However, the process was riddled with administrative difficulties and unavoidable delays. In some cases, village mayors refused to sign the necessary paperwork because there was insufficient space in local graveyards. Such circumstances "were just not envisaged," they explained.[14] The unfortunate situation left many French families frustrated and reluctantly resigned to leaving their deceased in a national cemetery.

Across the Channel, thousands participated in the largest British Legion pilgrimage to the First World War battlefields in August 1928. This mass exodus was motivated in part by the tenth anniversary of the armistice, the recent completion of Britain's war monuments, and the success of the American Legion pilgrimage the year before. Unlike their American predecessors, that is, veterans who had been the last to enter the fray but the first to return as heroes, men and women who joined the British Legion pilgrimage of 1928 distinguished themselves with attributes of "organisation, discipline, dignity and piety."[15] Originally, the British Legion planners had scheduled their pilgrimage for the summer of 1927 (just before the Americans), but the response was disappointing. Despite the minimal charge of only five British pounds, just 150 people participated; the organizers attributed the low numbers to cost: "Five pounds is a lot of money to most people and the idea of saving up week by week did not catch on."[16] A year later, a more robust response brought eleven thousand pilgrims from all across the United Kingdom back to the front.[17]

The 1928 British pilgrimage was considered a success by the British Legion because it fulfilled its objectives: it "consoled the bereaved, honoured the dead, renewed and fostered the comradeship of the war," and reminded the world of the valor and sacrifices of the nation during the war. It also provided an opportunity for the guardians of British war memory to reinforce traditional values that some may have felt were threatened by recent American celebrations in France. Implicit cultural comparisons to the American Legionnaires were frequently made in the British Legion's souvenir program, such as the following: "Their departure was typically British—there was no fuss; no flag-waving; no band; no cheering. They paraded outside the station with their respective companies. They marched or limped with their small handbags or their haversacks to their appointed platform. They were shepherded quietly and expeditiously into the 'A' train."[18]

The Americans were cultural interlopers amid a British and French piety that came together in defense of their dead, which were far more numerous. Did casualty statistics necessarily justify greater sensitivity and dignity? Presumably not to the individuals of any nation who lost loved ones to the war. Either way, the pervasive influence of Americanism across the Atlantic was unmistakable. How disappointing it must have been, then, for those on the 1928 British pilgrimage to pass under the triumphal welcoming arch at Vimy Ridge and notice that on it, the French artist had inadvertently portrayed American doughboys instead of depicting men of the Canadian forces.[19]

For Britons unable to join the middle classes on foreign pilgrimages, the Cenotaph and the grave of the Unknown Warrior in London served as a more accessible point of remembrance. Despite repeated requests in the House of Commons for the provision of free travel for relatives after the war, the British government claimed it "could not afford to pay the costs of assisting poor relatives."[20] This response is particularly striking since the British state was quite large with health insurance, unemployment benefits, and such, following the social reforms of the liberal government before the First World War.

Australia did not bring the dead home after the war, and as in other nations, resolution and acceptance of the reality of death were much harder in the absence of a grave.[21] Consequently, many pilgrims were drawn to the distant cemeteries on the first Australian War Graves pilgrimage in 1929. They participated despite receiving only minimal assistance from a government reluctant to become involved in an event that was not organized by the nation's official ex-servicemen's group but by a rival.[22]

Perhaps it was due to the lack of governmental support that pilgrims were exposed to several instances of rude behavior from French customs officials at Marseilles, protracted searches upon crossing the border between Belgium and France, and verbal abuse hurled by French bystanders. Relations between the Australians and the French further deteriorated when the mayor of the village quarreled with the pilgrims and suggested that they should have given money to the village rather than laying a wreath in the cemetery.[23] Although the Australian Memorial at Villers Bretonneux was not unveiled until 1938, the village served as the key commemorative site during the Australians' 1929 pilgrimage.

Like Britain, Canadians also erected temporary cenotaphs after the war and gathered in large numbers before local memorials to honor their dead. Then, in July 1936, five ocean liners carried more than sixty-four hundred Canadians across the Atlantic, where another two thousand pilgrims joined them in France.[24] The journey was, according to Lloyd, first proposed in 1927 following the American Legion's visit and was originally planned to coincide with the completion of the Canadian Memorial at Vimy Ridge. The Depression and other delays postponed the memorial's completion, which was originally expected in 1931 or 1932.[25] In contrast to American plans, structurally complete monuments were seen as a commemorative prerequisite by the Canadians, who considered the unveiling ceremony the high point of their visit.

Despite Canada's geographic proximity to the United States, the Canadians more closely resembled their British compatriots in that they were anxious to ensure that the 1936 pilgrimage retained a sense of dignity. Participants were asked to sign a pledge of agreement upon their formal application, to "conduct [themselves] during the entire trip in a proper manner, appropriate to such a pilgrimage."[26] King Edward VIII joined the pilgrims at Vimy Ridge, where he unveiled Canada's National Memorial, a reminder of the nation's vast contribution to the war effort. Vimy Memorial, erected by the people of Canada, commemorates sixty thousand dead and includes the names of over ten thousand Canadians who have no known burial place.[27]

Unlike the pilgrimages of other nations during the 1920s, preembarkation notes for the Canadians in 1936 included warnings against words or acts that showed intolerance or anything but "typical Canadian cheerfulness" toward the European nations.[28] Despite appeals to participants for tolerance of events on the world stage, the Canadian pilgrimage was marred from within by disagreements over language and among various ex-servicemen's organizations vying for control of the event.[29]

The American Legion pilgrimage of 1927 triggered an international surge in battlefield travel during those memorable anniversary years after the war, but this was not merely a competitive impulse. The antics of the Americans may have given rise to some disturbing fears among the former allies that memories of the war were weakening or had somehow become tainted by the Americans' cultural lightheartedness. The audacious claims of some of these former allies were intended to remind the Americans that they had not fought the war alone and represented a stronger compulsion to affirm the validity of their own collective war memories: that is, that the war had been worth fighting and that all the sacrifice had not been in vain.

Fears over the legitimacy of this ideal escalated with the arrival of each new pilgrimage, as frantic attempts to preserve a fragile world peace seemed destined to falter. Within a few short years, the concerns expressed by the Canadian organizers in 1936 proved warranted, as Europe became engulfed in another war.[30] The peace had lasted just long enough for nations to bury and memorialize their dead, and the pilgrimage movement ended as it had begun, with the Americans on foreign fields dedicating their monuments in the late 1930s.

The struggles witnessed by pilgrims of other nations—the inability or choice of governments not to support the pilgrims, bureaucratic wrangling with foreign hosts, language barriers and internal competition between pilgrimage organizers and participants alike—illustrate the range of potential problems that can plague such an ambitious endeavor. However, the mothers and widows who traveled overseas with the U.S. government between 1930 and 1933 experienced none of these difficulties. Their journey was defined by the government's impeccably smooth logistical planning and a glittering public-relations spin that accentuated the lavish fanfare accompanying each aspect of their journey while omitting any mention of the rigid restrictions that limited meaningful participation. As a result, the GSM pilgrimages resembled lottery prizes bestowed on a few fortunate winners, rather than inadequate compensation for such a regrettable loss. In the next chapter, I explore the contributing factors that shape this impression.

20

Mothers and Politics

It was certainly an advantage that the nation's largest and most highly publicized pilgrimage of 1927 was organized by the American Legion, since the U.S. government would most likely have reacted with indifference toward any other organization lacking its official endorsement. Several years prior, when the Legion made its first public mention of a movement aimed at "giving next of kin who are entitled to wear a gold star a trip to France," Congress had been debating the issue for months.[1] Pleas for organized, subsidized cemetery visits to Europe had dominated women's efforts almost as soon as the Armistice was signed, but it was not until December 1923 that the first bill was placed before Congress. Samuel Dickstein, a New York Democrat, introduced HR 4109 during the 68th Congress; the bill was then referred to the Committee on Military Affairs.[2]

Dickstein succeeded where other supporters—most notably, New York congressman Fiorello LaGuardia—had failed. In May 1919, LaGuardia had proposed a similar bill, but his timing was premature. The original legislation provided for the father, mother, or wife of the deceased serviceman to receive an expense-paid journey overseas, but LaGuardia claimed, "no matter what I introduced, I could not get a hearing."[3] The repatriation controversy undoubtedly worked against him in 1919, but perhaps just as significant was the absence of an effective mass-pilgrimage movement during this time of national upheaval. With the country embroiled in controversy over the ratification of the Versailles Treaty, battling communism on the domestic Red Scare front, arbitrating labor disputes, combating frequent racial violence, and negotiating reparations overseas, the formulation of an effective coalition for a mothers pilgrimage would have proven highly unlikely. Moreover, pilgrimages have a reflective, commemorative aspect relating to the past. In 1919–1920, the nation was enmeshed in its current problems; thus, the war did not yet belong to the past.

Another critical issue was the state of the Western Front after the war. If the Gold Star pilgrimages had proceeded when first proposed, the result might have been catastrophic for all concerned. Europe's scarred battlefields offered only remorse to anyone considering abandoning their loved ones to burial there. This was a heartbreaking period made worse by the anxious uncertainty that accompanied the government's postwar indecision over the disposition of American war dead. Once that issue was resolved, the agonizing and lengthy wait for the body's return could take years. For others, the decision to leave their deceased overseas came at an equally high price. There would be no funeral service, no headstone in a local cemetery, nothing left to venerate, and no closure so necessary in the grieving process. For those whose sons or husbands were officially known as "missing" or "unknown," the repatriation debate was a painful reminder of their added loss, and the relentless passage of time seldom offered solace or resolution. With this tragic episode behind them, most Americans looked to the future and the prospect of a new life as lobbying efforts for a federally sponsored pilgrimage reached heated proportions by 1928.

After Dickstein introduced the first bill, a "very careful review of the whole subject" was carried out by the army and published on May 3, 1924.[4] With zealous organizational efficiency, the military performed an extensive cost analysis, including staffing and logistical requirements, based on elaborate algebraic formulas. Officials concluded that $3,292,776 would be required to fund the pilgrimages if the War Department supervised the tours. That figure assumed that no mothers would be transported other than those of the known dead, and no mention was made of widows. The report estimated that 14,057 mothers living in the United States (average age of fifty-one and a half years) were eligible for the journey. Among the superfluity of data that allowed for a seemingly endless list of contingencies, there was a brief reminder that "age, diverse temperaments, and class in life of these mothers will greatly handicap enforcement of any rigid military rule or regulation." Therefore, "personal touch and kindly consideration will at all times be necessary."[5]

Mysteriously, the army's elaborate report was laid aside after its initial release, as the bill was voted out of committee by the close of 1924. That drew a swift and vociferous response from women across the nation's diverse sociocultural spectrum. The Speaker of the House, Frederick Gillett, was inundated with persuasive appeals beseeching him to "please permit consideration of this bill to pass for the sake of the dear mothers who have their loved one over their [*sic*]." In shaky, nearly illegible script, one woman expressed the views of so many: "Oh my dear sir how I long to see where they have laid my boy. . . . lord and master I leave all this with my savour [*sic*] who will guide it aright." The words of many women echoed a shared belief that what they were requesting was a "small thing for the government to do." It was a debt whose payment was considered long overdue. "The government did not stop to ask can you be spared but took them from us so that is the least they can do for the Gold Star Mother or wife of the boys." This mother revealed that her son had died at eighteen, "leaving a widowed mother with three little ones to be looked after."[6]

The notion that mothers as citizens of the nation had an obligation to send their sons to war is a profound and recurrent one that seems to have been revived at the height of the maternal welfare state that emerged during the Progressive Era.[7] Women extended their special domestic sphere out into the community through their reform activities as nationally organized women's groups. Their momentum strengthened during the early 1920s with the passage of social policies such as the mothers' pensions (known as widows' pensions) and the Sheppard-Towner Act of 1921.[8] This bill and its precedent, the Children's Bureau, were the direct results of effective political maneuvering by savvy women reformers. These civic activists, usually well-educated women of the elite and middle classes, were also leaders in the formation of remembrance associations devoted to the war's memory that flourished across the United States.[9]

Practical experience gained in the realm of earlier social-reform work proved beneficial to women in their battle for pilgrimage legislation throughout the mid- to late 1920s. The strength of their mobilization efforts was based on the development of an effective lobby with its dependence on agitation and publicity, bipartisan appeals to legislators through massive letter-writing campaigns, and the manipulation of public opinion. The GSM employed the same maternal rhetoric steeped in notions of selfless morality as that of earlier social reformers. As Theda Skocpol has observed, "Women had so long been regarded as guardians of morality that when they spoke with apparently unanimous conviction about the lofty purposes to be served by new social policies, their demands were hard for legislators to ignore."[10] When the horrors of war were retold within the context of the Patriotic Motherhood theme, the effect must have been all the more compelling. The time was right for another maternal crusade.

Women's groups were "at the height of their own organizational prowess and ideological self-confidence" during the early 1920s and were the "broadest force of the day working for the public interest."[11] So how can it be that war mothers were not equally successful in their struggle to obtain passage of the pilgrimage bill during their early campaign of 1923–1924? Their efforts were an extension of the same maternal ethos embraced by their counterparts lobbying for welfare compensation for poor mothers and children. Though benefiting a much smaller percentage of the public, Gold Star Mothers and their supporters hoped to provide a means of travel for women who could not otherwise afford to go to their son's grave.[12]

By the mid-1920s, Skocpol claims, "women's will and capacities to achieve further maternal policies diminished, just as powerful backlashes developed against policy gains that had already been achieved."[13] She cites the unsuccessful attempt by women reformers to persuade Congress to renew federal appropriations for the Sheppard-Towner public-health-care program as illustrative of this decreased power.

Gender historians are divided over the extent of political activity among women's organizations during these years. The feminist historian Nancy Cott contends that the tradition of female voluntarism continued to thrive throughout the interwar era. "It is highly probable that the greatest extent of associational activity in the whole history of American women" occurred between the two world wars, "after women became voters and before a great proportion of them entered the labor force."[14] The successful gains of the nation's war mothers by 1929 invites reconsideration of Skocpol's thesis regarding the longevity of the women's reform movement. However, one might also argue that the increasingly zealous patriotic motherhood ideals of the middle to late 1920s lent political momentum to their fight and that it was not solely the lobbying efforts of the women reformers.

Regardless of such civic-minded activism, in 1927 the nation heard President Calvin Coolidge make publicly clear that he "welcomed the withdrawal of the federal government" from the Sheppard-Towner bill, along with other "state-aid projects," during what was a generally conservative political climate.[15] The reluctance of Congress to provide funding for maternal health welfare may be attributed to the prevailing tension between the state and federal governments that characterized the 1920s. But could it not have also signaled a shift in the high-minded ideals regarding the accepted role of the patriotic mother? Were doubts afloat about her primary service to the state?[16] If motherhood ideology continued to maintain such a forceful grip on the public and national policymakers into the late 1920s, then why did mothers' pensions and other similar public-aid programs remain so poorly funded?

A closer assessment of the American War Mothers organizational history suggests that maternalism began to assume an increasingly pragmatic function, one that varied depending on the intended motive. Evidence of this evolutionary process may be observed by tracing the group's development from 1920, when the women held their first executive board meeting. Here, they agreed that their mission was to become "an international league of mothers to enforce peace."[17] The mothers unanimously endorsed the League of Nations, and although the deceased were still being repatriated from overseas at the time, these women were already wondering if they "could have the *Gold Star* [a newly built transport] take a load of mothers over to visit the graves in France."[18]

It was not long before these mothers gained administrative confidence, as they became more closely affiliated with the American Legion, War Department officials, and the White House, where they met with President Coolidge in 1925. Three years later, they joined four hundred women from other groups at a National Patriotic Conference in Washington, DC, where the secretary of war, Dwight L. Davis, congratulated them for their interest in national defense. The attentive audience applauded him as he spoke of his plan to bring the army into a closer relationship with the womanhood of the country.[19] Afterward, speakers from the War Department told the women, "This nation became a nation as a result of war and has been maintained as a nation only through the sacrifices of its citizens in many wars. . . . It will endure only so long as its people are willing to offer their lives, if necessary, in its service."[20]

By 1928, the organization's emphasis had shifted significantly. No longer in favor of international expansion, its resolutions now included support for a universal draft ("to eliminate slackers") and opposition to further reductions in military personnel.[21] As the organization matured, the war mothers grew increasingly aware of the benefits to be gained when they aligned their efforts with men, particularly those in positions of power. The women's participation in the struggle for the Gold Star pilgrimages illustrates the prominence they had attained by the close of the decade.

This collective cooperation with men in power was not without cost, however, as motherhood assumed an altered form of political currency with the approach of the tenth anniversary of the war. Peace advocates saw an opportunity to have women bring their "special skills" into the political arena as arbitrators, defenders of morality, and guardians of tranquillity. The International Council of Women, in its slim volume published in 1916, expressed these sentiments: "God made two, a man and a woman, to rule the home—the state is but a larger home. Woman must take her place right in states. The Mothering of the nations has been left out by legislatures, to the world's great detriment. Especially is the mother in her right place in determining international questions, for the lives of her sons are at stake."[22]

Those in the preparedness movement took an alternative position aligned with the military's view that such sentiments were naive and brought a dangerous softness to the national character. Instead, mothers held a special responsibility to prepare their sons for patriotic service and sacrifice to the nation if necessary.

Kathleen Kennedy suggests that for those women who pledged to uphold the ideals of patriotic motherhood, "preparedness offered a unique opportunity for national service, which they increasingly defined as a central component of motherhood and women's citizenship."[23] This yearning to serve the nation was evident in 1918 when the Women's Committee of the U.S. Council of National Defense supported the president's appeal for revised mourning practices. As shown previously, these committeewomen were eager to assist the war effort with the introduction of the gold star emblem and banner. In time, these women became increasingly frustrated over their public underutilization and the overemphasis on social-relief work, so they attempted to broaden their contribution to the war effort by tapping into the Americanization movement. White, middle-class women such as those of the American War Mothers continued to strengthen this faction with their preparedness programs throughout the decade.

In 1930, with the ideals of republican motherhood at a pinnacle, the American War Mothers held their annual Mother's Day ceremony at the Tomb of the Unknown Soldier. Once seated in the spacious amphitheater, the women heard the reassuring words, "As nations rose and flourished, those that honoured motherhood most rose highest and endured longest." Gold Star Mothers seated in the reserved front rows listened further for the War Department's worn but comforting reminder that, "loving their sons," they had nevertheless sent them to die if need be "on the holy cross of battle, fighting for humanity. The very blood that the mother has infused into her son's veins serves as a drum to whose throb they march away."[24]

No politician would risk publicly questioning the link between motherhood and civic obligation, but many would use the familiar motherhood rhetoric to further their own political stance on the nation's security and the risk of future wars. These political divisions soon provided a boost to the pilgrimage cause, one that women used to their fullest advantage.

21

Mathilda's Victory

In 1928, Congressman Thomas S. Butler, a representative from Pennsylvania, placed the familiar Gold Star pilgrimage legislation before the 70th Congress once more, when he reintroduced the bill to the Committee on Military Affairs.[1] Chairman John M. Morin, another Pennsylvanian, presided over the House committee hearings, and none other than the well-known Senator David Reed served as chairman of the Senate committee. Women's organizations, using their political expertise and favored position as war mothers, cultivated powerful and well-placed politicians such as Reed.[2]

While evidence suggesting Reed's direct responsibility for the promotion of and eventual passage of the Gold Star legislation is sketchy, his illustrious career, spanning more than twenty-five years, placed him in an ideal position to influence its success. Considering the plethora of international publicity surrounding the American Legion pilgrimage the year before, and the imminent completion of the battlefield monuments and cemeteries overseas, the timing for this motherhood legislation was ideal.

During the course of the bill's evolution, Reed's committee invited the testimony of countless persuasive supporters, including representatives of the newly founded Gold Star Mothers Association. Undoubtedly, the most aggressive rhetoric came from stalwart matriarch Mathilda Burling. Although her precise role as "national representative of the Association" frustrated many people and angered some, no one doubted Burling's ability to charm, cajole, and coerce all in her midst. Few remained neutral in the presence of her audacious personality. "She is one to be thrown out from the world," claimed one mother, adding, "she is a man's woman, a sneak," and perhaps the worst insult of all, "she is a very nasty politician."[3]

Mathilda Burling, wife of a New York policeman and mother of an enlisted soldier who died in 1918, claimed "executive" membership in the American Red Cross and "charter" membership in the American Legion, before appointing herself president of the Gold Star Service Association

Gold Star Mother matriarch Mathilda Burling, the wife of a New York policeman and mother of an enlisted soldier who died in 1918. Some people claimed she was a "very nasty politician." (Burial file of Private George B. Burling, Jr., Box 700, Cemeterial Division, Office of the QMG, RG 92, NA)

in 1924.[4] She chose to leave her son's remains buried in St. Mihiel American Cemetery, purportedly "at the [personal] request of our late President Roosevelt."[5] While some women despised Burling's presumptuous methods, others were quick to praise her. "Mrs. Burling has worked day and night for this bill for the last five or six years," testified one woman.[6]

Burling began lobbying for war mothers in 1924, when she wrote to the army asking for a flag on behalf of the mothers whose sons had no graves. That had not been standard practice, but the army graciously adopted her suggestion and responded accordingly.[7] By 1928, her activism was strongly focused on the mothers pilgrimage. She tried unsuccessfully to persuade General Pershing to discuss the pilgrimage bill with her, claiming that President Coolidge was very interested in the legislation.[8] Before explaining that he was otherwise engaged, the general reminded Burling of the "great sacrifice" the soldiers themselves had made while pointing out the many objections and difficulties that had arisen since the pilgrimage movement began.[9] A month later, Pershing wrote Burling again claiming to have read and approved the American Legion's resolution on the matter and saying "some satisfactory arrangements" should be made for "those who desire to go and who are unable to afford the expense." He advised her to seek the advice of congressional members as to how she should proceed.[10]

Burling's ties to the national Gold Star Mothers Association are vague, but they were certainly not congenial. Burling claimed to have conceived the idea of the pilgrimage, and she took credit for organizing the original Gold Star Association. After having been asked to leave her local GSM chapter, Burling founded her own mothers' organization and sought a separate state charter for her similarly named New York group, the American Gold Star Mothers of the World War, Inc. So successful were her efforts to publicize herself as the president of all Gold Star Mothers associations that the original group eventually brought a lawsuit against her.[11] The founder of the original Washington, DC, Gold Star Mothers organization, Mrs. George G. Seibold, considered Mathilda Burling's enrollment in that association, in 1927, to be "the greatest farce we have ever experienced." Seibold claimed, "Her one dollar fee was the most disastrous ever received."[12] By unanimous vote, Burling was dropped from membership for "disloyalty" on December 1, 1931, still owing two years' back membership dues.

These animosities seem to have been put aside during the congressional hearing, when Burling did not hesitate to resort to tactics that included an occasional jarring assertion such as, "Our boys were murdered, they were not given a fair chance to fight in a patriotic way." Generally, her commentary simply exploited patriotic motherhood ideals with unblushing forthrightness.[13] "As a mother whose only child lies over there, and who is authorized to represent the Gold Star Mothers of America," she began,

"I can not believe that the Senate of my country will deny us the privilege of paying a visit to those holy graves of our heroic sons abroad."[14] In May 1928, she pointed out to Senate committee members that the House of Representatives "was kind enough to favor this bill"; however, because many mothers had since died, it was "too late to favor them."[15] Burling's occasional use of such provocative rhetoric seems an odd method of building a coalition of maternal support.

When the original pilgrimage bill was proposed by Dickstein and the Gold Star Association, it stipulated that in case the mother was not living, the father could go; or if the mother and father were dead, a brother or sister or nearest of kin could participate. But by 1928, emphasis had altered significantly toward mothers as the primary recipient of the government's largesse.

Many of the women testifying on behalf of this legislation had already journeyed to the cemeteries in Europe, but Burling had not. "Eleven long years have passed since my boy, who was only a child in years, gave his life for the defence of this country," she said. "Each year I have lived in the hope that I would kneel before his grave." Then, using maternalism to its fullest advantage, she wept while adding, "It was our flesh and blood that enriched the foreign soil. After all it was the mothers who had won the war."[16]

By equating maternal loss with the sacrifice of their own flesh and blood, Burling and others claimed a privileged status that surpassed that of fathers and, even more significant, the status of widows.[17] Allegedly, mothers' claim to "sacrifice" carried more weight because they literally gave birth to soldiers, whereas the widows had no such indisputable tie to their dead men.[18]

Widowhood represented a murky, ambiguous area in the ideology of national sacrifice, and as a result, widows' entitlement to the evolving postwar memory was nearly overlooked. When debating the heated issue before the House, Congressman Butler pondered, "I was willing to include in the bill the unmarried widow. Have you any information there that will tell about the number? No, of course not." As an afterthought, Butler added, "unmarried widows were not mentioned in the other bill. . . . I suppose there will be a number of them."[19] This brought allegations from the war mothers that the widows were "not worthy" of the trip and that their presence would make "a junket" out of the pilgrimage. Mother love was "greater than anything in the world," they asserted, and more than one Gold Star Mother reminded her audience that many widows had already remarried, whereas "no mother lets another take the place of her boy."[20]

Gender did not necessarily serve as a supporting factor in the contest for national remembrance, as disgruntled letters illustrate.[21] "Will you please use your influence to kill bill HR 5494?" wrote one woman, complaining that it was "unpopular with most of the women's organizations of Essex, New Jersey."[22] Similarly, the Women's Overseas Service League referred to the pilgrimages as "shocking," whereas others claimed the bill would be "a flagrant misappropriation of public funds."[23] Some firmly believed that the government's previous offers to repatriate the dead had been "so adequate that any mother, wishing to see the grave of her son, would have taken advantage of them 10 years ago."[24]

Passage of this legislation inadvertently posed an ethical dilemma for Congress, since it implied the existence of a hierarchy of those considered most deserving of recognition. Mothers of the known dead were placed at the pinnacle of the remembrance pyramid, while widows, mothers of the unknown dead, fathers, the disabled, families, and veterans all jockeyed for positions within the structure. Negotiations were conducted within a system of assumptions that challenged the extent of one's wartime sacrifice. For some, authorization to participate in the pilgrimage was the ultimate measure of acknowledgment, while others sought financial remuneration. Either way, the contest was bound to breed disfavor and, frequently, contempt. Although politicians avoided expressions of ambivalence toward the pilgrimage proposal, they reminded their constituents that a considerable number of letters against the bill had been received.[25]

Nevertheless, on March 2, 1929, just weeks before leaving office and with nothing to gain in political terms, the notoriously frugal President Calvin Coolidge signed the "act to enable the mothers and widows of the deceased soldiers, sailors and marines of the American forces . . . interred in the cemeteries of Europe" to make their pilgrimage.[26] Historian Kurt Piehler contends that by the time the pilgrimage legislation reached the president's office, Coolidge could not resist the momentum favoring passage of this bill.[27] Unfortunately, scant documentation remains to substantiate Piehler's claim regarding this conservative president's decision, yet several speculative points may be posited.

Evidence suggests that the rhetorical sentiments of patriotic motherhood may not have been the overriding persuasive factor in the bill's passage. By 1928, the American Legion's endorsement of the GSM legislation represented a potential one million votes to the Republican Party.

Theodore Roosevelt, Jr., founding member of the American Legion and known supporter (like his father) of the overseas cemeteries, may have reminded the president of that fact, since he "liked nothing better than to advise Republican presidents and . . . also seems to have been in the Coolidge White House fairly often."[28] And though it may not have been an overriding inducement, Coolidge's memories of his mother's death when he was twelve years old, followed by the tragic death of his son, Calvin Jr., in 1924, may have helped soften the president's parsimonious tendencies.[29]

However, the international scene at the close of the decade may have lent the greatest weight toward the bill's success. Lindbergh completed his landmark flight from New York to Paris in 1927, a feat that triggered a much-needed surge of Franco-American amity, as did the settling of the war-reparations issue with Europe. As a further incentive toward peaceful relations, the United States joined France and sixty-one other nations in signing the multilateral Kellogg-Briand Pact (Pact of Paris) of August 1928. This instrument of national policy renounced war except in the case of self-defense and created a global atmosphere of optimism that lasting peace was possible.

Regardless of the president's motive, with internationalist Republican David Reed as committee chairman, and Pennsylvania's monuments dominating the battlefield by 1928, the legislation was destined to succeed. Moreover, pilgrimages offered politicians of both parties plenty of diplomatic potential. On January 27, 1928, Senator Robert Wagner (D-NY) told a House committee hearing,

> [The pilgrimages] will be a good thing for the cause of peace, in that Europe has thought for some time that we in the United States are entirely devoted to class materialism, and these mothers will show that this country has been . . . making a spiritual sacrifice due to the war. This pilgrimage will help in many ways. It will do far more to bring about a better understanding, showing that we have a spiritual side to us, than anything that has been done heretofore by our diplomats and other representatives.[30]

With so many people clamoring for a secure peace and the outlaw of war, supporters of the Gold Star legislation were quick to apply the language of peace to the pilgrimages within the context of international events. By identifying the pilgrimages as a peace mission, solidarity and public support for the proposition could more readily be assured.

Pacifist idealism had reached new heights. As 1928 ended, Coolidge noted the "prevalence of peace and good will" between the United States and the former Allies overseas, derived from "mutual understanding" and from "the knowledge that the problems which a short time ago appeared so ominous are yielding to the touch of manifest friendship."[31]

In March 1929, the American War Mothers used their national publication to proudly report the successful passage of the pilgrimage bill, stating that their organization had "worked valiantly to bring this great boon to the Gold Star Mother."[32] Yet none could have been more pleased with this success story than Mathilda Burling. *Time* magazine credited the "alert, energetic Mrs. Burling" with having "long ago conceived the idea" of the pilgrimages to France. "Her irrepressible efforts were more responsible for enactment of this legislation than any other individual's," the article boasted. Those who had supported the campaign through its long ordeal must have been less than amused to read that they were being considered "rivals" who had engaged in "petty politics" and reportedly criticized Burling's methods.[33]

The praises ringing from the pages of *Time* lack validity, since the pilgrimage idea was conceived before the outspoken matriarch joined the original Gold Star Association. However, Mathilda Burling deserves credit for her uncanny propensity toward self-promotion, matched by an aggressive manipulative approach that repeatedly gave her political advantage over her less savvy competitors.

As with other national commemorative efforts, the struggle for a pilgrimage to the overseas graves caused significant disunity among those who had been touched by the war experience. Whether for peace or military preparedness, assigning a political rationale to the Gold Star pilgrimages usurped their intended commemorative purpose. What had begun as a journey of mourning for those too poor to venture independently overseas had become a divisive mechanism for political voice.

As 1929 ended, funding had still not been allocated for the pilgrimages, but that did not quell the continuing debate over a multitude of ill-defined parameters. More than thirty different versions of this bill were debated, amended, and in some cases ratified before the spring of 1930.[34] Proposed modifications to the original bill ranged from budgetary objections to questions of logistics and more sensitive issues such as eligibility under the new legislation; many people believed fathers, stepmothers, and adoptive mothers should not be excluded.[35] Further objections concerning the logistical arrangements of the pilgrimage were also argued, since the original bill appointed the Red Cross and not the military as the organization most qualified to coordinate the details. When some in Congress and the War Department complained about the cost of the legislation, sponsors of proposed bills were quick to point out that mothers had actually saved the government money by not having their sons returned for burial.[36] Still others questioned how many days should be allocated for the journey and whether those unable to make the pilgrimage could receive a financial payment instead.

As Congress sat in judgment over the sensitive criteria that made one woman eligible for the pilgrimage and another not, hopes were repeatedly inflated and then dashed. "To insure a high moral standard," mothers living "out of wedlock" during the war were barred, as were widows who had since remarried.[37] Once that was resolved, adoptive mothers were scrutinized. The law stipulated that stepmothers would only be considered eligible if they had "stood in *loco parentis* to the decedent," and then only in certain conditions.[38] That technicality resulted in many sisters, aunts, and others being excluded from participation unless they could prove their relationship to the deceased. Such seemingly harsh restrictions served to keep costs down, but this ruling also reinforced a more subtle assumption. By placing greater significance on the biological mother, the government asserted that only "mothers of the blood" could be considered true bearers of the nation's heroes. This belief was such an integral part of the republican motherhood theme that it was incorporated into the bylaws of the American War Mothers Association, whereby adoptive mothers were forced to resign their membership.[39]

The largest class of ineligibles included the mothers of those who fought and died with the Allies before the entrance of the United States into the war. No provision was made for these women whose sons were thought to have violated the neutrality of the United States, thereby giving up their citizenship by joining the army of another nation.

Congress waited until May 1930 to pass a final amendment allowing passage for mothers and widows of those lost at sea and those whose bodies had not been located, and for women who had formerly visited the graves at their own expense. Prior to this amendment, the legislation had excluded nearly three thousand women.[40] But three years after the act was modified, only 729 women had accepted this last-minute invitation that had prevented them from joining the first year's pilgrimage.

In May 1930, when the first pilgrimage vessel finally sailed, it did so under the auspices of the War Department and not the Red Cross. The army's Quartermaster Corps, responsible for purchase and procurement of supplies and equipment (and the graves registration function) attended to all arrangements. Daily management of these details fell to the extremely professional, highly competent Colonel Richard T. Ellis, Officer-in-Charge of the Gold Star pilgrimages. By adapting popular theories of systems, management proficiency, and industrial organization, Ellis and his team streamlined the pilgrimage process using a highly efficient production-line approach. He fully recognized the immensity of his task, for which he readily admitted there was "no previous experience of a similar nature to use as a guide." His assignment, he realized, was to establish an organization that would function simultaneously "as a Hotel, Travel, Steamship and Wellfare [*sic*] Bureau."[41]

The primary challenge facing Ellis was the age of the pilgrims, since most ranged between sixty-one and sixty-five years, but many were over seventy and often in failing health. Other factors such as language barriers and the need for bilingual personnel presented additional challenges. Escort officer Colonel Oliver L. Spaulding reported that on a 1930 sailing, one of his passengers found herself quartered with two Polish women who could hardly speak English. He was forced to make a reassignment at once.[42] Within the first party of 231 to sail, 56 were of foreign birth, with the majority claiming Germany as their former homeland.[43]

Although the spring weather in France was reported to be "abominable," religion and ethnic concerns proved to be among the military's chief concerns, particularly for those of the Jewish faith. When Rose Hirsh and Lena Niditch of New York arrived on board, both women were adamant that they must "only be served with Koscher cooking."[44] The officer in charge reported that the procurement of such food created many difficulties. He wrote, "Either there are few Jews in France or they are not very orthodox where diet is concerned." Once they arrived in France, many of the Jewish pilgrims clearly "refused to eat anything that had not been blessed by a rabbi and in consequence necessitated the making of a trip around Paris hunting for Kosher restaurants."[45] Despite all the elaborate foresight, the military had not planned for such circumstances, nor were they prepared when Mrs. Niditch arrived at the Meuse-Argonne cemetery expecting to see a Jewish Star of David over her brother's grave and instead saw a cross marking his burial.[46]

One concern remained predominant on each sailing: the necessity to avoid "over-emphasis of the sentimental side in order to prevent morbidness or hysteria."[47] This policy included the moment-of-silence ceremony that took place during the crossing, when the captain brought the vessel to a complete stop in the mid-Atlantic. The chief steward ensured that the orchestra played appropriate sacred music, but like each of the officers in charge, he had been ordered that the occasion, though impressive, should be kept brief.[48]

"In order to keep emotional reaction at a minimum," the quartermaster general's report ordered that no ceremonies were permitted at the cemeteries. Rather, the War Department determined three other factors to be more crucial to a successful visit: "the arrangements necessary for the prompt and accurate conduct of the pilgrim to the grave in which she was interested, the distribution of flowers or wreaths, . . . [and] the taking of a photograph at the grave."[49] These guidelines set the general tone and character of all the GSM pilgrimages.

Of the 11,440 women deemed eligible, approximately 6,685 mothers and widows accepted the government's invitation.[50] The cost of the pilgrimages, scheduled to occur between May 1, 1930, and October 31, 1933, was originally estimated to be about three million dollars; however, the actual cost was over five million dollars.[51] Much of this funding was awarded to major American companies through lucrative contracts that included the United States Shipping Lines, whose fleet was presided over by Kermit Roosevelt (son of former president Theodore Roosevelt). Another contract went to Bailey, Banks & Biddle Co. of Philadelphia, for production of official medallions that were distributed to all the women who boarded the luxury liners.[52] No expense was spared to make their pilgrimage one of comfort and ease. From the moment they left their homes, all reasonable expenses were paid by the nation.

Before setting sail, escorting officers, who had been selected for their "superior judgment, common sense and tact," received a rousing welcome from the quartermaster general, Major General John L. DeWitt. "You must remember that you have been chosen because of certain qualifications. The most important of these is sobriety," he reminded them. DeWitt also instructed the men to be careful how they "deal[t] with" the pilgrims, emphasizing, "Many of the women making the voyage are so poor that they have been unable to buy even the suitcases that they are supposed to have."[53]

The government's publicity spinners had done their best to promote a democratic spirit and frequently reminded readers that Catholics, Protestants, and Jews—native born and foreign born—had all sacrificed their sons to the nation. Regardless of income or social level, the press releases repeated claims that the women were all guests of the U.S. government and were to be treated equally. Yet democratic ideals were overlooked as plans progressed to send black women to France in separate ships. General De Witt had not counted on the political backlash awaiting the War Department once these intentions were revealed.

General DeWitt's preoccupation with public relations was not unusual among the higher echelon of the image-conscious military establishment of this period.[54] From 1917, the army had begun to recognize the political capital to be gained by positively influencing public opinion, particularly since pockets of negativity still lingered over this pilgrimage legislation. With these critics in mind, Quartermaster DeWitt concluded, "we have nothing to conceal and we have everything to gain by making a proper impression on those correspondents whose writings reach the public through newspapers and periodicals."[55]

After the pilgrimages set sail, images of Native American Gold Star Mothers in full regalia were paraded before the cameras as "picturesque" symbols of American sacrifice, whereas the treatment of African American women made for less amusing press.[56] The protest that followed by the black community, though largely forgotten today, prefigured the civil rights movement that blossomed decades later.

22

Stars of Black and Gold

When the 71st Congress (1929–1931) opened on April 15, 1929, Oscar S. De Priest, a newly elected Republican from Illinois, prepared to take his seat. With the press and many African Americans looking on from the segregated visitors gallery, De Priest took the oath of office. He was the first black American elected to Congress in nearly three decades.[1]

As a House representative, De Priest regularly challenged the fixed segregationist practices on Capitol Hill, even as he endured the prejudices of some members, including those who refused to accept offices adjacent to his.[2] But when the First Lady refused to invite De Priest's wife, Jessie, to have tea with the spouses of other Republican congressmen, De Priest was furious. He was quick to ensure that the snub was widely publicized, until, in a highly symbolic gesture, Lou Henry Hoover invited Mrs. De Priest to join her at the president's residence. Also in attendance were the wives of the secretary of war and the attorney general. This marked the first time an African American woman had ever been entertained that way in the White House.[3]

The nation's reaction to the unprecedented invitation was swift. The Florida House of Representatives declared that the event was "both shameful and disgraceful" and that it threatened to "destroy the prestige of the Anglo-Saxon race." The Mississippi legislature condemned the tea invitation as "tending to destroy . . . racial integrity," and in North Carolina, the local *Tribune* concluded that Hoover would never carry the southern vote again. All across the South, thousands threatened to pull their votes from the Republican Party, claiming that Hoover had "no real regard for the feelings of Southern people." A few northern papers voiced impatience, claiming it was "high time" the South "got away from this un-American attitude," which it argued was "nothing more or less than a state of mind," but their views were nearly obscured by the opposition.[4]

Black voters had offered the Republican Party overwhelming support since the Civil War, but that backing began to erode under successive

Republican administrations throughout the 1920s. Disillusionment and the experiences of returning black servicemen from the recent war had awakened a new black American, one increasingly intolerant of the racial segregation still so prevalent throughout the United States. Then, in the spring of 1930, an unlikely minority of older, mostly poor, uneducated black women challenged the injustices of Jim Crow in what may have been the nation's earliest organized civil rights protest.[5]

Within months of the riotous remonstrations over Mrs. De Priest, the Hoover administration announced that the mothers and wives of black soldiers killed in the First World War and buried in Europe would be segregated from their white Gold Star counterparts during the pilgrimages. Secretary of War Patrick J. Hurley claimed that after careful consideration of the "interests of the pilgrims themselves," the women would be split into groups. He followed with an official statement that "no discrimination whatever will be made as between the various groups. Each group will receive equal accommodations, care and consideration."[6]

De Priest was quick to repeat the familiar accusations of the government's "un-American" activity, just as another African American, Walter White, brought the intervention of his organization, the NAACP, into the maelstrom.[7] White held a press conference in New York on Memorial Day weekend, just as the first ship of white women was sailing out of the nearby harbor. While addressing the press the next day in Washington, White explained that his organization had written to all eligible black Gold Star mothers and widows and was receiving an increasing number of responses from them.[8]

Consequently, hundreds of cards were sent to the secretary of war with signatures protesting the segregation policy. Without reservation, the preprinted message stated with clarity and force the hollowness of government slogans for democracy:

> Thirteen years after the victory, the War department would insult, by segregation, Mothers of fallen Negro Heroes in pilgrimage to their graves in France and Belgium. This is hypocrisy, not democracy. This is might, but not right. These fallen Heroes have surely given their most precious gift—life[—]in vain, and twelve million Negro Americans and their friends vigorously protest the imposition of this odious and un-American regulation.[9]

A separate letter was also sent directly to President Hoover in raging protest against the government's intention to segregate Gold Star Mothers.

Signed petitions, crossing state and regional boundaries, began arriving at the War Department, claiming that "the high principles of 1918 seem to have been forgotten." Others reminded the recipient that "the colored boys fought side by side with the white and they deserve the due respect." From Philadelphia, another resentful writer asked, "Must these noble women be jim-crowed, humiliated on such a sacred occasion?" Reverend E. J. Smith added, "if we fight and die together let us live together."[10]

Undeterred, the Hoover administration insisted that "mothers and widows would prefer to seek solace in their grief from companions of their own race."[11] Government press releases explained that because of the large numbers making the trip, it was "impracticable" to send the pilgrims in one body. "No discrimination whatever will be made," they insisted. But their rebuttal failed to satisfy black mothers, who continued to forward their petitions to President Hoover as part of the NAACP's efforts. In frustration they claimed they would decline to go at all unless the segregation ruling was abolished and all the women invited to sail in August 1930 could do so on equal terms. Although figures vary, approximately 1,593 black mothers and widows were deemed eligible to make the pilgrimage in total, but a mere 233 received invitations, due to death, remarriage, and ill health.[12]

Many people, like Mrs. Lora Cannon in Athens, Alabama, protested the government's position as an "insult to the living." She believed it "inconceivable that a Government founded upon the principles of fraternity, equality and even handed Justice, could so [c]ruelly wound the bleeding hearts of Mothers and widors [sic]." Another mother in Tennessee wrote, "don't put my name on the list for '32 or '33 for I will not make the trip. I can not have any part in the pleasures of going all I have now is Sadness."[13]

Publicly, the administration appeared unmoved by the protest, but behind this façade General DeWitt was concerned that the "considerable political pressure" might have a detrimental effect on the pilgrimages as a whole.[14] With acting Secretary of War Davison as intermediary, DeWitt was asked to respond to Hoover's question as to whether "some way could be devised whereby the mothers and widows themselves could bring about the segregation?" Various options were discussed, including the president's plan to send invitations out to white women, "offering them the choice of two ships, one of which would be the vessel that was to carry the colored mothers."[15] That way, Hoover believed that white women would appear responsible for the unpopular decision and not the

War Department. DeWitt expressed his view that if the current plan was changed, it would certainly be a failure. Practical logistical concerns and fears over more negative publicity prevented any change in the War Department's position, and the official line remained intact throughout all the pilgrimage years. Although no evidence suggests that white women threatened to boycott the pilgrimage, support for this early civil rights movement extended across America.

Petitioning efforts by the NAACP and threats that black voters would switch to the Democrats failed to sway the government's stance. Even the adept pen of W. E. B. Du Bois could not alter government policy. In a sharp assault, Du Bois referred to the more than six thousand African Americans whose "Black hands buried the putrid bodies of white American soldiers in France. [Yet,] Black mothers cannot go with white mothers to look at their graves."[16]

The extent to which most Americans knew of the black labor battalions' gruesome, repulsive, and unhealthy task during the summer of 1919 is unclear, but some observers remembered those days well. Black women assigned to the YMCA facility at the Meuse-Argonne American Cemetery watched them as they toiled day and night, week after week, "through drenching rain and parching heat." They wrote of the men's physical hardships, which were "nothing in comparison to the instances of discrimination 'that seared their souls like a hot iron, inflicted as they were at a time when these soldiers were rendering the American army and the nation a sacred service.'" As surrogate mothers officially tasked with feeding these young men, the women were struck by the sight of them returning at eventide, reverently "remov[ing] the boxes from the long lines of trucks and plac[ing] them on the hillside beside the waiting trenches that other soldiers had been digging all the long busy day." One of the YMCA women recalled that fear of mutiny ran high, as did the feeling of living "close to the edge of a smoldering crater."[17]

The fifty-four black mothers and widows who sailed out of New York in July 1930 were probably not fully aware of the conditions in which their sons and husbands had labored barely a dozen years before.[18] Had they known, they might still have been distracted from such thoughts by the glitz and glamour of their government-sponsored adventure. For the moment, maternal love coexisted with patriotism without protest.

When the black Gold Star Mothers arrived in New York, they were accommodated at the YWCA, rather than the more comfortable Hotel Pennsylvania, where white pilgrims stayed.[19] Each was allowed forty-eight hours

African American Gold Star Mothers of Party "K" who sailed from the U.S. on July 10, 1931. (Gold Star Pilgrimages, Quartermaster Files, RG 92, NA, Album 3)

to see the city before embarking on their voyage, which was accompanied by noticeably less fanfare than that of the white pilgrims.[20] Those who boarded the SS *American Merchant* hailed from a variety of states and represented almost every type of social background, from illiterate women to educated college graduates. For their journey, the War Department had assigned specially selected medical practitioners, including nurses, who were recruited from Harlem's hospitals, to dispense medical care to the passengers.[21]

General DeWitt had himself chartered their "B"-type freighter-passenger vessel, with a capacity of eighty-five cabin-class passengers, with the assumption that the voyages would go as planned. Publicly, his justification for this decision was that the government was unable to secure passage on any other transatlantic shipping company.[22] Once on board, the party had the entire ship, which allowed each mother access to the lower berth, so that no one was required to sleep on an upper bunk. According to their escort, Colonel Benjamin O. Davis, private rooms with bath were given to the older women.[23]

Colonel Davis, the army's highest-ranking black officer, claimed that it was an honor to be given the privilege of escorting the women, and he

Party E arriving at Gare des Invalides station in Paris where they were met by Noble Sissle and his orchestra. *Left to right:* Colonel Benjamin O. Davis, Mrs. Mitchell (the "Honor" Pilgrim), and Colonel Ellis. (Gold Star Pilgrimages, Quartermaster Files, RG 92, NA, Album 3)

brought his family along on the overseas crossing.[24] Before being asked to perform this special duty, Davis had been kept away from regular troops in assignments at black colleges and with black civilian components. At the time the pilgrimage offer came, he was a faculty member at Tuskegee Institute in Alabama, but he and his wife often spent their summers in Europe.

Once in France, the women rode in separate trains across the country-side to Paris, where they were greeted at the station by trumpeted notes of "Mammy" and other popular pieces.[25] Noble Sissle and his thirty-four-piece orchestra were waiting on the platform to welcome the women, with the veteran musician waving his baton in tailored elegance and grace in morning suit and white spats. "Bricktop," the black American female entertainer and genial proprietor of a Paris cabaret by the same name, joined Sissle with an assembled group of black Parisian women. They presented each pilgrim with a rose. Then, the band switched to "Onward Christian Soldiers," as the women were led away to their hotel.[26]

When questioned, Sissle told reporters that although he was opposed to segregation and he believed in fighting it, "those mothers should come to see the graves of their lost ones." He added, "I saw service during the war, and if I had fallen I would have liked to know that my mother had a chance to see my grave."[27]

The black Gold Star women enjoyed the same elegant restaurants and receptions offered on the white women's itinerary, but they benefited from one activity not experienced by their white counterparts. The entire party dined at Morgan's restaurant, where a Parisian "colored proprietor" had prepared a special meal of fried chicken and pie for them. He had also arranged for a "truck-load of watermelon" to be brought in from Algeria.[28] In the midst of all the attention showered on them, the women seemed to have little difficulty following General Pershing's advice when he welcomed them to France. He urged the bereaved mothers and widows to "try to get some pleasure and satisfaction out of the trip after they had mourned for their loves ones. 'The past cannot be recalled' he said."[29]

Walter White had hoped that when the mothers and widows understood the separate conditions that accompanied their travel, "they [would] repudiate the trip," but of all those who signed the petition against segregation, most seemed to do so without intending to decline the government's invitation.[30] The cost of forfeiting the once-in-a-lifetime offer had been too dear for the majority of black women to endure.

From the first sailings, the government appears to have held the upper hand, a pattern that continued each year thereafter. In 1930, 233 invitations were sent; 102 women accepted, 122 declined, and 9 did not reply. Of the declines, only 7 alleged discrimination, and 10 returned the government's form letter without comment. By comparison to their white counterparts, the aggregate number of eligible black women was too small to really make much of an impact on the government's attempts to segregate the pilgrimages. During the combined summers of 1930 and 1931, 168 black mothers and widows made the pilgrimage, compared to 5,251 white mothers during the same years.[31]

Major General Benjamin Cheatham, a retired quartermaster general, was recalled to active duty from May 10 to September 15, 1930, specifically to serve as general inspector for the pilgrimages. He and his quartermaster successor, General DeWitt, were ultimately responsible for the outcome of the pilgrimages, and together they welcomed expressions of gratitude from the black women as concurrence with their policies. General

Cheatham joined the initial voyage to oversee all details, believing that if the first group thoroughly enjoyed themselves, they would return home and spread the news to others. "It was I who . . . suggested sending them on a separate ship," he told the newspapers. "I am a Southerner. I knew the white people. I also know the colored people, and love them."[32] Both Cheatham and DeWitt comfortably assured the War Department that the women had been entirely satisfied "with all the arrangements made for their comfort, including the separate ship for them, and were most appreciative" of the government's offer.[33]

Indeed, many women did return from their pilgrimage without regret for having made such a compromise. One Georgia mother told reporters, "Every effort was made to get me not to come. I think it is a shame that some mothers were induced not to come by people who had nothing to lose, and who, if they were in our places, would certainly have come."[34] No one seems to have publicly challenged those who accepted the government's offer, which required of them a choice that white mothers and widows had not been asked to make.

Forced to choose between their race and national loyalty, motherhood proved to be the deciding factor. But, as in the past, the opportunity was lost for their common maternal bond to serve as a racially unifying force for all women. Their dead lay side by side in the overseas cemeteries, regardless of color; however, the pilgrims maintained the status that prevailed at home, where women's organizations were not racially integrated. To do so would have weakened the majority and their power.[35]

In exchange for allowing the exploitation of their motherhood status, black women received recognition and an opportunity to perpetuate the memory of those they had lost. Ultimately, both races participated in the pilgrimage on the government's terms, making the concessions it demanded and furthering ideologies that served its political ends.[36]

With the passing of each year's pilgrimage, the nation's black media continued to condemn the segregation. "I hope that you are as broad in dealing with this situation as the Negroes in this country were in helping to elect Mr. Roosevelt to office," wrote the editor of the *Chicago Review* in 1933.[37] Letters deploring the injustice continued to arrive at the War Department, but these efforts were no match for the expressions of gratitude from pilgrims who had made the exciting journey.[38] Returning women all agreed, "segregation or no segregation, [they] had done the right thing in making the trip."[39] The national protest continued to raise awareness but never managed to produce one integrated pilgrimage.

If Walter White's efforts had succeeded in 1930, the pilgrimages could not have gone ahead as a national venture, since doing so would have been unthinkable for the southern states. Estimates are that twenty-three women, no longer remembered, refused the government's offer at the urging of the NAACP. And although they may not have achieved their objective of an integrated pilgrimage, they succeeded in shifting the balance of power nationally by questioning the democratic principles over which the war had been fought.[40]

General John L. DeWitt's responsibility for the segregation of the Gold Star Mothers may also be long forgotten, but his role in spearheading the internment of Japanese Americans in camps during the Second World War has not been. Ironically, Representative Oscar De Priest lost his congressional seat in 1934 when he was defeated by Arthur W. Mitchell, the first black Democrat ever elected to Congress.[41]

23

Highballs on the High Seas

Where the welfare and comfort of the Gold Star mothers and widows were concerned, the army overlooked nothing to ensure the success of its high-profile public-relations venture. For the military escorts, the moments before sailing were fraught with detail. On the morning of departure, officers were responsible for inspecting all equipment, from coffins to deck chairs and from blankets and cushions to table settings and cabin assignments.[1] The paperwork was enormously time consuming and included passenger lists, baggage lists, passports, train assignments, customs and debarkation cards, and reports of innumerable variety. As the women climbed the gangplank, an identity badge pinned to their coat and a gold medal swaying from their neck, they could not have helped but notice all that had been organized on their behalf.

In preparation for the pilgrimages, Colonel Richard T. Ellis, the officer in charge, sought and received permission to rearrange French custom to suit the military and its American visitors. Throughout the journey, administrative inconveniences and standard French bureaucratic procedures were eliminated. Namely, allowances were made for American physicians to care for the pilgrims (foreigners were normally forbidden to practice in the country); between Cherbourg and Paris, special trains with additional dining cars were arranged for the group; all national museums and places of artistic interest granted access at reduced entrance fees; approval was obtained for cars to park in places usually prohibited; vehicles transporting the women were allowed to travel through the Bois de Boulogne (a privilege never previously agreed to); and Invalides Station (normally reserved for state occasions) was made available for the pilgrims' train.

Similar favors were also arranged with hotels to offer an "American breakfast" instead of the traditional light Continental fare. French bus companies were asked to provide "luxury" vehicles with the latest safety devices and blankets for the pilgrims. And since it was reported that insufficient toilet facilities could be located near the cemeteries, fashionable "rest houses" were constructed on the grounds. According to Colonel Ellis, these houses were akin to those "one would expect to find in an attractive country-club," yet they were completed in just ninety days.[2]

The order of departure by states was determined by First Lady Hoover, who drew lots to prioritize the invitation list early in 1930.[3] By May, women from all across the United States began arriving by train for embarkation in New York. Some were so poor that they lacked even the funds with which to purchase the needed clothing and additional accessories.[4] Others, such as Mrs. Louise Ziegler, were in poor health and had never traveled far from home before. Fearing that she could not make the pilgrimage alone, Ziegler requested and received permission for her daughter, Grace, to accompany her. In order to pay her own expenses, Grace agreed to write a series of articles for the local paper based on their adventure. Her lively descriptions capture their experiences throughout the pilgrimage, including their train journey from Durand, Illinois, in a parlor car to Chicago, where she noted that "Mamma got her first taste of real service." They grinned to each other as the porter hung their coats for them and put a cushion under their feet. Grace recalled, "I told her she [Louise] would have to get used to service, but I didn't realize then how much truth I spoke." Once they arrived in Chicago, a red-cap attendant and two train officials were waiting and guided them to their New York–bound train.[5]

Once the women were settled into their accommodation, usually the Hotel Pennsylvania, they were greeted by civic officials at a City Hall reception. The following day, they joined other passengers aboard luxury liners, but the mothers continued to receive every honor. By midmorning, bouillon was served on deck, and in the afternoon tea and sandwiches were available, in addition to a full lunch and lavish evening meals. Like other women not used to such luxury, Grace and her mother enjoyed the hot and cold "soft water" in their cabin, along with the ice water, electric heater and fan, and comfortable beds. "The floor was covered with a thick carpet and the walls were painted ivory," they remembered. There was a swimming pool with the sea "flowing in and out of the pool," which Louise Ziegler recalled was "very beautiful." They were especially taken by the "modernistic talkies" shown every night and the night club on board all decorated in red and gold. The dining hall and social room contained a balcony and grand staircase, and there were tea concerts each afternoon at four o'clock.[6]

Mrs. Fannie Thompson of Party "N" tossing a wreath overboard in memory of her son, Private Francis Condon, who was drowned when the SS *Ticonderoga* was torpedoed off the Irish Coast. (Gold Star Pilgrimages, Quartermaster Files, RG 92, NA, Album 1)

The absence of ceremony upon arrival at the graveside did not preclude observances on the high seas. Midway across the Atlantic, the ship's captain stopped the vessel in order to pay tribute to those who had perished at sea. The oldest mother was selected to toss a wreath overboard, and the chief steward assigned the orchestra to "render appropriate sacred music" as everyone observed a moment of silence. Afterward, a "hydrographic drift bottle" containing the names of all the ship's pilgrims was tossed overboard, presumably in an effort to avert any prolonged contemplation that might result in uncomfortable displays of emotion.[7]

Families who lost loved ones at sea appear to have been an afterthought to the legislators who amended the original Gold Star Pilgrimage Act of March 2, 1929. Over a year later, the law was extended to those buried at sea and those whose place of interment was unknown.[8] By the close of 1929, there were still 1,642 bodies of unknown soldiers buried in the eight permanent cemeteries and an additional 653 soldiers presumed to be dead but whose bodies were never recovered. Statistics vary considerably, but the army's Surgeon General Report for 1919 claims that 479 soldiers died en route overseas and were buried at sea, and another 675 members of the navy and Marine Corps were lost at sea. These figures increased the number of those eligible for the pilgrimage and raised costs an additional 10.8 percent.[9] However, the delay before the bill's final amendment gave Congress time to estimate the affordability of additional numbers and potential expenses based on the responses of the first group of women.

Although the calculated increase benefited hundreds of women, it also signaled a reluctance to acknowledge those who did not die a manly death on the battlefield but who fell victim to pneumonia or the flu. Loved ones at home, such as young Essie Bishop, were quick to defend men like her husband, Robert, who died of pneumonia before arriving overseas. Essie, widowed six months after marriage, wrote, "[He] was not in the service long enough to accomplish very much, . . . [but] I believe he would have made a brave soldier, any way. He was my soldier and I want my little boy to feel proud of his 'Daddy' even though he saw no active service."[10] Despite the nuanced apology often apparent in the words of the grieving, they were anxious to confirm that their loss was equally worthy of the same rites of remembrance. "Even though he died at sea before reaching the scene of actual battle," wrote one company commander, "he died a hero beloved by his fellow comrades and respected."[11]

For some families, an unknown grave in France was preferable to the thought of their loved one being buried at sea. When Leslie M. Gower of Clarksville, Tennessee, died of pneumonia on board a ship heading to France, the War Department's telegram announced that he had been buried at sea. But the official cable was later contradicted by news from the GRS that he was buried in France, a case still unresolved four years later, when Mr. Gower wrote, "I ask you as a special favor, when you clear up the error where my son was [buried] . . . keep it on record and not notify me about it as it has nearly broken his mothers [sic] heart to think he was buried at sea."[12]

As the historian Carol Byerly has noted, America's "ratio of deaths-from-disease to deaths-from-combat was worse than the other belligerents,"[13] a fact not particularly welcomed by the army's Medical Department. More than half the American dead had succumbed to disease, but the government endeavored to treat their deaths with the same honorable burial. Those who died of disease were buried right alongside those

General Sir Fabian Ware conversing with a pilgrim of Party "H" at the entrance to
the Hostess House of the Brookwood Cemetery in England, July 1930. (Gold Star Pilgrimages, Quartermaster Files, RG 92, NA, Album 2)

who died in combat, unless they happened to die on transports heading
overseas.

Once each pilgrimage party arrived at its first-class hotel in Paris or
London, the women would spend a week there and then travel to the cemeteries and other points of interest. Colonel Ellis had arranged for each
woman to receive a Michelin folding map on which were listed the key
places they visited. Along the way, the French and British governments
honored the women with formal functions presided over by General Pershing and military dignitaries of the host nation.

Generally, the itinerary remained the same for all groups, with the exception of one independently arranged "reunion" voyage of the 27th Division. After the first contingent of pilgrims got under way on May 7, 1930,
the second sailing was expected to follow with equal aplomb on May
13. This voyage was coordinated by the Honorable J. Mayhew "Colonel"
Wainwright (1864–1945), former staff officer with the 27th National Guard

Division and Republican representative for New York. Colonel Wainwright had persuaded the army to allow a group of Gold Star women to accompany veterans of the 27th Division who had served in the same unit as the women's deceased. He envisaged this sailing as a way of taking more of the mothers and widows overseas, including those previously excluded from the government's pilgrimage, if they chose to pay their own expenses.[14] With such attention to detail, it seemed nothing could go wrong, but the War Department had little control over accidents and mechanical failures occurring aboard the ships, nor had it sufficiently prepared for the late enrollment of passenger Mathilda Burling.[15]

Just as Wainwright's reunion voyage prepared to sail out of New York Harbor, an accident aboard another vessel required those Gold Star pilgrims to relocate onto the SS *Republic,* with the women and veterans of the 27th Division.[16] All were asked to share cabin space, thus making four to a stateroom. It was not long before the bickering began aboard the crowded ship, with many questioning the presence of the overbearing Burling on their "reunion" pilgrimage. There seemed to be no clear reason for her to have joined them, since her son had not been a member of the 27th Division. Some said that New York's mayor, Jimmy Walker, had invited her, while others were certain that "some Congressman had done it." One woman seemed to speak for many when she stated, "I think it would have been a most happy trip had Mrs. Burling not been there."[17]

The unfortunate individual chosen to escort these women was Lieutenant Colonel Stephen W. Winfree, a cavalry officer with a preference for civilian attire, an eye for young women, and a thirst for highballs. Winfree had been warned by the quartermaster general's office that the trip could be troublesome, and organizers explained that they would have gladly receded from the ordeal if it had been possible. The escorting officer was also informed that Mrs. Burling would be joining the voyage and that she was a "nuisance" who could pose problems for him. She was, in the words of his informants, a "woman politician."[18]

Mathilda Burling's political abilities had previously helped bring the pilgrimage legislation to fruition just as New Era American women were similarly attempting to carve out a place for themselves within the emerging state bureaucracy. By contrast, Burling's successful campaign on behalf of the Gold Star pilgrims depended on a narrow interpretation of maternalism, one confined to femininity, frailty, and nationalist ideals.[19] Her rhetorical pleas before Congress had reinforced the virtues of patriotic motherhood, and now, aboard ship, the military and her fellow passengers presumed that she would embrace her role as a mother rather than a politician. However, these expectations were quickly dashed.

Within weeks of the group's return to the United States on June 13, an official military investigation was launched in response to numerous complaints received by the War Department from women on board the crowded SS *Republic*. They wrote begrudgingly about the quality of their hotels and of the unsuitable conditions on the ship but also, more seriously, "of neglect and mismanagement . . . by Colonel Winfree." They accused their military escort of "drunkenness, failure to wear uniform and misconduct while on duty." That was a particularly serious accusation in view of the explicit attempts by the War Department to ensure that the pilgrimage be "successfully conducted in a manner to avoid any criticism on account of lack of services or attention."[20]

For more than a month during the summer of 1930, the War Department's Office of the Inspector General received the testimony of more than thirty individuals. Investigators were determined to keep the case confidential, so inquiry was confined to those who had had contact with Winfree—passengers and select military officers—in addition to the accused. It soon became clear that Mathilda Burling was the object of complaint as much as, if not more than, Winfree. Many women in their confusion mistakenly believed that Burling served in some official capacity with the War Department and that she had been solely responsible for the bill that made the Gold Star Mothers pilgrimage possible.[21] Ironically, Burling's abilities as a self-promoter and chief organizer risked endangering the success of the pilgrimage she had worked so hard to gain.

The inspector general's official report stated that "Mrs. Burling appear[ed] to have been active and aggressive from the time the pilgrims began to arrive in NY." She "frequented the hotels where the pilgrims were being accommodated and endeavored to perfect the GSM organization and to collect dues from them." In her efforts to "assume prominence among the pilgrims," she gave the impression that "she was clothed in some official authority on the trip." She was accused of insulting her fellow passengers, stirring discontent among the women by attempting to lead the group, and generally causing "friction" and "bitter resentment." "She's . . . constantly collecting money," alleged one woman. "She carries on as if she was sixteen years old." "She can't speak good English," said another, who claimed that Burling grabbed every man in sight and "would not leave him alone." "She had pictures taken with every man who was there." "It is out of place for a gold star mother dancing and joking every night and I was disgusted. I did not go to my son's wedding, I went to my son's grave," and on they grumbled.[22]

In her defense, Burling told the military examiners that Winfree gave all his time to "the young folks and not to the mothers." She explained that he was often out of uniform and that one night she had seen Winfree "standing at the bar very much under the influence of liquor and also drinking highballs." Burling's testimony revealed that she and her friend Mrs. Lawrence had chosen to venture into the hotel lobby around midnight to "mail some letters" when she saw Winfree enjoying a drink with a young woman, in his civilian clothes. When both mothers refused to imbibe, he reportedly told Burling, "You are a little virgin, a little white lily; I'd like to take you out and get you tight just to see what you would do." An indignant Burling turned to the bartender, and she claimed to have responded, "To think that I have left my only child over here and he was only eighteen."[23]

When she asked Winfree why he was not wearing his uniform, Burling testified that the officer replied, "What do you want me to do, wear the uniform and look like a porter and carry the mothers' pocketbooks and handbags?" Aside from Burling's companion, Mrs. Lawrence, there were no others present except for the bartender and the young lady drinking with the colonel. Burling alleged that Winfree even referred to the pilgrims as "finicky old women," before he expressed doubts about her own veracity: "I don't even know whether you have a boy over here or not." Burling's testimony continued for fifteen pages before reaching Winfree's last comment, spoken the night before they returned to the United States:

> It is women like you, foolish women like you, and men like Congressman O'Connor and his political friends who put over things like this. The idea asking the Government to send mothers over to their son's graves here. Why aren't you American mothers like the women over here in France[?] They go out and work every day and they have forgotten long ago about their son's being dead. Why all this fuss bringing the mothers all the way over here just to see their son's graves[?][24]

This last comment proved to be most devastating for the colonel, who was relieved of duty that summer for drunkenness, neglect, misconduct, and failure to wear his uniform. In his defence, Winfree told investigators that Mathilda Burling had been a "constant nuisance" to him throughout the tour and "did more to create discontent among the members of the party than any other factor."[25]

Without the testimony of impartial witnesses, we can never be certain what took place during that midnight encounter, but the military's swift response indicates that sufficient evidence existed to prevent them from taking a further risk with the accused. The outspoken cavalry officer had voiced, rather abrasively, what some in the military had previously only dared to allude to in their private memoranda. Major X. H. Price, the active-duty, long-serving secretary of the ABMC, spoke in similar derisive terms toward the amendment that allowed mothers and widows of the missing to join the trip to Europe. In the months preceding those congressional deliberations, Price wrote that allowing these additional women to join the pilgrimage was, in his opinion, "absurd and can only be considered as a reward for those who lost husbands and sons in Europe during the war and therefore could, with equal justice, be applied to the relatives of the men whose bodies were returned home."[26]

Both officers' words reveal frustration with America's prosperous postwar society, which undervalued and overlooked its surviving soldiers who continued to serve long after the armistice. Theirs was an organization in crisis, an army in limbo struggling to modernize without sufficient resources to do so. Throughout the 1920s, the military was subjected to relentless fiscal cuts, which, in addition to tight budgets, meant understaffed units and slow promotions. According to Edward Coffman, the military's transportation budget was stretched to the point that the chief of staff and his aide could not afford to travel in a Pullman compartment when they took the train to inspect posts. Military units had to beg outside local sources for office supplies, and even the daily ration of toilet paper was limited to three sheets for each soldier. Yet, while the military struggled, the indulgences and approbation shown the GSM was flaunted before the nation.[27]

Burling, for her part, was determined to perpetuate the republican motherhood image that had brought her the personal prestige and power to influence the nation's war memory. Winfree, on the other hand, questioned these maternal verisimilitudes and threatened her authority. In an ironic twist, fate had brought these two opposing forces together aboard the one vessel that sailed without the strict controls imposed on the other pilgrim ships.

Although Winfree denied all accusations against him, he succumbed to the manipulative political matriarch, who, it seemed, had at last gained the recognition she craved. But ultimately it was Winfree who exposed her greatest weakness before the others, that being her motherhood. When at last she reached St. Mihiel American Cemetery, the aim of more than ten years' work, Burling stood less than five minutes before the grave of her son because she was eager to attend a reception at another cemetery. She became indignant at Winfree's refusal to allow her to leave for what promised to be a more high-profile event. With hostility and angry impatience, Burling informed Winfree that this grave was, after all, only that of her stepson.[28]

The dramatic irony that Mathilda Burling brings to this scene through her admission is palpable. She stands as the antithesis of the republican mother image despite her skillful use of its patriotic rhetoric. Her driving ambition, though for an admirable cause, seems to have been fueled by her own need for self-aggrandizement, and as far as we know, no one but Winfree managed to confront her directly. Moreover, the tension these two characters brought to the moment exposes the fragility and possibly the crest of the republican motherhood myth. Had politics corrupted Mathilda Burling, or had the nation lost its innocence during those comfortable but cynical years of the 1920s?

Whereas the government strived to perpetuate the virtues of the Gold Star women, showering them with recognition and publicly rewarding them for their selfless sacrifice, popular culture of the period treated this image with a healthy dose of skepticism. In 1933, Hollywood brought the Gold Star Mothers saga to the silver screen in a humorous yet slightly melancholic portrayal entitled *Pilgrimage*.[29] The producer, John Ford, sets mother against widow in this unconventional story that illuminates the increasing resentment that many people felt toward the war by the mid-1930s. The leading character of the mother is depicted as a jealous, possessive woman who, angry and intolerant of her son's love for a local girl, sends him off to France, where he is killed. In one revealing scene, the aging mother of the deceased soldier is being persuaded by the mayor and others in her small rural community to join the pilgrimages. They insist that her participation will bring recognition to the area and serve as a remembrance of their contribution to the war effort. She reluctantly agrees to go, but once in France, she has no desire to visit her son's grave. Through an unlikely turn of events, she experiences a moment of epiphany at the film's end when she exclaims, "I killed him," as she accepts responsibility for her son's death.[30]

F. Scott Fitzgerald renders a somewhat more endearing portrait of the Gold Star Mothers in *Tender Is the Night*. While in Europe, Dick and Nicole Diver and their dissolute friends notice a party of women at another table and ask the waiter who they are. "Those are the gold-star muzzas," explains the waiter. "In their happy faces, the dignity that surrounded and pervaded the party, he perceived all the maturity of an older America," Fitzgerald writes. For a brief moment, Dick Diver muses that the mothers' presence and mourning for their dead adds beauty to the room, but then he shrugs off this illusion. "Almost with an effort he turned back to his two women at the table and faced the whole new world in which he believed," suggesting a sobering return to reality.[31]

By 1935, motherhood's sacred, privileged position had shifted. The transition is marked by a scathing satirical piece featured in *Esquire* magazine in which Philip Stevenson depicts the Gold Star pilgrims as cows. In thinly veiled repartee, self-righteous maternal figures "Mrs. Holstein" and "Mrs. Jersey" portray a disturbing lack of sadness or regret for having sent their sons to die. On the contrary, one of them suggests, "To Give Peace you must Endure Slaughter." With no pretense toward modesty, the speaker proclaims that nothing is too good for them since they (and not their sons) were the "Flower of the Flock, the Blue Ribbon Winners, the very Spirit of Giving." Addressing her bovine cohorts, the speaker recalls with distasteful candor that their sons should be remembered "all clean and pink and white and refrigerated. . . . Never once did I think of our boys as dead."[32]

Stevenson's fantasy implies that the Gold Star pilgrimage to the "Valley of the Departed" was an occasion for celebration and not sadness. Mrs. Jersey tells the group, "not one of us cried. It was really marvelous." Death is seen as clean and merciful to the speaker, who leaves her audience with a final thought: "If all the ladies in our little group could see this, they would never again pass resolutions asking to have Their Boys brought home." Instead, "They'd be delighted with how marvelous everything is done Over There."[33]

Government officials could not have predicted this drastic reversal of opinion and the harsh treatment soon to be doled out to the Gold Star Mothers and their long-awaited journey. The earnestness with which the War Department investigated the women's complaints, the extent of its logistical planning, the lavish accommodations it provided, and its carefully chosen staff reflect its determination to ensure the event's success.

The ambitious undertaking is certainly without precedent in the annals of national commemorative enterprise, particularly in light of its remarkable timing and the associated degree of financial investment. Even so, can one interpret this act of remembrance solely as a deed of sheer government benevolence following, as it does, more than a decade after the loss? Were the pilgrimages as designed by the War Department a success? Did they put a sense of closure to the grieving process? I turn now to the Gold Star pilgrims for their response.

24

A Personal Experience

The Gold Star pilgrimages were paraded before the world in a colorful array of guises and pretexts that included heartfelt images of democratic solidarity, American homogeneity, a peace mission, and a gesture from a grateful nation. But behind this public façade, shades of hypocrisy, petty politics, prejudice, and jealousy lingered, effectively obscuring what might have been a more authentic personal experience.

Were these pilgrimages, as conceived by the War Department, ever intended to serve as an opportunity for resolving grief? Perhaps the previous twelve years had healed old wounds so well that there was no need for resolution. On that voyage, aboard the floating microcosm of American society, death—purportedly the great equalizer—had mobilized the living, but had the women's pilgrimage truly brought them inner peace?

Reading through journals and other trace remnants left by the pilgrims, it becomes evident that for most of the women, thoughts of the deceased were overshadowed by the novelty of their adventure. Presumably, this journey would have prompted childhood memories and poignant reflections of last moments spent with their loved ones, and indeed they may have; however, these expressions, for the most part, are absent from the records. Could the emotive sight of thousands of white crosses have caused these pilgrims no evidence of pain? Officials prepared for fits of female hysteria, but of the more than six thousand who participated, only two women were admitted for mental health care.[1] Instead, a lacuna seems to have existed where grief should have been.

The women invited to join the pilgrimage had, for the most part, supported a nationalist ideology by agreeing to leave their sons and husbands buried overseas. Public expressions of grief would have been an admittance of doubt concerning the righteousness of their beloved's sacrifice and their own decision to leave the deceased buried so far from home. Nevertheless, by bringing these pilgrims face to face with their loss, the military risked triggering suppressed emotions that might have overshadowed the war's perceived accomplishments, something it earnestly hoped to avoid.

On the final night of the eastward crossing, before arriving in France, the women were feted with an elaborate farewell dinner. Grace Ziegler described in her journal the jovial atmosphere in the ship's luxurious dining hall, where they were given dunce caps, rattlers, and balloons. "We laughed ourselves sick over the sight of each other in our hats," Grace recalled.[2] After dinner, a photographer captured the moment that she predicted would probably be the "one delightful experience" of her mother's life.

Grace and her mother, Louise, a hard-working woman of German descent, compiled a scrapbook of their journey that showed no indication of remorse, sentimentality, or bitterness over the loss of Louise's only son. Except for the inclusion of a gold medal embossed with a star, their souvenirs were typical of most tourists: postcards, numerous photos, identity cards, brochures, and ribbons. In the margins, lively captions conveyed the lavish splendor and pampering bestowed on them; these were the trimmings that served to reinforce the value of the sacrifice they had made for the nation.

Once the pilgrims disembarked, the nearest encounter any of them had with funerary activities came from observing the ones taking place in France. Gold Star women were often fascinated by the melancholic events and recorded their observations with uncanny similarity to the American Legion auxiliary eyewitnesses years before. As they were leaving, the Zieglers watched a procession through the streets of Paris in which, Grace noticed, "The hearse was drawn by two black horses but all the people walked." She added, "The people wear black dresses. . . . It seems very depressing."[3]

The cultural differences between the old and new worlds are compelling and were clearly evident to the Americans, who seemed uncomfortable with the depth of emotion typically displayed in French mourning customs. Before leaving the ship, each woman was presented with a little silk sack made with the joined flags of France and the United States and filled with French soil. "We thought that you might like to take home with you this little memorial present, from your pious pilgrimage to France," the note read. The French cultural exchange association, La Bienvenue Française, had prepared the poignant offering in the belief that the American women would appreciate a sample of their nation's sacred ground during these pilgrimage days "of emotion" and remembrance.[4] The incongruity of this touching gesture with the party favors and souvenirs distributed by the shipping lines is telling.

During the war and the days immediately following the armistice, countless French and American women shared a close, mutual bond, particularly as firsthand information concerning the dead and missing was so anxiously sought by families in the United States. To facilitate this exchange, the American Red Cross recast an organization with its roots in Clara Barton's Civil War Soldier's Information Bureau and called it simply "the service of home communication." "Sensible, sympathetic women" known as "searchers" visited hospitals and military camps to obtain information concerning those soldiers who were missing and presumed dead, then they corresponded with families, passing on the circumstances of death and burial details.[5] This familiar obsession with the details surrounding the beloved's last moments alive may be perceived as macabre, but such understanding offered a sense of finality. It also helped the living make sense of what may have seemed like a questionable, if not meaningless, loss.[6]

In February 1919, Madame Thérèze H. Collinot, of Rouelles, a village in the Marne region, wrote to the Paris communication service hoping to learn more about the death of Lieutenant Vernon D. Hart, of the 90th Division. Hart, from Stamford, Texas, was billeted with the Collinot family before his tragic death on the morning of September 14, 1918, when a machine-gun bullet struck his mouth as he peered up over the rim of his shell hole. For months, Madame Collinot attempted to locate his burial place to convey this information to his mother, Mrs. Julia Duggan Hart.[7]

The two women began an endearing exchange that undoubtedly comforted both during those grief-stricken days soon after Vernon Hart's death: "Poor dear madame, poor unknown friend, I have known since the 28th of September that our dear Lieutenant and friend is no more—that he was killed on the Lorraine front. I have wept for him and I still weep; not a day passes that we do not speak of him and I never sleep without reliving in a dream the pleasant time which he spent here."[8] Eventually, Madame Collinot was able to relay the circumstances of Vernon's death to his mother and to reassure her that his grave was identified and cared for.

The women's friendship continued to strengthen as they shared family news as well as hopes that Mrs. Hart would soon have her son's body back home with her. The Collinot family, and others like them, assumed care of the American graves until they were removed from the area and consolidated into the national cemetery at Romagne-Montfaucon. Meanwhile, life in France had begun to return to normal, according to Madame

Collinot. News of weddings and birthday celebrations filled her letters, but with the Christmas holiday of 1920 came the lingering sadness of their loss. "In our little country we have suffered too much morally from the war to find holidays joyous. My husband was saying to me the other day, 'It seems to me that the dead reproach us for our gaiety.'" In closing, Madame Collinot added, "I have suffered in your grief. . . . To think of all this grieves me and I think only of it in the evenings now that the wind blows hard and the rains falls."[9]

Such profound expressions of pathos and suffering did not usually surface in the letters of Americans who attempted to comfort one another; instead, their letters were filled with words of strength, purpose, and courage. When Julia Hart's brother wrote to her months after Vernon's death, there was a striking dissimilarity with that of her French correspondent: "We must view his sorrow in a 'dispassionate' manner. . . . Meet your obligations to others; you must rise above despondency and conquer the conflicting sentiments that are overwhelming you. You must take facts as they really are. No sacrifice on your part can bring back the loss, but to make good the loss you must strive all the more."[10]

Julia Hart chose to have her son's body returned from France and buried in San Saba, Texas, where she was laid to rest beside him upon her death in 1970. Vernon's final burial place was never questioned by the Hart family, but others found this grim and weighty decision more than they could bear.

Mrs. Nancy Marsh, the fifty-two-year-old widow of an Episcopal chaplain from Nebraska, sailed on one of the last pilgrimages of 1933. After declining the government's invitation for several consecutive years, Mrs. Marsh agreed to go in 1933, accompanied by her sons. Judging from the many complaints brought against her by other passengers and accompanying officials, she was still carrying considerable anger and resentment over her husband's tragic death when she boarded the SS *Washington.*

Military reports claim that the widow chose not to wear her Gold Star badge and even removed the Gold Star marking on her deck chair. She replaced it with one she had written, which read, "Mrs. Marsh." Fellow passengers reported her to the authorities when she told them to take off their "dog tags," referring to the gold star badges furnished by the War Department. Nancy Marsh requested the doctor's attention numerous times with a variety of complaints but never seemed to be in her cabin when he and the nurse called. The physician's notes state that she was "a rather uncooperative patient."[11]

Memories of that tragic time nearly fifteen years before must have filled her mind during the long overseas crossing. Her husband, Lieutenant (The Reverend) Arthur H. Marsh, had died of bronchial pneumonia in October 1918, although the church news bulletin stated that he was "mortally wounded while ministering to the men of his command at the front."[12] Two months later, Marsh's widow wrote to the War Department urging officials to please send further facts concerning his death and place of burial since she knew only that he had died "from wounds received in action."[13] Early the following year, the chaplain who had presided over Lieutenant Marsh's burial wrote her that he died of the effects of gas at an American hospital.

Before becoming an Episcopal priest, Arthur Marsh had been Nebraska's first Rhodes Scholar. He studied for several years at Keble College, in Oxford, England, before returning to Washington, DC, where he married Nancy in 1914. Arthur Marsh's elderly parents were English, and although they were temporarily living in the United States at the time of their son's death, they planned to return home in the near future. Nancy, an educated woman from Virginia, wanted desperately to be near her husband's final resting place. In the midst of her painful indecision, she wrote to the War Department once more, hoping for guidance as she struggled with the distressing options:

> I cannot decide what to do. I find that my hand refuses to write the order that he stay "over there" and yet there seems nothing else to do. . . . There is just one thing that shows one ray of hope: can I be buried in France with him? If I could have that to look forward to, I think that I [could] endure the years and I can not write a card saying he is to stay unless I can go to him. . . . If you can help me you will brighten all my future years.[14]

Her letter crossed Chaplain Charles Pierce's desk in September 1919, well before the final policy for repatriation of the dead had been firmly established. Pierce had been asked to prepare an official response for the adjutant general, Major General P. C. Harris, in which he advised that no provision had been made for the burial of relatives in the overseas cemeteries. In official tones, Pierce suggested that the writer "arrive at her own decision" but added that she might "consider the wisdom of leaving her husband's body permanently in whatever [cemetery] may be chosen . . . [with] those who were his comrades in a historic struggle."[15] General

Harris added simply that he could not advise her, which was undoubtedly of little assistance to the distraught widow; however, he did suggest that she take her time replying, since it would "probably be some months" before the government was ready to begin the actual transportation of bodies to the United States.

Nancy Marsh could not have known that the person whom she had asked for advice had suffered his own cruel loss just two weeks after her husband was killed. Captain Charles Harris, the adjutant general's son, was struck by machine-gun fire and died in an enemy field hospital on October 20, 1918.[16] General Harris's experience with the Graves Registration Service was not one that might have prompted him to express great optimism in its care, however. When he learned in early 1919 that soldiers' remains in isolated graves were to be removed to a central cemetery, he wrote and asked that his son be permitted to rest where he was first interred, but his letter did not reach its recipient in time. Consequently, Captain Harris's body was inadvertently removed to the Romagne-sous-Montfaucon cemetery. While attempting to reassure the distressed Nancy Marsh of the government's superb care, Chaplain Pierce, as chief of the GRS, was forced to explain to the general that they were unable to locate his son's remains.

In the confusion, Harris's body was transferred to several different burial places while Pierce attempted to respond to yet another, eerily intuitive, plea from Nancy Marsh: "I hate to have his dear body handled in this manner, so carelessly as if it were not the core of my heart . . . and the hope of my life to come. Please help and tell me all you know about it."[17]

At last, in the spring of 1921, Nancy Marsh made her decision, but her final words to Charles Pierce hint that the long months of indecision had hardened her: "I have decided to leave my husband's body in France. At least I am almost reconciled to his death [and] had he lived they might have made an undertaker of him also."[18] Mrs. Marsh's cutting words suggest that the same lack of information that caused other reflective, sensitive family members such agonizing indecision had, likewise, taken its toll on her.

Uncertainty and doubt also plagued the General and Mrs. Harris, who watched with painful expectancy in Washington, DC, for news of their son's remains. In August 1921, the long-awaited hour finally arrived. The Harrises were driven to the pier at Hoboken, New Jersey, where a small room had been set aside with what was believed to be the remains of Captain Charles Harris. The General had not been satisfied with the identification process and asked to inspect the body himself, whereupon he observed various personal possessions and a marking on a piece of clothing. Mrs. Harris was able to identify the inscription, and from this evidence they "were satisfied that the identification was positive."[19]

This visual reassurance, though undoubtedly gruesome to behold, was a distinct advantage of rank and privilege to which few other families were entitled. Such material evidence put a sharp end to denial, yet thousands of Americans mourned without benefit of any physical remains, choosing instead a grave on foreign soil. Those families mourning soldiers who died without their identity intact, or whose remains were forever obliterated, were spared this agonizing decision since fate had made the final judgment.

The weight of the difficult postwar burial decision meant that for many families, the cemetery visit proved the climax of their pilgrimage experience. Consequently, officials had orchestrated this moment with the utmost precision, but for some, such as Belle Harner, who sailed with the Gold Star Mothers to France in the second year of the pilgrimages, there was no named grave to kneel before. Her son's body had never been recovered but was believed buried at the Oise-Aisne American Cemetery, where she visited on August 18, 1931. Her journal describes how each pilgrim relative of an unidentified soldier was given a large wreath of "natural flowers" and escorted to another part of the cemetery. Each woman was asked to choose a random headstone marking the burial place of an unknown, and there she laid her wreath.[20] Afterward, a photograph was taken of Mrs. Harner beside the headstone, just as it was done for the others. Mrs. Harner made no mention of the emotional impact of this visit, referring only to the rose wreath, the photographer, and the lovely gardens. There was no physical, identifiable remnant of her son's presence in this place and no satisfactory response to questions about the location of his death, despite Mrs. Harner's inquiry to her escort.

After Belle Harner noticed that the names of the unknown had not yet been inscribed on the chapel walls, she recorded her disappointment over the lack of any material representation to her son's memory. "When I was in France," she wrote, "I felt nearer to Marvin than at any other time. But, I still do not know the exact spot where he is. When the train pulled out of Paris, I felt like I was leaving him behind."[21] One cannot help but feel the sense of futility in Mrs. Harner's words as she returned home from her long journey without benefit of a grave, a place of death, or even an engraved name. Her experience testifies to the significance of physical remains or at least the desire for graven evidence of a former identity to those determined to preserve their memories.

Privately, some pilgrims' voices seem to suggest that things had still not been set aright. "I think it was heartbreaking to have to spend three successive days in the cemetery. If you could go one day and come back the next and say goodbye, but three days [are] too long and it was damp and cold there," wrote one mother. She added, "We expected to see something besides the graves on such a long trip."[22] Although her reaction is not rare, most women did view the pilgrimage in a positive light and expressed gratitude to the government, but this appreciation was often mingled with varying degrees of ambivalence:

I intended to write the Government to thank them for the privilege of standing at my son's grave and it was a great comfort to see the beautiful cemetery and I think they were very kind to us but I feel there was just a little bit something wrong. The 27th Division veterans had the best accommodations and service and . . . I heard that they hired the [SS] Republic outright and after Wall Street fell they took the mothers to help them out to pay for the ship and then treated them like dogs.[23]

In fact, the 27th Division had warmly invited the Gold Star women long before the October 1929 stock market crash, as its reunion brochure confirms.[24] Yet there remained for some of the women a lingering sense that their sacrifice may not have been appreciated. How much recognition would it take to atone for such a loss, if such expiation were even possible?

Few of the women who recorded their impressions failed to comment on the French cemeteries they passed. Remarks such as that expressed by Mrs. Harner were not unique: "I am sorry that the French have not been able to provide beautiful cemeteries for their dead. Those bleak wooden crosses make my heart bleed for the French Gold Star Mothers."[25] By contrast, most of the women were fascinated by the beauty of the American cemeteries and the care given to each grave there. Although souvenir itineraries and scrapbook photos reveal the presence of Gold Star pilgrims in front of monuments still under construction, the women's words rarely, if ever, mentioned visiting the spectacular ABMC sites. Sprinkled amid

Gold Star mothers and widows arriving at the Belleau Aisne Cemetery, undated.

recollections of French food, luxurious accommodation, and references to their traveling companions, the cemeteries dominated most memories. Thus, it seems that Pershing and his colleagues achieved their objective in making the American cemeteries a dominant feature of the heritage landscape.

On Memorial Day, the small American flags positioned by each grave showcased the freshly manicured lawns where the nation's dead lie buried. As dignitaries presided over ceremonies of rigid protocol, military guards fired volleys in solemn salute while men spoke from decorated platforms of the sacrifices previously made. The beauty and parklike settings of these cemeteries effectively hid the ugliness and morbidity of death, transforming grief into a softened, gilded version of loss while contributing to the myth of the fallen soldier.

If these women felt any anguish or doubt over their decision to leave loved ones buried so far from home, the sight of America's national cemeteries seems to have greatly eased their minds. "I am glad I have come," said one Texas woman. "Now I feel that my son rests at peace among his comrades, that he is a soldier."[26] Repeatedly, women recorded their gratitude and, more significant, a sense of peace and reassurance after witnessing the striking and well-maintained cemeteries. They appeared to gain strength from a belief that the same government that had cared enough to bring them on the pilgrimage would itself endure.

If, as the women's earnest avowals suggest, inner peace and emotional closure were attained upon seeing their loved one's grave, then the decision to leave bodies overseas had only prolonged the mourning process. Public recognition for their gold stars and countless patriotic orations had evidently not prevented years of lingering doubts concerning the choices they had made. For some, like Nancy Marsh, the painful decision to leave their beloved buried overseas brought years of nagging uncertainty. Despite what they had been told, time did not always heal their grief.[27]

Psychologists, philosophers, and laymen alike have considered the nature of mourning, yet the process remains largely a mystery, aside from the common consensus that grieving is a uniquely individual experience.[28] Elisabeth Kübler-Ross, a pioneer in grief therapy, posits that stoic attempts to camouflage our sorrow can fester in a myriad of ways. When the natural course of grieving death is compromised, as it was during those early wartime years, healing comes at a high price, if at all. By refusing to dwell on the human cost, Americans developed a memory of war that diminished rather than honored the sacrifice of life.

Of the more than eleven thousand women deemed eligible for the Gold Star pilgrimages, just over one-half that number accepted the government's generous offer.[29] Sadly, the others' rationale for refusing to revisit the past has been lost to the years. Questions regarding their resolution with such a terrible sacrifice remain obscured by time and lack of evidence, whereas the experiences of those who accepted the overseas invitation offer an opportunity for probing this unique saga.

The Gold Star mothers and widows pilgrimages were funded by taxpayers during some of the nation's worst years of deprivation and economic hardship. Although dissenting voices could be heard, they were faint amid the clamoring demands of a powerful coalition strengthened by a confluence of timing, circumstance, and a government determined to reinforce an image of power, wealth, and solidarity abroad.

Politically, ABMC members and federal supporters were eager to display their commemorative constructs that represented years of diligent study, labor, and expense; others in governmental circles saw the pilgrimages as a foreign-policy instrument capable of promoting peace. The War Department viewed the pilgrimages as an opportunity to display military professionalism, while attempting to balance compassion for the families of the war dead with an obligation to care for its own. Veterans and next of kin hoped that this return to the battlefield would reinforce their sacrifice, service, and ultimate victory, upon the nation's collective war memory. Among the women, activists perceived the fight for pilgrimage legislation as a vehicle for strengthening their political position, while others deemed it just recompense for performing their patriotic duty to the nation. Presumably, underlying all these intentions was the desire for resolution, an attempt to put the dead to rest at last.

Elisabeth Kübler-Ross and David Kessler, in their treatise *On Grief and Grieving*, note the standard definition of *closure* as the "act of closing or the state of being closed; a bringing to an end, a conclusion." The term normally refers to two different types of closures: "the first is the unrealistic wrap-up we expect after a loss," when grieving becomes a burden, one to be quickly overcome; the other "involves doing things that help put the loss in perspective, such as reviewing what happened and why" by filling in the missing information gaps.[30] Both modes of resolution were apparent among the bereft in the war's aftermath, but in our story, an additional form of closure emerges.

Within America, a lingering and disconcerting moral obligation could still be felt to the dead and to their families, who had made an additional sacrifice by leaving their loved ones in government hands. Time had shown that the democratic option previously offered to the next of kin had only minimally assuaged their grief. Although the nation appeared to have forgotten the war and moved on from its unpleasantness, the suffering and tragic loss of life had not been sufficiently resolved.

The government's grand gesture of honoring war losses with a sponsored pilgrimage certainly had its strengths, but such collective rituals, though beneficial for building nations, can never be truly personal. The grandness of the event—tainted as it was by political and racial overtones, occurring in a foreign land surrounded by unfamiliar customs and language, and under rigid constraints of a structured agenda—would surely have limited the potential for personal remembrance.

Moreover, the belated timing of the pilgrimages also worked against it, as many mothers had died or were in poor health; widows had since remarried; and as has been shown, memories of the nation's participation in the war had faded. Interest in the monuments was weakened since they were still under construction, and the names of the missing were merely sketches on an architect's plans.

Despite the diverse racial and ethnic backgrounds of the war's participants, little attempt was made to incorporate the service of women or minorities onto the national monuments or remembrance rituals. And although the American cemeteries undoubtedly made a striking impression, there were few personal inscriptions engraved onto the marble headstones, a welcome consolation offered by the British authorities to their families.[31] Lastly, appointing the military as responsible agent for the pilgrimages may have imparted a more rigid ambiance and tempo to the event, in sharp contrast to what may have resulted under the auspices of the alternative institution, the American Red Cross.

These factors combined to effectively diminish the impact of the nation's grand gesture, confirming Maurice Halbwachs's theory that the past is a social construction shaped by the concerns of the present.[32] Thus, the duration of memory as created by these women, the military, veterans, and the government could last only as long as the need remained and the groups producing it endured.[33]

American collective remembrance of the First World War was largely a politically motivated exercise, driven primarily by factions (some more successful than others), and each with its own agenda. It consisted of a series of negotiations and compromises sustained by democratic principles that, by their nature, systematically promoted self-interest, provided that national solidarity emerged relatively intact.

The American government never built monuments overseas again on the same grandiose scale, nor did it ever fund another Gold Star pilgrimage. After the last ship returned to U.S. shores in 1933, memories of these pilgrimages were for the most part overshadowed by time and later wars. And although European memory theorists may offer their hypotheses for reflection, their abstract and theoretical cultural approaches are insufficient for the messy nature of American democracy. Democratic process responds to the current wishes of its citizens and, as such, cannot by its very nature readily contribute to an enduring national remembrance.

Epilogue

"What will be thought of the great adventure of the War Department in returning thousands of dead to the United States in fifty years or a century from now . . . is impossible to say," mused Colonel Harry F. Rethers, chief of the Paris office of the Graves Registration Service in 1920. Optimistically, he predicted, "The story will serve to show the sincerity of men who honestly tried to carry out their mission well and who made the history they afterwards wrote."[1] The possibility that future generations might forget this war would have been considered an unspeakable tragedy by those who lived through it.

The U.S. repatriation policy and the heritage landscapes that men created in an attempt to remember the apocalypse of their era have endured. Ironically, memories of the First World War and its aftermath have been misplaced in favor of the multifarious Civil War monuments of reputed "bad taste." Nevertheless, these national icons share a powerful hold on popular memory, along with the uniform rows of identical Second World War headstones that emulate their more obscure predecessors.[2]

Repatriation of the dead from overseas battlefields after 1920 was the catalyst that drove American First World War commemoration. Yet democratic choice, initially offered to assuage the grief of the living, also contributed to a massive diffusion of memory. With more than 60 percent of the known dead scattered in graves throughout the United States, interest in overseas commemoration was undeniably diluted. Generations later, ABMC records offer precise details regarding the burial locations of those within their national cemeteries, whereas the government maintained no records of servicemen's graves once a body was released to families in the United States. In America's transient culture, this information readily disappeared, leaving no trace of the deceased.

Although a similar choice was offered to the public after the Second World War, conditions were radically different. The aims of that "just" war were clearly achieved, and America's role as a victorious power was firmly established by 1945; thus, the nation required few unifying commemorative structures to validate its contribution or to stir collective memory. When the ABMC met in 1947 to determine its second postwar direction, Senator David A. Reed, once more at the helm as chairman, stated that the erection of large monuments overseas was "unnecessary."[3]

In July 1958, the enigmatic Gold Star matriarch Mathilda Burling died in a New York nursing home at the age of seventy-eight.[4] Her death came just months after the remains of two unidentified American Second World War and Korean War servicemen were buried in Arlington National Cemetery's Tomb of the Unknown Soldier. These bodies were the last to rest there permanently, ending a practice that began in 1921, with disregard for Chaplain Charles Pierce's plea that the United States return all the bodies of the unknown to Arlington for interment. He believed that there was still a chance that identifications could be made, and until that time, the burials would become "a mecca for all the mothers of the land whose dead could not be given back to them."[5]

In July 1998, forty summers after those Second World War and Korean War burials, the remains of a Vietnam veteran buried in the Tomb of the Unknown fourteen years before were returned to his family and buried in St. Louis, Missouri. Scientists using cutting-edge mitochondrial DNA testing, identified the remains as those of U.S. Air Force pilot First Lieutenant Michael J. Blassie, effectively fulfilling Pierce's dream that one day no unknown soldier would ever be considered permanently unidentifiable.

Today, most Americans are probably unaware of the repatriation efforts of the GRS after the First World War, but they will indeed be familiar with images of soldiers' caskets being returned home from contemporary war zones. The recovery work of early graves-registration pioneers such as D. H. Rhodes and his unfortunate successor, Second Lieutenant V. M. Conway, lives on through the military organization called the Joint POW/MIA Accounting Command (JPAC) and the U.S. government's Central Identification Laboratory at Hickam Air Force Base, Hawaii. Each year American taxpayers contribute more than forty-six million dollars to sustain its mission of searching for, recovering, and identifying America's soldier dead.[6]

Although the majority of JPAC's efforts are currently focused on locating and identifying Second World War and Vietnam-era remains, the organization is occasionally asked to investigate finds believed to be from the 1914–1918 war. In 2006, a recovery team working on Second World War investigations in France was called to the vicinity of Prény Woods, where what was believed to be the remains of American First World War soldiers were uncovered. The JPAC team retrieved the remains and transported them back to its base in Hawaii, where they await positive identification.[7] This unique approach to commemoration adopted by the United States after the First World War and the accompanying expansion of the federal government's power constitute what may be the most persistent legacy of that conflict.

GRS chief Charles Pierce did not live to see his prophetic desires manifested, whereas Mathilda Burling witnessed the formation of the Gold Star Wives organization in 1946. One hundred war widows established the nationwide affiliation from a local New York charter. The Second World War left 73,527 American widows, with more than one-half of this number mothers of young children.[8] One of the group's immediate goals was to work for increases in the benefits paid to widows from fifty dollars per month to sixty dollars, and to see the orphans' pension of fifteen dollars per month raised to eighteen dollars.

Today there are approximately 150 Gold Star Mothers chapters in the United States and between ten thousand and eleven thousand members (men and women) of the Gold Star Wives of America, in more than sixty active chapters. In addition to the gold star pins awarded by the Department of Defense to family members of the deceased, a range of products are now available—flags, auto magnets, window decals, bumper stickers, and baseball caps—all bearing the recognizable gold and blue stars.

As in the past, these organizations are counterbalanced by the aspirations of collectives such as the Gold Star Families for Peace, led by the outspoken Cindy Sheehan, mother of an American soldier killed in the Iraq conflict. When asked about her group's purpose, Sheehan responded that it was formed "to be a unique voice to spread the word about the lies and betrayals that killed our children and . . . [to] put a human face on the suffering of [war]." She added, "Look in your hearts, look at the truth about this immoral war and work for Peace."[9]

Sheehan's message is strikingly similar to the reflections of another mother more than eighty years ago who poignantly questioned and grieved her son's death on the Marne: "There are many mothers who, exchanging their boys for the little glitter of gold stars, have not yet been able to find a way through the bitterness and rebellion in their hearts to have the power to say, 'I shall help, by every word I utter, by all the mental assertion I am capable of, by every means I have, to make another war impossible.'"[10]

Despite such pledges of peace, as of September 2006, there were nearly 125,000 U.S. war dead from the First and Second World Wars and the Mexican-American War interred in the ABMC cemeteries. Additionally, there are 94,000 U.S. servicemen and women commemorated by name on Tablets of the Missing from the world wars and the Korean and Vietnam wars.[11]

The ABMC continues its work of "commemorating the achievements and sacrifices of U.S. armed forces where they have served overseas since April 6, 1917." The commission now manages twenty-four permanent American military cemeteries; twenty-five federal memorials, monuments, and markers; and seven nonfederal memorials. Aside from the *American Armies and Battlefields in Europe* guidebook, there remains no official U.S. published history of the First World War.

Notes

NOTES TO THE PREFACE

1. Lisa M. Budreau, "Over Where?" *American in Britain*, May–June 1998, 34-35.

2. Jay Winter, *Sites of Memory, Sites of Mourning* (Cambridge: Cambridge University Press, 1998), 52.

3. "Meditation XVII," by John Donne, includes the oft-quoted line, "Ask not for whom the bell tolls, it tolls for thee." John Donne from "Devotions upon Emergent Occasions" (1623), XVII.

NOTES TO THE INTRODUCTION

1. Ellis W. Hawley, *The Great War and the Search for a Modern Order* (New York: St. Martin's, 1979), 50; David Kennedy, *Over Here: The First World War and American Society* (New York: Oxford University Press, 1980), 17, 24.

2. George L. Mosse, *Fallen Soldiers: Reshaping the Memory of the World Wars* (Oxford: Oxford University Press, 1990), 6, 7. George Mosse explains that the military cemetery came to function as a central symbol. The myth was designed to "mask war and to legitimise the war experience; it was meant to displace the reality of war. The memory of the war was refashioned into a sacred experience." Ibid., 7.

3. This reference was taken from a recent study of collective memory in which the author, quite convincingly, "distinguishes between 'continuity' as commemoration or pedigree from 'discontinuity,' i.e. events so traumatic as to erase their antecedents or so useful as to warrant them being remembered in place of earlier events." David Henige, review of *Time Maps: Collective Memory and the Social Shape of the Past*, by Eviatar Zerubavel, *Journal of Interdisciplinary History* 35, no. 1 (2004): 113–114. Also see Stephen Bertman's discussion of culture and national identity presented in *Cultural Amnesia: America's Future and the Crisis of Memory* (Westport, CT: Praeger, 2000), 15.

NOTES TO CHAPTER 1

1. Doran Cart, "Liberty Memorial Museum of World War One," *Dusty Shelf* (Kansas City Area Archivists) 19, no. 3 (1999-2000): 10. I am indebted to Doran Cart for drawing my attention to the Kendall Collection. This material also appeared in my article "The Politics of Remembrance: The Gold Star Mothers' Pilgrimage and America's Fading Memory of the Great War," *Journal of Military History* 72, no. 2 (April 2008): 371–411.

2. War Department, Adjutant General's Office to Mr. B. F. Kendall, Shenandoah, Iowa, August 15, 1918, Gold Star Mothers Collection, Estella Kendall Papers, Liberty Memorial Museum, Kansas City, Missouri.

3. Chaplain 168th Infantry Regiment, Roscoe C. Hatch, HQ 168th Inf., AEF, to Mrs. M. F. Kendall, August 30, 1918, Kendall Papers.

4. Before the number of repatriated dead reached a peak in mid-1921, more than thirteen thousand families had changed their minds and decided to leave remains overseas. "Sentiment Changes on Soldier Dead," *New York Times* (hereafter *NYT*), May 15, 1921, sec. 2, 1:7.

5. War Department to Mrs. Estella M. Kendall, April 16, 1919, Kendall Papers.

6. Unfortunately, no record of Mrs. Kendall's response exists, only the reply from the War Department, June 5, 1921. War Department to Mrs. B. F. Kendall, August 7, 1923, Kendall Papers. The Meuse-Argonne American Cemetery sits approximately twenty-three miles northwest of Verdun, France.

7. See "Returning Remains to America," in "Graves Registration Service History" (draft version), Chapter IX, Box 4, 1917–1922, Cemeterial Division, Office of the QMG, RG 92, NA. Figures varied over the years from between 30,902, stated in *American Armies and Battlefields in Europe,* 2nd ed. (Washington, DC: U.S. Government Printing Office, 1938), 459 (hereafter *ABMC Guide*), to current figures of 31,945. See Mark Meigs, *Optimism at Armageddon* (London: Macmillan, 1997), 181.

8. The *ABMC Guide* states that the number remaining "unknown" is 4,431, a figure that includes 1,643 buried in unidentified graves in Europe, 1,537 whose grave is the sea, and 1,250 whose remains are nonrecoverable. However, the book was published in 1938, and figures have since risen. *ABMC Guide*, 459.

9. Although the reference to the deceased is most often expressed in masculine terms, approximately 143 women serving in the Army Nurse Corps also died overseas during the war. Their bodies were eligible for repatriation or burial overseas, and mothers were similarly invited to join the GSM pilgrimage. Nelle F. Rote, *Nurse Helen Fairchild: WWI 1917–1918* (Lewisburg, PA: Fisher Fairchild, 2004), 248–265; Lettie Gavin, *American Women in World War I* (Boulder: University Press of Colorado, 1997), 249–252.

10. The cost of the pilgrimages was originally estimated to be about $3 million; however, the actual expenditure was $5,386,367. War Department, Washington, DC, to The President, April 18, 1933, President Franklin D. Roosevelt's "Official File 461," Gold Star Mothers, 1933–1945, FDR Library, Hyde Park, NY. For original estimate, see *NYT*, July 7, 1929, 9:4.

11. Jay Winter, *Sites of Memory, Sites of Mourning* (Cambridge: Cambridge University Press, 1998), 101.

12. In the Fox film production *Pilgrimage,* Henrietta Crosman plays Hannah Jessop, an embittered, widowed mother who loses her son to the war (story by I. A. R. Wylie, directed by John Ford, released in 1933). *NYT*, June 25, 1933; "The Screen," *NYT*, July 13, 1933; Tag Gallagher, *John Ford: The Man and His Films* (Berkeley: University of California Press, 1986), 75.

NOTES TO CHAPTER 2

1. The question of casualties is difficult to calculate. Current Department of Defense statistics from "Principal Wars in Which the U.S. Participated" states 116,516 deaths are attributable to the First World War. See http://siadapp.dmdc.osd.mil/personnel/casualty/wcprincipal.pdf (May 2009). The 1919 figures are taken from Memo from the War Department to the Office of the QMC, Col. Chambers, dated May 15, 1919, from H. R. Lemly, Major, QMC, Entry 1915, Box 26, General H. L. Rogers's Private File, 1919–1923, RG 92, NA.

2. Meigs, *Optimism at Armageddon*, 145.

3. QMG to Secretary of War, War Department, September 20, 1917, and Pershing cablegram to Adjutant General at the War Department, March 1918, Cemeterial Division Correspondence, 1917–1922, Entry 1941 (hereafter Cemeterial Division), Office of the QMG, RG 92, NA.

4. "To Bring Back Our Dead," *NYT*, September 5, 1918, 10:6; G. Kurt Piehler, *Remembering War the American Way* (Washington, DC: Smithsonian Institution Press, 1995), 95.

5. Newton Diehl Baker (December 3, 1871–December 25, 1937), a Democrat and notable figure in the Progressive Movement, never served in a public position again despite being considered a candidate for the Democratic nomination for president in 1924, 1928, and 1932. Daniel R. Beaver, *Newton D. Baker and the American War Effort, 1917–1919* (Lincoln: University of Nebraska Press, 1966).

6. *History of the American Graves Registration Service*, vol. 1, to September 1920, preface by H. F. Rethers, 7, U.S. Army War College, Carlisle Barracks, PA.

7. After the Second World War, America suffered 359,000 fatalities, of which 281,000 were recovered and given burial in temporary cemeteries overseas. Once again, families decided disposition of the dead. See Edward Steere, "National Cemeteries and Memorials in Global Conflict," *Quartermaster Review*, November–December 1953. A figure of thirty million dollars for the cost of repatriation is found in General Correspondence, 1917–1925, Entry 37A, Records of the Office of the Adjutant General (hereafter cited as AGO General Correspondence), RG 407, NA. Original estimates were five hundred dollars per body.

NOTES TO CHAPTER 3

1. *Report of the Surgeon General U.S. Army to the Secretary of War*, vol. 2 (Washington, DC: U.S. Government Printing Office, 1919), 1641.

2. Erna Risch, *Quartermaster Support of the Army: A History of the Corps, 1775–1939* (Washington, DC: Quartermaster Historian's Office, Office of the QMG, U.S. Army, 1962), 692; *ABMC Guide* states twenty-four hundred cemeteries (459).

3. Miss Lola Seyton to Office of QMG, November 24, 1918, File 293.8, RG 407, NA.

4. Mrs. Fannie Greenwood, Richton, Mississippi, to War Department, January 10, 1919, File 293.8, AGO General Correspondence, RG 407, NA; and Mrs. Fannie Greenwood, Kila, Miss., August 13, 1919, burial file for C. Greenwood, Entry 1942, RG 92, NA.

5. Mrs. Ethel Goldman to Major General John F. O'Ryan, December 7, 1918, New York City, and Fannie Myers to Chief, GRS, March 17, 1919, Greenville, SC, 27th Division, Entry 1241, Correspondence Files, Entry 1241 (hereafter AEF Records), RG 120, NA.

6. The QMG of the Army to the Secretary of War, September 20, 1917, Washington, DC, Correspondence of the Cemeterial Division, Entry 1941, RG 92, NA (emphasis added).

7. It was believed that Charon only accepted the dead who were buried or burned with proper rites and only if they paid him an obolus (coin) for their passage. For that reason a corpse always had a coin placed under the tongue. Micha F. Lindemans, "Charon," *Encyclopedia Mythica*, http://www.pantheon.org/articles/c/charon.html. Charon is also mentioned in Dante's *Inferno* (book 3, line 78) and Virgil's *Aeneid* (book 6, line 369).

NOTES TO CHAPTER 4

1. Kristin L. Hoganson, *Fighting for American Manhood* (New Haven, CT: Yale University Press, 1998), 6; Graham A. Cosmas, *An Army for Empire: The United States Army in the Spanish-American War* (Shippensburg, PA: White Mane, 1994 [first published in 1971]).

2. From 1899 to 1902, 4,234 died, although figures vary considerably. Hoganson, *Fighting for American Manhood*, 7.

3. Margaret Leech, *In the Days of McKinley* (New York: Harper, 1959), 333.

4. Cosmas, *Army for Empire*, 297.

5. *NYT*, March 31, 1899, 14:1; "686 Dead Heroes Arrive," *NYT*, March 30, 1899, 3:5. *Army Almanac* claims there were 747 casketed remains. *The Army Almanac: A Book of Facts Concerning the Army of the United States* (Washington, DC: U.S. Government Printing Office, 1950), 684.

6. "President McKinley's Order," *NYT*, April 5, 1899, 5:1.

7. "686 Dead Heroes Arrive," *NYT*, March 30, 1899, 3:5. The Spanish-American War remains "among the most militarily successful conflicts fought by the United States" (Piehler, *Remembering War*, 40).

8. "Soldier Dead Removed," *NYT*, March 31, 1899, 14:1.

9. Gary Laderman, *The Sacred Remains: American Attitudes toward Death, 1799–1883* (New Haven, CT: Yale University Press, 1996), 167–168.

10. Philippe Ariès, *The Hour of Our Death*, trans. Helen Weaver (London: Penguin, 1981), 598; Jessica Mitford, *The American Way of Death Revisited* (New York: Virago, 1998), 157–158.

11. Until the eighteenth century, few people except the very rich were buried in coffins. The casket was strictly a phenomenon of modern America, unknown in other parts of the world. Mitford, *American Way of Death Revisited*, 145–146.

12. General E. Stephen Otis (1838–1909), Manila, to Adj. General of the War Department, Washington, DC, April 1, 1899, *Correspondence Relating to the War with Spain*, vol. 2 (Washington, DC: Center of Military History, U.S Army, U.S. Government Printing Office, 1902), 955.

13. "Grief soon subsides, and the older the bill gets, the harder it is to collect." Mitford, *American Way of Death Revisited*, 149, quoting W. P. Hohenschuh, author of *Modern Funeral*, published in 1900.

14. D. H. Rhodes, Insp., National Cemeteries, to the QMG of the Army, Washington, DC, September 30, 1901, Entry 677, Office of the QMG, RG 92, NA.

15. Ibid., 5.

16. Ibid., 7. F. S. Croggon, Superintendent, U.S. Burial Corps, to the Chief, QM, Division of the Philippines, Manila, P.I., April 1, 1903, 1–4, Entry 677, Office of the QMG, RG 92, NA.

17. In March 1903, Pierce asked Assistant Surgeon General Harry Lippincott to write a letter of reference to the Adjutant General in Washington, DC, in which Lippincott praised Pierce's work in Manila. He commends Pierce and includes an extract of Special Order No. 85, dated March 29, 1899, through Major General Otis, requesting the services of Captain C. C. Pierce. This was, no doubt, an attempt to counter Rhodes's incriminating report. Office of the Chief Surgeon, Governor's Island, New York, March 27, 1903, to the Adjutant General, U.S. Army, ACP File, Adjutant General's Office, RG 94, NA. Edward Steere, *The Graves Registration Service in World War II* (Washington, DC: U.S. Government Printing Office, 1951), 11.

18. Rhodes to the QMG of the Army, 47.

19. Ibid., 48. David Rhodes (1849–1932) was landscape gardener of the National Cemeteries for more than fifty years. He was buried in Arlington National Cemetery. "David H. Rhodes," Arlington National Cemetery website, http://www.arlingtoncemetery.net/dhrhodes.htm.

20. Steere, *Graves Registration Service*, 11.

21. In December 1899, all the artillery, infantry, and cavalry colonels and almost 70 percent of the lieutenant colonels and majors, as well as thirty-seven captains, were Civil War veterans. Coffman attributes this condition to the "long stagnant interwar period of slow promotion combined with a late retirement age of sixty-four." Edward M. Coffman, *The Regulars: The American Army* (Cambridge, MA: Belknap Press of Harvard University Press, 2004), 50.

22. The discussion here relies on the introduction of Winter's study in cognitive and social psychology as it appears in Jay Winter and Emmanuel Sivan, eds., *War and Remembrance in the Twentieth Century* (Cambridge: Cambridge University Press, 1999), 12.

23. See Bertman, *Cultural Amnesia*, 15.

NOTES TO CHAPTER 5

1. Pershing wrote his autobiography in 1931; it won the 1932 Pulitzer Prize. John J. Pershing, *My Experiences in the World War*, vol. 1 (Blue Ridge Summit, PA: Tab Books, 1989), 7–8.

2. Ibid., 8. Pershing believed that the United States should have taken the precaution in the spring of 1916 to organize and equip an army of half a million combat troops, readying them to sail to France in April 1917.

3. Telegram from War Department, Captain T. A. Baldwin, Jr., to QMG, San Antonio, TX, May 10, 1916, telegram May 15, 1916, signed "Sharpe, War Dept.," and telegram May 14, 1916, to QMC, Fort Sam Houston, TX, signed Rogers, Box 1345, General Correspondence Geographic File, 1922–1935, Mexico, Office of the QMG, RG 92, NA.

4. See documentation on Herman E. Kirby, originally buried near La Joya, Chihuahua, Mexico. Letter to Secretary of State from American Consul in Mexico, October 13, 1925, in ibid.

5. Erna Risch, *Quartermaster Support of the Army: A History of the Corps, 1775–1939* (Washington, DC: Quartermaster Historian's Office, Office of the QMG, U.S. Army, 1962), 689–690.

6. HR 5410, 65th Congress, 1st Session, July 13, 1917. J. Hampton Moore (1864–1950) was opposed to the United States' entering war. He left office to become mayor of Philadelphia in 1920. Moore Papers, collection 1541, Historical Society of Pennsylvania.

7. French Ministry of the Interior memo, quoted in correspondence to the Chief of the French Military Mission, from the Commander in Chief of the AEF, February 8, 1919, Series 293, AEF Records, RG 120, NA.

8. Sous-Secretaire d'État de l'Administration de la Guerre to LTC C. C. Pierce, Chief, Graves Reg., February 21, 1919, Series 293, AEF Records, RG 120, NA.

9. Ibid.

10. A December 1917 conference attended by Captain Chettle, October 1918, Box 1082, WG 164, Catalogue no. 268, CWGC. Chettle was a collaborator of Fabian Ware's since the early days in France; he served as director of records for the IWGC. See Philip Longworth, *The Unending Vigil* (London: Leo Cooper, 1967), 76–77.

11. Fabian Ware to W. C. Bridgeman, Esq., MP, Board of Trade, Whitehall Gdns., London, September 4, 1919, Box 1082, WG 1294/3, Pt. 1, Catalogue no. 268, and Intendant General, Chef des l'Offfice des Sepultures Militaires, to the Commissaire General aux Affaires de Guerre Franco-Americaines, Paris, February 25, 1919 (signature illegible), CWGC. Also from General, SOS [General Harbord], March 3, 1919, Entry 1649 (hereafter SOS Records), AEF Records, RG 120, NA.

12. Pershing confidential cable to the Chief of Staff and Secretary of War, March 1, 1919, Series 293, Entry 476, Confidential Cablegrams Sent from General Pershing to the Adjutant General, 1917–1919, AEF Records, RG 120, NA.

13. J. G. Harbord to the Chief of the French Military Mission, February 8, 1919, SOS Records, RG 407, NA (emphasis added).

14. James Harbord wrote, "No nightmare that I ever had had shown me as Commanding General of the SOS." And he wrote, "It is unnecessary to say that I regretted very bitterly that the General [Pershing] thought it was necessary to send me back here." Harbord to Brig. General Chas. M. Saltzman, Chief Signal Officer, Washington, DC, September 18, 1918, and September 25, 1918, pp. 219, 203, vol. 8, 1917–23, James G. Harbord Papers, Manuscript Department, LOC.

15. L. A. Shipman, Major, QMC, to Chief, American GRS, QMC, in Europe, June 23, 1920, Entry 441, Correspondence of the Purchase, Storage, and Traffic Division, 1918–1920, War Department General and Special Staffs, RG 165, NA.

16. "Sur le Projet de Loi Interdisant L'Exhumation et le Transport des Corps Militaires" ("Note on the Law Forbidding the Exhumation and Transport of Military Dead"), Imprimerie Nationale, 1919, Paris, O Piece, 9499, Drawer 522, Bibliothèque de documentation internationale contemporaine (BDIC), University of Paris X, Nanterre (translation is mine).

17. American Representatives to French National Commission (signed LTC Pierce) to Cmdr. in Chief, AEF, April 6, 1919, Tours, France, SOS Records, AEF Records, RG 120, NA.

18. Confidential memo, Major A. L. Ingpen, IWGC, Brussels, to Vice Chairman, March 30, 1920, Box 1083, WG 1294/3, Pt. 2, CWGC.

19. Captain Chettle, October 1918, Box 1082, WG 164, Catalogue no. 268, CWGC.

20. Thomas W. Laqueur, "Memory and Naming in the Great War," in John R. Gillis, ed., *Commemorations: The Politics of National Identity* (Princeton, NJ: Princeton University Press, 1994), 152; Elizabeth G. Grossman, "Architecture for a Public Client: The Monuments and Chapels of the American Battle Monuments Commission," *Journal of the Society of Architectural Historians* 43, no. 2 (May 1984): 119. For correspondence from families in Britain, see G. H. Wakeman, Esq., to Director of Graves Registration & Inquiries, November 22, 1918, Wakeman Collection, Imperial War Museum. For Parliamentary debate on British repatriation, see House of Commons Debate (5th series), May 4, 1920, vol. 128, cc 199–72, Hansard (Her Majesty's Stationery Office, UK).

21. Fabian Arthur Goulstone Ware, born in Bristol, England, on June 17, 1869. Information Sheet, *Fabian Ware: Founder of the Commonwealth War Graves Commission* (Berkshire, UK: CWGC, 1999); Fabian A. G. Ware, *The Immortal Heritage* (Cambridge: Cambridge University Press, 1937). For history of CWGC, see Longworth, *Unending Vigil*.

22. Ian Beckett notes that Ware also directed that there should be no distinction between officers and men. Ian F. W. Beckett, *The Great War, 1914–1918* (Essex, UK: Longman, 2001), 432.

23. Ware to Bridgeman, September 4, 1919.

24. W. P. Coleman, Col. (Infantry), to Chief, GRS, October 13, 1919, File 1917–1925, AGO General Correspondence, RG 407, NA.

25. Col. Leon Kromer, Chief, GRS in Europe, to HQ, American Forces in France, Office of the Chief Quartermaster Graves Registration Service, 12 rue Boissy D'Anglais, Paris, October 13, 1919, SOS Records, AEF Records, RG 120, NA.

26. "Our Soldier Dead Must Stay in France," *NYT*, November 25, 1919, 17:2.

27. American Representatives to French National Commission (signed LTC Pierce) to Cmdr. in Chief, AEF, April 6, 1919, Tours, France, SOS Records, AEF Records, RG 120, NA.

28. War Department, Adj. General's Office, Washington, DC, March 11, 1919, Series 293, SOS Records, AEF Records, RG 120, NA.

29. "Find Wide Desire for Return of Dead," *NYT*, January 24, 1920, 7; "40,000 Ask Return of Dead," *NYT*, November 14, 1919, 12:8.

30. Testimony of Col. Chas. Pierce to O. E. Bland, February 5, 1920, Foreign Expenditures Subcommittee, House of Representatives, 66th Congress, 2nd Session, on War Expenditures, vol. 3, serial 4, parts 51–74 (Washington, DC: U.S. Government Printing Office, 1920): 3441–3499.

31. "The Legion's Care of the Home-Coming Dead," *American Legion Weekly*, May 26, 1922, 24.

32. Mosse, *Myth of the War Experience*, 78.

33. John E. Kowalewski, Buffalo, NY, June 29, 1920, Pvt. Walter Kowalewski, Co. D, 133rd Inf., Box 2743, Entry 1941, Cemeterial Division, Office of the OMG, RG 92, NA.

34. Samuel Greenblatt to SOS, June 12, 1919, Harry Greenblatt, Box 2743, Entry 1941, Cemeterial Division, Office of the QMG, RG 92, NA.

35. War Department, Adjutant General's Office, Washington, DC, to The Commanding General, AEF, France, April 1, 1919, Series 293.8, Burials and Reinterment, AGO General Correspondence, RG 407, NA.

36. Major General John O'Ryan to Col. M. D. Bryant, HQ 27th Div., December 16, 1918, Series E.2133, File 107th Infantry, U.S. Army Mobile Commands, RG 391, NA.

37. HQ, 107th Infantry Amer. Ex. Forces, France, December 26, 1918, in ibid.

38. The chaplain was referring to a chaplains' meeting of the 42nd Division, January 24, 1919. Chaplains Harrington and Nash, 150th and 151st FA, 42nd Div., to the Senior GHQ Chaplain, AEF, Entry 597, Chaplain's Office Files, AEF Records, RG 120, NA.

39. J. G. Harbord, second endorsement dated April 28, 1919, to Robert C. Davis, "Disposition of the bodies of deceased soldiers of the [AEF]," appearing on a memo from Robert C.

Davis, Adjutant General, Commander-in-chief, to the Adjutant General of the Army, May 6, 1919, Box 566, RG 120, NA.

40. Harbord's endorsement to Robert C. Davis, Adj. Gen., to Cmdr. in Chief, AEF, May 6, 1919, in ibid.

41. "Senate Votes for Cemetery for Our Dead in France," *NYT,* June 13, 1919, 17.

42. "Problem of the Vanquished Victor," *NYT,* April 27, 1919, 6; "Speedy Recovery Shown by France," *NYT,* August 30, 1920, 17; "Warns of Reports Harmful to France," *NYT,* March 24, 1919, 5; Robert J. Young, *Marketing Marianne: French Propaganda in America, 1900–1940* (New Brunswick, NJ: Rutgers University Press, 2004), 76.

43. *History of the American Graves Registration Service, Q.M.C. in Europe* (hereafter *GRS History*), vol. 1, to September 1920, U.S. Army publication, 115.

44. Ibid., 118.

45. Bart Ziino, *A Distant Grief: Australians, War Graves and the Great War* (Crawley: University of Western Australia Press, 2007), 3–4.

46. Young states that this security made it easier for Americans to contemplate accommodation with the Germans. *Marketing Marianne,* 76.

47. "Find Wide Desire for Return of Dead," *NYT,* January 24, 1920; "40,000 Ask Return of Dead," *NYT,* November 14, 1919, 12:8. Of the 74,770 questionnaires sent out, 63,708 answers were received by January 1920.

48. "Objection to Bringing Home Soldier Dead," *NYT,* January 18, 1920, sec. 8, 11:8.

49. Baker to the Secretary of State, October 20, 1919, War Department, Series 293.8, AGO General Correspondence, RG 407, NA; "American Officials Are Pressing for Permission to Exhume Their Bodies," *NYT,* November 23, 1919, 7.

50. "Limits Removal of Dead," *NYT,* December 28, 1919, 21:2; and Note on the Military Graves, July 1, 1919, O Piece, 5822, Drawer 522, "des États-Unis, Tombes Militaire," Paris-Imprimerie Nationale, 1919, BDIC, University of Paris X, Nanterre.

51. Oscar E. Bland, referring to testimony by Col. Chas. Pierce, House of Representatives, HR 9927, *Congressional Record* (October 14, 1919): 6917; and testimony of Pierce to Bland, February 5, 1920.

52. Secretary of War's statement read before Congress on October 14, 1919, *Congressional Record* (October 14, 1919): 6917.

53. War Department memo to Mr. Ralph Hayes, Ass't to the Secretary, from Medical Corps Executive Officer, Col. C. R. Darnall, May 24, 1920, Box 3, Cemeterial Division, Office of the QMG, RG 92, NA.

NOTES TO CHAPTER 6

1. House Rep. Clement C. Dickinson of Missouri, House of Representatives, 66th Congress, 2nd Session, *Congressional Record* 59 (January 27, 1920): pt. 2:2132–2133.

2. The French Army reported that fifty thousand burials within the Zone of Interior (combat zone) had been destroyed. *GRS History,* 1:27.

3. Maj. Gen. M. W. Ireland, "Field Operations," *The Medical Department of the United States Army in the World War,* vol. 8 (Washington, DC: U.S. Government Printing Office, 1925), 389.

4. Ibid.

5. *GRS History,* 1:28.

6. Letter dated January 18, 1931, burial file for Sgt. Winfield A. Jackson, Box 2457A, Office of the QMG, RG 92, NA.

7. Field Marshal Sir D. Haig, Cmdr.-in-Chief, British Armies in France to the Secretary, War Office, London, GHQ, March 14, 1919, Box 1082, WG 1294/3, pt. 1, Catalogue no. 268, CWGC.

8. J. E. Talbot, Principal Assistant Secretary of the IWGC, November 11, 1918, WG 164, Catalogue no. 268, Box 1082, CWGC.

9. U.S. government statistics in 1920 claimed that the British had more than 3,000 cemeteries on the Western Front. *GRS History*, 2:29. More recently, Bart Ziino claims that the IWGC constructed some 1,850 cemeteries around the world, more than half on the former front in France and Belgium. Ziino, *Distant Grief*, 3.

10. Arthur E. Barbeau and Florette Henri, *The Unknown Soldiers: African-American Troops in World War I*, 2nd ed. (New York: Da Capo, 1996), 165.

11. Meigs, *Optimism at Armageddon*, 178; see also "Colored Yanks Bury Dead as They Sing Old Song," *Cleveland Advocate*, September 28, 1918, 1.

12. Meigs, *Optimism at Armageddon*, 178. Also *GRS History*, vol. 1, U.S. Army publication.

13. *GRS History*, 1:35.

14. William G. Shepherd, "Graves Registration Service History" (draft version).

15. Barbeau and Henri, *Unknown Soldiers*, 104–105.

16. "Oh Lord! How Long?" *Cleveland Advocate*, December 15, 1917, 8.

17. Newton Baker, John J. Pershing, and Theodore Roosevelt, preface to *Scott's Official History of the American Negro in the World War*, by Emmett J. Scott (Washington, DC: U.S. Government Printing Office, 1919), 15. Scott served as special assistant to the secretary of war, and his white-washed narrative includes a preface by Newton Baker, Gen. John J. Pershing, and "the late" Col. Theodore Roosevelt.

18. Barbeau and Henri, *Unknown Soldiers*, 179. W. E. B. Du Bois had written privately to a college-administrator ally about Moton, "I am continually astonished by his lack of courage." Quoted in David Levering Lewis, *W. E. B. Du Bois* (New York: Holt, 2000), 27.

19. "25,000 of Our Dead in One Cemetery," *NYT*, April 15, 1919, 9:3.

20. Ormond A. Forte, "Death Is Swallowed Up in Victory," *Cleveland Advocate*, October 19, 1918, 8.

21. Scott, *Scott's Official History*, 320.

22. "25,000 of Our Dead in One Cemetery."

23. Barbeau and Henri, *Unknown Soldiers*, 176–178.

24. Ibid., 22–23.

25. Ibid., 26; *NYT*, July 29, 1917, 1; "A Negro's March with Muffled Drums," *Survey* 38 (August 4, 1917): 405; and *Washington Bee*, July 14, 1917, 1.

26. Barbeau and Henri, *Unknown Soldiers*, 178, 182, 184.

27. The exact nature of Buckner's crime is not documented. James E. Watson, Senator from Indiana, to Mr. C. J. Prentiss, December 26, 1929, burial file for Private William Buckner of Co. B, 313th Labor Battalion, Box 669, Office of the QMG, RG 92, NA.

28. Barbeau and Henri, *Unknown Soldiers*, 180.

29. Lewis, *W. E. B. Du Bois*, 2, 14.

30. Piehler, *Remembering War*, 105.

31. ASA Irwin, Cpt., QMC, to Quartermaster Supply Officer, ref.: Jas. E. Smith, Pvt., Co. A, 372nd Infantry, and Kenneth Hawkins, Pvt., Medical Detachment, 349th Infantry, June 17, 1921, Cemeterial Division, Office of the QMG, RG 92, NA.

32. Black soldiers and Filipinos were said to have got along so well with one another that some black soldiers chose to settle on the island after the war. Coffman, *Regulars*, 48.

33. See also Hoganson, *Fighting for American Manhood*, footnote 213.

NOTES TO CHAPTER 7

1. The government simplified the naturalization process by setting up courts at the army camps, making it possible for aliens to gain U.S. citizenship quickly. B. Crowell and R. F. Wilson, *How America Went to War: An Account from Official Sources of the Nation's War Activities, 1917–1920* (New Haven, CT: Yale University Press, 1921), 204–205.

2. Nancy Gentile Ford, *Americans All! Foreign-Born Soldiers in World War I* (College Station: Texas A&M University Press, 2001), 44.

3. *GRS History*, 1:94.

4. Statistics for Italy: 301 bodies shipped; for Ireland: 64 bodies shipped. Czechoslovakia had the least, with 4 bodies—all shipped by August 1922. Ibid., 3:15–16.

5. Burial file of Pietro DiPalma [should be dePalma], Box 1321, Office of the QMG, RG 92, NA.

6. *GRS History*, 3:23.

7. Ibid., 3:15.

8. H. F. Rethers, Col., Paris, to QMC, Washington, DC, May 25, 1921, Wasil Kovaswick, Box 2743, Cemeterial Division, Office of the QMG, RG 92, NA.

9. "Location of Graves and Disposition of Bodies of American Soldiers Who Died Overseas," Special Report of Statistical Branch, General Staff, War Department, January 15, 1920 (Washington, DC: U.S. Government Printing Office, 1920), 5.

10. Second Lieutenant V. M. Conway, Sworn Notarized Statement, signed shortly after his discharge in November 1919, Corr. Relating to Cemeteries, File 293.8, Report of Lt. Conway, RG 92, NA. For Russia details, see Max Boot, *The Savage Wars of Peace* (New York: Perseus Books, 2002), 205–220.

11. Conway, statement.

12. The SS *Lake Daraga* was the first repatriation ship to return to the United States, with 111 American dead on November 12, 1919. *American Legion Weekly*, May 26, 1922, 24.

13. "Bringing Our Dead Home from Russia," *NYT*, November 14, 1919, 14:4; and Piehler, *Remembering War*, 97.

14. Two further expeditions, both initiated by American veterans, returned to the Archangel region in 1929 and again in 1934. My thanks to Jennifer Keene for drawing my attention to the material in the Walter F. Dundun Papers, "Reminiscences, 1969" folder, at the Bentley Historical Library, University of Michigan.

15. The precise number of coffins brought back to the United States changes with each account. Cpt. H. R. Lemley, USA, Retired, Chief of Cemeterial Branch, December 11, 1919, Box 29, Cemeterial Division, Office of the QMG, RG 92, NA; "They Ask to Know," *American Legion Weekly*, June 15, 1923.

16. After the war, there were approximately 11,600 "foreigners" buried in the United Kingdom, of whom 2,600 were German. The majority of Americans who were buried in the United Kingdom died there during the flu epidemic and upon the wrecks of the ships *Otranto* and *Tuscania*. Letter to the Secretary, Ministry of Transport, Whitehall Gdns., December 13, 1919, Box 1057, WG 843/3/1, Catalogue no. 508, CWGC; and *GRS History*, 1:152.

17. *GRS History*, 2:63.

18. The ten European countries were England, Ireland, Scotland, Belgium, Luxembourg, Germany, Austria, Serbia, Russia, and Italy. In Great Britain alone, there were ninety-three cemeteries where Americans were buried. "Location of Graves and Disposition of Bodies," 5, "Graves Registration Service History" (draft version).

19. *GRS History*, 1:101.

20. "Rep. LaGuardia of NY Introduced Bill," *NYT*, May 20, 1919, 4:4.

21. "Topics of the Times" (editorial), *NYT*, December 22, 1919, 14.

22. Ibid.

23. Piehler, *Remembering War*, 95; Meigs, *Optimism at Armageddon*, 180–181.

24. *NYT*, August 1, 1919, 15:6.

25. Piehler, *Remembering War*, 95; editorial, *NYT*, December 19, 1919, 14:4; "Brent Wants Dead to Stay," *NYT*, January 16, 1920, 8:8.

26. American Legion resolution, passed in Minneapolis, 1919, "American Military Dead Overseas," in "A Report to the Secretary of War," Ralph Hayes, Washington, May 14, 1920, 24.

27. Theodore Roosevelt, New York Office, *Kansas City Star,* Madison Avenue, November 2, 1918, to Col. Chas. Pierce, Quentin Roosevelt file, Box 180, ABMC Records, RG 117, NA. A similar letter was also published in its entirety in the *NYT* on November 18, 1918, in ibid.

28. Editorial, *NYT,* December 19, 1919, 14:4; *NYT,* January 26, 1920, 8; Meigs, *Optimism at Armageddon,* 180.

29. "Paying the Debt," *American Legion Weekly,* May 26, 1922, 7, 8.

30. "Would Keep Our Dead," *NYT,* May 30, 1919, 7:4.

31. "Brent Wants Dead to Stay."

32. Mosse, *Myth of the War Experience,* 90, 92; Winter, *Sites of Memory,* 119.

33. Donald Smythe, "Honoring the Nation's Dead," *American History Illustrated* 16, no. 2 (May 1981): 29.

34. J. D. Foster to Chairman, Bring Home Our Soldier Dead League (hereafter "Bring Home League"), to Hon. Newton D. Baker, November 1919, File 293.8, Cemeterial Division, Office of the QMG, RG 92, NA.

35. Ibid.

36. Meigs, *Optimism at Armageddon,* 180.

37. Ibid.; Piehler, *Remembering War,* 97; Rep. John W. Rainey of Illinois, U.S. House of Representatives, 66th Congress, 2nd Session, *Congressional Record* 59 (February 6, 1920): pt. 3:2562–2567.

38. Fabian Ware to B. C. MacDermot, Esq., November 8, 1941, Box 3026, File A/53/3, pt. 1, CWGC.

39. Winter, *Sites of Memory,* 26.

40. John Pettegrew, "'The Soldier's Faith': Turn-of-the-Century Memory of the Civil War and the Emergence of Modern American Nationalism," *Journal of Contemporary History* 31, no. 1 (1996): 49–73.

NOTES TO CHAPTER 8

1. Testimony of Pierce before Expenditures Subcommittee, 3496–3497.

2. J. G. Harbord, Maj. Gen., to Cmdr. in Chief, G-4, March 5, 1919, Entry 1649, Series 293, SOS Records, AEF Records, RG 120, NA; Adj. Gen'l of the Army to Commanding Gen'l, AEF, "Disposition of the bodies," April 1, 1919, and second endorsement to memo, of May 6, 1919, Robert C. Davis, Adj. Gen'l to Chief of Staff, War Department, Sub-group AEF, File E6, RG 120, NA.

3. Chief, GRS, HQ, SOS, AEF, to CQM, AEF, ref.: Disposition of American dead in the AEF, December 4, 1918, Entry 1889, General Correspondence, 1922–1935, Office of the QMG, RG 92, NA.

4. To refer to the funeral industry as "inexperienced" is a curious and seemingly unsupportable claim and reflects Pierce's deep animosity toward his "competition." Ibid.

5. Testimony of Pierce, 3446.

6. Ibid., 3447.

7. This estimation was later reduced as families changed their minds and chose an overseas burial instead. "Concerning Return of Bodies of American Soldiers," Secretary of War to Hon. J. W. Wadsworth, Jr., Chairman, Committee on Military Affairs, U.S. Senate (Washington, DC: U.S. Government Printing Office, March 1920).

8. There were three assistant secretaries of war authorized by Congress during the war. Hayes was a special assistant secretary appointed specifically to handle the graves negotiations in France. War Expenditures hearings before Subcommittee No. 3 (Foreign Expenditures) of the Select Committee on Expenditures in the War Department, House of Representatives, 66th Congress, 1st Session, on War Expenditures, Serial 4, Part 51 (Washington, DC: U.S. Government

Printing Office, 1920), 3126. *GRS History*, 1:114–124. These suggestions were originally put forward by Pierce in his December 4, 1918, memo to CQM, AEF, re.: Disposition of American dead in the AEF.

9. See "Returning Remains to America," *GRS History*, 1:114–124.

10. "Sentiment Changes on Soldier Dead," *NYT*, May 15, 1921, sec. 2, 1:7.

11. This figure is compared with only 164 changes to permanent overseas burials. *GRS History*, 3:64.

12. Mr. and Mrs. Isaac Smith to Cemeterial Division, April 1921, burial file of James W. Smith, Box 4551, Office of the QMG, RG 92, NA.

13. Mrs. Mary E. Shannon, Brooklyn, NY, to Cemeterial Division, July 19, 1920, burial file of Thomas J. E. Shannon, Office of the QMG, RG 92, NA.

14. Private August Sudbeck, November 11, 1919, July 9, 1919, War Department; Donavin W. Sudbeck, Hartington, Nebraska, October 31, 2001, to American Cemetery, Waregem, Belgium, ABMC Cemetery Archives.

15. "Our Dead in France" (editorial), *NYT*, April 17, 1921, sec. 2, 20:1. Wister penned the popular novel *The Virginian*.

16. "Unpardonable" (editorial), *American Legion Weekly*, September 9, 1921, 12; "13,000 Change Their Minds," *NYT*, April 16, 1921, 1:4.

17. "Only 2 Unclaimed Soldier Dead Here," *NYT*, April 16, 1921, 1:4.

18. "Return of U.S. Dead," *NYT*, January 4, 1920, sec. 2, 1:1.

19. "Capt's Father Returns," *NYT*, May 23, 1921, 23:1.

20. "Only 2 Unclaimed Soldier Dead Here."

21. "Body of Newark Lad, Killed in the Argonne," *NYT*, August 8, 1921, 1:6.

22. A. B. Pouch, Nat'l Pres., to Hon. Newton D. Baker, August 20, 1920, QMG Sub-Group, Corr. Relating to Cemeteries, File 293.8, Series "Bring Home League," RG 92, NA.

23. Ibid.; J. D. Foster to Hon. Newton D. Baker, November 1919, in ibid. Foster penned a series of letters, petitions, and telegrams to Baker form November 1919 to mid-1920 demanding that the government act more aggressively to return the dead.

24. Pierce returned temporarily to Washington in December 1919. Pouch to Pierce, January 4, 1921, in ibid.

25. Foster's visit coincided with the lifting of French restrictions that month.

26. Charles C. Pierce to Col. Harry F. Rethers, Chief, GRS in Europe, March 10, 1920, QMG Sub-Group, Corresp. Relating to Cemeteries, File 293.8, Series "Bring Home League," RG 92, NA. Pierce's response is surprising considering an earlier comment he made in 1918 that sharply criticized the practice of "commercialized patriotism" with its "adoption of patented disinfectants and all sorts of 'freak' devices for the shipment of bodies." Chief, GRS, to CQM, AEF, December 4, 1918, Disposition of American Dead, RG 92, NA.

27. J. D. Foster to Col. Chas. C. Pierce, U.S. Army, March 15, 1920, QMG Sub-Group, Corresp. Relating to Cemeteries, File 293.8, Series "Bring Home League," RG 92, NA. Senate bill 3588 would have advanced Pierce permanently to the rank of colonel. *Register of the Army of the United States for 1919* (Washington, DC: U.S. Government Printing Office, 1919).

28. No charges or further evidence of wrongdoing were ever pressed against Charles Pierce, who died the following year. Testimony of Andrew Durbin, Clerk, and Captains Robertson and Tompkins, IG Report, April 1920. War Department Memo, March 24, 1920, from Intel Officer, 461 8th Ave., New York, to Military Intel Division, Washington, DC, Subject Cemeterial Division, Box 772, Office of IG Correspondence, 1917–34, RG 159, NA.

29. Commanding Officer, Maj. L. A. Shipman, GRS, to Chief, QMC, in Europe, June 23, 1920, Sub-Group PST Division, File 293.8, RG 165, NA.

30. Mrs. Chas. C. Pierce died one month prior, April 23, 1921, of pneumonia. Burial file of Charles C. Pierce, Entry 1941, Office of the QMG, RG 92, NA.

31. War Department figures claim 46,304 were returned. January 1931, Box 345, RG 407, NA; and *GRS History*, 3:101.

32. "Objection to Bringing Home," *NYT*, January 18, 1920, sec. 8, 11:8; regarding the figure of thirty million dollars, see Corresp. Relating to Cemeteries, Box 345, RG 407, NA; and Piehler, *Remembering War*, 96.

33. "Pleas for Unknown," *NYT*, May 31, 1920, 3. As if to confirm this woman's perceptive judgment, all the unknown from World War II were returned to the United States for burial in national cemeteries. "These Honored Dead," *Army Information Digest* 1, no. 4 (August 1946): 30.

NOTES TO CHAPTER 9

1. Despite the arrival of the first U.S. troops in the summer of 1917, they did not reach the front line until late October, early November. See Meirion Harries and Susie Harries, *The Last Days of Innocence: America at War, 1917–1918* (New York: Random House, 1997), 5; *ABMC Guide*, 423; Pershing, *My Experiences in the World War*, 217–218.

2. Pershing, *My Experiences in the World War*, 218.

3. Harries and Harries, *Last Days of Innocence*, 5.

4. W. S. McClatchey, Chief Clerk, County of Allegheny, Pittsburgh, PA, to Newton Baker, November 21, 1917, QMG Sub Group, burial file of Thomas Enright (Enright, Hay, and Gresham burial files), RG 92, NA.

5. Henry G. Sharpe, QMG, to Mr. W. S. McClatchey, Chief Clerk, Pittsburgh, PA, November 26, 1917, in ibid.

6. "Patriotic mother" to Mr. Baker, Sec. of War, Pittsburgh, PA, War Department stamp November 20, 1917, in burial file of Thomas Enright.

7. Ibid.

8. Ibid.

9. Steere, *Graves Registration Service*, 150.

10. Cecilia Elizabeth O'Leary suggests that the United States "re-invented itself as a modern nation-state after the Civil War by mobilizing a romanticized militarism." Claire Bond Potter, review of *To Die For: The Paradox of American Patriotism*, by Cecilia Elizabeth O'Leary, *American History* 28, no. 1 (2000): 55–62.

11. Piehler, *Remembering War*, 58.

12. "The South supplied the sentiment; the North the organization." "The Beginnings and Results of Memorial Day," *American Legion Weekly*, May 26, 1922, 16; For GAR, see David W. Blight, *Race and Reunion: The Civil War in American Memory* (Cambridge, MA: Belknap Press of Harvard University Press, 2001), 157.

13. Piehler, *Remembering War*, 58. The legacy of prisoner abuses and deaths among northerners also helped foster the popularity of Memorial Day rituals. For accounts of life in southern prisons, Robert H. Kellogg, *Life and Death in Rebel Prisons* (Hartford, CT: Stebbins, 1865).

14. "The Beginnings and Results of Memorial Day."

15. References to Clara Barton by historian James M. McPherson all refer solely to her nursing contribution. James M. McPherson, *The Illustrated Battle Cry of Freedom* (Oxford: Oxford University Press, 2003), 413, 414, 457. At the other extreme, David Blight claims Barton "led" the Andersonville expedition to record names of the dead, along with Dorence Atwater. In truth, she accompanied the graves officer. Blight, *Race and Reunion*, 153.

16. Stephen B. Oates, *A Woman of Valor: Clara Barton and the Civil War* (New York: Free Press, 1994), 295, 368; Percy H. Epler, *The Life of Clara Barton* (New York: Macmillan, 1917), 111, 113.

17. Quoted in Oates, *Woman of Valor*, 296, 305, 312.

18. Barton's reaction is reminiscent of D. H. Rhodes's when he observed the methods of Charles Pierce in the Philippines. Ibid., 368.

19. The WRC is still in existence today and was incorporated by an act of the 87th Congress, September 7, 1962. Blight, *Race and Reunion*, 71–72. See also GAR, Department of Oregon, Women's Relief Corps, Meade Corps No. 18 records, 1889–1916, University of Oregon Scholars' Bank.

20. Hoganson claims that when Barton arrived in Cuba, military officers initially rejected her offer of aid, so she set to work assisting the Cuban forces. The situation illustrates the military's tendency to resist civilian interference and substantiates Hoganson's claim that American military prowess was entwined with images of manhood and virility. Hoganson, *Fighting for American Manhood*, 126.

21. Epler, *Life of Clara Barton*, 283–286.

22. Ibid., 316.

23. Hoganson, *Fighting for American Manhood*, 22.

24. Barton was a member of the Potomac Corps of the WRC. Epler, *Life of Clara Barton*, 376.

25. Blight, *Race and Reunion*, 158.

26. See W. Fitzhugh Brundage, "White Women and the Politics of Historical Memory in the New South, 1880–1920," in J. Dailey, G. E. Gilmore, and B. Simon, eds., *Jumpin' Jim Crow: Southern Politics from Civil War to Civil Rights*, 115–139 (Princeton, NJ: Princeton University Press, 2000).

27. Ibid., 126.

28. Ibid., 115. Also Gaines Foster, *Ghosts of the Confederacy: Defeat, the Lost Cause, and the Emergency of the New South, 1865–1913* (New York: Oxford University Press, 1987); and Theda Skocpol, "Organization Despite Adversity: The Origins and Development of African American Fraternal Associations," *Social Science History* 28, no. 3 (Fall 2004): 367–437.

29. Blight, *Race and Reunion*, 278.

30. Brundage, "White Women and the Politics of Historical Memory," 118–119.

31. Joan Marie Johnson, "'Ye Gave Them a Stone': African American Women's Clubs, the Frederick Douglass Home, and the Black Mammy Monument," *Journal of Women's History* 17, no. 1 (2005): 63.

32. Ibid., 62–86. The UDC and other groups had led numerous campaigns for a Mammy monument before this proposal, from as early as 1905. Also see Blight, *Race and Reunion*, 288; and Kirk Savage, "The Politics of Memory: Black Emancipation and the Civil War Monument," in John R. Gillis, ed., *Commemorations: The Politics of National Identity* (Princeton, NJ: Princeton University Press, 1994), 127.

33. Johnson, "Ye Gave Them a Stone," 72.

34. Blight, *Race and Reunion*, 288.

35. Johnson, "Ye Gave Them a Stone," 76.

36. Ibid., 69. Art historian Kirk Savage says, "blacks simply did not have the cultural privilege to seek this form of legitimacy, and whites did not care to give it to them." Savage, "Politics of Memory," 136.

37. Savage, "Politics of Memory," 135.

38. Blight, *Race and Reunion*, 193.

39. There were exceptions, such as the Shaw Memorial in Boston (1897), which was dedicated to Colonel Robert Gould Shaw and the black Massachusetts 54th and 55th Infantry and the 5th Cavalry. Ibid., 338–345. Another exception is the Freedman's Memorial by Thomas Ball (1876), in Washington, DC. Savage, "Politics of Memory," 128, 136–137, 139.

40. Blight, *Race and Reunion*, 312; Pettegrew, "Soldier's Faith."

41. Blight, *Race and Reunion*, 154; Jim Weeks, *Gettysburg: Memory, Market, and an American Shrine* (Princeton, NJ: Princeton University Press, 2003), 18–53

42. Blight, *Race and Reunion*, 31.

NOTES TO CHAPTER 10

1. The speaker was Mrs. Louis DeKoven Bowen, chairman of the Woman's Committee, an auxiliary branch of the parent body, the Council of National Defense. "Gold Star as Mourning," *NYT*, November 13, 1917, 7:3.

2. Ibid.

3. "'Mourning' Is Harmful," *NYT*, November 14, 1917, 14:5.

4. Ibid. The editorial concludes with a chilling comment that "the well-advised do not put it on [mourning dress] except when not to do so would too much offend the sensibilities of their neighbors."

5. British-born Samuel Gompers was a staunch advocate of the war and a presidential appointee to the powerful Council of National Defense. "The Bad Effect of Mourning," *NYT* (editorial), November 18, 1917, sec. 2, 2:7; and "Samuel Gompers (1850–1924)," AFL-CIO website, http://www.aflcio.org/aboutus/history/gompers.cfm (accessed June 2008).

6. Woodrow Wilson to Dr. Anna Howard Shaw, May 16, 1918, in *The Papers of Woodrow Wilson*, ed. Arthur Link, 69 vols. (Princeton, NJ: Princeton University Press, 1966–94), 48:28; Wilson's papers are held at the LOC. Shaw earned the Distinguished Service Medal for her work with this committee. She was also a leader in the woman's suffrage movement. Anna Howard Shaw, with the collaboration of Elizabeth Jordan, *The Story of a Pioneer* (New York: Harper & Brothers, 1915).

7. Ibid.

8. "President Approves . . . Bands," *NYT*, May 26, 1918, 18:5.

9. Caroline Seaman Read to Woodrow Wilson, May 3, 1918, in *Papers of Woodrow Wilson*, 48:28 (emphasis added).

10. Ibid.

11. Wilson to Shaw, May 16, 1918, in *Papers of Woodrow Wilson*, 48:28.

12. Jalland's primary focus is on Britain's middle and upper classes. Pat Jalland, *Death in the Victorian Family* (Oxford: Oxford University Press, 1999), 370.

13. Ibid., 372.

14. Ibid., citing Dr. Robert MacKenna, who argued this point in his 1916 study, *The Adventure of Death*, on pages 2 and 28.

15. Ibid., 373.

16. Ibid., 376; Sarah Tarlow, *Bereavement and Commemoration* (Oxford, UK: Blackwell, 1999), 152.

17. Ariès, *Hour of Our Death*, 560.

18. In Australia, the public face of grief was equally stoical: women were advised not to "falter or shrink from pain," according to Brian Ziino. Moreover, Australian women were also encouraged to abandon conventional mourning dress for a small enameled badge as the outward and visible sign of grief. Ziino, *Distant Grief*, 17; Joy Damousi, *The Labour of Loss: Mourning, Memory and Wartime Bereavement in Australia* (Cambridge: Cambridge University Press, 1999), on pride, p. 49, and on wearing a badge of mourning, p. 54.

19. Sigmund Freud, "Mourning and Melancholia," in *Standard Edition of the Works of Sigmund Freud*, vol. 14, trans. and ed. James Strachey (London: Hogarth, 2001), 245.

20. Winter, *Sites of Memory*, 115; Jay Winter and Emmanuel Sivan, "Setting the Framework," in Winter and Sivan, *War and Remembrance*, 32.

21. John R. Gillis, introduction to Gillis, *Commemorations*, 7.

22. For more on collective memory, see David Thelen, "Memory and American History," *Journal of American History* 75, no. 4 (March 1989): 1117; Maurice Halbwachs, *On Collective Memory*, ed. and trans. Lewis A. Coser (Chicago: University of Chicago Press, 1992), 34; Winter and Sivan, "Setting the Framework," 23–29.

NOTES TO CHAPTER 11

1. Britain was the first to bury its Unknown Soldier, in November 1920; France did so in January 1921, followed by Belgium in November 1922. The American unknown soldier was the only unidentified First World War soldier returned to the United States, and he arrived before the repatriated identified dead were buried. Meigs, *Optimism at Armageddon*, 143–147; Mosse, *Fallen Soldiers*, 94–98; Piehler, *Remembering War*, 118; and Adjutant General's Office, Policy and Precedent file, Series 729, RG 407, NA.

2. Meigs, *Optimism at Armageddon*, 147; "The Tomb of the Unknowns," Arlington National Cemetery website, http://www.arlingtoncemetery.net/tombofun.htm.

3. Congressman Hamilton Fish, Jr., believed the burial should take place on Memorial Day in order to promote regional reconciliation. Adjutant General's Office, Policy and Precedent file, Series 729, RG 407, NA; and Piehler, *Remembering War*, 118.

4. Charles C. Pierce, memo for the QMG, February 8, 1921, Box 87, Unknown Soldier File, ABMC Records, RG 117, NA.

5. Ibid., 2. Secretary of War Newton Baker forwarded Pierce's request to U.S. senator James W. Wadsworth with the comment, "I am not in favor of his recommendation." Baker to Hon. James W. Wadsworth, Jr., February 12, 1921, in ibid.

6. Quoted from Baker's speech in Cleveland, Ohio, on April 26, 1918, Box 244, Speeches File for 1918, p. 24, Newton D. Baker Papers, LOC.

7. Census figures show that in 1917 the American population included 4,662,000 people born within the boundaries of the Central Powers. John Higham, *Strangers in the Land* (New York: Atheneum, 1963), 213.

8. Piehler, *Remembering War*, 121.

9. Ron Robin, *Enclaves of America: The Rhetoric of American Political Architecture Abroad, 1900–1965* (Princeton, NJ: Princeton University Press, 1992), 36. European memory historians have been enforcing this relationship for years. Consider the work of Benedict Anderson, Eric Hobsbawm, and Annette Becker, to name just a few.

10. William E. Leuchtenburg, *The Perils of Prosperity, 1914–32* (Chicago: University of Chicago Press, 1958), 87; Hawley, *Great War*, 44.

11. Leuchtenburg, *Perils of Prosperity*, 51–52.

12. Ibid., 56–57; also Thomas A. Bailey, "The Supreme Infanticide," in Davis R. B. Ross, Alden T. Vaughan, and John B. Duff, eds., *Progress, War, and Reaction: 1900–1933* (New York: Thomas Y. Crowell, 1970), 155.

13. Selig Adler, *The Isolationist Impulse: Its Twentieth-Century Reaction* (London: Abelard-Schuman, 1957), 100; Leuchtenburg, *Perils of Prosperity*, 60.

14. Adler, *Isolationist Impulse*, 96, 64; Ferguson, *Colossus*, 52–53.

15. "There was little in the American experience to make men realize that wars, unlike prize fights, do not stop at the sound of the gong." Adler, *Isolationist Impulse*, 98.

16. Robert H. Ferrell, *Peace in Their Time* (New Haven, CT: Yale University Press, 1952), 40.

17. Robin, *Enclaves of America*, 33. By November 1920, the Allies had borrowed $9,466,283,000; by 1929, compound interest brought the total to more than $11 billion. Harries and Harries, *Last Days of Innocence*, 428.

18. Warren I. Cohen, *Empire without Tears: America's Foreign Relations, 1921–1933* (Philadelphia: Temple University Press, 1987).

19. Leuchtenburg, *Perils of Prosperity*, 104–119.

20. Robin, *Enclaves of America*, 65.

21. Ibid., 36. Annette Becker also describes U.S. departure from its traditional isolationism, claiming that Americans "rejected, at least temporarily, their separation, their isolationism."

Annette Becker, *Les Monuments aux Morts Memoire de la Grande Guerre* (Paris: Editions Errance, 1988), 137 (translation mine).

22. John Milton Cooper, Jr., "The Great War and American Memory," *Virginia Quarterly Review* 79 (Winter 2003): 77.

23. Ibid., 77–78. Cooper appears to be referring primarily to Senator William E. Borah, who became chairman of the Foreign Relations Committee in 1924.

24. Currently, over thirteen hundred bronze and granite monuments mark the Civil War positions where Americans fought. Pennsylvania monuments outnumber those of all other states. Frederick W. Hawthorne, *Gettysburg: Stories of Men and Monuments as Told by Battlefield Guides* (Gettysburg, PA: Association of Licensed Battlefield Guides, 1988), 7.

25. Smythe, "Honoring the Nation's Dead," 27.

26. Robin asserts that "America's place under the sun acquired meaning only by comparison with the British, French and German examples, as well as less ambitious models." Robin, *Enclaves of America*, 65.

NOTES TO CHAPTER 12

1. Webb C. Hayes (1856–1934), an Ohio native and veteran of several U.S. wars. Military collecting and preservation played an important role in Hayes's life and began at an early age. Colonel (Ret.) Webb C. Hayes to QMG, U.S. Army, Paris, December 7, 1918, Entry 1889, Series 1922–1935, Office of the QMG, RG 92, NA; Stacy Alexander Paxson, "Nation's Monuments on Cuban Battlefields," *Army and Navy Life* 8, no. 10 (April 1906): 9–21; Thomas J. Brady, "Webb C. Hayes: Gilded Age Ideologue or Adventurer?" *Northwest Ohio Quarterly* 66, no. 3 (Summer 1994): 130–146; and Hayes Collection at the Rutherford B. Hayes Presidential Center, Fremont, Ohio.

2. "Remarks on the organization of the American Battlefield Commissions for marking the places where the American soldiers fell . . . ," supplement to letter from Hayes to QMG, December 7, 1918, p. 3.

3. Hayes to QMG, December 7, 1918.

4. Ibid., 2. Hayes considered the return of remains after the Spanish-American War to be an exception and attributed the response to the "too kind-hearted President and Secretary of War [who] allowed their feelings to get the better of their judgment." Ibid.

5. Pershing, memo to Chief of the General Staff, March 9, 1919, File 21971, Series E6, AEF Records, RG 120, NA.

6. Brig. Gen. Fox Conner, Ass't Chief of Staff, to General Moseley, April 17, 1919, Re: Marking the Battlefields, in ibid.

7. Brigadier General George Van Horn Moseley returned to Washington, DC, where in 1929 he served as military adviser to the assistant secretary of war. His assistant staff officer was Major Dwight D. Eisenhower. Carlo D'Este, *Eisenhower: A Soldier's Life* (New York: Holt, 2002), 197. Quotation from G. Van Horn Moseley, memo for Deputy Chief of Staff, April 1919, File 21971, Series E6, AEF Records, RG 120, NA.

8. Palmer had studied military organization at the Staff College in 1910. Smythe claims that Palmer was "a scholarly American officer." Smythe, "Honoring the Nation's Dead," 27–28.

9. Ralph Hayes, "The Care of the Fallen," A Report to the Secretary of War on American Military Dead Overseas (Washington, DC: May 14, 1920), 42; "Crosses" Memo, W. H. Hart, QMG, to the Assistant Secretary of War, March 13, 1924, 4, QM 293.7, General Correspondence, 1922–35, Box 143, RG 92, NA.

10. Frank Bartlett Willis (1871–1928), forty-seventh governor of Ohio (Rep.), served in the House of Representatives from 1911 to 1915. Biographical Directory of the United States Congress, http://bioguide.congress.gov/biosearch.

11. James William Husted (1870–1925), New York (Rep.), House representative from 1915 to 1922. Biographical Directory of the United States Congress; "Memorial Highway in France and Belgium: Bill for an American Commission," Folder 22, Box 15, Hayes Collection No. 4 at the Rutherford B. Hayes Presidential Center, Fremont, Ohio.

12. Hayes to QMG, December 7, 1918; also Appendix III, History of Legislation, File 21971, Series E6, AEF Records, RG 120, NA.

13. See the New York City society's official letterhead in the Hayes Collection. These two bills were S 2864 and HR 9634. "Memorial Highway in France and Belgium, Bill for an American Commission"; Appendix III, History of Legislation.

14. For example, see statement of Rear Admiral T. J. Cowie, U.S. Navy (Commander of the Military Order of the World War), to Hon. Stephen G. Porter, Chairman of the Committee on Foreign Affairs, House of Representatives, 67th Congress, 2nd and 3rd Sessions, on HR 9634 and HR 10801, "For the Creation of an American Battle Monuments Commission," December 14, 1922, 62; also H. P. Caemmerer, Secretary and Executive Officer, the Commission of Fine Arts, to Hon. Stephen G. Porter, November 28, 1922, in ibid.

15. The plan called for eighty relief maps and fifty outline-sketch plaques. Memo for the Chief of Staff, War Department, May 16, 1921, 5; "Suitable memorials to the American Soldier in Europe," Treasury Department, Bureau of the Budget, 67th Congress, 2nd Session, House of Representatives, Document No. 197, February 23, 1922, 2.

16. This abrupt change resulted after a conference between the secretary of war and members of the Foreign Affairs Committee. Perhaps members wanted to avoid the more powerful American Legion. Appendix III, History of Legislation, with Memo for the Chief of Staff, signed W. G. Haan, Maj. Gen., Ass't Chief of Staff, May 16, 1921, 2, War Department Document 14765, File 21971, Series E6, AEF Records, RG 120, NA.

17. Haan document, 23.

18. Not until 1924 would any allocation of bonuses be finally agreed on and no payments made until 1945. Harries and Harries, *Last Days of Innocence*, 456.

19. Jennifer Keene, *Doughboys, the Great War, and the Remaking of America* (Baltimore: Johns Hopkins University Press, 2000), 162–165.

20. Hawley, *Great War*, 77.

21. Appendix III, History of Legislation, 3. A vote was not taken at the first hearing.

22. Memo for Chief of Staff, War Department, from J. M. Palmer, Brigadier General, May 16, 1921, ABMC Minutes and Agendas, RG 117, NA.

23. Memo, ref.: "First meeting of American Battle Monuments Commission," September 1, 1923, X. H. Price, Secretary, ABMC Minutes and Agendas, RG 117, NA. Letters had been sent to the White House from the public endorsing Hamilton Fish (he also received the majority of recommendations from congressional members, but he was not appointed to the commission). J. M. Palmer, memo to Secretary of War, April 7, 1923, in ibid.

NOTES TO CHAPTER 13

1. Although a senator was recommended to serve on the commission, no specific name was mentioned; Senator David Reed filled that position. However, Representative Stephen G. Porter, chairman of the Foreign Affairs Committee, prepared the original legislation, and his name was later suggested, but he was not chosen as an ABMC member. Both Porter and Reed represented the Pittsburgh constituency.

2. Reed was appointed to the Senate seat, rather than elected, when Senator William Evans Crow died. Letters to the editor, *Time*, December 16, 1929, 4, Microform no. 02914, LOC.

3. *Time*, December 16, 1929, 4–8. David Aiken Reed (1880–1953) was acting chief of staff of the United Section of Inter-Allied Armistice Commission and American representative on the Allied Economic Commission. As U.S. senator from Pennsylvania, 1922–1935, he was chairman of the Senate Committee on Military Affairs (70th through 72nd Congresses) and a member of the Finance, Foreign Affairs, and Immigration committees. He also served as U.S. delegate to the London Naval Conference of 1930.

4. The *Time* article revealed that Reed was well known as an "instinctive aristocrat" who made "no appeal to the common people [and] never attempt[ed] to identify himself falsely with them." Ibid., 8.

5. See ABMC Minutes and Agendas; and "Erection of a Monument in France to Commemorate the Valiant Services of the 93rd Div. of AEF," hearings before the Committee on Foreign Affairs, 69th Congress, 1st Session, on HR 9694, March 3, 4, 5, 1926 (Washington, DC: U.S. Government Printing Office, 1926), 20.

6. See Francis Russell, *The Shadow of Blooming Grove: Warren G. Harding in His Times* (New York: McGraw-Hill, 1968); also Robert H. Ferrell, *The Strange Deaths of President Harding* (Columbia: University of Missouri Press, 1996).

7. Hawley, *Great War*, 74. Under the leadership of Charles R. Forbes, the agency defrauded the government and cost taxpayers some two hundred million dollars. Senator Reed was also chairman of the committee investigating the Veterans' Bureau. Minutes of the third meeting of the ABMC, November 8, 1923, Box 1A, File: Index to Records of Proceedings of the ABMC, September 21, 1923, to September 4, 1924, ABMC Records, RG 117, NA.

8. *Time*, December 16, 1929, 6.

9. The officer claimed that many naval graves had been overlooked in the reburial process and that even when the next of kin requested burial in an American cemetery, their wish had often been ignored. The result was that the government was relieved of responsibility for their graves. Minutes of the third meeting of the ABMC.

10. A motion was passed at the first ABMC meeting that the discussions and votes of members not be made public without special authority from the commission. Memo, First Meeting of American Battle Monuments Commission, September 1, 1923, 2, ABMC Minutes and Agendas, ABMC Records, RG 117, NA.

11. When the ABMC legislation was passed, only two days remained before Congress adjourned, leaving the commission without any fiscal appropriation until the next session. Appendix III, History of Legislation, 4, ABMC Records, RG 117, NA.

12. Minutes of the third meeting of the ABMC, November 8, 1923, 9, ABMC Minutes and Agendas, ABMC Records, RG 117, NA.

13. Charles E. Hughes, Department of State, to Major X. H. Price, Secretary, December 13, 1923 (letter included with minutes of the fourth meeting of ABMC, January 30, 1924), Minutes of ABMC, 1923–24, ABMC Records, RG 117, NA.

14. The commission's expenses for this visit were included in its 1924 budget request for $650,000. Pierce to Pershing, February 1, 1924, Annual Report of the ABMC, fiscal year ending June 30, 1925, 1, ABMC Records, RG 117, NA.

15. Burial count as of April 1930 mentioned in attachment to "Establishment and Present Status" memo of April 17, 1923, by a board composed of the assistant secretary of war, General Pershing, and the quartermaster general. Cemetery Expenditures, April 25, 1930, Box 772, 333.9, U.S. Army Records of the Inspector General, RG 159, NA.

16. Monro MacCloskey, Brig. Gen. (USAF retired), *Hallowed Ground: Our National Cemeteries* (New York: Richards Rosen, 1968), 50. Pierce and Pershing's early cemetery plans; see "Crosses" memorandum to the Assistant Secretary of War, from W. H. Hart, QMG, March 13, 1924, Box 143, Subject file 1922–35, General Correspondence, "Crosses," Vol. 2 (1924), RG 92, NA; "Establishment and Present Status" memo of April 17, 1923; and Frank E. Vandiver, *Black Jack: The Life and Times of John J. Pershing* (College Station: Texas A&M University Press, 1977), 2:1064.

17. The decision to leave Americans buried in England was a rather late one. See "Report of Major General John F. O'Ryan [former commander of 27th U.S. Division], on Duty Abroad," August 16, 1920, a published pamphlet (Albany, NY: J. B. Lyon, 1923), 40.

18. Ariès, *Hour of Our Death*, 477–478.

19. By August 1928, there were 135 "do not disturb" cases in Europe, the majority of which were in very poor condition, "causing the government much criticism." John T. Harris, Maj., Memorandum for Major Dabney, April 23, 1931, War Department, Washington, DC, QMC; J. McClintock, Maj., QMC, to Mr. William Blise, Iron Belt, Wisconsin, November 6, 1928; and Lt. Col. Arthur D. Budd, Hartford, Connecticut, to QMG, ref.: William S. Ely, n.d.; all in "Disposition of Remains," GRS Records, RG 92, NA.

20. *GRS History*, 1:103.

21. Ministère de la Guerre des pensions, March 18, 1922, to Le President du Conseil, Ministère des Affaires étrangères, direction des Affaires politique et commerciale, sous direction d'amérique, Series: Papiers d'agents, Sous series: Jules Jusserand Collection, vol. 19 (1808–1939), Ministère des Affaires étrangères, Paris. Also see memo for the commission, ref.: "Acquisition of land in France," August 17, 1926, ABMC Memo No. 49, reference to American Ambassador's letter, Box 87, ABMC Records, RG 117, NA.

22. Initially, Congress granted $856,680, but after an urgent request from the GRS chief in Europe, an additional $143,320 was added, making a total of $1 million. For expenditures, see War Department to the Secretary of State, October 29, 1923, 851.1231/9, M560, microfilm reel 38, Records of the Department of State, RG 59, NA; Public Resolution No. 44, 67th Congress, amended by Public Resolution No. 385, 67th Congress, January 22, 1923, "Establishment and Present Status," in Cemetery Expenditures, April 25, 1930, Box 772, GRS (3), 333.9, U.S. Army Records of the Inspector General, RG 159, NA; Translation of French Law, December 29, 1915, "Acquisition of Land for Cemeteries," Office of the Assistant Chief of Staff, Entry 283, AEF Records, RG 120, NA; and Series: Correspondence politique et commerciale/B-Amérique, Sous series: Jules Jusserand Collection, vol. 19, Ministère des Affaires étrangères, Archives Diplomatiques, Amérique 1918–1929, États-Unis, 171, Armee, Cimetieres, ceremonies, monuments militaries Americans en France, Janvier 1922–Mai 1924, Ministère des Affaires étrangères, Paris.

23. H. F. Rethers to the President of the Council of Ministry of Foreign Affairs, December 9, 1921, Amérique 1918–1929, 170, Mars 1919–Décembre 1921, Ministère des Affaires étrangères, Paris.

24. X. H. Price to Mr. Ambassador, "Acquisition of Land in France," Memo, ABMC Correspondence, RG 117, NA.

25. Longworth, *Unending Vigil*, 11.

26. There is no record of compensation amounts or payments. Correspondence between Mlle. Malvina Delespaul and Monsieur le President de la Commission d'hygiene, Courtrai, February 18, 1922, and February 20, 1922; Administration Communale de Waereghem, May 22, 1919; and Service des Sepultures Militaires, May 9, 1922; all in Waregem Town Archives, Belgium.

27. Article 225 of the Versailles Treaty of Peace declared that all governments must agree to respect and maintain the graves of soldiers and sailors who died as prisoners of war and were buried in Germany. "Burial of British Soldiers," House of Commons Debate, July 8, 1919, Vol. 117, cc1593-4, Hansard (HMSO), UK.

28. GHS Pinsent, Esq., Treasury, to Fabian Ware, Imperial War Graves Commission, Baker Street, London, August 24, 1920, Memorials and Graves 1921–23, T161/596 Treasury, "Allied Graves in the UK . . . maintenance of," War Office Records, National Archives, Kew, England.

29. Fabian Ware, Major-General, Vice-Chairman, IWGC, to "My dear Pinsent," September 2, 1920, T161/596, S2555, Grave Space, War Office Records, National Archives, Kew, England.

30. This identification problem had been ongoing. See Benj. L. Jacobson to Third Assistant Secretary of War, August 19, 1918, Entry 1941, RG 92, NA. Also General Pershing's orders via

cablegram, July 29, 1918, restating instructions issued the previous February, Entry 194, Col. Harry Cutler, Chair, JWB, to Acting Chief of Staff, G-1, April 5, 1919, 9, RG 92, NA; Commander-in-chief Reports, Entry 22, Folder 69, RG 120, NA.

31. John Paul Tyler, Sr., Chaplain, 82nd Div., to Senior G.H.Q, Chaplain's Office, AEF, Report for the Month of August 1918, Chaplains' Reports, 82nd Div., Entry 597, AEF Records, RG 120, NA; Rabbi Lee J. Levinger, *A Jewish Chaplain in France* (New York: Macmillan, 1921), 110. By the Second World War, all soldier identity tags displayed religious affiliation.

32. Pvt. Samuel J. Rudak, Co. G, 102nd U.S. Inf., AEF, to Hon. Nathan Barnert, May 23, 1918, Entry 1941, RG 92.

33. Frederick Palmer, *Newton D. Baker: America at War*, vol. 1 (New York: Dodd, Mead, 1931), 323–324.

34. This is a conservative estimate, according to Rabbi Levinger in *Jewish Chaplain in France*, 17 and 121.

35. AEF Commander-in-Chief's Report, Part 8, Activities of G-1, Appendix G, Report of Jewish Welfare Board, April 5, 1919, Entry 22, Folder 69, AEF Records, RG 120, NA.

36. Levinger, *Jewish Chaplain in France*, 7.

37. Hart, quoting an endorsement dated July 24, 1919, addressed to the Cemeterial Branch, signed by C. C. Pierce, "Crosses" memorandum (see n. 19).

38. "Crosses" memorandum. Kurt Piehler suggests that the shepherd's crook was proposed before the cross.

39. Meeting minutes quoted from August 30, 1920, and November 8, 1920, in "Crosses" memorandum.

40. November 8, 1920, meeting of the War Memorials Council, as quoted in "Crosses" memorandum.

41. Minutes from the third ABMC meeting, November 8, 1923, ABMC Records, RG 117, NA.

42. Index to Records of Proceedings of the ABMC.

43. Third meeting motion by Reed took place on November 8, 1923; Mrs. Bentley's cable from the GSM association, see minutes of the nineteenth meeting of the ABMC, June 3, 1926; for Gold Star Fathers association position on headstones, see comment from Mr. A. S. McCaskey, minutes of the twentieth meeting of the ABMC, October 7, 1926, all in Box 1A, File: Index to Records of Proceedings of the ABMC, September 21, 1923, to September 4, 1924, ABMC Records, RG 117, NA. For the general agreement of the GSM and Gold Star Fathers associations, see "Crosses" memorandum.

44. Annual Report of the ABMC, June 1925, 4.

45. Ibid., 6.

46. "Information Obtained at Conference with Chief," unsigned and undated, Box 87, ABMC Records, RG 117, NA; also David W. Lloyd, *Battlefield Tourism: Pilgrimage and the Commemoration of the Great War in Britain, Australia and Canada, 1919–1939* (Oxford, UK: Berg, 1998), 124.

47. "Pershing Reports on War Memorials," *NYT*, June 12, 1928, 28.

48. Minutes of the twenty-third meeting of the ABMC, February 1927, Box 1A, File: Index to Records of Proceedings of the ABMC, and ABMC Minutes, June 3, 1926, RG 117, NA; also Grossman, "Architecture for a Public Client," 141.

49. Cyrus Adler to Charles Moore, Esq., October 1, 1928; and Chas. A. Platt to H. P. Caemmerer, CFA, August 15, 1928, Project Files, Box 6, American Cemeteries, Europe, Jewish Welfare Board, Tomb of the Unknown Soldier, Commission of Fine Arts (CFA), RG 66, NA.

50. The Johnson-Reed Act was also named for Albert Johnson, formerly a newspaper editor and a vehement nativist famed for his opposition to the Industrial Workers of the World. Higham, *Strangers in the Land*, 321.

51. Reuben Fink, "Visas, Immigration, and Official Anti-Semitism," *Nation* 112, no. 2920 (June 22, 1921): 870; Higham, *Strangers in the Land*, 315, 316, 318, 325.

52. X. H. Price to General John J. Pershing, February 1, 1924, 2, Pershing Correspondence File, Entry 5, ABMC Records, RG 117, NA.

53. Robin, *Enclaves of America*, 33.

54. Each British national cemetery also has its Cross of Sacrifice with a sword set on it, and the Stone of Remembrance bearing the carved biblical quotation, "Their name liveth for evermore."

55. Serial numbers did not appear on the headstones. See secretary of war's recommendation to ABMC, dated December 7, 1925, that the army serial numbers of deceased soldiers be omitted from headstones in Europe. No explanation is given. Minutes of the sixteenth meeting of the ABMC, December 14, 1925, Box 1A, File: Index to Records of Proceedings of the ABMC, September 21, 1923, to September 4, 1924, ABMC Records, RG 117, NA; William C. Moore, "The Division of the Dead," *American Legion Weekly*, May 26, 1922, 4.

56. E. E. Davis, Exec. Ass't, GRS, to Mr. Charles J. Holland, Attorney and Counsellor at Law, 350 Madison Ave., NY, burial file of Private William J. Bergen, RG 92, NA.

57. F. Mossop, Serjeant, 25188, 1st Bn, the King's (Liverpool Regiment), "Debt of Honour Register," CWGC database of Americans serving with British forces, Maidenhead, England.

58. "Forty-First Annual G.A.R. Program for Memorial Day," Sewickley Cemetery, May 30, 1921, Sewickley, PA.

59. The AOMDA was incorporated in 1952 and is still active. American Overseas Memorial Day Association, January 23, 1923, F. Drake to General John J. Pershing; Pershing to Mr. W. H. Brevoort [*sic*], Paris, France, March 21, 1923; F. E. Drake to W. H. Bevoort, The Travellers' Club, March 9, 1923, Overseas Memorial Day Assoc., Pershing Papers, Manuscript Division, LOC.

60. Annual maintenance costs were estimated at five thousand dollars per year in 1922. Although operations and maintenance costs are not broken down individually by cemetery, expenses for U.S. cemeteries and memorials in 2005 were $53,770,464. Annual fiscal appropriations total more than $36 million for salaries and expenses. Cemetery visitor figures are not listed. See American Battle Monuments Commission, Fiscal Year 2006 Annual Report, 30.

NOTES TO CHAPTER 14

1. Higham, *Strangers in the Land*, 308.

2. Ibid., 270.

3. Higham claims that Jews "faced a sustained agitation that singled them out from the other new immigrant groups blanketed by racial nativism—an agitation that reckoned them the most dangerous force undermining the nation." Ibid., 278.

4. The estimate of immigrant volunteers is taken from Ford, *Americans All!* 30; Higham, *Strangers in the Land*, 277.

5. Creel's words, quoted in Elizabeth Stevenson, *Babbitts and Bohemians: The American 1920s* (New York: Macmillan, 1967), 42.

6. Ibid.

7. Ibid., 48.

8. Jules Abels, *In the Time of Silent Cal* (New York: G. P. Putnam's Sons, 1969), 48.

9. Ibid.

10. Ibid., 9.

11. Rogers was actually referring to the worsening economic crisis in 1931. Quoted in John F. Wukovits, ed., *The 1920s* (San Diego, CA: Greenhaven, 2000), 232.

12. Knox also shared a law practice with James Reed (David Reed's father). Andrew Mellon was their client and the third-richest man in the United States, after Henry Ford and John D. Rockefeller. He was sixty-five years old when appointed. David Cannadine, *Mellon: An American Life* (New York: Knopf, 2006), 214.

13. Abels, *In the Time of Silent Cal*, 220, 223.

14. Cannadine, *Mellon*, xiii; and Robert H. Ferrell, *The Presidency of Calvin Coolidge* (Lawrence: University Press of Kansas, 1998), chap. 1, esp. 21; Stevenson, *Babbitts and Bohemians*, 116.

15. Abels, *In the Time of Silent Cal*, 42.

16. For more on partisan indifference, see David E. Kyvig, *Daily Life in the United States, 1920–1940*, 2nd ed. (Chicago: Ivan R. Dee, 2004), 165.

17. By comparison, Kyvig states that the 2000 census found 281.4 million Americans. Ibid., 10–11.

18. Ibid., 11.

19. Ibid., 19; Cannadine, *Mellon*, 107.

20. Cannadine, *Mellon*, 489, 597.

21. Letters to the editor, "Pennsylvania's Reed," *Time*, December 16, 1929, 8.

22. Reed was specifically referring to those veterans in hospitals. "Sought to Expel Reed from Legion," *NYT*, March 6, 1927, 20:1.

23. Cannadine is quoting from an article written in 1930 by journalist R. L. Duffus. *Mellon*, 433.

24. Ibid., 597, 232.

25. Cannadine records Reed's contemporaries depicting him as a "Mellon puppet" (ibid., 489); see the *Time* magazine article that states his "interests [were] closely allied with those of Andrew William Mellon." "Pennsylvania's Reed," *Time*, December 16, 1929. Amity Shlaes calls Reed "Mellon's old spokesman" in *The Forgotten Man: A New History of the Great Depression* (New York: HarperCollins, 2007), 210; and for Mellon's influence on Reed, see Abels, *In the Time of Silent Cal*, 225.

26. Cannadine, *Mellon*, 442–443.

27. Apparently, one reason Mellon had agreed to accept the treasury position in the first place was the assurance from his friend Knox that he would champion his policies in the state and defend his interests in the upper house. Ibid., 294.

28. In Pershing's absence, Reed suggested that a temporary chairman be elected. The motion was made by Captain R. G. Woodside, a Pittsburgh native who listed that city's sheriff's office as his address. Woodside was then elected vice chairman. Record of Proceedings, minutes of the first meeting of the ABMC, September 1, 1923, 1, ABMC Minutes, ABMC Records, RG 117, NA.

29. This strategy was refined by the board appointed by the secretary of war in 1920. The War Department's project was estimated to cost $538,103 and was planned for completion in five years. Hearings before the Committee on Foreign Affairs, 67th Congress, 2nd and 3rd Sessions, on HR 9634 and HR 10801, part 2 (Washington, DC: U.S. Government Printing Office, 1923), 7.

30. General J. G. Harbord, who commanded the 2nd Division, cites details of each monument in a letter published in "Pleads for Upkeep of War Monuments," *NYT*, December 14, 1930, sec. 1, 9:4.

31. The 2nd Division alone had twenty-two boulders. Annual Report of the ABMC, June 1925.

32. The 3rd Division's monument in Château-Thierry was destroyed by bombardment in 1940, but a new structure was later placed at a different location in the town. Annual Report of the ABMC, June 1925, 27; a photo of 3rd Division monument taken August 11, 1940, accompanied "Diary Notes, Monday, July 8, 1940," 3rd Division File, Division Monuments, AEF Records, RG 120, NA.

33. Colonel (later Major General) Frank Parker commanded the 18th I.R. and 1st Infantry Brigade, 1st Division, during the war and would have been more than a casual observer of such activities. Interview with Col. Frank Parker, Infantry, 1st Division, signed by X. H. Price, Major, Corps of Engineers, War Department, December 22, 1921, Box 1230, File 21971, AEF Records, RG 120, NA.

34. Some of the more or less permanent monuments were given attention and later maintained under the ABMC. Annual Report of the ABMC, June 1925, 40.

35. Major General Charles P. Summerall commanded the 1st Division from July to October 1918 and then commanded the V Corps. He was later chief of staff. Summerall-Price correspondence, February 9, 13, 1926, and March 16, 1926, Box 1230, File 21971, AEF Records, RG 120, NA.

36. This motion was introduced by Senator Reed. Minutes of the seventeenth meeting of the ABMC, March 29, 1926, ABMC Minutes, Box 26, WWI monument and memorial files, ABMC Records, RG 117, NA.

37. ABMC minutes from 1923 to 1933 and Divisional AEF files, RG 120, NA; "Federal Help Sought to Save War Markers," *NYT*, November 8, 1931, sec. 5, 6:3; *NYT* editorials, November 26, 1931, sec. 4, 26:4; "Pleads for Upkeep of War Monuments," *NYT*, December 14, 1930, sec. 1, 9:4. The 1st, 2nd, and 5th Divisions erected the greatest number of war monuments, with those of the 2nd and 5th alone numbering in excess of sixty-four.

38. "Federal Help Sought to Save War Markers."

39. Ibid.

40. Ibid.

41. William Charles Moore, "The Division of the Dead," *American Legion Weekly*, May 26, 1922, no. 21: 4.

42. Charles Moore, "War Memorials Bad and Good," *American Legion Weekly*, September 8, 1922, 15. On the *Spirit of the American Doughboy* statue by Ernest Moore Viquesney, see *American Legion Weekly* magazines for the early 1920s.

43. Jennifer Wingate, "Over the Top: The Doughboy in World War I Memorials and Visual Culture," *American Art* 19, no. 2 (2005): 29–32.

44. C. Moore, "War Memorials Bad and Good," 14.

45. R. A. Long, founding president of the Liberty Memorial Association, stated, "From its inception it was intended that this memorial should represent . . . a living expression for all time of the gratitude of a grateful people to those . . . who gave their lives in defense of liberty and our country." "The Liberty Memorial," History of the Memorial, http://www.theworldwar.org/s/110/display (2009).

46. C. Moore, "War Memorials Bad and Good," 15. The Kansas City Memorial was designed by Harold Van Buren Magonigle (1867–1935), also known for the McKinley memorial in Canton, Ohio. See "Accession Sheet," no. 38M77, Magonigle Papers, Rare Book and Manuscript Division, New York Public Library; also available online at http://www.nypl.org/research/chss/spe/rbk (2009).

47. "East and West Meet," *New York Times Magazine*, August 22, 1926, IV, 8:1.

48. In a rather obtuse fashion, one *New York Times* editorial read, "Let Kansas City have it that way, the essential thing is that while New York's War Memorial—which New York would call just that—is still a dream of patriots and a hope deferred of architects and artists, Kansas City's Peace-After-the-War Memorial is a thing of solid stone." Ibid.

49. Minutes of the seventeenth meeting of the ABMC. Once Reed's motion passed, it was decided that a statement should be prepared for the press giving the matter "as wide publicity as possible." Piehler, *Remembering War*, 98; "Limit Set on War Memorials Built," *Washington Post*, April 26, 1926, 2.

50. "Limit Set on War Memorials Built."

51. This was the first memorial on the Mall to list the names of women and African Americans with white men from the District. Mark D. Richards, "DC Service in WWI and DC World War Memorial," May 26, 2002, http://www.dcwatch.com/richards (2008); Programs File, Box 6, Gold Star Mothers Papers, Collections of the Manuscript Division, LOC; and Bobbie Brewster, "The Forgotten Tribute," *Washington Post*, April 11, 2004, B8.

52. *The Washington Star*, July 27, 1926, cited in Richards, "DC Service in WWI and DC World War Memorial" (located in the Washingtoniana Room of the DC Public Library, 1930s scrapbook, "Memorials and Monuments in Washington, DC").

53. Walter J. Fenton to W. Myers, Esq., editorial in *New York Herald Tribune,* September 4, 1924, Committee on Memorials, Box 87, RG 117, NA.

54. Joseph H. Hanken, VFW Headquarters, to Frank B. Kellogg, Sec. of State, July 31, 1928, and F. W. Van Duyne, Col., QMC, September 5, 1928, memo, State Department Records, RG 59, NA.

55. D. Kennedy, *Over Here,* 218.

56. For parades as instruments of nationalism, see Jürgen Heideking, Geneviève Fabre, and Kai Dreisbach, introduction to Heideking, Fabre, and Dreisbach, eds., *Celebrating Ethnicity and Nation: American Festive Culture from the Revolution to the Early 20th Century* (New York: Berghahn Books, 2001), 46.

57. See Ferrell, *Peace in Their Time.*

58. Despite years of political lobbying and campaigning by the Legion, Congress did not vote Armistice Day a federal holiday until 1938.

59. The quotation is from Isaiah in the Old Testament. "Memorial Dedicated over Legion's Protest," *NYT,* November 12, 1927, 4:3.

60. Details from Michael O'Brien in the Western Front Association magazine, *Stand To!* 65 (September 2002): 20–22.

61. The only overseas memorial dedicated after the war in memory of American women was a home for destitute French girls (Katherine Baker Memorial), built and dedicated in April 1927 at Issy-les-Moulineaux, France. Vol. 1320, Records of Foreign Service Posts, Diplomatic Posts (Consular Files), RG 84, NA; and Charles Moore, "Fallen on the Field of Honor: I—War Memorials," *Outlook,* February 18, 1920, 275; Moore claimed there was "no apparent desire to commemorate the women who went to war."

62. Wingate, "Over the Top," 41.

63. Wukovits, *The 1920s,* 157.

64. Barbeau and Henri, *Unknown Soldiers,* 188.

65. Keene, *Doughboys,* 156.

66. Johnson was posthumously awarded the Purple Heart in 1996.

67. Walter White, Secretary, NAACP, to Winthrop Adams, Esq., U.S. Veterans Bureau, April 26, 1928, Box C-376, NAACP Records, LOC.

68. Sgt. Bernard O. Henderson, Newport News, VA, to Dr. W. E. B. Du Bois, NY, December 18, 1918, in ibid.

69. The lead organizing member was Theodore Roosevelt, Jr., son of the late president. Piehler, *Remembering War,* 111.

70. Louisiana, Alabama, Georgia, and Mississippi were included among states that refused to grant charters to "colored Posts"; however, there were some southern states that did grant charters. Assistant Secretary, J. Wesley Samuels, Esq., Everett, Washington, March 30, 1921, "Military General" subject file, 1921 (Jan.–May), NAACP Records, LOC; also Alex A. Govern, Chairman, Baton Rouge, Louisiana, to Mr. Walter White, Secretary NAACP, October 11, 1934, in ibid.

71. Piehler, *Remembering War,* 113; Keene, *Doughboys,* 156.

72. John Bodnar, *Remaking America: Public Memory, Commemoration, and Patriotism in the Twentieth Century* (Princeton, NJ: Princeton University Press, 1992), 86.

73. Ibid. The *Washington Post* announced that a fund of one hundred thousand dollars was appropriated by the Indiana General Assembly for prizes and expenses for a competition for architects to design the Legion headquarters. See "$50,000 for Memorial Plans," *Washington Post,* March 11, 1921, 6.

74. Bodnar, *Remaking America,* 88.

75. Halbwachs believed the same was true for the Christian community returning to Jerusalem. He noted that enemies of emergent Christianity tried to destroy places of pilgrimage in an attempt to maintain order and wipe out memories that threatened their own reputation. Halbwachs, *On Collective Memory,* 202–203.

76. The order was never pressed. "Sought to Expel Reed from Legion," *NYT*, March 6, 1927, 20:1.

NOTES TO CHAPTER 15

1. Annual Report of the ABMC, June 1925, 35.

2. Ibid., 35–36.

3. The estimated cost for this monument was $350,000. Ibid., 36.

4. Price to Pershing, Rio de Janeiro, Brazil, December 31, 1924, Pershing Correspondence File, Entry 5, ABMC Records, RG 117, NA; and Annual Report of the ABMC, June 1925, 38.

5. Grossman, "Architecture for a Public Client," 126. Elizabeth Grossman's article on Cret originates from her Ph.D. dissertation, "Paul Philippe Cret: Rationalism and Imagery in American Architecture" (Brown University, 1980). Her work on Cret's architecture in biographical form is entitled *The Civic Architecture of Paul Cret* (Cambridge: Cambridge University Press, 1996). Also Annual Report of the ABMC, June 1925, 46.

6. Price to Pershing, December 31, 1924, 1–2. Cret was in France when war broke out and remained there in the army for five years, returning to Philadelphia after being discharged. He was awarded the Croix de Guerre for his wartime Franco-American liaison efforts and died in 1945. Cret was a consulting architect for the ABMC from 1923 to 1945. *Philadelphia Evening Public Ledger*, August 25, 1919, File: "Quentin Roosevelt Grave," Box 180, ABMC Records, RG 117, NA.

7. Paul P. Cret and Thomas Atherton had designed for Pennsylvania the fountain at Nantillois (1925), the bridge at Fismes (1928), and the memorial park at Varennes (1927). Grossman states that this work helped Cret to get his ABMC appointment. Grossman, "Architecture for a Public Client," 124, 126. Minutes of the eleventh meeting of the ABMC, November 22, 1924, RG 117, NA. Cret was also commissioned by the Roosevelt family to design the memorial fountain to their son, Quentin, in the village of Chamery, France, in 1919. *Philadelphia Evening Bulletin*, September 1920; *Evening Public Ledger*, August 25, 1919., file News Clippings, Box 180, ABMC Records, RG 117, NA.

8. During the war, Price had organized, trained, and taken to France the 53rd National Field Artillery Brigade of the 28th Division. Price was a builder who constructed homes and apartments in Philadelphia and Pittsburgh. He was actually a colonel in command of the Pennsylvania National Guard and upon retirement was promoted to general. Anne Wiegle (Price was her great uncle) to the author, September 2008. See newsclippings from Delaware County Historical Society, Chester, PA.

9. Price to Pershing, December 31, 1924. Minutes of the twentieth meeting of the ABMC. Cost of plan taken from Annual Report of the ABMC, June 1925, 42.

10. Minutes of the fifteenth meeting of the ABMC, November 4, 1925, RG 117, NA; Annual Report of the ABMC, June 1925, 44.

11. Grossman, "Architecture for a Public Client," 126.

12. Robin, *Enclaves of America*, 55; Piehler, *Remembering War*, 100.

13. Noted in a review of Cret's work at the University of Texas, Austin, "Paul Philippe Cret (1876–1945)," by Christopher Long, at http://www.utexas.edu/toursmainbuilding/people/cret.html (2009).

14. Robin, *Enclaves of America*, 50; Grossman, "Architecture for a Public Client," 139.

15. Minutes state that "a discussion of the disadvantages of competitions" took place at the fifteenth ABMC meeting.

16. Stevenson, *Babbitts and Bohemians*, 119; Nathan Miller, *New World Coming: The 1920s and the Making of Modern America* (New York: Scribner, 2003), 164. In 1922, Congress created the World War Foreign Debt Commission, which renegotiated the Allied debt to the United

States (for war loans) and added the interest—payable over sixty-two years—to the principal, thus doubling the amount owed the United States (making it over twenty-two billion dollars). By 1932, most European countries had defaulted on their war debts. See Ferrell, *Peace in Their Time*, 40–42; and George Brown Tindall, *America*, vol. 2, 2nd ed. (New York: Norton, 1988), 1152.

17. See letters and petitions addressed to "Monsieur le depute," signed by the French secretary general and employees from Fevre & Co., dated October 4, 1927. The correspondence refers to the loss of work during a period when "France is in an economic crisis," which resulted in many unemployed laborers. File 173, Armies and Cemeteries, February 1927–December 1929, Amérique 1918–1929, États-Unis, Quai d'Orsay, Paris (translation mine).

18. Today, the small stone church stands on the main road into the village and bears a commemorative plaque to the 26th Division. John Sherburne, Overseas Memorial, Inc., to Major X. H. Price, May 11, 1926, 26th Div. File, Division Memorials, Division Monuments, AEF Records, RG 120, NA.

19. Price to General John H. Sherburne, Chairman, Y.D. Overseas memorial, July 24, 1926, in ibid.

20. MacArthur was promoted to major general in 1925, the year of this letter. It may have been written while he was serving one of two tours as commander of corps areas in the States. MacArthur to "my dear Johnson," Third Corps Area, U.S. Army, Baltimore, MD, September 15, 1925, 2, Meeting Minutes and Agenda, 1923, Box 1, ABMC Records, RG 117, NA.

21. Ibid.

22. James E. Mangum, Chief Clerk, to Major X. H. Price, "Estimates of appropriations," June 4, 1925, Box 87, ABMC Records, RG 117, NA.

23. Ibid., 2; Mangum to Price, "Estimates of Appropriation, fiscal year 1927," July 16, 1925, in ibid.

24. Testimony of Chairman Stephen G. Porter, hearings before the Committee on Foreign Affairs, House of Representatives, 69th Congress, 1st Session, on HR 9694, March 3, 1926, "Authorizing the Erection of a Monument to . . . the 93rd Division of the AEF" (Washington, DC: U.S. Government Printing Office, 1926), 4; and John J. Pershing, "To the Ages," *American Legion Monthly*, June 1934, 8.

25. The black guardsmen numbered between fifty-one hundred and fifty-six hundred men and were considered a problem because white guardsmen rejected black units, and consequently, there was no place for odd infantry regiments in the military hierarchical structure. The army's solution was to tack on a fourth regiment, composed of draftees, and call the combined organization the 93rd Division (provisional). See Barbeau and Henri, *Unknown Soldiers*, chap. 5.

26. "Monument in France to Ninety-Third Division," hearings before the Committee on Foreign Affairs, House of Representatives, HR 9694, 69th Congress, 1st Session, March 3, 4, 5, 1926, "Authorizing the Erection of a Monument to . . . the 93rd Division of the AEF" (Washington, DC: U.S. Government Printing Office, 1926), 19.

27. Fish was referring to the 27th and 30th Divisions.

28. Fish testimony, HR 9694 hearing, 23.

29. The Foreign Affairs Committee was told that the War Department's previous projected budget of five hundred thousand dollars was a "pitifully insufficient sum, and we found we would have to spend at least $3,000,000 to do it adequately." Testimony, HR 9694 hearing, 8.

30. Ibid., 22.

31. Thomas Atherton and Paul P. Cret to Lt. Gov. David J. Davis, June 12, 1926, and X. H. Price to Dr. Paul P. Cret, June 11, 1926, 79th Division Memorial file, Division Monuments, AEF Records, RG 120, NA; minutes of the twentieth meeting of the ABMC.

32. In February 2001, a monument was finally dedicated to the 369th New York black regiment in the village of Sechault, France.

33. HR 9694 hearing, 34–35.

34. Nancy was chosen because the city was centrally located in relation to the American sectors and was reputedly "the largest and most beautiful town in the area." Annual Report of the ABMC, June 1925, 37.

35. The article was translated by Major Price and appeared in both *l'Immeuble* and *la Construction* on May 23, 1926. The letter was written to the people of Nancy by a Monsieur Bruntz, a local man, who Price insisted "should not be taken seriously." See memorandum no. 41, Box 87, ABMC Records, RG 117, NA.

36. Major Price to J. J. Pershing, December 19, 1932, Box 7, File 201, ABMC Records, RG 117, NA.

37. The ABMC Annual Report of 1925 estimates the monument cost would be $130,000.

38. Price to Pershing, December 19, 1932.

39. Minutes of the twentieth meeting of the ABMC.

40. The ABMC was not able to persuade the French to reverse the decision to preserve the ruins and was unwilling to seek a new site. Grossman, "Architecture for a Public Client," 129; Minutes of the twenty-third meeting of the ABMC, February 1927, RG 117, NA.

41. Grossman notes at least three different requests from Pershing to the architect for changes to the Montfaucon column, which was previously designed to reach a mere 180 feet. Grossman, "Architecture for a Public Client," 131. At one point in the monument's construction the entire vertical column had to be hoisted and turned on improvised rollers so that the blocks in the base could be better fitted together. The incident occurred in the middle of winter with high winds. As told in Major General Thomas North's draft manuscript "One Soldier's Job," Part 1, p. 23, undated and unpublished. (North was ABMC Secretary, September 26, 1946, to April 30, 1968.) ABMC Cemetery Archives, Waregem, Belgium, courtesy of Chris Sims.

42. Ibid., 127, quoting a letter from Paul Cret to John Russell Pope, April 28, 1926.

43. Ministry for Foreign Affairs, Div. of Political and Commercial Affairs, signed by Comte F. Dejean, C, American Section at the Foreign Office, June 10, 1927, Volume 1320, Records of Foreign Service Posts, Diplomatic Posts, France (Consular files), RG 84, NA.

44. Sheldon Whitehouse, Charge d'Affaires, American Embassy, Paris, June 14, 1927, in ibid.

45. "Will Honor Our Troops," *NYT*, September 4, 1932, 30:4.

46. Pershing was said to have "objected bitterly" to this monument and "demanded" the French premier, André Tardieu, have it destroyed, even though the monument was constructed on privately owned ground. "Gold Star Mothers Charge 'Desecration,'" *NYT*, December 14, 1931, 12:6 (emphasis added).

47. "French Group Resists Pershing on Memorial," *NYT*, August 12, 1930, 16:4; Minutes of the thirty-first meeting of the ABMC, December 20, 1929, RG 117, NA.

48. "Gold Star Mothers Charge 'Desecration'"; minutes of the thirty-first meeting of the ABMC; Memorial Photo of Gold Star Mothers at the dedication ceremony in Nantillois, France, August 18, 1930, *Chicago Daily Tribune*, Paris edition.

49. Minutes of the twenty-seventh meeting of the ABMC, June 26, 1928, RG 117, NA.

50. Minutes of the eighteenth meeting of the ABMC, May 5, 1926, RG 117, NA.

51. Minutes of the seventeenth meeting of the ABMC.

52. D. A. Reed to Dr. Emmett J. Scott, May 12, 1926, Box 28, ABMC Records, RG 117, NA.

53. Minutes of the thirty-third meeting of the ABMC, December 1, 1930, RG 117, NA.

54. John J. Pershing, Chairman, Memorandum for the Commission, December 31, 1931, Box 87, ABMC Records, RG 117, NA.

55. Pershing was informed that the commissioner, R. G. Woodside, had "probably disposed satisfactorily of all the busybodies in that organization who continued to inquire about dedications." Mark M. Boatner, Jr., Cpt., Corps of Engineers, to Pershing, December 2, 1935, Box 87, ABMC Records, RG 117, NA.

56. Cannadine, *Mellon*, 449.

57. Miller, *New World Coming*, 384. MacArthur was assisted by Major Dwight D. Eisenhower, who had supervised the completion of the *ABMC Guide Book*, published in 1927.

58. Pershing announced to the press that work on the monuments was nearly finished and that the headquarters in France would be broken up. "Commission to Disband," *NYT*, August 13, 1933, 28:3; MacCloskey, *Hallowed Ground*, 51.

59. Cannadine, *Mellon*, 442–443.

60. "Our National War Memorials in Europe," *National Geographic Magazine* 65, no. 1 (January 1934): 1–36. Regardless of the quality of the professional relationship between Pershing and Reed by 1934, Pershing wrote to Reed expressing his sympathy in warm terms: "I had no idea that things would turn out for you as they have. I need not tell you how very much I regret the outcome." J. J. Pershing to Senator David A. Reed, Paris, November 25, 1934, David A. Reed Scrapbooks, vol. 6, Department of Rare Books and Special Collections, Princeton University Library, Princeton, NJ.

61. John J. Pershing, "To the Ages," *American Legion Monthly*, June 1934, 40.

62. Cannadine, *Mellon*, 590, referring to "The Last of the Romans," by Joseph Hudnut, dean of Harvard's Graduate School of Design.

63. Ibid.

64. Aline B. Louchheim, "Memorials to Our War Dead Abroad," *NYT*, January 15, 1950, 2:10; John Canady, "The World's Worst Sculpture," *NYT*, July 25, 1965.

65. Canady, "World's Worst Sculpture."

66. Winter and Sivan, *War and Remembrance*, 16.

NOTES TO CHAPTER 16

1. "On to Paris," *American Legion Weekly*, May 1927, 73.

2. Philip Von Blon and Marquis James, "The AEF Comes Home," *American Legion Monthly*, December 1927, 78, 71.

3. Membership figures had declined in 1927 from a previous 845,186 in 1920. Dixon Wecter, *When Johnny Comes Marching Home* (Cambridge, MA: Houghton Mifflin, 1944), 446.

4. Ibid., 427.

5. Ibid., 312. Upon discharge, soldiers received a sixty-dollar bonus.

6. Ibid., 362–363.

7. Harries and Harries, *Last Days of Innocence*, 446.

8. Ibid., 446. There is no indication whether this ex-sailor was a member of the Legion. This kind of unofficial action was not only condoned but often reinforced at both state and federal levels. See F. Scott Fitzgerald's "May Day," in *The Stories of F. Scott Fitzgerald*, vol. 1 (Middlesex, UK: Penguin, 1969). For the American Legion and the Red Scare, see M. J. Heale, *American Anti-communism: Combating the Enemy Within* (Baltimore: Johns Hopkins University Press, 1990); John Lax and William Pencak, "Creating the American Legion," *South Atlantic Quarterly* 81, no. 1 (Winter 1982): 43–46.

9. Wray R. Johnson, "Black American Radicalism and the First World War: The Secret Files of the Military Intelligence Division," *Armed Forces & Society* 26, no. 1 (Fall 1999): 27–53; Harries and Harries, *Last Days of Innocence*, 445; Lewis, W. E. B. Du Bois, chap. 6.

10. William Pencak, *For God and Country: The American Legion, 1919–1941* (Boston: Northeastern University Press, 1989), 68–69.

11. Wecter notes that the majority of members were "generous Americans with better-than-average incomes." Wecter, *When Johnny Comes Marching Home*, 438, 444.

12. Ibid., 443–453.

13. Ibid., 449.

14. Wecter, *When Johnny Comes Marching Home*, 449. The assistant secretary of war defended the men saying, "After every one of our national conventions all the radical sheets in this country rave about the 'rowdies' of the American Legion. We are better behaved by a mile than half the national gatherings which no one thinks of criticizing." "MacNider Attacks Critics of Legion," *NYT*, August 13, 1927, 15:4.

15. "Note pour le Cabinet du Ministre," August 27, 1928, vol. 282, American Legion Series, Amérique 1918–1919, États-Unis, Ministère des Affaires, Paris (translation mine).

16. Whitney Walton, "Internationalism and the Junior Year Abroad: American Students in France in the 1920s and 1930s," *Diplomatic History* 29, no. 2 (April 2005): 257, 258.

17. Ibid., 271. In 1937, the United States began to federally subsidize foreign exchanges to certain countries.

NOTES TO CHAPTER 17

1. Lloyd, *Battlefield Tourism*, 114.

2. Ibid.

3. *American Legion Weekly*, April 11, 1924, 10.

4. John J. Pershing, "Our National War Memorials in Europe," *National Geographic Magazine* 65, no. 1 (January 1934): 8–9.

5. Ibid., 9; see also Donald Smythe, *Honoring the Nation's Dead*, 28.

6. *A Guide to the American Battle Fields of Europe* (1927 version), 245. Precisely 20,468 copies of the guide book were published in 1927. About 7,000 of those copies were purchased on boats sailing to Europe. ABMC, Information Bulletin No. 9, November 17, 1927, signed X. H. Price, Guidebook, Box 87, ABMC Records, RG 117, NA.

7. Ernest P. Bicknell, Deputy Commissioner to Europe American Red Cross, to Mr. F. P. Keppel, Director, Foreign Opns., A.R.C., Washington, DC, August 12, 1920, American Red Cross Records, File 619.1, Series 1917–34, RG 200, NA.

8. Harvey Levenstein, *Seductive Journey: American Tourists in France from Jefferson to the Jazz Age* (Chicago: University of Chicago Press, 1998), 225. "It is not a cheap undertaking for a single tourist, nor for a short holiday," stated Lieutenant Colonel H. deWatteville, in "A Motor Tour along the Western Front," *Army Quarterly* 16 (January 1928): 401.

9. Hugh Clout, *After the Ruins* (Exeter, UK: University of Exeter Press, 1996), 274.

10. Lloyd, *Battlefield Tourism*, 102, 103.

11. Levenstein, *Seductive Journey*, 224–225. The American manager of the Paris hotel Crillon published a joint proposal with a group of "Chicago and New York millionaires for inaugurating a chain of high-class American hotels in France," complete with "autobus and touring car service for tourists visiting the front." "American Plans Chain of Hotels for U.S. Tourists," undated newsclipping, Manuscript Division, AC #1286, Miscellaneous World War I Collection, Tennessee State Library and Archives, Nashville, TN.

12. DeWatteville, "Motor Tour," 394. Tourism declined because "the scenes of destruction were no longer as inherently interesting as they had been" (Lloyd, *Battlefield Tourism*, 105); the former battlefields "were remarkably resilient" and did not retain many traces of the battles that had been fought on them (Levenstein, *Seductive Journey*, 225–227).

13. Tobias Döring, "Travelling in Transience: The Semiotics of Necro-Tourism," in Hartmut Berghoff, Barbara Korte, Ralf Schneider, and Christopher Harvie, eds., *The Making of Modern Tourism: The Cultural History of the British Experience, 1600–2000* (London: Palgrave, 2002), 250.

14. Ibid., 265.

15. Ibid., 256–257.

16. DeWatteville, "Motor Tour," 398.

17. Ibid.

18. Minutes of the nineteenth meeting of the ABMC.

19. "Row on Row, They Await the Pilgrims," NYT, May 11, 1930, sec. 4, 24–28.

NOTES TO CHAPTER 18

1. Truman had been a captain in a field artillery unit. Monte M. Poen, ed., Letters Home by Harry Truman (New York: G. P. Putnam's Sons, 1984), 71–72.

2. This appeal to peace was never mentioned again in future correspondence. France Convention Committee, AL Headquarters, Richmond, VA, to the French Ministry, September 1, 1925, File 284, États-Unis, vol. 1, 1923–1927, Ministère des Affaires étrangères, Paris.

3. French expenditures ultimately exceeded this estimate, costing 1,912,670 francs. National Commander to President du Conseil, Ministère des Affaires étrangères, September 19, 1924; Note pour le Commandant Jamet, February 16, 1925; and French Convention Committee, AL Headquarters, September 1, 1925, all in ibid.

4. American Legion Monthly, December 11, 1925, and January 22, 1926.

5. Editorial, American Legion Monthly, June 1927, 28.

6. Palmer D. Edmunds, "Should We Forget the War?" American Legion Weekly, December 5, 1925, 14, 16; also Lax and Pencak, "Creating the American Legion," 46.

7. For more on the Legion and preservation of war memory, see Keene, Doughboys.

8. American Legion Monthly, June 1927, 28.

9. "Legion Should Postpone Paris Reunion," Washington News, September 8, 1926.

10. "French Sympathy Swings to Legion," NYT, August 26, 1927, 1:7, 8:3; "Paris Assures Fete for Legion," NYT, September 6, 1927, 19:1; and Levenstein, Seductive Journey, 272.

11. Initially, 21,746 people booked passage, but many later canceled. "Keeping Step," American Legion Monthly, December 1927, 46; Information Bulletin No. 9.

12. John J. Wicker, Jr., A.L. National Travel Director, to French Ministry, May 28, 1926, File 284, États-Unis, vol. 1, 1923–1927, Ministère des Affaires étrangères, Paris.

13. Volume 1322, January 1927, Consular Files, Records of Foreign Service Posts, RG 84, NA.

14. An additional 1,747 people met the Legionnaires upon their arrival in Paris, for a total of 19,991. "Keeping Step," 46.

15. Philip Von Blon and Marquis James, "The A.E.F. Comes Home," American Legion Monthly, December 1927, 32.

16. Ibid.

17. Pencak, For God and Country, 99; D. Kennedy, Over Here, 365.

18. This percentage is based on twenty thousand attendees (an approximate figure) against the seven hundred thousand official membership estimates for 1927.

19. Veterans' antics at the Gettysburg summer encampments of the nineteenth century included staged burlesque parades and "plays based on Philadelphia tradition that originated with English colonists." These practices "borrowed on pre-modern Christmas traditions involving costumed, sometimes transvestite, 'fantasticals' and 'callithumpians' who temporarily inverted the social order." Floats, noisemakers, and kazoo bands were the norm. James Weeks, "A Different View of Gettysburg," Civil War History 50, no. 2 (2004): 186–187.

20. Lloyd, Battlefield Tourism, 107.

21. Honorable Sheldon Whitehouse, Chargé d'Affaires, American Embassy, Paris, to Secretary of State, September 1927, Volume 1322, Records of Foreign Service Posts, Diplomatic Posts, France, RG 84, NA.

22. Ibid.

23. D. Kennedy, Over Here, 365.

24. "Legionnaires March Charms Paris Press," *NYT*, September 21, 1927, 2:5, 6.

25. John J. Pershing, Foreword, Paris, 1927, to American Legion, Box 12, Pershing Papers, 1904–1948, Collection of the Manuscript Division, LOC. Pershing considered the event "the greatest goodwill pilgrimage in history," according to Pencak, *For God and Country*, 98.

26. "Paris Ejects American for Aiding Artist Whose Legion Souvenir Shocked France," *NYT*, August 29, 1927, 1:2; Levenstein, *Seductive Journey*, 274; D. Kennedy, *Over Here*, 364–366; Beckett, *Great War*, 437. Twenty-eight Legionnaires were hauled before the special tribunal created for conventioneers for "drunkenness in its wildest forms." Pencak, *For God and Country*, 98.

27. Meuse-Argonne American Cemetery is the largest American cemetery in Europe. It contains just over fourteen thousand graves. *ABMC Guide*, 457–472.

28. Others reportedly left Paris for Verdun and nearby cemeteries "by immense motorcars." "Veterans at Verdun Bow before the Dead," *NYT*, September 21, 1927, 2:3; see also "Legionnaires Visit Comrades' Graves," *NYT*, September 21, 1927, 2.

29. Von Blon and James, "The A.E.F. Comes Home," *American Legion Monthly*, December 1927, 78.

30. Mrs. Levi M. Hall, Report of Trip to the National Convention of the American Legion Auxiliary in Paris, France, September 1927, Gold Star Mothers Collection, private collection of Holly Fenelon.

31. Ibid., 3.

32. Ibid., 3, 5, 11.

33. Ibid., 4, 18.

34. Linda K. Kerber, *Toward an Intellectual History of Women* (Chapel Hill: University of North Carolina Press, 1997), 58. See also Rebecca J. Plant, "The Repeal of Mother Love: Momism and the Reconstruction of Motherhood in Philip Wylie's America" (Ph.D. diss., Johns Hopkins University, 2001), 117.

35. "Therefore Be It Resolved," *American Legion Monthly*, December 1928, 74; "A Gold Star Pilgrimage," *American Legion Weekly*, April 11, 1924, 10. The Legion's first public mention of a movement aimed at giving next of kin a trip to France was made in April 1924.

36. On this quality of pilgrimages, see Phil Cousineau, *The Art of Pilgrimage: The Seeker's Guide to Making Travel Sacred* (Berkeley, CA: Conari, 1998), xxii, xxiii.

NOTES TO CHAPTER 19

1. "Row on Row, They Await the Pilgrims," *NYT*, May 11, 1930, sec. 4, 24–28; other sources claim that 234 women were onboard. "Gold Star Sailing," *Time*, May 19, 1930.

2. By 1924, approximately one thousand women had already made the journey overseas to the cemeteries where their sons and husbands were buried. Army 1924 report, reprinted in the published hearing of the House of Representatives Committee on Military Affairs, 70th Congress, "To authorize Mothers and Unmarried Widows of Deceased World War Veterans Buried in Europe to Visit the Graves," Washington, DC, January 27, 1928, 12, GSM Pilgrimage, QMC, RG 92, NA.

3. Association letterhead dated February 15, 1924, from the Gold Star Association of America to Hon. A. Platt Andrew, Congressman 6th District, Massachusetts, File: HR68A-H131, 68th Congress, House Committee on Military Affairs, RG 233, NA. Also Statement of Mrs. Frederick Gudebrod, Secretary of the Gold Star Association, hearing before a Subcommittee of the Committee on Military Affairs, U.S. Senate, 70th Congress, 2nd Session, on HR 5494, S 2681, S 5332, Part 2, February 12, 1929 (Washington, DC: U.S. Government Printing Office, 1929), 3, Records of the U.S. House of Representatives, 68th Congress, Box 383, RG 233, NA.

4. American Gold Star Mothers Records, Applications for Membership, Box 2, 1928–1943, LOC.

5. Australia's Minister for Defence, Senator George Pearce, declared that the badge would be "simple in design but chaste." Damousi, *Labour of Loss*, 26.

6. Ibid., 30.

7. In 1923, there was a strongly supported movement afoot in Australia that bereaved relatives should be helped to visit the graves overseas. It was argued that a pilgrimage "would achieve the peace of the world." But only one group comprised of four mothers was actually assisted to visit the battlefields, in 1924. Lloyd, *Battlefield Tourism*, 194–198.

8. Damousi, *Labour of Loss*, 35.

9. Lloyd, *Battlefield Tourism*, 187–198; Damousi, *Labour of Loss*, 26–45.

10. This incident occurred during an Anzac Day ceremony in 1938, when women's participation was said to have "destroyed the significance of the occasion." Damousi, *Labour of Loss*, 36–37.

11. Emma Kessler Sweet, San Francisco, to Senator Hiram Bingham, hearing before U.S. Senate Subcommittee on Military Affairs, on HR 5494, "To Authorize Mothers and Unmarried Widows of Deceased World War Veterans in Europe to Visit the Graves," 70th Congress, 1st Session, May 14, 1928, 19, RG 92, NA.

12. Mrs. Ethel Nock, Member of the Committee of Legislation, American War Mothers, hearing before U.S. Senate Subcommittee on Military Affairs, on HR 5494, S 2681, S 5332, Part 2, U.S. Senate, 70th Congress, 2nd Session, February 12, 1929, 5.

13. By December 1920, only 120,000 requests for bodies had been received. Secretary General of the Anglo-French Mixed Committee, IWGC, Paris, to the Land and Legal Advisor, France and Belgium, October 12, 1920, General file, Box 1083, WG 1294, pt. 3, CWGC.

14. *LePhare*, October 8, 1920, 2; November 11, 1920, 2; November 30, 1920, 1:5, in L'Espace Multimédia Médiathèque, Calais, France.

15. Words of the Burgomaster of Ypres, quoted by Admiral of the Fleet Earl Jellicoe, in the souvenir program. The author notes that "no extra Gendarmes did duty . . . during these two days." "They are not necessary," declared the French authorities, "for the British [are] a disciplined people." *The Battlefields Pilgrimage: A Souvenir of the Battlefields Pilgrimage*, August 1928, 7, 44.

16. Ibid., 13.

17. Some people suspected that the presence of Legion president Field-Marshal Earl Haig might have enticed many to join since he was scheduled to lead the pilgrim "army" past the new Menin Gate. Haig died before the pilgrimage departure. Ibid., 13, 17, 19.

18. British pilgrims were provided with packed lunches each day and their guides were War Graves gardeners. Ibid., 13, Ibid., 60–61.

19. An undisclosed number of Canadians joined the British pilgrimage of 1928, when the Vimy Ridge monument was still merely a huge concrete base. Major A. Waller, in ibid., 37.

20. Those costs were calculated to be as high as two million pounds. Lloyd, *Battlefield Tourism*, 38. Britain's St. Barnabus Society also assisted pilgrims with their journey to the former battlefields. See Lt. Malcolm W. Wakeman collection, 67/305/1, Department of Documents, Imperial War Museum (IWM), London.

21. On the effects of the absence of a body, see Damousi, *Labour of Loss*, 16.

22. Lloyd, *Battlefield Tourism*, 195–196.

23. One hundred pilgrims participated. Ibid., 197–198.

24. Pierre Berton, *Vimy* (Toronto: McClelland and Stewart, 1986), chap. 4. All Canadian pilgrims paid their own expenses. *Guidebook to Vimy*, by Veterans Limited, Ottawa, ed. John Hundevad, Collection of Vernon Kingsley Gill, Misc. 53 (816), Department of Documents, IWM. Lloyd, *Battlefield Tourism*, 199, 188.

25. Lloyd, *Battlefield Tourism*, 199.

26. Application No. 3431, Collection of Vernon Kingsley Gill, Misc. 53 (816), Department of Documents, IWM.

27. *Guidebook to Vimy*, 39, 41, 67.

28. The Canadian pilgrimage overlapped with the eleventh Olympic Games, held in Berlin. "General Information," in ibid., 18–19.

29. Language divided the participants, who included both British and French Canadians. Lloyd, *Battlefield Tourism*, 202.

30. It was perhaps no coincidence that the "Peace Light Memorial" at Gettysburg, designed by former ABMC architect Paul Cret, was dedicated in 1938. The monument was initially proposed in 1913 by more than fifty-five thousand northern and southern veterans who expressed their desire to construct a lasting symbol to the unity of the nation—a monument to peace. It was dedicated on July 3 during the last major reunion of Civil War veterans. Hawthorne, *Gettysburg*, 27.

NOTES TO CHAPTER 20

1. The American Legion mentioned the pilgrimages in April 1924, but they were not specifically intended for women over other family members since the Gold Star Association (and not the GSM) claimed responsibility for initiating the bill. "A Gold Star Pilgrimage," *American Legion Weekly*, April 11, 1924, 10. HR 4109 remained in discussion throughout each session until May 29, 1924 (HR 4147, HR 9223, and HR 9538). Box 345, Misc. File 1922–1935, GSM Pilgrimage files, Series E-1896, Office of the QMG, RG 92, NA.

2. Samuel Dickstein, a Lithuanian immigrant, served as Democratic representative, 1922–1946. He was chairman of the House Committee on Immigration and Naturalization and later known for initiating the McCormack-Dickstein Committee (1934–35) and the creation of the House Un-American Activities Committee. Box 345, Misc. File 1922–1935, GSM Pilgrimage files, Series E-1896, Office of the QMG, RG 92, NA; Allen Weinstein and Alexander Vassiliev, *The Haunted Wood: Soviet Espionage in America* (New York: Random House, 1999). See letters of petition from the Gold Star Association members, January and February 1924, Committee on Military Affairs, 68th Congress, file HR68A-H13.1, RG 233, NA.

3. U.S. Congress, House, Committee on Military Affairs, January 27, 1928, "To Authorize Mothers and Unmarried Widows of Deceased World War Veterans Buried in Europe to Visit the Graves," 70th Congress, 1st Session, January 27, 1928, 27, includes a copy of HR 239, May 9, 1919, introduced in the 68th Congress by F. LaGuardia.

There were two bills introduced in the 70th Congress that concerned the GSM pilgrimage. HR 5494 was introduced by Representative Butler of Pennsylvania on December 5, 1927. An amended version of the bill was reported by the House Committee on Military Affairs on February 2, 1928, and passed the House on February 20, 1928. It was then referred to the Senate Committee on Military Affairs. Although the bill was discussed on the floor of the Senate on April 28, 1928, it was not reported for consideration by the committee. The second bill was S 5332, which was introduced by Senator D. A. Reed on January 12, 1929. The bill was referred to the Senate Committee on Military Affairs, which reported an amended version on February 22. The bill as amended was approved by the Senate on February 28. The House approved the bill by unanimous consent on March 1, 1929.

4. Reprinted in the published hearing "To Authorize Mothers," House of Representatives Committee on Military Affairs, Washington, DC, January 27, 1928.

5. Presumably, "class in life" referred to those women who could not afford to pay for the journey themselves. Ibid., 13.

6. Letter from Mrs. Chas. Ditter, January 10, 1925; letter from Mrs. G. Brother, January 12, 1925, city and state illegible; letter from Mrs. Elizabeth Britton, January 12, 1925, New York; and

letter from Mrs. Johanna Wolbertz, NYC, January 12, 1925; all in U.S. House of Representatives, 68th Congress, Box 383, file HR68A-H13.1, RG 233, NA.

7. Theda Skocpol, *Protecting Soldiers and Mothers* (Cambridge, MA: Belknap Press of Harvard University Press, 1992), 451; Kerber traces the American model of Republican Motherhood back to the early republic. She states, "there developed the consensus that a mother could not be a citizen but that she might serve a political purpose." Kerber, *Toward an Intellectual History of Women*, 61.

8. Skocpol, *Protecting Soldiers and Mothers*, 329–331. Legislation enacted between 1911 and 1920 authorized local governments to make regular payments directly to impoverished mothers of dependent children. The Sheppard-Towner Act, considered America's first explicit federal social-welfare legislation, had a budget of one million dollars funded annually for five years. The same allocation was later granted for the Gold Star pilgrimages, which lasted three years.

9. Many women chose the American Legion auxiliaries as a platform for their social activism, but their focus was aimed less on women than on benefits for veterans and children.

10. Skocpol, *Protecting Soldiers and Mothers*, 368–369.

11. Ibid., 372. "The Progressive Era was the time when the nationwide political mobilization of American middle-class women reached its height." Ibid., 319.

12. Hon. Hamilton Fish, Jr., NY, House of Representatives, Committee on Military Affairs, "To Authorize Mothers and Unmarried Widows of Deceased World War Veterans Buried in Europe to Visit the Graves," 70th Congress, 1st Session, January 27, 1928, 22. By 1928, the economic status of the mother was emphasized. One New York senator told his audience that the government's role was to "do for the citizen the things he can not do for himself." He added, "These mothers, most of them, are very poor." Hearing before the U.S. Senate Subcommittee on Military Affairs, "To Authorize Mothers and Unmarried Widows of Deceased World War Veterans Buried in Europe to Visit the Graves," 70th Congress, 1st Session, May 14, 1928, 3.

13. Skocpol, *Protecting Soldiers and Mothers*, 319.

14. Nancy F. Cott, *The Grounding of Modern Feminism* (New Haven, CT: Yale University Press, 1987), 14.

15. Skocpol, *Protecting Soldiers and Mothers*, 514. Opponents of the bill believed the states should take over the cost of the program, but many also condemned what they termed "an imported socialistic scheme." Skocpol claims, "the overall political climate in 1926–27 was more conservative than that in 1921." No permanent entitlement to the services of the legislation had ever been established. Skocpol, *Protecting Soldiers and Mothers*, 500, 513, 521.

16. Kathleen Kennedy, *Disloyal Mothers and Scurrilous Citizens: Women and Subversion during World War I* (Bloomington: Indiana University Press, 1999), 16–17.

17. The AWM membership was open to all mothers with children who had served in the war. Minutes of the First Meeting of the Executive Board of the National American War Mothers, Louisville, Kentucky, September 29–30, 1920, 2. N. A.W.M. Archives, Washington, DC.

18. Ibid.

19. "National Patriotic Conference," *American War Mother* 5, no. 1 (March 1928): 8.

20. Colonel Charles B. Robbins, Assistant Secretary of War, quoted in ibid., 9.

21. *American War Mother* 5, no. 1 (March 1928): 11; Resolution 4, *American War Mother* 2, no. 9 (November 1925).

22. J. S. Hallowes and the International Council of Women, *Mothers of Men and Militarism* (London: Headley Brothers, 1916), 25.

23. K. Kennedy, *Disloyal Mothers*, 1. Kennedy notes that in the days leading up to America's entry into the war, the Wilson administration worried that "women, especially those in the prewar women's peace movement, might constitute a subversive element in the nation, detrimental to wartime unity and the smooth functioning of selective service." Wilson's appeal to women in

1918 suggesting alternative mourning practices illustrates his attempt to gain their support for the war in traditional ways. Ibid., 4 (quoting Wilson).

24. "Davison Pays Tribute to U.S. War Mothers," *Washington Post*, May 12, 1930, 1.

NOTES TO CHAPTER 21

1. House of Representatives, Committee on Military Affairs, "To Authorize Mothers and Unmarried Widows of Deceased World War Veterans Buried in Europe to Visit the Graves," 70th Congress, 1st Session, January 27, 1928.

2. Skocpol, *Protecting Soldiers and Mothers,* 319.

3. Anna Stein, Brooklyn, NY, Box 1149, Correspondence, 1917–1934, p. 32, File 333.9, Winfree, Series E26, Inspector General's Office, RG 159, NA.

4. Burling's son, Private George B. Burling, Jr., died of Graves' Disease (known then as "Exophtalmic goiter") on February 13, 1918. Burling burial file, Box 700, Cemeterial Division, Office of the QMG, RG 92, NA.

5. Burling referencing a condolence letter she received from Theodore Roosevelt, in the hearing before the Subcommittee on Military Affairs, on HR 5494, S 2681, S 5332, Part 2, U.S. Senate, 70th Congress, 2nd Session, February 12, 1929, 25.

6. Mrs. Jennie F. Walsh, hearing before Senate Subcommittee on Military Affairs, May 14, 1928, 5.

7. It was customary for the army to give each mother or widow a flag when the soldier was buried. Apparently, none was given to those NOK of an unknown. Mathilda Burling to William H. Hart, QMG, Washington, DC, January 23, 1924, Hart Burial Files, Entry 1942, RG 92, NA.

8. Mathilda Burling to General John J. Pershing, Western Union Telegraph Co., December 6, 1928, Box 37, Pershing Papers, LOC.

9. The general made specific reference to the poorer mothers as being most deserving of the trip abroad. John J. Pershing to Mathilda Burling, November 28, 1928, and Burling to Pershing, December 6, 1928, both in Box 37, Pershing Papers, LOC.

10. John J. Pershing to Mathilda Burling, December 11, 1928, in ibid.

11. Legal inquiries began as early as 1932 by E. M. H. Guedry, national chairman of the original American Gold Star Mothers. The wrangling continued into 1939 and was finally resolved in March 1948, when Supreme Court Justice Aaron Steuer granted a petition by the American GSM to permanently restrain Burling "from representing herself as national president of the similar organization." Burling died ten years later. *NYT*, March 12, 1948, 25; *NYT*, July 22, 1958, 27. E. M. H. Guedry to J. M. Kenyon, Kenyon & MacFarland, January 6, 1933, Guedry to J. J. Scully, Scully, Scully & O'Brien, January 9, 1939, both in Box 6, GSM Collection, LOC.

12. Mrs. G. G. Seibold, Washington, DC, to Mrs. E. M. H. Guedry, January 26, 1939, in ibid.

13. Burling claimed to be representing "mothers throughout the country, in general." Mrs. Mathilda Burling, hearing before U.S. Senate Subcommittee on Military Affairs, on HR 5494, S 2681, S 5332, Part 2, 70th Congress, 2nd Session, February 12, 1929.

14. Mrs. Mathilda A. Burling, hearing before U.S. Senate Subcommittee on Military Affairs, May 14, 1928, 4.

15. Ibid. (The House had passed the bill on February 20, 1928, without debate. The Senate, on the other hand, debated the bill for months.)

16. Ibid.

17. Plant notes that mothers presented the loss of their sons in a highly possessive manner, claiming, in a sense, that these bodies were their own. Plant, "Repeal of Mother Love," 147.

18. Damousi, *Labour of Loss,* 70.

19. House of Representatives, Committee on Military Affairs, "To Authorize Mothers," January 27, 1928, 70th Congress, 1st Session, 17.

20. Mrs. Ethel Nock, hearing before U.S. Senate Subcommittee on Military Affairs, May 14, 1928, 10.

21. Historians generally agree that by 1926–27, politicians were aware that women did not vote as a bloc. Skocpol, *Protecting Soldiers and Mothers*, 521; Molly Ladd-Taylor, "'My Work Came Out of Agony and Grief': Mothers and the Making of the Sheppard-Towner Act," in Seth Koven and Sonya Michel, eds., *Mothers of a New World* (New York: Routledge, 1993), 337; Plant, "Repeal of Mother Love," 121.

22. Maud W. Danforth to Hon. Hiram Gingham, East Orange, NJ, May 14, 1928, in Senate hearings on HR 5494, May 14, 1928, 26.

23. See "Other Uses for $5,000,000" (editorial), *NYT*, February 8, 1930, 14:7; *NYT* editorials, January 17 and 22, 1933, letters to the editor; and letters read during the hearings on HR 5494, 70th Congress, 2nd Session, February 12, 1929, part 2, p. 23, of Montclair Women's Club, February 8, 1929.

24. This woman also claimed that the pilgrimages were undignified. Helena H. Ingalls to Hon. Hiram Bingham, U.S. Senate, NY, hearing before U.S. Senate Subcommittee on Military Affairs, May 14, 1928, 26–27.

25. Senator Hiram Bingham speaking at the hearing before the U.S. Senate Subcommittee on Military Affairs, May 14, 1928, 24.

26. The law specifying that the president take office on January 20 rather than the traditional March 4 was not enacted until 1933. Eve Zibart, "Every Four Years: The Real Political Parties," *Washington Post*, January 14, 2005, 27–29.

27. "A Gold Star pilgrimage to France proved impossible to resist politically." Piehler, *Remembering War*, 102, and email to the author, March 13, 2004.

28. Ferrell, *The Presidency of Calvin Coolidge*, 109.

29. Virginia Coolidge died of tuberculosis, "leaving a void in the boy's life that was never filled," according to Nathan Miller, *New World Coming*, 129. Years later, the president's wife experienced enormous grief over their son's death, possibly influencing her husband's decision to approve this legislation. Also, on the anniversary of their son's death, Mrs. Coolidge wrote a song, entitled "The Open Door," that was sung by Gold Star Mothers during services at Arlington Cemetery in 1930. "Gold Star Mothers Honored," *Washington Post*, May 12, 1930, 3:2.

30. Robert F. Wagner (U.S. Senator) to Hon. John J. Boylan, House Office Building, Washington, DC, January 26, 1928, letter to House reprinted in Committee of Military Affairs hearing, "To Authorize Mothers and Unmarried Widows of Deceased World War Vets Buried in Europe to Visit Graves," which took place on January 27, 1928, 28–29.

31. Hawley, *Great War*, 110–111, quoting President Coolidge in a report to Congress in December 1928; also Ferrell, *The Presidency of Calvin Coolidge*, 227.

32. Mrs. Ethel Nock was the editor and vice president of the local chapter of American War Mothers in the District of Columbia. *American War Mother* 6, no. 1 (March 1929): 10; and testimony before the Senate, hearings before a Subcommittee of the Committee of Military Affairs, U.S. Senate, on HR 5494, 70th Congress, 2nd Session, February 12, 1929, 5–15.

33. "National Affairs," *Time*, May 19, 1930, 13.

34. A list of proposed legislation begins with HR 4109, 68th Congress, December 20, 1923, and ends with Public Resolution No. 227, 71st Congress (HR 4138), May 15, 1930, Box 345, Misc. File 1922–1935, GSM Pilgrimage files, E-1896, Office of the QMG, RG 92, NA.

35. Piehler, *Remembering War*, 102.

36. Congressman J. Mayhew Wainwright (New York): "We are dealing with a little sentimental recognition of the mothers who did not put the Government to that expense [repatriation]. Rep. Hamilton Fish, Jr. (NY), believed the pilgrimages would not cost more than $1,000,000. This is not going to break the Treasury. I do not think that there are more than 2,500 or 3,000 at

the most that will want to go." House Committee on Military Affairs, January 27, 1928, 22. Also Piehler, *Remembering War*, 102.

37. "National Affairs," 12.

38. War Department, John T. Harris, Major, to Mrs. Stella E. Smith, Dumont, NJ, June 28, 1929, and burial file of Corporal Orville J. Miller, Iowa, March 24, 1933, Cemeterial Division, Office of the QMG, RG 92, NA.

39. Both the Gold Star Mothers and the earlier American War Mothers Association maintained this rigid policy at various times. The GSM group applied for a charter after its incorporation, when it specified, "we mean and require that she be the author of the dead patriot's being; not a step-mother; not a foster-mother nor one by adoption but the blood Mother of the son or daughter who paid the supreme sacrifice." Re: Bill S 459 and HR 9, undated, Scrapbook No. 9, Box 7, GSM Collection, LOC; also first meeting of the Executive Board of the National American War Mothers, Louisville, Kentucky, September 29–30, 1920, 20, American War Mothers Archives, Washington, DC; and Ethel Nock, hearing before U.S. Senate Subcommittee on Military Affairs, February 12, 1929.

40. The precise number of additional women who benefited is difficult to calculate, but it raised the approximate cost another 11 percent. "Status of Gold Star Mothers," *Army and Navy Register*, November 30, 1929, 509; and "Pilgrimage for the Mothers and Widows," House Document No. 140, 71st Congress, 2nd Session (Washington, DC: U.S. Government Printing Office, 1930) (see Letter of Transmittal, Patrick J. Hurley, War Department, December 6, 1929), iii.

41. Ellis documented his work equally well, leaving numerous after-action reports. Col. Richard Ellis, "Report on the Activities in Europe of the American Pilgrimage Gold Star Mothers and Widows, 1930," March 7, 1931, Box 8, 1922–1935 file, GSM Pilgrimage files, RG 92, NA.

42. Report by Col. Spaulding, September 11, 1930, General Staff misc., Box 361, NY Report, 1930, and "Languages" file, GSM Pilgrimage files, RG 92, NA.

43. Ellis, "Report on the Activities."

44. Liaison Report, Party "E" Westbound, August 18, 1933, GSM Pilgrimage files, RG 92, NA.

45. Liaison report, unsigned, file: American Pilgrimage: GSM & Widows, NY 1930–1933, Office of the QMG, RG 92, NA.

46. Her brother was killed instantly while eating his noon meal in October 1918. "Change of Cross," August 8, 1933, R. H. Jordan, Lt. Col., QMC, burial file of Pvt. Nathan Yellman, Cemeterial Division, Office of the QMG, RG 92, NA.

47. Ellis, "Report on the Activities," sec. 1, p. 2.

48. Liaison Detail, S.S. American Merchant, July 9, 1931, Benjamin O. Davis, Sr., Papers, ID No. 93, U.S. Army Military History Institute, Carlisle Army War College, PA.

49. Ellis, "Report on the activities," 19.

50. This final figure comes from War Department, Washington, DC, to The President, April 18, 1933, President Franklin D. Roosevelt's "Official File 461," Gold Star Mothers, 1933–1945, FDR Library, Hyde Park, NY. Reports of the number of eligible women differ significantly. "High U.S. Officers Speak at Banquet for War Mothers," *Washington Post*, September 1930, 18; John J. Noll, "Crosses," *American Legion Monthly*, September 1930, 14; Major Louis C. Wilson, QMC, "The War Mother Goes 'Over There,'" *Quartermaster Review*, May–June 1930, 21.

51. The exact cost was $5,386,367.00. War Department, Washington, DC, to The President, April 18, 1933. Original estimate was reported in the *NYT*, July 7, 1929, 9:4.

52. "Contracts for Gold Star Mothers," Box 380, GSM Pilgrimage files, RG 92, NA. Total contracts for medals during three years were worth approximately fifteen thousand dollars.

53. Major General J. L. DeWitt, QMG, "Instructions for the Officers," New York City, April 10, 1931, 4, Benjamin O. Davis Collection, No. 19, U.S. Army Historical Institute, Army War College, Carlisle, PA; *Time*, April 28, 1930, 11; and "23 Sail to Plan Gold Star Tours," *Brooklyn Daily Times*, April 16, 1930.

54. Coffman, *Regulars,* chap. 5, "The Managerial Revolution."

55. "Other Uses for $5,000,000," *NYT,* February 7, 1930. Concerns over the "unjustifiable" public spending seem to have dominated the negative comments in the press, along with suggestions that the money might have been better used in veterans' hospitals. DeWitt, "Instructions for the Officers"; *Time,* April 28, 1930, 11; and *NYT* editorials for January 17, 22, and 25, 1933.

56. "Indian Gold Star Mother Here," *Chicago Daily News,* Paris edition, May 27, 1933; "Winnebago Woman Here Seeks Grave of Warrior Son," *New York Herald,* Paris edition, May 27, 1933.

NOTES TO CHAPTER 22

1. Oscar Stanton De Priest (1871–1951), born in Florence, Alabama. "Oscar Stanton De Priest," Black Americans in Congress website, http://baic.house.gov/member-profiles/profile. html?intID=28.

2. At least two (unnamed) southern members insisted they would not serve adjacent to De Priest. Bruce A. Ragsdale and Joel D. Treese, *Black Americans in Congress, 1870–1989,* Office of the Historian, U.S. House of Representatives (Washington, DC: U.S. Government Printing Office, 1990), 35–37.

3. W. E. B. Du Bois, "The Facts," *Crisis,* September 1929, 298.

4. Newspaper excerpts are based on the *Crisis* survey article by Du Bois, ibid., 298–317.

5. See also Serrano, "Poignant Protest."

6. Admitting discrimination would have violated *Plessy v. Ferguson,* which adopted a "separate but equal" constitutional standard. Quotation from Major General B. F. Cheatham, USA, Retired, "Report War Mothers Pilgrimage" to QMG, Washington, DC, August 9, 1930, 2, Quartermaster Files, GSM Pilgrimage file, RG 92, NA; "Capital Rebuffs Gold Star Negroes," *NYT,* May 30, 1930.

7. De Priest quoted in Serrano, "Poignant Protest," 33. While in France in the late 1920s, Walter White (1893–1955) wrote a highly acclaimed study of lynchings in America, *Rope and Faggot* (1929), reprinted by the University of Notre Dame Press in 2002. On life in Paris for African Americans, see Levenstein, *Seductive Journey,* 264.

8. Early numbers for those eligible for the pilgrimage vary from 600 to 624, and then increase to 1,593, by 1933. Serrano, "Poignant Protest"; "Gold Star Mothers and Widows," *Afro American,* Baltimore edition, January 18, 1930; J. L. DeWitt, QMC, March 16, 1932, "Correspondence," in Box 345, "Segregation" file, GSM Pilgrimage files, RG 92, NA.

9. Walter White to Secretary of War (1930), Quartermaster Files, Boxes 348 and 380, "Segregation" file, GSM Pilgrimage files, RG 92, NA. White claims to have learned of the government's plan to segregate participating black women in March 1930. He then wrote to the War Department and obtained confirmation of the ruling. "Capital Rebuffs Gold Star Negroes."

10. Walter White, letter to President of the United States (1930), GSM Pilgrimage files, Box 348, RG 92, NA. Quotations here from Wm. G. Childs, Darby, PA; Dorothey Dennis; and Mrs. Georgina Ford, Philadelphia, PA. See manila cards addressed to Hon. P. J. Hurley, summer of 1930, in Box 380, "Segregation" file, GSM Pilgrimage files, RG 92, NA.

11. F. H. Payne, Ass't Secretary of War, to Mrs. M. E. Mallette, President, Keith Improvement Assoc., Chicago, Illinois, June 30, 1930, Box 345, "Segregation" file, GSM Pilgrimage files, RG 92, NA.

12. In some cases, the government simply had no way to locate these next of kin. "Colored Gold Star Pilgrimage," revised July 17, 1930 (unsigned), Box 348, "Segregation" file, GSM Pilgrimage file, RG 92, NA.

13. Mrs. Lora Lee Cannon, Athens, Alabama, to Sec. of War, May 22, 1930, and Mrs. Hattie Cowon of Hartsville, TN, August 17, 1931, Cemeterial Division, Office of the QMG, RG 92, NA.

14. DeWitt, Memorandum for the Diary, May 1, 1930, "Segregation" file, RG 92, NA. Hoover was likely to be at least moderately concerned about the racial discontent, since blacks had voted

approximately 70 percent Republican. See Nancy J. Weiss, *Farewell to the Party of Lincoln: Black Politics in the Age of FDR* (Princeton, NJ: Princeton University Press, 1983).

15. DeWitt, Memorandum for the Diary, May 1, 1930. Fears that American Shipping Lines might bring legal action against the government for reneging on its contract prevented further discussions of integrating the ships. Officials of the U.S. lines were never consulted on this matter. DeWitt, Memorandum for the Diary, April 29, 1930.

16. W. E. B. Du Bois, "As the Crow Flies," *Crisis* 37, no. 7 (July 1930): 221.

17. Addie W. Hunton and Kathryn M. Johnson were the second and third black women of only nineteen permitted to go to France to serve two hundred thousand black soldiers. Gavin, *American Women in World War I*, 139–141.

18. In 1930, two groups made the pilgrimage, one of fifty-four pilgrims and another of forty. Second endorsement, J. L. DeWitt, War Department, to the Adjutant General, May 2, 1932, "Segregation" file, GSM Pilgrimage file, RG 92, NA.

19. Mothers were housed at the Emma Ransom House (YWCA residence house) and the Hotel Dumas, 205 West 135th Street, Box 348, "Segregation" file, GSM Pilgrimage file, RG 92, NA.

20. Regarding the YWCA residence in New York, see Box 3, Hotel Pennsylvania file, and Box 348, GSM Pilgrimage files, RG 92, NA; also DeWitt, Memorandum for the Diary, April 29, 1930; "Negro Gold Star Mothers in France," *NYT*, June 20, 1932, 14:2.

21. Several French-speaking black nurses from Harlem Hospital in New York were recruited. Fred R. Moore to Col. Williams, June 13, 1930, Box 3, Hotel Pennsylvania file, GSM Pilgrimage files, RG 92, NA.

22. Correspondence shows that if the U.S. shipping lines had agreed to accommodate the black women, they would have lost money during the height of the tourist season from white passengers who refused to sail. By purchasing separate sailings for the black women, the government assured them against lost revenue. "Colored Mothers Given Special Ship," *Washington Post*, July 11, 1930, 1; DeWitt, Memorandum for the Diary, April 29, 1930, and J. L. DeWitt, Memo to Secretary of War, May 1, 1930, "Segregation" file, GSM Pilgrimage files, RG 92, NA.

23. "Gold Star War Mothers Talk for the Afro," *Afro-American*, August 9, 1930, Box 348, GSM Pilgrimage files, RG 92, NA.

24. Benjamin O. Davis, Sr., was promoted to colonel on February 18, 1930, just months before the pilgrimage. On October 25, 1940, he was promoted to brigadier general, making him the first African American general in the U.S. Army. Marvin E. Fletcher, *America's First Black General: Benjamin O. Davis, Sr., 1880–1970* (Lawrence: University Press of Kansas, 1989).

25. "55 Negro Mothers Feted," *Chicago Tribune*, Paris edition, July 22, 1930; "Jazz Tunes Cheer Colored Mothers," *New York Herald*, Paris edition, August 26, 1930; Tyler Stovall, *Paris Noir* (Boston: Houghton Mifflin, 1996), 86–87; also see G. Kurt Piehler, "The War Dead and the Gold Star," in Gillis, *Commemorations*, 179–180.

26. "Gold Star War Mothers Talk for the Afro." Ada Louise Smith, known as "Bricktop," was born in Alderson, West Virginia. Her nightclub, Chez Bricktop, on Rue Pigalle in Paris, opened in 1926 and welcomed elite guests such as Cole Porter, the Duke and Duchess of Windsor, F. Scott Fitzgerald, and Josephine Baker. Bricktop's red hair and cigars were her signature. She was eighty-nine years old when she died in 1984. *Huntington Herald-Dispatch*, February 2, 1984, West Virginia Archives & History, West Virginia Division of Culture and History, http://www.wvculture.org/History/Notewv/brictop. The African American musician and lyricist Noble Sissle (1889–1975) started in vaudeville and then enlisted in the army in 1917 with fellow black musician James Reese Europe, where they recruited a highly successful military band. African American Registry website, http://www.aaregistry.com/african_american_history/1000/A_musical_legend_Noble_Sissle.

27. "Cabled Story to U.S. Colored Newspapers," by J. A. Rogers, "Segregation" file, GSM Pilgrimage files, RG 92, NA; "Gold Star War Mothers Talk for the Afro."

28. "55 Negro Mothers Feted"; "Cheatham Started Jim-Crow," n.d., Scrapbook of newsclippings, Box 348, GSM Pilgrimage files, RG 92, NA.

29. "Gold Star War Mothers Talk for the Afro."

30. Serrano quotes a memo DeWitt wrote to his assistant, Colonel W. R. Gibson: "It is a known fact that these colored women are below the average in intelligence and it is my opinion that many of them have signed this letter without intending to decline the invitation to make the pilgrimage." Serrano adds, "sadly, he was right." "Poignant Protest," 19.

31. "Colored Gold Star Pilgrimage."

32. Benjamin Franklin Cheatham (1867–1944) came from a distinguished Tennessee family. He was appointed quartermaster general by President Coolidge in 1926, and as such, he supervised the GRS, which was still identifying and burying the American dead. He was recalled to active duty to oversee the pilgrimage at the request of his successor, Major General DeWitt. "Benjamin Franklin Cheatham, Maj. General, U.S. Army," Arlington National Cemetery website, http://www.arlingtoncemetery.net/bfcheat.htm. "Cheatham Started Jim-Crow."

33. Cheatham, "Report War Mothers Pilgrimage."

34. Mrs. W. D. Rush of Atlanta, interviewed by the *Afro-American*, August 9, 1930, Gold Star Pilgrimages Scrapbook, GSM Pilgrimage files, RG 92, NA.

35. When the AWM's president was asked about black mothers joining in 1920, she responded, "There are Southern women here. Don't bring that up. The colored women have not asked to be organized." Minutes of the first meeting of the Executive Board of the National War Mothers, September 29–30, 1920, N. A.W.M. Archives, Washington, DC.

36. For more on the politics of motherhood, see Ann Phoenix, Anne Woollett, and Eva Lloyd, eds., *Motherhood: Meanings, Practices and Ideologies* (London: Sage, 1991), 16.

37. Perry C. Thompson, Editor, to Hon. George H. Dern, Secretary of War, May 9, 1933, File 319.1, Report on 27th Div., Box 345, 1930 GSM Pilgrimage files, QMC, RG 92, NA. Regarding the GSM pilgrimage splitting the black vote, see Lester A. Walton, "Vote for Roosevelt," *Crisis*, May 1929, 343; "Division of Negro Vote Is Discussed," *Washington Post*, October 12, 1930; and Serrano, "Poignant Protest," 16.

38. Preprinted cards addressed to the Secretary of War in Box 380, GSM Pilgrimage files, RG 92, NA.

39. "No regrets for Jim Crow Visit, they all Declare," in "Gold Star War Mothers Talk for the Afro," *Afro-American*, August 9, 1930, Box 348, "Newsclippings Scrapbook," "Segregation," GSM Pilgrimage files, RG 92, NA

40. DeWitt's report to the Secretary of War, May 20, 1930, File 319, GSM Scrapbook; see also the *Afro-American*, Baltimore edition, January 18, 1930, April 4, 1931; and *Washington Tribune*, June 5, 1931, all in Box 348, "Newsclippings Scrapbook," "Segregation," GSM Pilgrimage files, RG 92, NA.

41. De Priest was ousted after the Democrats extended their control over the House and Senate in the wake of Franklin D. Roosevelt's election in 1932. "Behind Barbed Wire," *NYT*, September 11, 1988; Serrano, "Poignant Protest," 16.

NOTES TO CHAPTER 23

1. The War Department insisted that coffins be provided in case of death during the pilgrimages. War Department to Colonel Benjamin O. Davis, Subject: Liaison Detail, July 9, 1931, Davis Papers, U.S. Army Historical Institute, Carlisle, PA. Funeral details were also prearranged with a New York business that stood ready if called. Funerals file, New York, Box 6, GSM Pilgrimage files, RG 92, NA.

2. Col. Richard Ellis, "Report on the Activities in Europe of the American Pilgrimage Gold Star Mothers and Widows, 1930," March 7, 1931, 16, Correspondence, GSM Pilgrimages to Europe, Entry 1905 (Paris Office), RG 92, NA.

3. The drawing took place in the Green Room of the White House on February 7, 1930, in front of Generals Pershing and Cheatham and other dignitaries. Box 345, GSM Pilgrimage files, RG 92, NA.

4. One unnamed mother of an enlisted man lost at sea was able to join the pilgrimage after receiving donations from the Coast Guard Academy's canteen profits. F. C. Billard to Superintendent, Academy, June 16, 1931, General Correspondence of the U.S. Guard, 1910–1953, RG 26, NA.

5. Fred M. Ziegler, Co. D, 132 Infantry, 33rd Division, was killed on October 11, 1918. Grace Ziegler to QMG, January 25, 1932, Fred M. Ziegler Collection, courtesy of Ed Bliss and Alison Davis Wood, WILL-TV, Urbana, IL.

6. Ibid.

7. Daily orders, July 9, 1931, Pilgrimage of War Mothers and Widows (GSM), 1930–1933 (Inspection Reports), Benjamin O. Davis Papers, U.S. Army Military History Institute, U.S. Army War College, Carlisle Barracks, PA.

8. HR 4135 was enacted May 30, 1930. "Status of Gold Star Mothers," *Army and Navy Register*, November 30, 1929, 509; Report of the Quartermaster General Pilgrimage, vol. 1, March 1929 to June 1931, Box 380, GSM Pilgrimage files, RG 92, NA.

9. *Report of the Surgeon General, U.S. Army*, vol. 2 (Washington, DC: U.S. Government Printing Office, 1919), 2051; for naval losses, see "Status of Gold Star Mothers."

10. Mrs. Essie Bishop, Tate, TN (referring to Robert Bishop, who died December 1918, at Camp Wadsworth, Spartanburg, SC), December 1922, TN World War I, "Gold Star Questionnaires," 1918–1924, RG 53, Tennessee State Library and Archives.

11. Second Lieutenant Rudolph S. Adler, Lt. Quartermaster Corps, Motor Truck Co. 536, to Mr. J. H. Graves, RFD #3, Westmoreland, TN (referring to Private Willie B. Graves), n.d., in ibid.

12. J. W. Gower, Clarksville, TN, to Mr. John T. Moore (referring to Leslie M. Gower), Reel No. 3, February 21, 1923, in ibid.

13. "This [disease ratio] was more than in any other army in the Great War." Carol R. Byerly, *Fever of War: The Influenza Epidemic in the U.S. Army during World War I* (New York: New York University Press, 2005), 132. Byerly notes that Congress "discontinued burial at sea of soldiers who died in transport in late 1917." Ibid., 129.

14. Individual fares for the Reunion Tour ranged from $293 to $346 per person, depending on berth and deck level. "27th Division Back to the Front" brochure, Thos. Cook & Son, Entry 65, War Department General and Special Staff, RG 165, NA; General B. F. Cheatham to Mr. Brig. Gen. Kincaid, formerly Adj. Gen. of NY State, dated October 12, 1929, Misc. File, 1922–1935, Box 380, ref.: 27th Division voyage with GSM, Office of the QMG, RG 92, NA.

15. "Mrs. Mathilda Burling, together with a number of other mothers and widows whose sons or husbands were not members of the 27th Division, made the pilgrimage . . . at their own request." A. D. Hughes, Cpt. QMC, to Mrs. Alice V. Domes, July 12, 1930, Burial Files, Series 1942, Office of the QMG, RG 92, NA.

16. Six hundred 27th Division veterans were on board along with two hundred New York National Guardsmen and nearly two hundred Gold Star Mothers. "23 Sail to Plan Gold Star Tours," *Brooklyn Daily Times*, April 16, 1930; "More War Mothers Leave for France," *NYT*, May 14, 1930, 16:2; Inspector General Investigation Report, July 19, 1930, Correspondence 1917–1934, Box 1149, Winfree, Stephen W., GSM, Inspector General's Office, RG 159, NA.

17. Testimony of Mrs. Church, July 1930, Inspector General Division, Governors Island, NY, Correspondence, 1917–1934, Box 1149, Inspector General's Office, RG 159, NA.

18. Winfree testimony, July 11, 1930, RG 159, NA.

19. On the links between maternalism and Americanism, see K. Kennedy, *Disloyal Mothers,*

3.

20. Since this was not the standard Gold Star Mothers pilgrimage voyage, the War Department was particularly nervous about its success. The quotation appeared in a letter to Colonel A. E. Williams, Officer in Charge Port of Embarkations, Mothers and Widows Pilgrimage Office, 225 West 34th Street, NY, May 12, 1930, Box 380, Misc. File 1922–1935, Office of the QMG, RG 92, NA.

21. Alice V. Domes to War Department, Franklinville, NY, July 6, 1930, burial file of Pvt. Claude J. Domes, Cemeterial Division, Office of the QMG, RG 92, NA.

22. See testimony of Mrs. Stein, pp. 33, 34, and Mrs. Church, pp. 120–122, in Office of the Inspector General Correspondence, 1917–1934, Box 1149, File 333.9, Winfree, Stephen W., RG 159, NA.

23. Burling testimony, June 21, 1930, in ibid., 7–15.

24. Ibid.

25. Winfree was relieved from duty with the pilgrimages on August 15, 1930, and sent to a Texas cavalry unit. War Department, S.O. #189, confidential report, B. F. Cheatham, Major General, Investigating Officer to the Adjutant General, U.S. Army, Washington, DC, June 30, 1930, Inspector General's Office, 1917–1934, Winfree File, Series E26, RG 159, NA.

26. Extract copy from letter to Mr. Mangum from Major Price, February 10, 1930, Letter No. 1015-P, Records relating to interment, ABMC Records, RG 117, NA.

27. The cavalry was also in transition, as tanks were being brought in to replace the more traditional horses. Coffman, *Regulars*, 233, 234.

28. Winfree claimed that Burling became hostile when he refused her permission to join the press, General Pershing, and others at the Somme American Cemetery at Bony, France. Testimony of Col. Winfree, 190; of Mrs. Lawrence, 68; and of Mrs. Stein, 33.

29. *Pilgrimage*, a Fox production, was produced by John Ford, starred Henrietta Crosman, and premiered at the Gaiety Theater in New York on July 13, 1933. The movie makes no reference to the black mothers. T. Gallagher, *John Ford*, 75; and *NYT*, July 13 and 16, 1933. Full review, *NYT*, June 25 and July 11, 1933.

30. I am grateful to Professor Michael Birdwell of Tennessee Technical University, Cookeville, for sharing his insightful analysis of this movie. Email to the author, May 18, 2003.

31. F. Scott Fitzgerald, *Tender Is the Night* (first published by Scribner's as a serial in 1934 and published as a book in 1939), preface by Malcolm Cowley (London: Penguin, 1974), 168. Also Edwin S. Fussell, "Fitzgerald's Brave New World," *ELH* (English Literary History) 19, no. 4 (December 1952): 304.

32. "Gold Star Mother," *Esquire* 3 (December 1935): 205; and Plant, "Repeal of Mother Love," 155.

33. "Gold Star Mother," 205.

NOTES TO CHAPTER 24

1. Normally, the American Hospital of Paris was used for all hospitalization except nervous and mental disorders. Unfortunately, there are no details on these two women admitted to the Sanatarium de la Medical. Report for Paris office, 1930, Box 8, Entry 1905, General Correspondence of the Paris Office, GSM and Widows' Pilgrimage to Europe, 1930–33, GSM, RG 92, NA.

2. Grace Ziegler (quoting her diary) to the QMG, Durand, Illinois, January 25, 1932, Ziegler Collection.

3. Ibid.

4. The official letter from La Bienvenue Française accompanied each bag of soil and included the signatures of many of its members. Paris, Summer 1933, Ziegler and Kendall Collections.

5. By the armistice, the bureau (comprising one hundred searchers) was receiving an average of thirty thousand queries a week. "Opens New Relief Bureau," *NYT*, March 18, 1918; and "Red Cross Prison Work," *NYT*, November 11, 1918.

6. Elisabeth Kübler-Ross and David Kessler, *On Grief and Grieving* (New York: Scribner, 2005), 158.

7. Lieutenant Vernon Hart, 360th Infantry Regiment, was killed in the fierce Meuse-Argonne fighting near Villers-sous-Prény. See photos of his detachment coming out of the line the following day in the *ABMC Guide*, 140–141. Vernon Duggan Hart Papers, Folder 6, Box 3, 1837–1969, Julie Duggan Hart Papers, Southwest Collection Library, Texas Tech University, Lubbock.

8. Mdme. Collinot, Rouelle par Auberine, Haute, Marne, to Mrs. Julia C. Hart, Stamford, TX, November 4, 1918, in ibid.

9. Collinot to Hart, December 3, 1920, in ibid.

10. Malour Duggan to "My dear sister," Villaines, France, August 1, 1919, Folder 4, Box 3, Miscellaneous, Julie Duggan Hart Papers.

11. Excerpt from liaison report, June 8, 1933. Burial file of Arthur H. Marsh, Box 3090, Cemeterial Division, Office of the QMG, RG 92, NA.

12. Arthur H. Marsh, chaplain, 18th Infantry, 1st Division, was gassed as his unit was going into position and was transferred to an American hospital in Vittel. The bronchial pneumonia that was diagnosed would, presumably, have been caused by the gas. Church bulletin quote in *The Crozier* ("The official organ of the Church in the Diocese of Nebraska") 19, no. 11 (November 1918); and Chaplain Hughes to Nancy Marsh, February 11, 1919, burial file of Marsh.

13. Hughes to Marsh, February 11, 1919; in his letter to Mrs. Marsh, the chaplain refers to a letter from the Red Cross dated December 26, 1918, to the family and wife of Marsh, informing them of Arthur's death from wounds.

14. Nancy Marsh to P. C. Harris, Adjutant General, War Department, September 1919, burial file of Marsh.

15. Col. Chas. Pierce to Adj. General Harris, September 1919, as endorsement, burial file of Marsh.

16. Captain Charles B. Harris, 6th Engineers, 3rd Division, of Cedartown, Georgia, was killed at Claire Chenes Woods, France, while operating a captured enemy machine gun. His grave was located when the Americans captured Sedan. Burial file of Charles B. Harris, Cemeterial Division, Office of the QMG, RG 92, NA. I am indebted to Cedartown resident Millard Greer for sharing his research and drawing my attention to this case.

17. Nancy Marsh to Chaplain Chas. Pierce, January 1921, burial file of Marsh.

18. Nancy Marsh to Col. Charles Pierce, March 14, 1921, burial file of Marsh.

19. Memo for Col. Penrose, J. F. Butler, Capt., Infantry, August 8, 1921, War Department, burial file of Harris.

20. "The Personal Travel Journal of Mrs. Belle M. Harner, a Gold Star Mother of the Great War," from the collection of William Dienna, Phoenixville, PA, Fenelon Collection.

21. Ibid.

22. Witness referred to throughout the testimony simply as "Mrs. Lawrence," 68, in Office of the Inspector General Correspondence, 1917–1934, Box 1149, File 333.9, Winfree, Stephen W., RG 159, NA.

23. Mrs. Davidson, Long Island, NY, 58, in ibid.

24. *27th Division Back to the Front, 1930*, Official Travel Arrangements for the visit to the European Battlefields (U.S. Lines and Thos. Cook & Son, June 24, 1929), Entry 65, MID File, Records of the War Department General and Special Staffs, RG 165, NA.

25. "Journal of Mrs. Belle M. Harner"; see also "Gold Star Mothers Undaunted by Rains," *Washington Post*, May 25, 1930, 15.

26. "War Mothers Feel That Sons in Fitting Resting Places," n.d., in Julia Duggan Hart Papers.

27. "You don't ever bring the grief over a loved one to a close," write Kübler-Ross and Kessler, in *On Grief and Grieving*, 158.

28. I am speaking of classics such as Sigmund Freud ("Mourning and Melancholia," 1914–1916); C. S. Lewis, *A Grief Observed* (San Francisco: Harper & Row, 1961); and the extensive works of Elisabeth Kübler-Ross.

29. By the close of 1929, the number of mothers and widows entitled to make the pilgrimage was 11,440. It was further estimated that 6,730 desired to make the pilgrimage. By 1933, a total of 6,685 women had sailed to Europe on the Gold Star pilgrimages, at an average cost per woman of $960. Patrick J. Hurley, Sec. of War, December 6, 1929, Letter of Transmittal, "Pilgrimage for the Mothers and Widows" (Washington, DC: U.S. Government Printing Office, 1930), iii; and War Department to the President, April 18, 1933, President's Personal file, PPF 1534: American Gold Star Mothers, Franklin D. Roosevelt Library, Hyde Park, NY.

30. Kübler-Ross and Kessler, *On Grief and Grieving*, 102, 157–158.

31. According to Major General Thomas North, secretary of the ABMC (1946–1968), the next of kin were permitted to specify a personal epithet up to fifty letters, but the response was "light," and "phrases such as 'Killed in Action' tended to create invidious distinctions, so the practice was abandoned." "General North's Manuscript" (undated and unpublished), from "One Soldier's Job," Part I, 8, ABMC, Waregem Archives, Belgium.

32. Halbwachs, *On Collective Memory*, 25.

33. Collective memory is "embedded in the social structure, and changes when social bonds weaken or dissolve, or when new bonds replace them." Winter and Sivan, *War and Remembrance*, 24.

NOTES TO THE EPILOGUE

1. By this time, Charles Pierce had been reassigned to Washington, DC. Rethers, preface to *GRS History*, 2.

2. National monuments are conspicuously absent from the battlefields of the Second World War.

3. It was the sense of the ABMC that the permanent cemeteries, with their memorial chapels, would "constitute monuments to the military operations as well as memorials to the dead." Minutes of the fiftieth meeting of the ABMC, May 15, 1947, Box 1, ABMC Meeting Minutes and Agenda, 1923–1993, ABMC Records, RG 117, NA.

4. "Mrs. Mathilda Burling Is Dead," *NYT*, July 22, 1958, 27.

5. Charles C. Pierce, Lt. Col., C, Cemeterial Division, Memorandum for the Quartermaster General, February 8, 1921, Box 87, ABMC Unknown Soldier File, ABMC Records RG 117, NA.

6. Figure quoted by the Central Identification Laboratory's Public Affairs Office, Hickam AFB, Hawaii, 2005.

7. The author served as team leader for this JPAC recovery mission during the late summer and autumn of 2006.

8. I am grateful to Marie Jordan, the organization's founder, for providing this information. Of the widow figure, 38,427, or 52.3 percent, were mothers. The largest percentage of widows was between the ages of twenty-five and thirty-five (47.9 percent), but there were 148 war widows over sixty years of age. *The Gold Star* 1, no. 4, special reprint edition (November 1946), statistics on p. 2.

9. "Memorial Day Interview: Gold Star Families for Peace," interview with Cindy Sheehan, May 30, 2005, by Kevin B. Zeese, at LewRockwell.com, http://www.lewrockwell.com/orig6/zeese2.html.

10. These are the words of Mrs. Deerling, whose son had died ten years earlier in the Meuse-Argonne battles. Janet Mabie, "A Gold-Star Mother Speaks from Her Heart," *Christian Herald*, February 2, 1929, 114, in Julia Duggan Hart Papers.

11. The Tablets of the Missing also include names of those lost or buried at sea. Other aspects of the ABMC mission include the operation and maintenance of military burial grounds in foreign countries and controlling the design and construction of memorials, monuments, and markers by other U.S. citizens and organizations. Annual Report of the ABMC, 2006, 5.

Selected Bibliography

MANUSCRIPT AND ARCHIVAL SOURCES

Belgium
Flanders Field, American Cemetery, Waregem
Waregem Town Archives

United States
American Legion Archives, Indianapolis, Indiana
American War Mothers Archives, Washington, DC
Herbert Hoover Presidential Library, West Branch, Iowa
Liberty Memorial Museum in Kansas City, Missouri
    Gold Star Mothers Collection (Estella Kendall Papers)
Library of Congress, Washington, DC
    Manuscript Department
        Papers of Newton D. Baker (Microfilm, Reels 3, 5, 6, 8, 9, 13)
        Papers of James G. Harbord (Vol. 8)
        NAACP Collection, Boxes 374, 376
        Papers of John J. Pershing
        U.S. Quartermaster's Department (MMC 2341)
    Microfilm Room
        Time, Micro #02914
Library of the Kentucky Historical Society, Frankfort
    Mexican War Archival Collection
Library of the University of North Carolina at Chapel Hill
    The Manuscripts Department, Southern Historical Collection
        Lawrence D. Tyson Papers, #1173, Folder 507
National Archives and Records Administration (NARA), Washington, DC
    Legislative Archives
        Congressional Records, House and Senate Journals
        Hearing Transcripts
National Archives II (NARA), College Park, Maryland
    RG 59: Records of the Department of State Relating to Internal Affairs of France, 1910–1929
    RG 66: Commission of Fine Arts
    RG 84: Records of Foreign Service Posts, Diplomatic Posts (France)
    RG 92: Office of the Quartermaster General
    RG 117: American Battle Monuments Commission
    RG 120: American Expeditionary Forces
    RG 159: Records of the Office of the Inspector General
    RG 165: Records of the War Department General and Special Staffs

RG 200: American Red Cross Files
RG 233: Records of Committee Papers
RG 391: U.S. Army Mobile Commands
RG 407: Office of the Adjutant General
National Museum of American Jewish Military History, Washington, DC
 Jewish War Veterans Convention File, Box 1A
Princeton University Archives, Seeley G. Mudd Manuscript Library, Princeton, New Jersey
 David Aiken Reed Scrapbooks
Franklin D. Roosevelt Library, Hyde Park, New York
 Gold Star Mothers files
Tennessee State Library and Archives
 RG 53: World War I Gold Star Questionnaires, 1918–1924 (microfilm)
Texas Tech University, Lubbock, Texas
 Julia Duggan Hart Papers, Southwest Collection/Special Collections Library
  Box 1, file 11
  Box 3, files 1, 4, 5, 6
U.S. Army Military History Institute, U.S. Army Heritage and Education Center, U.S. Army War
 College, Carlisle Barracks, Pennsylvania
 Benjamin O. Davis, Sr., Papers
 Davis, Arthur J., Lecture UB396.3, D38 1925

France
Bibliothèque de documentation internationale contemporaine (BDIC), University of Paris X,
 Nanterre
 Cote: S Piece 5552
 Q Piece 49, 2898
 O Piece 9778, 5822, 9499
Centre de recherche de l'Historial de la Grande Guerre, Peronne
L'Espace Culture Multimédia de la Médiathèque, Calais
 Newspapers: *Le Petit Calaisien, La Phare,* and *L'Avenir*
Ministère des Affairs étrangères, Quai d'Orsay, Paris
 L'Amérique, 1918–1929 (series)
  États-Unis (sous series), vols. 170, 171, 172, 282, 283, 284, 285
 Papiers d'agents (series)
  Jules Jusserand (sous series), vol. 19 (1808–1939)
Le Service de la Documentation Historique de la Croix-Rouge Française (French Red Cross
 Archives), Paris
Archives de la Guerre, Service Historique de l'Armée de Terre, Château de Vincennes, Paris

Great Britain
Commonwealth War Graves Commission (CWGC), Maidenhead, Berkshire
 WG 1122, WG 269, WG 843, WG 1612, WG 1778, WG 1122, WG 1502/1, WG 1294/3,
 A/53/3, and MU1
Imperial War Museum, London
 Department of Documents
 Misc. 816, Misc. 30 (541), Wakeman 67/305/1
Public Record Office (National Archives), Kew
 WO 32/3790, 14805, 14806, 3134, 3135, 3136, 3145, 4845, 5765
 T1/12195, 12298, 125554, T161/596, 23, 261
 FO 6112/306
 HO 45/21621, 11080, 419854, HO 144/22305, 23415, 23427, 23428

Private Collections
Gold Star Mothers Collection, Holly Fenelon, Whittier, California
Fred M. Ziegler Collection, Edward Bliss, Florida (courtesy of Alison Davis Wood, WILL-TV, 300 N. Goodwin Ave., Urbana, IL)

PRINTED PRIMARY SOURCES

Haug, Henrietta L. "Gold Star Mothers: A collection of notes recording the Personal Histories of the Gold Star Mothers of Illinois." Brussels, Illinois, 1941.
"Information for Visitors Going to American Graves in France: American Guide Book to France." London, n.d.
O'Ryan, John F. *Report of Major General John F. O'Ryan on Duty Abroad, August 16, 1920.* Albany, NY: J. B. Lyon Company, 1923.
A Souvenir of the Battlefields Pilgrimage. London: British Legion, 1928.
St. Barnabas Hostel. "The St. Barnabas Pilgrimage to the Battlefields and War Cemeteries of Gallipoli and Salonika." London, 1926.
United States Lines and Thos. Cook & Son. *27th Division Back to the Front, 1930.* Official Travel Arrangements for the visit to European Battlefields, 1929.

NEWSPAPERS

Afro-American
Chicago Daily Tribune
Kansas City Times
New York Herald
New York Times
L'Ouevre
Washington Post
Washington Times

SECONDARY SOURCES

Abels, Jules. *In the Time of Silent Cal: A Retrospective History of the 1920's.* New York: G. P. Putnam's Sons, 1969.
Adler, Selig. *The Isolationist Impulse: Its Twentieth-Century Reaction.* London: Abelard-Schuman, 1957.
American Battle Monuments Commission. *American Armies and Battlefields in Europe.* 2nd ed. Washington, DC: U.S. Government Printing Office, 1938.
Ariès, Philippe. *The Hour of Our Death.* Trans. Helen Weaver. London: Penguin, 1981.
Ashplant, T. G., Graham Dawson, and Michael Roper. *The Politics of War Memory and Commemoration.* London: Routledge, 2000.
Audoin-Rouzeau, and Annette Becker. *1914–1918: Understanding the Great War.* Translation by Catherine Temerson. London: Profile Books, 2000.
Bailey, Thomas A. "The Supreme Infanticide." In Davis R. B. Ross et al., eds., *Progress, War, and Reaction: 1900–1933.* New York: Thomas Y. Crowell, 1970.
Barbeau, Arthur E., and Florette Henri. *The Unknown Soldiers: African-American Troops in World War I.* 2nd ed. New York: Da Capo, 1996. First published in 1974.
Beaver, Daniel R. *Newton D. Baker and the American War Effort, 1917–1919.* Lincoln: University of Nebraska Press, 1966.
Becker, Annette. *Guerre et la Foi (War and Faith: The Religious Imagination in France, 1914–1930).* Oxford, UK: Berg, 1998.

———. *Les Monuments aux Morts: Memoire de la Grande Guerre* (*Monuments of the Great War*). Paris: Editions Errance, 1988.

Beckett, Ian F. W. *The Great War, 1914–1918*. Essex, UK: Longman, 2001.

———. *The Victorians at War*. London: Hambledon and London, 2003.

Berghoff, Hartmut, Barbara Korte, Ralf Schneider, and C. Harvie, eds. *The Making of Modern Tourism: The Cultural History of the British Experience, 1600–2000*. London: Palgrave, 2002.

Bertman, Stephen. *Cultural Amnesia: America's Future and the Crisis of Memory*. Westport, CT: Praeger, 2000.

Berton, Pierre. *Vimy*. Toronto: McClelland and Stewart, 1986.

Blight, David W. *Race and Reunion: The Civil War in American Memory*. Cambridge, MA: Belknap Press of Harvard University Press, 2001.

Bodnar, John, ed. *Bonds of Affection: Americans Define Their Patriotism*. Princeton, NJ: Princeton University Press, 1996.

———. *Remaking America: Public Memory, Commemoration, and Patriotism in the Twentieth Century*. Princeton, NJ: Princeton University Press, 1992.

Boot, Max. *The Savage Wars of Peace*. New York: Perseus Books, 2002.

Bourke, Joanna. *Dismembering the Male: Men's Bodies, Britain and the Great War*. London: Reaktion Books, 1996.

Brady, Thomas J. "Webb C. Hayes: Gilded Age Ideologue or Adventurer?" *Northwest Ohio Quarterly* 66, no. 3 (Summer 1994).

Brundage, W. Fitzhugh. "White Women and the Politics of Historical Memory in the New South, 1880–1920." In J. Dailey, G. E. Gilmore, and B. Simon, eds., *Jumpin' Jim Crow: Southern Politics from Civil War to Civil Rights*. Princeton, NJ: Princeton University Press, 2000.

Budreau, Lisa. "Over Where?" *American in Britain*, May–June 1998.

———. "The Politics of Remembrance: The Gold Star Mothers' Pilgrimage and America's Fading Memory of the Great War." *Journal of Military History* 72, no. 2 (April 2008): 371–411.

Bushaway, Bob. "Name Upon Name: The Great War and Remembrance." In Roy Porter, ed., *Myths of the English*. Cambridge, UK: Polity, 1992.

Byerly, Carol R. *Fever of War: The Influenza Epidemic in the U.S. Army during World War I*. New York: New York University Press, 2005.

Cannadine, David. *Mellon: An American Life*. New York: Knopf, 2006.

Cart, Doran. "Liberty Memorial Museum of World War One." *Dusty Shelf* (Kansas City Area Archivists) 19, no. 3 (1999–2000).

Carwardine, Richard. *Lincoln: A Life of Purpose and Power*. Bloomington: Indiana University Press, 2000.

Cather, Willa. *One of Ours*. New York: Vintage Books, 1971. First published in 1922 by Knopf.

Ciesielski, Greg. "Knights of Columbus Grave Locating Service," *Military Postal History Society Bulletin* 41 (Fall 2002).

Clark, Mary Sine. "'If They Consent to Leave Them over There': The European Pilgrimages of World War I Mothers and Widows from Virginia." *Virginia Cavalcade* 50, no. 3 (Summer 2001).

Clout, Hugh. *After the Ruins: Restoring the Countryside of Northern France after the Great War*. Exeter, UK: University of Exeter Press, 1996.

Coffman, Edward M. *The Regulars: The American Army*. Cambridge, MA: Belknap Press of Harvard University Press, 2004.

———. *The War to End All Wars*. Lexington: University Press of Kentucky, 1998.

Cohen, Warren I. *Empire without Tears: America's Foreign Relations, 1921–1933*. Philadelphia: Temple University Press, 1987.

Connerton, Paul. *How Societies Remember*. Cambridge: Cambridge University Press, 1989.

Coombs, Rose E. B. *Before Endeavours Fade: A Guide to the Battlefields of the First World War.* London: Battle of Britain Prints International, 1977.

Cooper, John Milton, Jr. "The Great War and American Memory." *Virginia Quarterly Review,* Summer 2003.

Cosmas, Graham A. *An Army for Empire: The United States Army in the Spanish-American War.* Shippensburg, PA: White Mane, 1994. First published in 1971 by University of Missouri Press.

Cott, Nancy F. *The Grounding of Modern Feminism.* New Haven, CT: Yale University Press, 1987.

Cousineau, Phil. *The Art of Pilgrimage: The Seeker's Guide to Making Travel Sacred.* Berkeley, CA: Conari, 1998.

Crowell, B., and R. F. Wilson. *How America Went to War: An Account from Official Sources of the Nation's War Activities, 1917–1920.* New Haven, CT: Yale University Press, 1921.

Cuhaj, George S. "Gold Star Mothers—Their Voyages and Their Medals." *TAMS Journal* (Official Organ of the Token and Medal Society) 20, no. 6 (December 1980): 236–241.

Damousi, Joy. *The Labour of Loss: Mourning, Memory and Wartime Bereavement in Australia.* Cambridge: Cambridge University Press, 1999.

———. *Living with the Aftermath: Trauma, Nostalgia and Grief in Post-war Australia.* Cambridge: Cambridge University Press, 2001.

D'Este, Carlo. *Eisenhower: A Soldier's Life.* New York: Holt, 2002.

deWatteville, Lt. Col. H. "A Motor Tour along the Western Front." *Army Quarterly* 16 (January 1928).

Dickson, Paul, and Thomas B. Allen. *The Bonus Army.* New York: Walker, 2004.

Döring, Tobias. "Travelling in Transience: The Semiotics of Necro-Tourism." In Hartmut Berghoff, Barbara Korte, Ralf Schneider, and Christopher Harvie, eds., *The Making of Modern Tourism.* London: Palgrave, 2002.

Du Bois, W. E. B. "As the Crow Flies." *Crisis* 37, no. 7 (July 1930).

Edmunds, Palmer D. "Should We Forget the War?" *American Legion Monthly,* May 1927.

Eksteins, Modris. *Rites of Spring.* Boston: Houghton Mifflin, 1989.

Elshtain, Jean B. *Women and War.* New York: Basic Books, 1987.

Epler, Percy H. *The Life of Clara Barton.* New York: Macmillan, 1917.

Faust, Drew Gilpin. *This Republic of Suffering: Death and the American Civil War.* New York: Knopf, 2008.

Feldstein, Ruth. *Motherhood in Black and White: Race and Sex in American Liberalism, 1930–1965.* Ithaca, NY: Cornell University Press, 2000.

Ferguson, Niall. *Colossus: The Rise and Fall of the American Empire.* New York: Penguin, 2004.

Ferrell, Robert H. *Peace in Their Time: The Origins of the Kellogg-Briand Pact.* New Haven, CT: Yale University Press, 1952.

———. *The Presidency of Calvin Coolidge.* Lawrence: University Press of Kansas, 1998.

———. *The Strange Deaths of President Harding.* Columbia: University of Missouri Press, 1996.

Feuer, A. B. *The Santiago Campaign of 1898. A Soldier's View of the Spanish-American War.* Westport, CT: Praeger, 1993.

Fink, Reuben. "Visas, Immigration, and Official Anti-Semitism." *Nation* 112, no. 2920 (June 22, 1921).

Fitzgerald, F. Scott. "May Day." In *The Stories of F. Scott Fitzgerald.* Vol. 1. Middlesex, UK: Penguin, 1969.

———. *Tender Is the Night.* Preface by Malcolm Cowley. London: Penguin, 1974. First published 1939.

Fletcher, Marvin E. *America's First Black General: Benjamin O. Davis, Sr., 1880–1970.* Lawrence: University Press of Kansas, 1989.

Ford, Nancy Gentile. *Americans All! Foreign-Born Soldiers in World War I.* College Station: Texas A&M University Press, 2001.

Förster, Stig, and Jörg Nagler. *On the Road to Total War: The American Civil War and the German Wars of Unification, 1861–1871.* Cambridge: Cambridge University Press, 1997.

Foster, Gaines. *Ghosts of the Confederacy: Defeat, the Lost Cause, and the Emergency of the New South, 1865–1913.* New York: Oxford University Press, 1987.

Freud, Sigmund. *The Standard Edition of the Complete Psychological Works of Sigmund Freud.* Vol. 14. Trans. and ed. James Strachey. London: Hogarth, 2001.

Fussell, Edwin S. "Fitzgerald's Brave New World." *ELH* (English Literary History) 19, no. 4 (December 1952).

Fussell, Paul. *Abroad: British Literary Traveling between the Wars.* Oxford: Oxford University Press, 1980.

——. *The Great War and Modern Memory.* Oxford: Oxford University Press, 1975.

——, ed. *The Norton Book of Travel.* New York: Norton, 1987.

Gallagher, Gary W. *The Myth of the Lost Cause and Civil War History.* Bloomington: Indiana University Press, 2000.

Gallagher, Tag. *John Ford: The Man and His Films.* Berkeley: University of California Press, 1986.

Gavin, Lettie. *American Women in World War I.* Boulder: University Press of Colorado, 1997.

Gillis, John R., ed. *Commemorations: The Politics of National Identity.* Princeton, NJ: Princeton University Press, 1994.

Ginsburgh, Robert. "This, Too, Is America." *American Legion Monthly,* November 1933, 16–19, 49–52.

Glassberg, David. "Monuments and Memories." *American Quarterly* 43, no. 1 (March 1991): 143–156.

Gledhill, Christine, ed. *Home Is Where the Heart Is: Studies in Melodrama and the Woman's Film.* London: BFI, 1987.

"A Gold Star Pilgrimage" (editorial). *American Legion Weekly,* April 11, 1924, 10.

Graham, John W. *The Gold Star Mother Pilgrimages of the 1930s.* Jefferson, NC: McFarland, 2005.

Graham, Stephen. *The Challenge of the Dead: An Impression of France and the Battlefields Just after the War.* London: Ernest Benn, 1930.

Grainger, Roger. *The Social Symbolism of Grief and Mourning.* London: Jessica Kingsley, 1998.

Grayzel, Susan R. *Women and the First World War.* London: Pearson, 2002.

Gregory, Adrian. *The Silence of Memory: Armistice Day, 1919–1946.* Oxford, UK: Berg, 1994.

Grossman, Elizabeth G. "Architecture for a Public Client: The Monuments and Chapels of the American Battle Monuments Commission." *Journal of the Society of Architectural Historians* 43, no. 2 (May 1984): 119–143.

——. *The Civic Architecture of Paul Cret.* Cambridge: Cambridge University Press, 1996.

A Guide to the American Battle Fields in Europe, 1st ed. Washington, DC: Government Printing Office, 1927.

Halbwachs, Maurice. *On Collective Memory.* Ed. and trans. Lewis A. Coser. Chicago: University of Chicago Press, 1992.

Hallowes, J. S., and the International Council of Women. *Mothers of Men and Militarism.* London: Headley Brothers, 1916.

Harries, Meirion, and Susie Harries. *The Last Days of Innocence: America at War, 1917–1918.* New York: Random House, 1997.

Hawley, Ellis W. *The Great War and the Search for a Modern Order: A History of the American People and Their Institutions, 1917–1933.* New York: St. Martin's, 1979.

Hawthorne, Frederick W. *Gettysburg: Stories of Men and Monuments as Told by Battlefield Guides.* Gettysburg, PA: Association of Licensed Battlefield Guides, 1988.

Heale, M. J. *American Anti-communism: Combating the Enemy Within.* Baltimore: Johns Hopkins University Press, 1990.

Heideking, Jürgen, Geneviève Fabre, and Kai Dreisbach, eds. *Celebrating Ethnicity and Nation: American Festive Culture from the Revolution to the Early 20th Century.* New York: Berghahn Books, 2001.

Higham, John. *Strangers in the Land: Patterns of American Nativism, 1860-1925.* New York: Atheneum, 1963.

Higham, Robin, and Donald J. Mrozek. *A Guide to the Sources of United States Military History.* New Haven, CT: Archon Books, 1998.

Higonnet, Margaret R., Sonya Michel, et al. *Behind the Lines, Gender and the Two World Wars.* New Haven, CT: Yale University Press, 1987.

History of the American Graves Registration Service. Preface by H. F. Rethers. U.S. Army Graves Registration Service, 1921.

Hobsbawm, Eric, and Terrence Ranger, eds. *The Invention of Tradition.* Cambridge: Cambridge University Press, 1983.

Hoganson, Kristin L. *Fighting for American Manhood: How Gender Politics Provoked the Spanish-American and Philippine-American Wars.* New Haven, CT: Yale University Press, 1998.

Hutchison, Graham Seton. *Pilgrimage.* London: Rich & Cowan, 1935.

Jalland, Pat. *Death in the Victorian Family.* Oxford: Oxford University Press, 1999.

Johnson, Douglas W. *Battlefields of World War I Western Fronts.* New York: Oxford University Press, 1921.

Johnson, Joan Marie. "'Ye Gave Them a Stone': African American Women's Clubs, the Frederick Douglass Home, and the Black Mammy Monument." *Journal of Women's History* 17, no. 1 (2005).

Johnson, Wray R. "Black American Radicalism and the First World War: The Secret Files of the Military Intelligence Division." *Armed Forces & Society* 26, no. 1 (Fall 1999): 27-53.

Kaplan, E. Ann. *Motherhood and Representation.* London: Routledge, 1992.

Kearl, Michael C., and Anoel Rinaldi. "The Political Uses of the Dead as Symbols in Contemporary Civil Religions." *Social Forces* 61, no. 3 (March 1983).

Keene, Jennifer D. *Doughboys, the Great War, and the Remaking of America.* Baltimore: Johns Hopkins University Press, 2000.

———. "Optimism at Armageddon: Voices of American Participants in the First World War" (review). *Journal of Social History* (Spring 1999).

———. "Women's Identities at War: Gender, Motherhood, and Politics in Britain and France during the First World War." *Journal of Social History* 34, no. 4 (Summer 2001).

Kellogg, Robert H. *Life and Death in Rebel Prisons.* Hartford, CT: Stebbins, 1865.

Kelly, Patrick J. "The Election of 1896 and the Restructuring of Civil War Memory." *Civil War History* 49, no. 3 (2003).

Kennedy, David M. *Freedom from Fear: The American People in Depression and War, 1929-1945.* Oxford: Oxford University Press, 1999.

———. *Over Here: The First World War and American Society.* New York: Oxford University Press, 1980.

Kennedy, Kathleen. *Disloyal Mothers and Scurrilous Citizens: Women and Subversion during World War I.* Bloomington: Indiana University Press, 1999.

Kephart, William M. "Status after Death." *American Sociological Review* 15, no. 5 (October 1950): 635-643.

Kerber, Linda K. *Toward an Intellectual History of Women.* Chapel Hill: University of North Carolina Press, 1997.

Kerber, Linda K., and Jane DeHart Mathews, ed. *Women's America: Refocusing the Past.* New York: Oxford University Press, 1982.

Kipling, Rudyard. *The Graves of the Fallen: Imperial War Graves Commission.* London: HMSO, 1919.

Klein, Maury. *Rainbow's End: The Crash of 1929.* New York: Oxford University Press, 2001.

Klein, Yvonne, ed. *Beyond the Home Front: Women's Autobiographical Writing of the Two World Wars.* Bristol, UK: Arrowsmith, 1997.

Klement, Frank L. *The Gettysburg Soldiers' Cemetery and Lincoln's Address.* Shippensburg, PA: White Mane, 1993.

Koven, Seth, and Sonya Michel, eds. *Mothers of a New World.* New York: Routledge, 1993.

Kübler-Ross, Elisabeth, and David Kessler. *On Grief and Grieving.* New York: Scribner, 2005.

Kyvig, David E. *Daily Life in the United States, 1920–1940.* 2nd ed. Chicago: Ivan R. Dee, 2004.

Ladd-Taylor, Molly. "'My Work Came Out of Agony and Grief': Mothers and the Making of the Sheppard-Towner Act." In Seth Koven and Sonya Michel, eds., *Mothers of a New World.* New York: Routledge, 1993.

Laderman, Gary. *The Sacred Remains: American Attitudes toward Death, 1799–1883.* New Haven, CT: Yale University Press, 1996.

Laffin, John. *A Western Front Companion 1914–1918.* Stroud, UK: Alan Sutton, 1995.

Laqueur, Thomas W. "Memory and Naming in the Great War." In John R. Gillis, ed., *Commemorations: The Politics of National Identity.* Princeton, NJ: Princeton University Press, 1994.

Laubach, Lt. Col. Jas. H. "A Brief History of the Gold Star Pilgrimages." *Quartermaster Review,* September–October 1933.

Lax, John, and William Pencak. "Creating the American Legion." *South Atlantic Quarterly* 81, no. 1 (Winter 1982).

Leech, Margaret. *In the Days of McKinley.* New York: Harper, 1959.

Leuchtenburg, William E. *The Perils of Prosperity, 1914–32.* Chicago: University of Chicago Press, 1972. First published 1958.

Levenstein, Harvey. *Seductive Journey: American Tourists in France from Jefferson to the Jazz Age.* Chicago: University of Chicago Press, 1998.

Levinger, Lee J. *A Jewish Chaplain in France.* New York: Macmillan, 1921.

Lewis, C. S. *A Grief Observed.* San Francisco: Harper & Row, 1961.

Lewis, David Levering. *W. E. B. Du Bois: The Fight for Equality and the American Century, 1919–1963.* New York: Holt, 2000.

Linenthal, Edward T. *Sacred Ground: Americans and Their Battlefields.* Champaign: University of Illinois Press, 1991.

Lloyd, David W. *Battlefield Tourism: Pilgrimage and the Commemoration of the Great War in Britain, Australia and Canada, 1919–1939.* Oxford, UK: Berg, 1998.

Locke, Alain, ed. *The New Negro: An Interpretation.* New York: Albert and Charles Boni, 1925.

Longworth, Philip. *The Unending Vigil: A History of the Commonwealth War Graves Commission, 1917–1967.* London: Leo Cooper, 1967.

MacCloskey, Monro. *Hallowed Ground: Our National Cemeteries.* New York: Richards Rosen, 1968.

Macmillan, Margaret. *Peacemakers.* London: John Murray, 2002.

Marvel, William. *Andersonville: The Last Depot.* Chapel Hill: University of North Carolina Press, 1994.

May, Henry F. *The End of American Innocence: A Study of the First Years of Our Own Time, 1912–1917.* Preface by David Hollinger. New York: Columbia University Press, 1992.

Mayo, James M. *War Memorials as Political Landscape: The American Experience and Beyond.* New York: Praeger, 1984.

McGiffert, Michael, ed. *The Character of Americans.* Homewood, IL: Dorsey, 1964.

McPherson, James M. *Battle Cry of Freedom.* New York: Oxford University Press, 1988.

———. *The Illustrated Battle Cry of Freedom.* New York: Oxford University Press, 2003.

Meigs, Mark. *Optimism at Armageddon: Voices of American Participants in the First World War.* London: Macmillan, 1997.

Metcalf, Peter, and Richard Huntington. *Celebrations of Death: The Anthropology of Mortuary Ritual.* 2nd ed. Cambridge: Cambridge University Press, 1991.

Miller, Nathan. *New World Coming: The 1920s and the Making of Modern America.* New York: Scribner, 2003.

Mitford, Jessica. *The American Way of Death Revisited.* New York: Virago, 1998.

Musicant, Ivan. *Empire by Default: The Spanish-American War and the Dawn of the American Century.* New York: Holt, 1998.

Moore, Charles. "Fallen on the Field of Honor." *Outlook,* February 18, 1920, 275–278.

———. "War Memorials Bad and Good." *American Legion Weekly,* September 8, 1922, 14–16.

Moore, William Charles. "The Division of the Dead." *American Legion Weekly,* May 26, 1922.

Mosier, John. *The Myth of the Great War: A New Military History of World War I.* New York: HarperCollins, 2001.

Mosse, George L. *Fallen Soldiers.* Oxford: Oxford University Press, 1990.

———. "Two World Wars and the Myth of the War Experience." *Journal of Contemporary History* 21, no. 4 (October 1986): 491–513.

"Mother Goes 'Over There'" (editorial). *Quartermaster Review* 9, no. 3 (November–December 1929).

"National Affairs." *Time,* May 19, 1930.

"National Patriotic Conference." *American War Mother* 5, no. 1 (March 1928); 6, no. 1 (March 1929).

Noll, John J. "Crosses." *American Legion Monthly,* September 1930.

Oates, Stephen B. *A Woman of Valor: Clara Barton and the Civil War.* New York: Free Press, 1994.

O'Leary, Cecilia Elizabeth. *To Die For: The Paradox of American Patriotism.* Princeton, NJ: Princeton University Press, 1999.

"On to Paris" (editorial). *American Legion Monthly,* May 1927.

O'Shea, Stephen. *Back to the Front: An Accidental Historian Walks the Trenches of World War I.* New York: Avon Books, 1996.

Palmer, Frederick. *Newton D. Baker: America at War.* Vol. 1. New York: Dodd, Mead, 1931.

Paxson, Stacy Alexander. "Nation's Monuments on Cuban Battlefields." *Army and Navy Life* 8, no. 10 (April 1906).

Pencak, William. *For God and Country: The American Legion, 1919–1941.* Boston: Northeastern University Press, 1989.

Perkins, Kathy A. *Black Female Playwrights: An Anthology of Plays before 1950.* Bloomington: Indiana University Press, 1990.

Pershing, John J. *My Experiences in the World War, Volume 1.* Blue Ridge Summit, PA: Tab Books, 1989. First published in 1931 by Harper & Row.

———. "Our National War Memorials in Europe." *National Geographic Magazine* 65, no. 1 (January 1934).

Peterkin, Julia. *Roll, Jordan, Roll.* Photo studies by Doris Ulmann. London: Jonathan Cape, 1934.

Pettegrew, John. "'The Soldier's Faith': Turn-of-the-Century Memory of the Civil War and the Emergence of Modern American Nationalism." *Journal of Contemporary History* 31, no. 1 (1996): 49–73.

Phoenix, Ann, Anne Woollett, and Eva Lloyd, eds. *Motherhood: Meanings, Practices and Ideologies.* London: Sage, 1991.

Piehler, G. Kurt. *Remembering War the American Way.* Washington, DC: Smithsonian Institution Press, 1995.

———. "The War Dead and the Gold Star." In John R. Gillis, ed., *Commemorations: The Politics of National Identity.* Princeton, NJ: Princeton University Press, 1994.

Poen, Monte M., ed. *Letters Home by Harry Truman.* New York: G. P. Putnam's Sons, 1984.

Porter, Roy, ed. *Myths of the English*. Cambridge, UK: Polity, 1992.

Potter, Claire Bond. Review of *To Die For: The Paradox of American Patriotism*, by Cecilia Elizabeth O'Leary. *American History* 28, no. 1 (2000): 55–62.

Potter, Constance. "World War I Gold Star Mothers Pilgrimages, Part 1." *Prologue* 31 (Summer 1999).

———. "World War I Gold Star Mothers Pilgrimages, Part 2." *Prologue* 31 (Fall 1999).

Remini, Robert V. *Henry Clay: Statesman for the Union*. New York: Norton, 1991.

Renehan, Edward J. *The Lion's Pride: Theodore Roosevelt and His Family in Peace and War*. Oxford: Oxford University Press, 1998.

Resek, Carl, ed. *War and the Intellectuals: Collected Essays, 1915–1919*. 1964. Indianapolis: Hackett, 1999.

Risch, Erna. *Quartermaster Support of the Army: A History of the Corps, 1775–1939*. Washington, DC: Quartermaster Historian's Office, Office of the QM General, 1962.

———. *Quartermaster Support of the Army, 1775–1939*. Center for Military History, 1989.

Robin, Ron. *Enclaves of America: The Rhetoric of American Political Architecture Abroad, 1900–1965*. Princeton, NJ: Princeton University Press, 1992.

Rollins, Peter C., and John E. O'Connor, eds. *Hollywood's World War I Motion Picture Images*. Bowling Green, OH: Bowling Green State University Popular Press, 1997.

Rote, Nelle F. *Nurse Helen Fairchild: WWI 1917–1918*. Lewisburg, PA: Fisher Fairchild, 2004.

Rothman, Barbara Katz. *Recreating Motherhood: Ideology and Technology in a Patriarchal Society*. New York: Norton, 1989.

Rowbotham, Sheila. *A Century of Women: The History of Women in Britain and the United States*. London: Viking, 1997.

Russell, Francis. *The Shadow of Blooming Grove: Warren G. Harding in His Times*. New York: McGraw-Hill, 1968.

Sandweiss, Martha A., Rick Stewart, and Ben W. Huseman. *Eyewitness to War: Prints and Daguerreotypes of the Mexican War, 1846–1848*. Washington, DC: Smithsonian Institution Press, 1989.

Savage, Kirk. "The Politics of Memory: Black Emancipation and the Civil War Monument." In John R. Gillis, ed., *Commemorations: The Politics of National Identity*. Princeton, NJ: Princeton University Press, 1994.

Schlesinger, Arthur M., Jr., ed. *The Almanac of American History*. New York: Bramhall House, 1983.

Scott, Emmett J. *Scott's Official History of the American Negro in the World War*. Washington, DC: U.S. Government Printing Office, 1919.

Serrano, Richard A. "Poignant Protest." *Los Angeles Times Magazine*, September 15, 2002.

Service, Robert W. *Rhymes of a Red Cross Man*. New York: Barse & Hopkins, 1916.

Seton-Watson, Hugh. *Nations and States: An Enquiry into the Origins of Nations and the Politics of Nationalism*. London: Methuen, 1977.

Sheffield, Gary. *Forgotten Victory, the First World War: Myths and Realities*. London: Headline Review, 2002.

Shlaes, Amity. *The Forgotten Man: A New History of the Great Depression*. New York: HarperCollins, 2007.

Skocpol, Theda. "Organization Despite Adversity: The Origins and Development of African American Fraternal Associations." *Social Science History* 28, no. 3 (Fall 2004): 367–437.

———. *Protecting Soldiers and Mothers: The Political Origins of Social Policy in the United States*. Cambridge, MA: Belknap Press of Harvard University Press, 1992.

Sloane, David C. *The Last Great Necessity*. Baltimore: Johns Hopkins University Press, 1991.

Smith, Anthony D. *Nationalism and Modernism: A Critical Survey of Recent Theories of Nations and Nationalism*. London: Routledge, 1998.

Smith, Gene. *Still Quiet on the Western Front 50 Years Later*. New York: William Morrow, 1965.

Smythe, Donald. "Honoring the Nation's Dead." *American History Illustrated* 16, no. 2 (May 1981).

St. Barnabas Hostel. *The St Barnabas Pilgrimage to the Battlefields and War Cemeteries of Gallipoli and Salonika*. London: St. Barnabas Hostel, 1926.

Steere, Edward. "Genesis of Graves Registration, 1861–1870." *Military Affairs* (published by the American Military Institute, Washington, DC) 12, no. 3 (Fall 1948).

———. *The Graves Registration Service in World War II*. Washington, DC: U.S. Government Printing Office, 1951.

———. "National Cemeteries and Memorials in Global Conflict." *Quartermaster Review*, November–December 1953.

Steiner, Rudolf. *The Dead Are with Us*. Trans. D. S. Osmond. 1918. London: Rudolf Steiner, 1995.

Stevenson, Elizabeth. *Babbitts and Bohemians: The American 1920s*. New York: Macmillan, 1967.

Stovall, Tyler. *Paris Noir: African Americans in the City of Light*. Boston: Houghton Mifflin, 1996.

Strachan, Hew. *The Oxford Illustrated History of the First World War*. Oxford York: Oxford University Press, 1998.

Stroebe, Wolfgang, and Margaret S. *Bereavement and Health: the Psychological and Physical Consequences of Partner Loss*. Cambridge: Cambridge University Press, 1987.

Sutton, Robert K., ed. *Rally on the High Ground: The National Park Service Symposium on the Civil War*. Fort Washington, PA: Eastern National, 2001.

Tarlow, Sarah. *Bereavement and Commemoration: An Archaeology of Mortality*. Oxford, UK: Blackwell, 1999.

Taylor, H. A. *Goodbye to the Battlefields*. London: S. Paul, 1930.

Thelen, David. "Memory and American History." *Journal of American History* 75, no. 4 (March 1989): 1117–1129.

"Therefore Be It Resolved." *American Legion Monthly*, December 1928.

Thomas, Lowell. *Woodfill of the Regulars: A True Story of Adventure from the Arctic to the Argonne*. London: Heinemann, 1930.

Thompson, James Westfall. "The Aftermath of the Black Death and the Aftermath of the Great War." *American Journal of Sociology* 26, no. 5 (March 1921).

Tindall, George Brown. *America*. Vol. 2. 2nd ed. New York: Norton, 1988.

The Treaty of Versailles and After: Annotations of the Text of the Treaty. Washington, DC: U.S. Government Printing Office, 1947.

Turner, Frederick Jackson. "The Significance of the Frontier in American History." In Michael McGiffert, ed., *The Character of Americans*. Homewood, IL: Dorsey, 1964.

Viviani, Christian. "Who Is without Sin? The Maternal Melodrama in American Film, 1930–39." In Christine Gledhill, ed., *Home Is Where the Heart Is: Studies in Melodrama and the Woman's Film*. London: BFI, 1987.

Von Blon, Philip, and Marquis James. "The A.E.F. Comes Home." *American Legion Quarterly*, December 1927.

Vorenberg, Michael. "Recovered Memory of the Civil War." *Reviews in American History* 29, no. 4 (2001).

Walton, Whitney. "Internationalism and the Junior Year Abroad: American Students in France in the 1920s and 1930s." *Diplomatic History* 29, no. 2 (April 2005).

Ware, Fabian A. G. *The Immortal Heritage: Work and Policy of the Imperial War Graves Commission during 20 Years, 1917–1937*. Cambridge: Cambridge University Press, 1937.

Wecter, Dixon. *When Johnny Comes Marching Home*. Cambridge, MA: Houghton Mifflin, 1944.

Weeks, Jim. "A Different View of Gettysburg: Play, Memory, and Race at the Civil War's Greatest Shrine." *Civil War History* 50, no. 2 (2004).

———. *Gettysburg: Memory, Market, and an American Shrine*. Princeton, NJ: Princeton University Press, 2003.

Weinstein, Allen, and Alexander Vassiliev. *The Haunted Wood: Soviet Espionage in America*. New York: Random House, 1999.

Weiss, Nancy J. *Farewell to the Party of Lincoln: Black Politics in the Age of FDR*. Princeton, NJ: Princeton University Press, 1983.

Whalen, Robert Weldon. *Bitter Wounds: German Victims of the Great War, 1914–1939*. Ithaca, NY: Cornell University Press, 1984.

White, Walter. *A Man Called White*. New York: Viking, 1948.

Wilson, Major Louis C. "The War Mother Goes 'Over There.'" *Quartermaster Review*, May–June 1930.

Winder, Bruce. *Mr. Polk's Army*. College Station: Texas A&M University Press, 1999.

Wingate, Jennifer. "Over the Top: The Doughboy in World War I Memorials and Visual Culture." *American Art* 19, no. 2 (2005): 26–47.

Winter, Jay. *Sites of Memory, Sites of Mourning: The Great War in European Cultural History*. Cambridge: Cambridge University Press, 1998.

Winter, Jay, and Emmanuel Sivan, eds. *War and Remembrance in the Twentieth Century*. Cambridge: Cambridge University Press, 2000.

Wukovits, John F., ed. *The 1920s*. San Diego, CA, Greenhaven, 2000.

Wylie, Philip. *Generation of Vipers*. New York: Rinehart, 1942.

Young, Robert J. *Marketing Marianne: French Propaganda in America, 1900–1940*. New Brunswick, NJ: Rutgers University Press, 2004.

Ziino, Bart. *A Distant Grief: Australians, War Graves and the Great War*. Crawley: University of Western Australia Press, 2007.

UNPUBLISHED THESES AND PAPERS

Abroe, Mary Munsell. "All the Profound Scenes, Federal Preservation of Civil War battlefields, 1861–1990." Loyola University of Chicago, 1996.

Byerly, Carol R. "The Politics of Disease and War: Infectious Disease in the United States Army during World War I." University of Colorado, 2001.

Frank, Lucy. "Being Only Out of Sight: Sarah Piatt, Elizabeth Stuart Phelps and the Problem of Mourning in Post-bellum America." Paper presented at British Association of American Studies conference, Oxford, UK, April 2002.

Hall, Levi (Mrs.). "Report of Trip to the National Convention of the American Legion Auxiliary in Paris, France, Sept 1927." Association report. Holly Fenelon Collection.

Harner, Belle M. "The Personal Travel Journal of Mrs. Belle M. Harner, a Gold Star Mother of the Great War." William Dienna Collection. Phoenixville, PA.

Kiesling, Eugenia. "The U.S. Army's Approach to Historical Staff Rides." Society for Military History Conference. University of Calgary, Canada, 2001.

Krowl, Michelle A. "To Strengthen the Bonds of This Grand and Re-united Country: Reburial, Reconciliation, and the Legacy of the American Civil War." American Historical Association Conference, Washington, DC, 2004.

Piehler, G. Kurt. "Remembering War the American Way: 1783 to the Present." American Studies, Fine Arts, Rutgers State University, 1991.

Plant, Rebecca J. "The Repeal of Mother Love: Momism and the Reconstruction of Motherhood in Philip Wylie's America." Ph.D. diss., Johns Hopkins University, 2001.

Index

Accountability, government, 6, 9, 24

Adjusted Compensation bill, 169. *See also* Bonus Bill

Adler, Cyrus, 125

African Americans, 8, 9, 133; and American Legion, 168, 180; anger at discrimination, 56; and Black Mammy 92; and Bolshevism, 168; and Civil War, 60–61, 93; contributions of, 72; and Gettysburg, 61; Gold Star Mothers, 210, 212–215; and GRS, 53, 53–58, 212; and hypocrisy, 60, 145; lynchings, 58, 61; memorialization of, 144; and memory, 92, 93, 216; and motherhood, 216; mothers, 212; musicians, 130; and patriotism, 146; and Pershing, 34, 56, and pilgrimages, 208, 212–217; pilgrimage eligibility, 211; and pilgrimage segregation, 211; and race riots, 58; regiments, 144, 145, 154, 156; segregated graves, 61; and segregation, 209, 212; soldiers, 57, 59, 126; and Spanish-American War 28, 61; terms of service, 60; veterans, 9, 34, 60, 93, 145, 168, 180, 209; voters, 209; widows, 212; women, 9, 93, 124–126; and Young Men's Christian Association, 212

Air Force, U.S., 243

Alger, Russell A., 27, 38

Ambivalence, postwar, 104, 163

"America China Relief Expedition of 1900" (Boxer Rebellion), 107

American Armies and Battlefields in Europe: A Guide to the American Battlefields in Europe, 173, 182, 244

American Battle Monuments Commission (ABMC), 5, 6, 8, 160, 161, 243; and commemoration, 160, 172, 239; conflicts with, 152–155, 175; control over monuments, 152, 153, 155, 156; costs of, 7, 154; creation of, 111; criticism of memorials,

162–163; and headstones, 123–126; leadership of, 111, 113–116, 119, 132; and memorials, 133, 134, 136–138, 140, 157; monument plan, 146, 148–149, 150, 151; and mothers, 226; numbers interred, 244; numbers missing in action, 244; records of, 242; and Second World War, 243; and site selection, 146, 147, 157, 158

American Expeditionary Forces (AEF), 19, 20, 34, 38, 73, 107, 112, 121, 127

American Field of Honor Association, 69, 70, 97, 98, 100

American Gold Star Mothers of the World War, Inc., 200

American Gold Star Mothers, Inc., 185

American government, 7, 25, 41, 60, 85, 104, 106, 118, 146, 156, 160, 170, 177, 191, 192, 227, 228, 241; and pilgrimages, 239. *See also* Congress; Legislation, pilgrimage

American Legion, 8, 44, 88, 111, 123, 127; agenda of, 142, 169; and African Americans, 168, 182; Auxiliary, 180, 182, 231; behavior of, 180–182, 190; and British Legion, 188; and Burling, Mathilda, 198; events of, 169; and Gold Star Mothers, 184; and legislation, 200; and lobbying, 169; and mothers, 196; Paris Convention, 170, 176, 177, 179–184, 189, 190, 192, 198; and membership, 168; and monuments, 138, 141, 142, 146, 160; and Nationalism, 167; and pilgrimages, 170, 185, 186; and pilgrimage legislation, 202; and politics, 169; role of, 69, 168–169, 177; and segregation, 145, 182; and States Rights, 145, 168; and WMC, 122

American Legion Monthly, 161, 176, 178, 180

American Legion Weekly, 138

American Merchant, 213

About the Author

LISA BUDREAU is a research historian at the Office of Medical History, Office of the Surgeon General, Army Medical Department in Falls Church, Virginia. She holds a doctorate from Oxford University, England, and she has published and lectured in Europe and the United States on a variety of First World War topics. (See www.bodiesofwar.com for further details.)

CPSIA information can be obtained at www.ICGtesting.com

235424LV00001B/7/P

9 780814 799901